NATIVE PERSISTENCE AT A CALIFORNIA MISSION OUTPOST

NATIVE PERSISTENCE AT A CALIFORNIA MISSION OUTPOST

The Bioarchaeology and History of
the Asistencia de San Pedro y San Pablo

EDITED BY
Jelmer W. Eerkens, Lee M. Panich,
Christopher Canzonieri, and Christopher Zimmer

Foreword by The Amah Mutsun Tribal Band of Mission San Juan Bautista

UNIVERSITY OF FLORIDA PRESS

Gainesville

Cover: *Asistencia* by Mary Bresnahan, 1994. San Mateo County Historical Association Collection (1995.47).

This book is freely available in an open access digital edition thanks to the generous support by the University of California Davis Library. Additional financial support was provided by the Office of the Provost, Santa Clara University.

Copyright 2025 by Jelmer W. Eerkens, Lee M. Panich, Christopher Canzonieri, and Christopher Zimmer
The text of this book is licensed under a Creative Commons Attribution-NonCommercial-NoDerivatives 4.0 International License (CC BY-NC-ND 4.0): https://creativecommons.org/licenses/by-nc-nd/4.0/

To use this book, or parts of this book, in any way not covered by the license, please contact University of Florida Press at our website at http://upress.ufl.edu.

Published in the United States of America

30 29 28 27 26 25   6 5 4 3 2 1

DOI: https://doi.org/10.5744/9781683405474

Library of Congress Cataloging-in-Publication Data
Names: Eerkens, Jelmer W. editor | Panich, Lee M., 1978– editor | Canzonieri, Christopher editor | Zimmer, Christopher, (tribal representative) editor
Title: Native persistence at a California mission outpost : the bioarchaeology and history of the Asistencia de San Pedro y San Pablo / edited by Jelmer W. Eerkens, Lee M. Panich, Christopher Canzonieri, and Christopher Zimmer ; foreword by the Amah Mutsun Tribal Band of Mission San Juan Bautista.
Description: 1. | Gainesville : University of Florida Press, [2025] | Includes bibliographical references and index.
Identifiers: LCCN 2024053283 (print) | LCCN 2024053284 (ebook) | ISBN 9781683405023 hardback | ISBN 9781683405085 paperback | ISBN 9781683405238 ebook | ISBN 9781683405474 pdf
Subjects: LCSH: Catholic Church—Missions—California | Indians of North America—Missions—California | Ohlone Indians—Missions—California | Missions, Spanish—California—History | BISAC: SOCIAL SCIENCE / Archaeology | SOCIAL SCIENCE / Anthropology / Cultural & Social
Classification: LCC F868.S156 N386 2025 (print) | LCC F868.S156 (ebook) | DDC 979.4/01—dc23/eng/20250326
LC record available at https://lccn.loc.gov/2024053283
LC ebook record available at https://lccn.loc.gov/2024053284

University of Florida Press
2046 NE Waldo Road
Suite 2100
Gainesville, FL 32609
http://upress.ufl.edu

GPSR EU Authorized Representative: Mare Nostrum Group B.V., Mauritskade 21D, 1091 GC Amsterdam, The Netherlands, gpsr@mare-nostrum.co.uk

CONTENTS

List of Figures   vii
List of Tables   ix
Foreword   xi
Acknowledgments   xiii

1. Introduction: Situating the Asistencia de San Pedro y San Pablo   1
   Jelmer W. Eerkens, Lee M. Panich, Christopher Canzonieri, and Christopher Zimmer

2. A Brief History of Archival and Archaeological Research at the Asistencia de San Pedro y San Pablo   8
   Lee M. Panich

3. Life and the Biological Consequences therein at the Mission Period Site of Asistencia de San Pedro y San Pablo (CA-SMA-71/H), 1787–1794   33
   Alyson Caine, Christopher Canzonieri, and Christine Marshall

4. Proteomic Sex Estimation and Detection of Immune Proteins in Tooth Enamel at the Asistencia de San Pedro y San Pablo (CA-SMA-71/H)   71
   Tammy Buonasera, Diana Malarchik, Jelmer W. Eerkens, Christopher Canzonieri, and Glendon Parker

5. San Pedro y San Pablo as a Venue for Cultural Persistence: Mortuary Practices and Exchange Networks on the Margins of the Mission System   83
   Lee M. Panich, Melody Tannam, and Jelmer W. Eerkens

6. Dietary Persistence and Change in California's Mission Period: Stable Isotope Evidence from Tooth and Bone from Asistencia de San Pedro y San Pablo (CA-SMA-71/H)   113
   Jelmer W. Eerkens, Christopher Canzonieri, and Jason Miszaniec

7. Proteomic Analysis of Dental Calculus as Insight into Mission Period Diets in California   138

   Kyle Burk, Glendon Parker, Jelmer W. Eerkens, Christopher Canzonieri, Christopher Zimmer, Monica V. Arellano, and Alan Leventhal

8. Biochemical Ethnobotany of Ohlone Plant Use during the Mission Period   157

   Mario Zimmermann, Shannon Tushingham, Anna Berim, and David R. Gang

9. Examining Heavy Metal Exposure at Asistencia de San Pedro y San Pablo during the Mission Period in Northern California   176

   Diana Malarchik, Jelmer W. Eerkens, Christopher Canzonieri, Christopher Zimmer, Tanya M. Smith, Christine Austin, and Austin Cole

10. Dental Biodistance and Kinship at Asistencia de San Pedro y San Pablo   196

    Kristen A. Broehl-Droke

11. Peopling the Past: Life Histories of Native Residents of the Asistencia de San Pedro y San Pablo   207

    Lee M. Panich, Beth Armstrong, and Christopher Canzonieri

12. Persistence of Traditional Lifeways, and Change, during the California Mission Period at Asistencia de San Pedro y San Pablo   226

    Jelmer W. Eerkens, Lee M. Panich, Christopher Canzonieri, and Christopher Zimmer

Appendix: Images of Human Skeletal Remains   241

List of Contributors   247

Index   251

FIGURES

2.1. Greater San Francisco Bay region with missions and other places mentioned in text   9
2.2. A diseño from an unsuccessful land grant petition   15
2.3. Plan map of excavations at the Sánchez Adobe, ca. 1950–1990   18
2.4. Map of 2016–2018 utility trench excavation and location of fifteen human burials   20
3.1. Distribution of age-at-death by sex   46
4.1. Relationship of total IgG peptide signal intensity to SA peptide intensity for tooth enamel   77
4.2. Relative IgG levels by age for tooth enamel   78
4.3. Amelogenin X intensities normalized by sample weight for tooth enamel   79
5.1. Shell beads from San Pedro y San Pablo   86
5.2. Comparison of isotopic analysis of selected Olivella beads   89
5.3. Jet and glass beads from San Pedro y San Pablo   91
5.4. Pestles from San Pedro y San Pablo   97
5.5. Basalt metate found during construction monitoring   98
5.6. Drawing of bundle of belongings found with Burial 15   100
6.1. Isotopic model and previous human C and N isotopes   118
6.2. Animal bone C and N isotopes   123
6.3. Isotopic life histories for Burials 2, 6, 8, and 13   127
6.4. Comparison of isotopic composition of precontact and Mission Period diets   129
8.1. Mass spectrum of calculus from Burial 11   164
8.2. Partial least squares–discriminant analysis for visualizing patterns among individual burials   166
8.3. Loading plot for Residues-Sex PLSDA   167
9.1. Box and whisker plots showing metal levels in parts per million   185

9.2. LA-ICP-MS maps showing lead, copper, and zinc concentrations for Burial 2 first molar   186

9.3. LA-ICP-MS maps showing lead, copper, and zinc concentrations for Burial 14 first molar   187

9.4. LA-ICP-MS maps showing lead, copper, and zinc concentrations for Burial 11 first molar   188

10.1. Dendrogram showing biological affinity between individuals   201

11.1. Entries in the Mission San Francisco death records for Olcóx and Jagessém   210

11.2. Entries in the Mission San Francisco death records for Mauricio and Julírbe   211

11.3. Simplified kinship diagram showing the relationships between Jagessém, Yunnénis, Julírbe, and Mauricio   215

11.4. Plan map of burials with traditional Ohlone names in italics, Spanish baptismal name, and date of death   223

A.1. Preservation of Burial 2 with pathological alterations shaded in black   242

A.2. Burial 3, right innominate bone with alterations at iliac crest   243

A.3. Occlusal view of staining on dentition from Burial 14   243

A.4. Cross section of first molar of Burial 2   244

A.5. Cross section of first molar of Burial 14   244

A.6. Cross section of first molar of Burial 11   244

TABLES

2.1. Age and gender distribution for individuals buried at San Pedro y San Pablo   14

3.1. Summary of demographic profile of the fifteen individuals   36

3.2. Pathological alterations present at CA-SMA-71/H by burial   48

3.3. Crude prevalence of dental diseases from California Indigenous archaeological samples   57

4.1. Proteomic sex estimation for individuals at San Pedro y San Pablo   75

4.2. Serum albumin, IgG, and C-reactive protein in enamel intensity for individuals at San Pedro y San Pablo   77

5.1. Overview of shell beads from San Pedro y San Pablo   87

5.2. Distribution of measured clamshell disk dead subtypes   87

5.3. Glass beads from San Pedro y San Pablo   93

5.4. Results of specialized obsidian studies of flaked stone tools from Burial 15   96

5.5. Funerary offerings by burial number   99

6.1. Results of stable isotope analyses from faunal remains   121

6.2. Bone collagen isotopes from San Pedro y San Pablo humans   124

6.3. Age of weaning estimates, and $\delta^{13}C$ and $\delta^{15}N$ values across different life history windows   125

7.1. Individuals and samples included in calculus proteomic study   142

7.2. Proteomic results from Mission Period human dental calculus at the asistencia   147

7.3. Proteomic results from precontact human dental calculus in San Francisco Bay Area   149

8.1. Biomarker data from dental calculus samples   163

9.1. Results from bulk heavy metal analysis for each individual in parts per million, as well as an average of published averages from modern teeth   183

11.1. Potential matches between archaeological data and historical data for individuals buried at San Pedro y San Pablo   209
11.2. Potential matches for Burial 7 and Burial 16   213

FOREWORD

We, The Amah Mutsun Tribal Band of Mission San Juan Bautista, California, as the state-appointed Most Likely Descendants (MLDs) for the Asistencia de San Pedro y San Pablo, commonly known as the Sánchez Adobe, Pacifica California, are excited to have supported and contributed to the various analytical studies in this volume.

The research within this volume provides information regarding the overall health, diet, and lifeways of our ancestors who were forced into the California Mission System. We are honored to have been involved in this multidisciplinary study demonstrating collaboration between Indigenous groups and archaeologists. We hope these projects will continue to foster positive and beneficial relationships between Native American Communities and archaeologists.

While we understand that the study of ancestral remains can raise ethical and emotional issues, we felt that their inadvertent disturbance offered a unique opportunity to know more about their lives. We felt it was important to share this knowledge with the public to help keep them in our collective memories. Now that the studies are complete, we are grateful to the San Mateo County Parks for allowing us to rebury the ancestors and their belongings as closely as possible to their original resting place.

ACKNOWLEDGMENTS

We thank the staff of the County of San Mateo Parks Department for their assistance at the Sánchez Adobe Park, site of the former Asistencia de San Pedro y San Pablo. In particular, special thanks go to Matthew Del Carlo (Ranger IV), Gregory Escoto (Ranger III), Darrick Emil (Ranger III), Kody Morello (Ranger II), Ronnie Cardoza (Equipment Operator), and Becky Christ (Site Manager Sánchez Adobe, San Mateo County Historical Association). Additionally, thanks to the following park staff who assisted: Kenneth Crampton, Travis Hanson, Thomas Hart, Mark Rogers, Daniela Todorcevic, and Matthew Tolmasoff.

We thank Andrew Galvan of the Ohlone Indian Tribe, Beth Armstrong, and Desiree Vigil, Tribal Monitors. Ms. Armstrong also assisted in excavating and recovering the burials and accessing mission documents. We thank Dominic Canzonieri, who assisted in excavating and recovering burials, and Basin Research Associates, Inc.: Dr. Colin I. Busby provided project management during the archaeological recovery phase; Dr. Donna Garaventa provided background research; Melody Tannam assisted in the burial recovery and helped with artifact analysis, artifact photography, site mapping, and graphics; and Stuart Guedon provided archaeological monitoring support during construction activities.

We thank Mary Puckett at the University of Florida Press for assisting us through the publication process, and Sarah Peelo and an anonymous reviewer for providing valuable feedback on earlier drafts of the book.

The County of San Mateo Parks Department provided funding for archaeological services undertaken by Basin Research Associates, Inc. for the Sánchez Adobe Interpretive Center Project, 2018–2022 under an On-Call Professional Services Agreement. Portions of the specialized studies were funded by grants from the National Science Foundation to Panich (BCS 1559666) and Eerkens (BCS 1220048 and BCS 2021256).

Finally, and most importantly, we thank the Amah Mutsun Tribal Band of Mission San Juan Bautista, Chairwoman Irenne Zwierlein, Michelle Zimmer, and Christopher Zimmer, for none of these studies would have been possible without their keen interest, approval, and collaboration.

1

Introduction

Situating the Asistencia de San Pedro y San Pablo

JELMER W. EERKENS, LEE M. PANICH,
CHRISTOPHER CANZONIERI, AND CHRISTOPHER ZIMMER

During mechanical excavation in 2016 for utility improvements at the Sánchez Adobe Park in Pacifica, California, workers made a surprising discovery: human skeletal remains. While it was known that this was the location of an eighteenth-century Spanish mission outpost, archaeologists and historians had never precisely determined the location of the associated cemetery—despite more than seventy years of research on the site. After the unanticipated discovery, archaeologists worked with tribal representatives to carefully mitigate the damage of the utility work that threatened the cemetery. Ultimately, a total of fifteen individuals and any associated grave goods had to be temporarily exhumed. All were Native Californians from nearby Ohlone communities who were buried at the site—what was then known as the Asistencia de San Pedro y San Pablo—sometime between 1786 and 1800. This book offers an unprecedented look into their lives during the early years of colonization on California's Pacific Coast.

The following chapters emerge from a long-standing and collaborative relationship with the Amah Mutsun Tribal Band of Mission San Juan Bautista, who were appointed as the Most Likely Descendants (MLD) for the site by California's Native American Heritage Commission. In conjunction with the tribe, a research plan was developed to learn more about Ohlone life at the Asistencia de San Pedro y San Pablo. This work involved careful collaboration with the tribe, logistic support from the San Mateo County Department of Parks and San Mateo County Historical Association, as well as coordination by archaeologists from Basin Research, the cultural resource management consultants who oversaw the project. Researchers from several universities with expertise in a range of fields were then recruited to conduct specialized studies that would reveal more about the lives of the fifteen individuals whose graves were disturbed by the construction activities and, by extension, their friends and family who also lived and died at the site. These studies, described in the chapters that follow, present new information about the health, diet, and social relationships of Native people living at a satellite mission during a critical phase of the expansion of the Franciscan mission system in the greater San Francisco Bay Area.

This work is part of a wave of research across California, and the Americas more broadly, that moves beyond a narrow focus on the impacts of colonialism suffered by Native populations toward a more nuanced examination of how Native individuals and families drew on long-standing cultural knowledge and social relationships to navigate the challenges of the times (e.g., Panich and Gonzalez 2021). When applied to the study of Spanish colonialism, in particular, many researchers employ a landscape perspective to understand how Native communities dealt with the imposition of Spanish colonial missions established in their varied homelands. Recent archaeological work at California mission sites, for example, has demonstrated that Native people maintained important continuities in ceremonial practices, diet, technological traditions, community structure, and regional exchange networks (Brown et al. 2023; Hull and Douglass 2018; Lightfoot 2005; Noe 2023; Panich and Schneider 2014; Panich et al. 2014; Panich et al. 2018; Peelo et al. 2018; Popper 2016; Potter et al. 2021). Outside of the missions, archaeological research has similarly revealed how Native people remained connected to ancestral homelands in various ways, often through manipulation of colonial policies that allowed them to visit sites of refuge in hinterlands (Byrd et al. 2018; Bernard et al. 2014; Reddy 2015; Schneider 2015a, 2015b, 2021).

These twenty-first-century studies and views contrast markedly with earlier twentieth-century perspectives that were based largely on analysis of historical documents written by the Spanish (see discussion in Lightfoot 2005; Panich 2013; Schneider et al. 2020). That earlier research emphasized the dramatic changes to Native lifestyles brought about by the establishment of the mission system, with Spanish as actors of change and Native people as passive receivers of Euroamerican technologies, behaviors, and identities. Studies in this volume attempt to use scientific data to evaluate the *extent* to which lifeways persisted or changed for the individuals uncovered at the asistencia, and take a more nuanced approach to understanding experiences of individuals who were buried at this location. To meet these goals, the chapters here employ a range of cutting-edge archaeometric techniques to highlight especially the health, diet, social connections, and medicinal practices of the fifteen baptized individuals buried at the asistencia.

The chapters of this book are organized in sections. The first two chapters, including this one, provide an introduction and a historical background. The next set of chapters, 3–10, use different analytical approaches to build up profiles for the fifteen individuals. These chapters include osteological and paleopathological studies (Caine et al., chapter 3), proteomic sex estimation and evaluation of childhood stress from proteins preserved in dental enamel (Buonasera et al., chapter 4), mortuary analysis, especially of obsidian and beads, as insight into social status and regional connections (Panich et al., chapter 5), stable isotope analysis to evaluate diet of both humans and animals (Eerkens et al., chapter 6), proteomic studies of dental calculus to reconstruct diet (Burk et al., chapter 7), liquid chromatography of dental calculus to identify plant residues and biomarkers as insight into medicinal practices (Zimmermann et al., chapter 8), measurement of heavy metals in teeth as insight into tool use and activity patterns (Malarchik et al., chapter 9), and biodistance analysis of dental traits to examine potential genetic relatedness between individuals (Broehl-Droke, chapter 10). We had originally planned to conduct ancient DNA analyses and include results in this volume. Unfortunately, due to COVID and other delays, that work has not been completed at the time of this writing.

The final two chapters of the volume bring together results of the various studies. Chapter 11 (Panich et al.) matches bioarchaeological results presented in previous chapters to the historical mission records from the asistencia in an attempt to identify individuals by name. Combining the historical and archaeological records in this way, the authors build a life history for each person. The final chapter (Eerkens et al.) examines patterns within the fifteen individuals, by sex, age, and social status, to provide context to what life was like for individuals buried at the asistencia, and presumably more broadly within the mission system. The study examines how these different social categories intersected with either the persistence of traditional cultural practices or engagement with novel opportunities within the mission.

While bioarchaeological studies of cemeteries dating to the Mission Period are comparatively rare in California, such work in other geographic locations similarly points to the potential to use individual life histories to reveal more complex patterns of persistence and struggle in comparable colonial settings (Murphy and Klaus 2017; Stojanowski 2013; Tica and Martin 2019; and Walker et al. 1988). What is particularly valuable about the studies in this book is that mission death records indicate that just 152 individuals in total were buried at the asistencia. Thus, with the fifteen individuals in this study, approximately 10 percent of the total burial population is represented. Further, by comparing bioarchaeological information, such as age, sex, and pathologies, to demographic information provided in the death records, chapter 11 makes tentative identifications for eight of the fifteen individuals in the study.

In most bioarchaeological studies, the dead are anonymous. However, for the Asistencia de San Pedro y San Pablo individuals, we have an unprecedented opportunity to give names to the skeletal remains. By linking the bioarchaeological and historical records, in an archaeoforensic context, we greatly extend what we know about the fifteen individuals. For example, we know information about their familial history, such as their natal village and names of their parents, and can place them on the landscape at particular dates in time, such as when and where they were baptized, and in some cases when and where they were born. Such work humanizes the archaeological record, portraying each burial as an individual with a unique lived experience and life history. Together, the contributions in this edited volume offer a set of innovative bioarchaeological, archaeometric, and mortuary studies for those who were disturbed during construction activity and reveal previously unknown details about their lives at the nexus of Native and colonial worlds in the late 1700s.

We are aware of the sensitivity surrounding images of Native American skeletal remains, particularly within some Tribal Nations and among some nontribal advocates. As scientists, we also recognize the importance of presenting evidence to support particular claims, and of creating information that future studies could potentially incorporate within larger comparative data sets to test new hypotheses. Chapter 3 of this book discusses particular osteological evidence that suggests the presence of particular pathogens and stressors within the asistencia population. Likewise, chapter 9 presents information on the distribution of different elements, such as lead and zinc, in teeth, and includes images of cross-sectioned teeth. After much discussion among ourselves and the tribe, we decided such images were not gratuitous, but were a necessary component of the research and presentation. However, we put the images of human skeletal remains in an appendix of the book, rather than within the chapter, so that readers would not unexpectedly be confronted with such images. Instead, interested readers who would like to consult the images can flip to the appendix (in hard copy), or download the appendix (if viewing digital).

Human societies around the world have a range of behaviors and traditions to remember and celebrate their ancestors, such as erecting statues, creating national holidays, displaying portraits, building cemeteries, and telling and retelling stories. Societies have engaged in these behaviors for millennia. Archaeology has only been practiced as a discipline for about two hundred years, and thus is a more recent addition to this list. The methods are different (i.e., we use science, survey, and excavation), but we have the same ultimate goal. Archaeology helps us commemorate, and understand, the people who came before us.

Through the studies in this volume, we remember and honor the fifteen Ohlone ancestors who lived through a dramatic period of change and continuity in California's history. We celebrate them here by retelling some of the details of their lives.

References

Bernard, Julienne, David W. Robinson, and Fraser Sturt
2014   Points of Refuge in the South Central California Hinterlands. In *Indigenous Landscapes and Spanish Missions: New Perspectives from Archaeology and Ethnohistory*, edited by L. M. Panich, T. D. Schneider, 154–171. University of Arizona Press, Tucson.
Brown, Kaitlin M., Marirose Meyer, Elena Hancock, Nicolasa I. Sandoval, and Glenn J. Farris
2023   Status and Social Stratification at Mission La Purísima Concepción: An Intra-Site Investigation of Residential Space within the Chumash Rancheria 'Amuwu. *International Journal of Historical Archaeology* 27:506–542.
Byrd, Brian F., Shannon DeArmond, and Laurel Engbring
2018   Re-Visualizing Indigenous Persistence during Colonization from the Perspective of Traditional Settlements in the San Francisco Bay-Delta Area. *Journal of California and Great Basin Anthropology* 38(2):163–190.
Hull, Kathleen L., and John G. Douglass, eds.
2018   *Forging Communities in Colonial Alta California*. University of Arizona Press, Tucson.
Lightfoot, Kent G.
2005   *Indians, Missionaries, and Merchants: The Legacy of Colonial Encounters on the California Frontiers*. University of California Press, Berkeley.
Murphy, Melissa S., and Haagen D. Klaus, eds.
2017   *Colonized Bodies, Worlds Transformed: Toward a Global Bioarchaeology of Colonialism*. University Press of Florida, Gainesville.
Noe, Sarah J.
2023   Subsistence and Persistence: Indigenous Foodways Within Mission Santa Clara de Asís. *California Archaeology* 15(1):69–107.
Panich, Lee M.
2013   Archaeologies of Persistence: Reconsidering the Legacies of Colonialism in Native North America. *American Antiquity* 78(1):105–122.

Panich, Lee M., and Sara L. Gonzalez, eds.
2021   *Routledge Handbook of the Archaeology of Indigenous-Colonial Interaction in the Americas.* Routledge, London.

Panich, Lee M., and Tsim D. Schneider, eds.
2014   *Indigenous Landscapes and Spanish Missions: New Perspectives from Archaeology and Ethnohistory.* University of Arizona Press, Tucson.

Panich, Lee M., H. Afaghani, and N. Mathwich
2014   Assessing the Diversity of Mission Populations through the Comparison of Native American Residences at Mission Santa Clara de Asis. *International Journal of Historical Archaeology* 18:467–488.

Panich, Lee M., Rebecca Allen, and Andrew A. Galvan
2018   The Archaeology of Native American Persistence at Mission San José. *Journal of California and Great Basin Anthropology* 38(1):11–29.

Peelo, Sarah, Linda J. Hylkema, John Ellison, Clinton M. Blount, Mark G. Hylkema, Margie Maher, Tom Garlinghouse, Dustin McKenzie, Stella D'Oro, and Melinda Berge
2018   Persistence in the Indian Ranchería at Mission Santa Clara de Asís. *Journal of California and Great Basin Anthropology* 38(2):207–234.

Popper, Virginia S.
2016   Change and Persistence: Mission Neophyte Foodways at Selected Colonial Alta California Institutions. *Journal of California and Great Basin Anthropology* 36(1):5–25.

Potter, James M., Tiffany Clark, and Seetha Reddy
2021   Subsistence and Ritual: Faunal and Plant Exploitation at the Mission Santa Clara de Asís Ranchería (CA-SCL-30H). *California Archaeology* 13(2):203–225.

Reddy, Seetha N.
2015   Feeding Family and Ancestors: Persistence of Traditional Native American Lifeways during the Mission Period in Coastal Southern California. *Journal of Anthropological Archaeology* 37:48–66.

Schneider, Tsim D.
2015a   Placing Refuge and the Archaeology of Indigenous Hinterlands in Colonial California. *American Antiquity* 80(4):695–713.
2015b   Envisioning Colonial Landscapes Using Mission Registers, Radiocarbon, and Stable Isotopes: An Experimental Approach from San Francisco Bay. *American Antiquity* 80(3):511–529.
2021   *The Archaeology of Refuge and Recourse: Coast Miwok Resilience and Indigenous Hinterlands in Colonial California.* University of Arizona Press, Tucson.

Schneider, Tsim D., Khal Schneider, and Lee M. Panich
2020   Scaling Invisible Walls: Reasserting Indigenous Persistence in Mission-Era California. *The Public Historian* 42 (2): 97–120.

Stojanowski, Christopher M.
2013   *Mission Cemeteries, Mission Peoples: Historical and Evolutionary Dimensions of Intracemetery Bioarchaeology in Spanish Florida.* University Press of Florida, Gainesville.

Tica, Cristina I., and Debra L. Martin, eds.
2019   *Bioarchaeology of Frontiers and Borderlands.* University Press of Florida, Gainesville.
Walker, Phillip L., John R. Johnson, and Patricia M. Lambert
1988   Age and Sex Biases in the Preservation of Human Skeletal Remains. *American Journal of Physical Anthropology* 76:183–188.

2

A Brief History of Archival and Archaeological Research at the Asistencia de San Pedro y San Pablo

Lee M. Panich

Given the great potential of the information revealed through the collaborative study of the individuals from the Asistencia de San Pedro y San Pablo, this chapter seeks to establish a baseline of historical and archaeological information regarding the role of the site in both Native and colonial histories. We also offer a detailed discussion of regional research questions that will contextualize the chapters that follow.

When Franciscan missionaries established the Asistencia de San Pedro y San Pablo in 1786, their proselytization efforts in the greater San Francisco Bay region were only a decade old. They had come to Alta California slightly earlier, beginning in 1769, as part of a plan to hold the territory for Spain against encroachment by other colonial powers in the Pacific. Alongside military presidios and civilian pueblos, or towns, the missions were a critical part of the Spanish colonial plan, intended to convert Native Californians not only to Roman Catholic Christianity but also to a more Euro-American lifestyle. To do so, the Franciscans relied on a policy of *reducción* in which individuals and families from myriad tribal communities would be resettled at particular mission sites where they could be closely monitored as they learned the intricacies of Catholic doctrine, the Spanish language, and agriculture. With these guiding principles in mind, Mission San Francisco de Asís—locally known as Mission Dolores—became the first Spanish mission of the San Francisco Bay region in 1776 (Milliken 1995; Newell 2009; Panich 2020).

The Franciscans and other Spanish authorities, however, had misjudged the environmental and political realities of life on the San Francisco Peninsula. By the mid-1780s, they realized that the location of Mission San Fran-

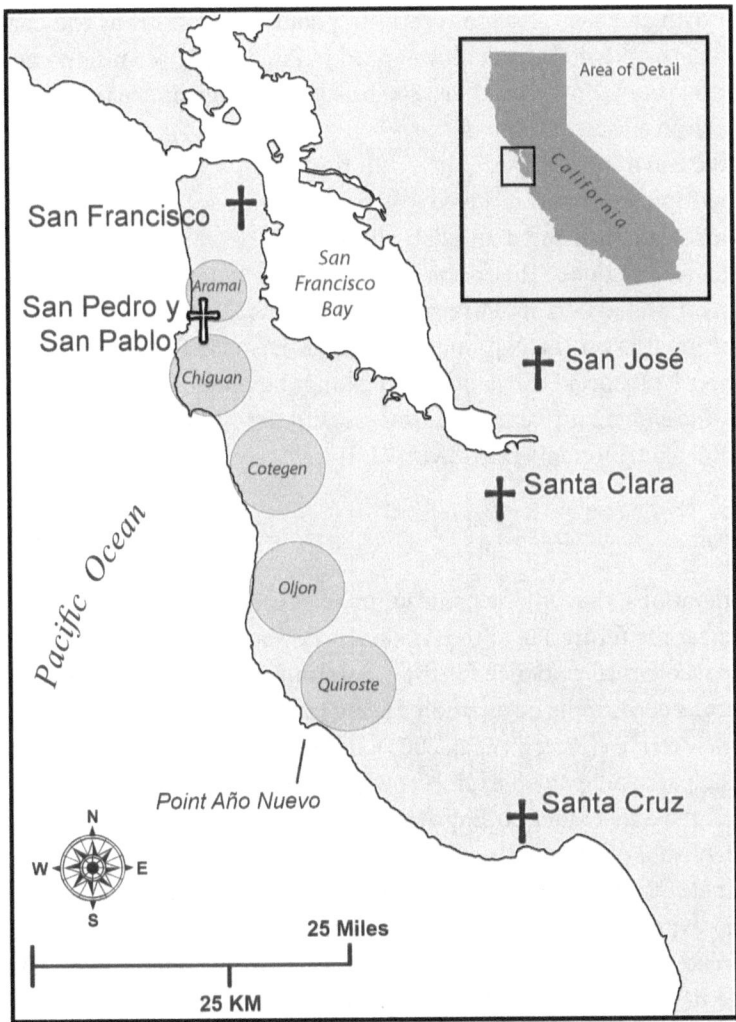

Figure 2.1. Map of the greater San Francisco Bay region with missions and other places mentioned in text. Approximate tribal territories are in shaded circles.

cisco offered only limited agricultural potential and, perhaps more troubling, that the Native residents of coastal territories were not particularly inclined to join the new mission community. As a remedy, the Franciscans established San Pedro y San Pablo in 1786 as an asistencia, or sub-mission, of Mission San Francisco in a fertile valley near the peninsula's Pacific shores, in what is the present-day town of Pacifica (figure 2.1). The fledgling outpost was near the Ohlone village of Pruristac and had direct access to other Ohlone communities further south along the coast who were resistant to colonization (Milliken

1979). With the twin goals of recruiting Native people from the coast and bolstering the mission's agricultural production, the site seemingly prospered for several years. However, after 1800 or so, the asistencia seems to have transitioned into a less prominent role.

As the missions were secularized in the 1830s, a colonist, Francisco Sánchez, petitioned for and received title to the former asistencia and surrounding lands. He constructed an adobe home at the site, which is today known as the Sánchez Adobe. The adobe and immediately surrounding property has been a San Mateo County Park since 1947 and is California Historical Landmark #391. It is on the National Register of Historic Places, as the Sánchez Adobe Park Historic District, encompassing the nineteenth-century Sánchez Adobe, the eighteenth-century asistencia, and the Ohlone village of Pruristac. Its California trinomial is CA-SMA-71/H.

Pruristac

For generations, the Ohlone community of Pruristac occupied the San Pedro Valley near the future site of the Asistencia de San Pedro y San Pablo. Precontact archaeological evidence for the community is scant, but obsidian hydration results confirm its occupation during much of the late precontact period (~1000–1769 CE) (Pastron et al. 2005). Indeed, residents of Pruristac encountered the party of Spanish explorers who, in the autumn of 1769, first reconnoitered the San Francisco Bay Area by land. The Spanish, however, would not establish a permanent presence in the region for several years, and it is likely that local Ohlone people continued to live in traditional ways even as colonial expeditions increasingly passed through their territories. One such party visited the Pruristac homelands in 1774. In a moment of foreshadowing, the missionary Francisco Palóu recorded his impression that the valley would make an excellent site for a mission "for it does not lack land, water, or pasture for cattle" (Milliken 1979:14–18).

Mission San Francisco de Asís was founded in 1776, altering the political geography of the San Francisco Peninsula. While the residents of Pruristac and their neighbors remained outside of direct colonial control, they were undoubtedly troubled by the growing Spanish presence near their homelands. The first Native individuals from Pruristac to be baptized were two sons of the community's captain, Yaguéche. Their baptisms were recorded at Mission San Francisco in February of 1779 while their father held out for another four years (Early California Population Project 2022: SFD Baptisms 92, 93, and 319). People from the area, including the nearby Punta de Almejas, trickled in to the mission over the coming years, but only a handful of individuals from

Pruristac were baptized in any given year through 1785. This pattern was consistent with the broader context of recruitment at Mission San Francisco. By the end of the first decade after its founding, most of the unbaptized Native people of the San Francisco Peninsula still lived some distance from the mission itself. While the Franciscans no doubt desired a faster pace of baptism, they were hindered by the fact that the main mission site was not conducive to agriculture and could not produce enough food for the growing congregation (Milliken 1979:23; Newell 2009:170).

The Asistencia de San Pedro y San Pablo

With the founding of the Asistencia de San Pedro y San Pablo, the interrelated problems of new baptisms and food supply were quickly remedied. The outstation extended the reach of the mission closer to autonomous villages along the Pacific coast and provided a site with more agricultural potential. The Franciscans seem to have identified the area around Pruristac as a possible agricultural outpost in the early 1780s, but it was not until 1786 that work began on the Asistencia de San Pedro y San Pablo. During that year, the Franciscans harnessed enough Native labor to have them construct a granary, a chapel, and other buildings. Records indicate that some of the structures were initially built using the palisada (wattle and daub) technique, but that laborers also amassed adobe bricks for future construction projects. Construction was more or less completed by 1789, with the site taking on the form of a sub-mission, complete with its own adobe quadrangle, agricultural activities, and cemetery (Jackson and Castillo 1995:152; Newell 2009:170).

The Franciscans were likely pleased with the asistencia's performance over the first few years. In 1787, some ninety acres were under cultivation and twenty-five baptisms were recorded at San Pedro y San Pablo. That year also marked the first Catholic burials at the site. The question of missionary oversight remains open, but it appears that one of the Franciscans assigned to Mission San Francisco—roughly twenty kilometers to the north—performed mass at San Pedro y San Pablo every Sunday, with the potential of remaining for longer stays during the harvest season. Crops reported to have been sown at San Pedro include maize, wheat, beans, and barley, along with a vineyard and orchard that included fruits such as peach, pear, and quince (Chavez et al. 1974; Early California Population Project 2022; Milliken 1979). Despite the sizable investment in infrastructure, the population dynamics of the site are not well understood. Reports of construction at San Pedro y San Pablo, for example, ended in 1789 without any mention of residential structures intended for Native residents, such as the kinds of adobe dormitories common at the main missions. In fact, some scholars have suggested that San Pedro y San Pablo was not even a residential site and that Native people associated with it continued to live in their home villages (Newell 2009:172). Still, the sacramental records indicate that approximately a hundred sixty baptisms, a hundred fifty deaths, and thirty-five marriages were performed at the asistencia between its founding and 1800. The Native people associated with the outstation were largely from coastal Ohlone communities, stretching as far south as Point Año Nuevo (Early California Population Project 2022; Milliken 1995:102; Newell 2009:170–172).

Indeed, the sacramental registers—including baptisms, marriages, and deaths—give a broad sense of the tribal origins of Native families and individuals who lived and died at San Pedro y San Pablo. A sizable number were individuals were from the community of Pruristac, which was the closest named settlement to the asistencia. These people and their neighbors, including those who were said to hail from the Punta de Almejas, formed a larger tribal entity that Milliken and colleagues (2009) call Aramai. The Native population associated with the outstation also included a significant proportion of people from further south, including the regions around Half Moon Bay and San Gregorio. These individuals and families were originally from communities that were part of the Chiguan, Cotegen, Oljon, and Quiroste tribal groups. Even though Mission Santa Clara would have been the geographically closest mission for most of these communities, at least until the founding of Mission Santa Cruz in 1791, the Asistencia de San Pedro y San Pablo likely offered several advantages, including its coastal location and lack of a full-time missionary (Milliken et al. 2009; Newell 2009).

More than 90 percent of the sacraments—baptism, marriage, and burial—performed at San Pedro y San Pablo took place between 1787 and 1792, with a significant decrease in baptisms and marriages from the early months of 1792 onward. The cause of this dramatic shift is not entirely clear. One possibility is that an outbreak of disease struck the outpost, as suggested by a sharp increase in burials at San Pedro y San Pablo in 1792 (Milliken 1979:31–33). Events further down the coast may have also contributed to the near abandonment of San Pedro y San Pablo. First was the founding of Mission Santa Cruz in 1791, which competed directly with the asistencia for the recruitment of coastal people, who were also being baptized at Mission Santa Clara at the southern extent of San Francisco Bay. A second series of events involved the leader of the powerful Quiroste tribe—a man named Charquin—who was baptized at San Pedro y San Pablo in late 1791 before quickly turning against the mission system. Instead of residing at the asistencia or at Mission San Francisco, he withdrew to his home village of Mitenne where he attracted a sizable contingent of Native people who had fled the nearby missions. By early 1793, tensions between Charquin's refuge community and colonial authorities came to a head, and it is possible that the Franciscans curtailed their activities at San Pedro y San Pablo as a precautionary measure (Milliken 1979:33; Milliken 1995:115–116; Rizzo-Martinez 2022:58–60).

Despite the unrest, Native people did continue to work at San Pedro y San Pablo in the following years. Mission records, for example, indicate that the outpost remained a crucial source of agricultural production for Mission San Francisco throughout the 1790s even as the Franciscans shifted some cultivation to San Mateo along the bay shore (Milliken 1979:33–35). The mission's sacramental records reveal fifteen additional burials that took place at the asistencia between 1795 and the end of the century. Two baptisms and two marriages were also performed at the outstation during those years (Early California Population Project 2022). Nearly all of these recorded events took place in autumn or early winter, perhaps suggesting that the site was most intensively occupied at harvest time.

All told, we identified a total of 152 Native individuals who were laid to rest at the Asistencia de San Pedro y San Pablo. For this analysis, we consulted the death records for Mission San Francisco de Asís using the Early California Population Project (2022) and the mission records database compiled by the late Randall Milliken, with selected cross-referencing of the original records that are held in San Francisco. Earlier scholars have suggested a comparable, but slightly smaller, total of approximately 135 Native individuals who were buried at the site between 1786 and 1794 (Milliken 1979; Newell 2009). The source of the discrepancy is unclear, but the addition of the later burials dating to 1795–1800 seems to account for the majority of the difference. All of the burials were individuals from Ohlone communities, most of which were located along the coast from the asistencia southward toward Santa Cruz. As noted, these home communities included Pruristac itself as well as villages belonging to the Chiguan, Cotegen, Oljon, and Quiroste tribal groups.

Demographic data offer some additional context for life at the asistencia. The majority, some 56 percent, of those who were buried at San Pedro y San Pablo were listed as being female. This is in keeping with broader patterns at the California missions in which a disproportionate number of women died compared to men (Jackson 1992; Jackson and Castillo 1995). Generally speaking, childbirth was especially dangerous given the suppression of traditional healing practices and the prevalence of infections spread through sexual assaults committed by colonial men against Native women. Children were also particularly at risk for infections of various kinds. Multiple individuals listed in the death records were noted as being newborns, and a full

Table 2.1. Age and gender distribution for individuals buried at San Pedro y San Pablo

Description	Age Range	Female	Male	Total
Infant	0–3	30	22	52
Child	4–12	15	17	32
Adolescent	13–17	7	4	11
Young Adult	18–25	6	5	11
Young/Middle Adult	26–35	14	5	19
Middle Adult	36–45	9	8	17
Mature Adult	46+	4	6	10
Total		85	67	152

Note: Age ranges reflect those used in the bioarchaeological analysis presented in this volume (following Boylston and Roberts 1996).

third of the individuals buried at the site died in the first three years of life. Indeed, over 63 percent of the documented burials at San Pedro y San Pablo were individuals younger than 18. These numbers contributed to the dismal overall statistics for Mission San Francisco, where Native children born into the colonial system only had an average life expectancy of 4.8 years. The figure for 1793, at the height of San Pedro y San Pablo, was a shocking 0.8 years at birth (Jackson 1992).

After the Asistencia

There is a significant gap in the documentary record for San Pedro y San Pablo following the last burials recorded there in the year 1800. In fact, some of the documents from the late 1790s and early 1800s suggest a shift in agricultural production from cultivation—which would require more permanent occupation—to cattle raising. Yet, sporadic accounts confirm that the site remained a part of the colonial landscape, including one report from 1823 claiming that the famed Coast Miwok bandit Pomponio was active in the area of San Pedro y San Pablo (Brown 1975:9). Still, the question of permanent occupation remains. After the year 1800, almost three decades passed without mention of Native people at the site. The next, and last, record of Native people's presence was in 1828, when it was said that some twenty-six Native individuals were living there, including men, women, and children. Yet, just six years later, a colonist petitioning to be granted the lands of San Pedro y San Pablo reported that the site was "vacant and unoccupied." An inventory of Mission San Francisco from 1835 made no mention of San Pedro y San Pablo (Chavez et al. 1974:11; Milliken 1979:33–36; Milliken et al. 2009:128–129).

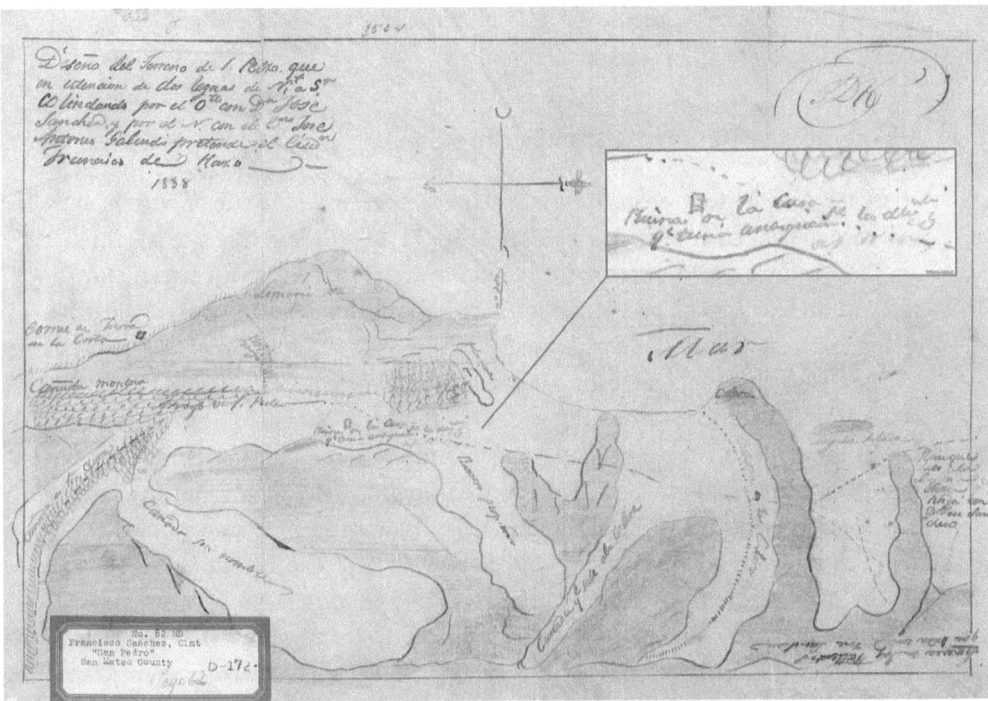

Figure 2.2. A diseño from an unsuccessful land grant petition from Francisco de Haro in 1838. Note: The map shows the former asistencia with the caption "Ruina de la casa que tenia antiguamente la misn de Sn Franco" (Ruins of the structure formerly held by Mission San Francisco). The map was later used as evidence in the adjudication of the land grant to Francisco Sánchez. Courtesy of the Bancroft Library, University of California, Berkeley.

Over the course of the 1830s and 1840s, the Franciscan missions were gradually secularized, a process in which the mission congregations were converted to parish churches, and mission lands and property were distributed among colonists and surviving Native people. In 1839, Francisco Sánchez, a former solider and colonial official, received a grant from the Mexican governor of California for nearly nine thousand acres he was already occupying near the former asistencia (figure 2.2; Alvarado 1839). Sánchez and his family soon constructed their own two-story adobe home—what is today known as the Sánchez Adobe—though the documentary record is silent on the state of the earlier structures at that time or whether any Native people still lived in the area. Certainly, Sánchez, like other proprietors of California's vast ranchos, would have relied heavily on Native people for labor. After Sánchez's death in 1862, the rancho lands were sold off. The adobe itself eventually served a number of other roles, including a hotel, artichoke warehouse, and speakeasy (Culp 2002; Dietz 1979; Drake 1952).

Archaeological Research at San Pedro y San Pablo

There is a long history of archaeological investigations at the site of what is today known as the Sánchez Adobe (CA-SMA-71/H). Though the site is named for the residence of a later historical occupant, Francisco Sánchez, historians and archaeologists had long wondered about the possibility of an earlier historic-era occupation of at the site.

The first archaeological testing of the site occurred in 1950, before the existence of the asistencia was confirmed. Conducted as field school for San Mateo Junior College, the excavations revealed cobblestone foundation remnants as well as some 2,200 artifacts. These are only poorly reported but included two Spanish coins from the 1790s and other materials, such as ceramics and items of adornment, that could conceivably date to the Mission Period. A nearby shell midden was also tested but was said to contain only "chert chips," revealing no firm connection to the asistencia that was reported to be in the area (Drake 1952; Drake and Pilling 1950). A few years later, historian Alan K. Brown discovered documentary evidence that the Sánchez Adobe site was indeed the location of the Asistencia de San Pedro y San Pablo. Further testing by an archaeologist from San Francisco State University in 1970 was inconclusive but offered the idea that the existing Sánchez Adobe could have been constructed directly atop the earlier asistencia structures (Chavez et al. 1974:1–12; Dietz 1979:1–10).

Just a few years later, archaeologists were finally able to provide firm evidence of the asistencia at the site of the later Sánchez Adobe. In 1974, backhoe trenches were placed across the "area, which was believed, by all parties who have sought to reconstruct the outpost quadrangle, to be the site of the outpost" (Chavez 1974:13). The results confirmed the presence of subsurface deposits, primarily cobblestone foundations, that related to the asistencia. Interestingly, few artifacts related to the eighteenth-century use of the site were encountered in or around the foundations, though the excavators themselves acknowledged that the use of the backhoe likely limited the potential for small finds. A human cranium was discovered during the trenching, but no effort was made to expose the entire interment. Though it now seems likely that the cranium was part of the mission-era cemetery, the archaeologists at the time believed the skeletal remains were associated with the site's precontact deposits (Chavez et al. 1974).

Archaeologists returned to the site in 1978, conducting areal excavations to expose the foundations that had been previously documented. The standing Sánchez Adobe, they found, may have been built over a portion of the former mission outpost, but significant foundation remnants extended to the south and east. Portions of nine rooms of the asistencia's quadrangle were exposed. Researchers believed them to represent the priest's and foreman's quarters, the kitchen, one of the granaries, as well as additional rooms of unknown function. Other features included a drainage ditch and possible cistern. As with the earlier excavations, few artifacts were noted that conclusively date to the late eighteenth or early nineteenth centuries. Of note were an obsidian biface fragment found in the overburden and a groundstone pestle fragment that had been incorporated into the foundation of the quadrangle. Various sherds of colonial-era ceramics were found—including locally produced earthenware and imported wares such as majolica. But the vast majority of the approximately nine thousand artifacts were related to more recent uses of the site (Dietz 1979).

In 1990, additional archaeological excavations were undertaken to ascertain the function of particular rooms, chart the extent of the granary, and to evaluate the condition of the previously excavated portions of the quadrangle. As in earlier projects, backhoe trenches were used to test different areas of the site (Wickstrom et al. 1990). Like nearly all of the previous work at the site, this project also focused on architectural features, as was common for the historical archaeology of Spanish colonial sites in California throughout the second half of the twentieth century (Allen 2010). Intrusive pits containing more recent materials were found to be cut into the former asistencia structure, but excavators did note artifacts dating to the Mission Period. These included several groundstone fragments, six Olivella shell beads (including Class A spire-lopped and Class B end-ground varieties), two blue glass beads of unknown type, and a metal religious medallion in the shape of a cross featuring a crucified Christ on one side and the Virgin Mary on the other. Sherds of majolica and lead-glazed earthenwares were among a small assemblage of ceramics (Costello 1990; Wickstrom et al. 1990). Of interest for the present study, the report's final summary states, "It is known that a cemetery was created for the interment of persons who died at the outpost of San Pedro y San Pablo. The location of this cemetery is yet to be identified" (Wickstrom et al. 1990:6–2).

During the early to mid-2000s, a number of construction projects on and near the property required archaeological monitoring and mitigation (Campbell et al. 2017:22–24). While some materials associated with the asistencia

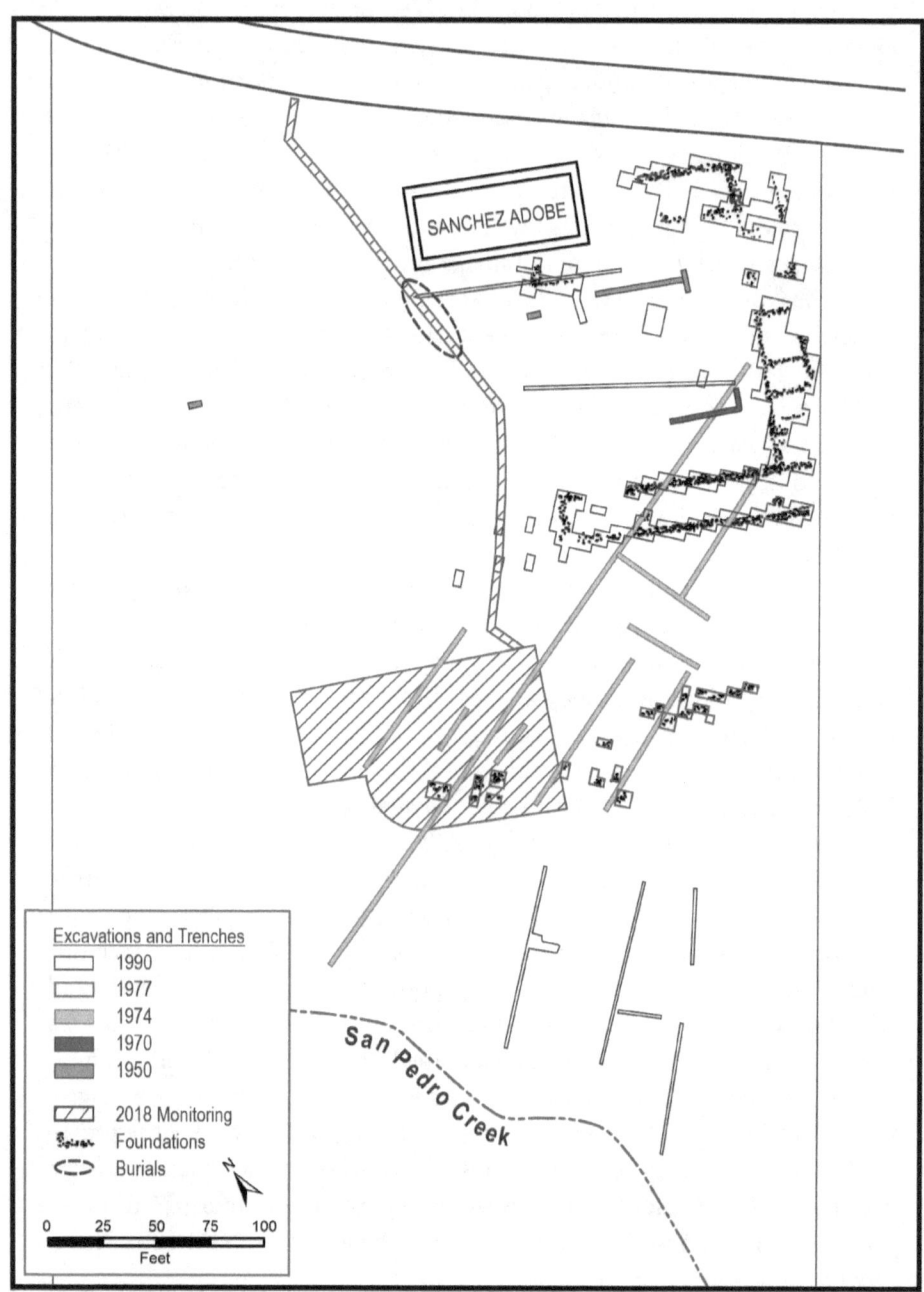

Figure 2.3. Plan map of excavations at the Sánchez Adobe, ca. 1950–90. Shown are the foundations of the Asistencia de San Pedro y San Pablo.

were uncovered, no major features were discovered. A single excavation unit in the nearby shell midden yielded the partial remains of a mule deer that had been butchered using metal tools. Excavators also recovered a small sample (n=24) of lithic debitage—chert, chalcedony, and obsidian—as well as a fragment of a chert corner-notched arrow point. The three obsidian flakes all originated from the Napa Valley source area, though obsidian hydration analysis suggests that they were created in precontact times (Pastron et al. 2005:24–25). Surprisingly, more than a half-century of archaeology, including several large-scale excavations, was conducted at the site of Asistencia de San Pedro y San Pablo without confirmation of the cemetery location (figure 2.3).

This changed in 2016 and 2017, when testing and geophysical survey related to utility improvements at the Sánchez Adobe Park revealed the presence of intact deposits, including a Native burial, at the site. Materials recovered from midden deposits included several flaked and ground stone tools, marine shell from a range of species, and faunal remains from wild and domesticated animals. Excavators also uncovered a thermal feature, which returned radiocarbon dates spanning the postcontact period of occupation for the site, suggesting that it could have been associated with the asistencia or later cattle ranching activities. A small archaeobotanical analysis was conducted on soil from the feature, revealing both native and introduced species. Of particular interest were seeds of *Chenopodium* (goosefoot), *Arctostaphylos* (manzanita), and Fabaceae (legumes) (Campbell et al. 2017; Kováčik 2017). Human skeletal remains, representing a single burial, were inadvertently discovered during this work but were not excavated.

Based on the findings from 2016 to 2017, and in keeping with the needs of the park's utility upgrade project, further archaeological monitoring and mitigation took place in 2018. At that time, additional burials were impacted, necessitating the recordation and excavation of fifteen individuals (see figure 2.4), though the single burial recorded in the previous project could not be rediscovered. For the purposes of estimating the minimum number of individual (MNI) and providing a data set for the palaeoepidemical study, a comprehensive inventory was conducted of those elements recovered from the discrete burials, as well as for isolated bone. Bioarchaeologists employed inventory standards developed by Buikstra and Ubelaker (1994:17–20) and Marshall (1999). Throughout the testing of 2016–17 and the burial recovery that followed, project personnel worked closely with Native American monitors from the Ohlone Indian Tribe, namely Andrew Galvan and Desiree Vigil, as well as with Christopher Zimmer of the Amah Mutsun Tribal Band of Mission San Juan Bautista, who was designated the Most Likely Descendant (MLD) by California's Native American Heritage Commission.

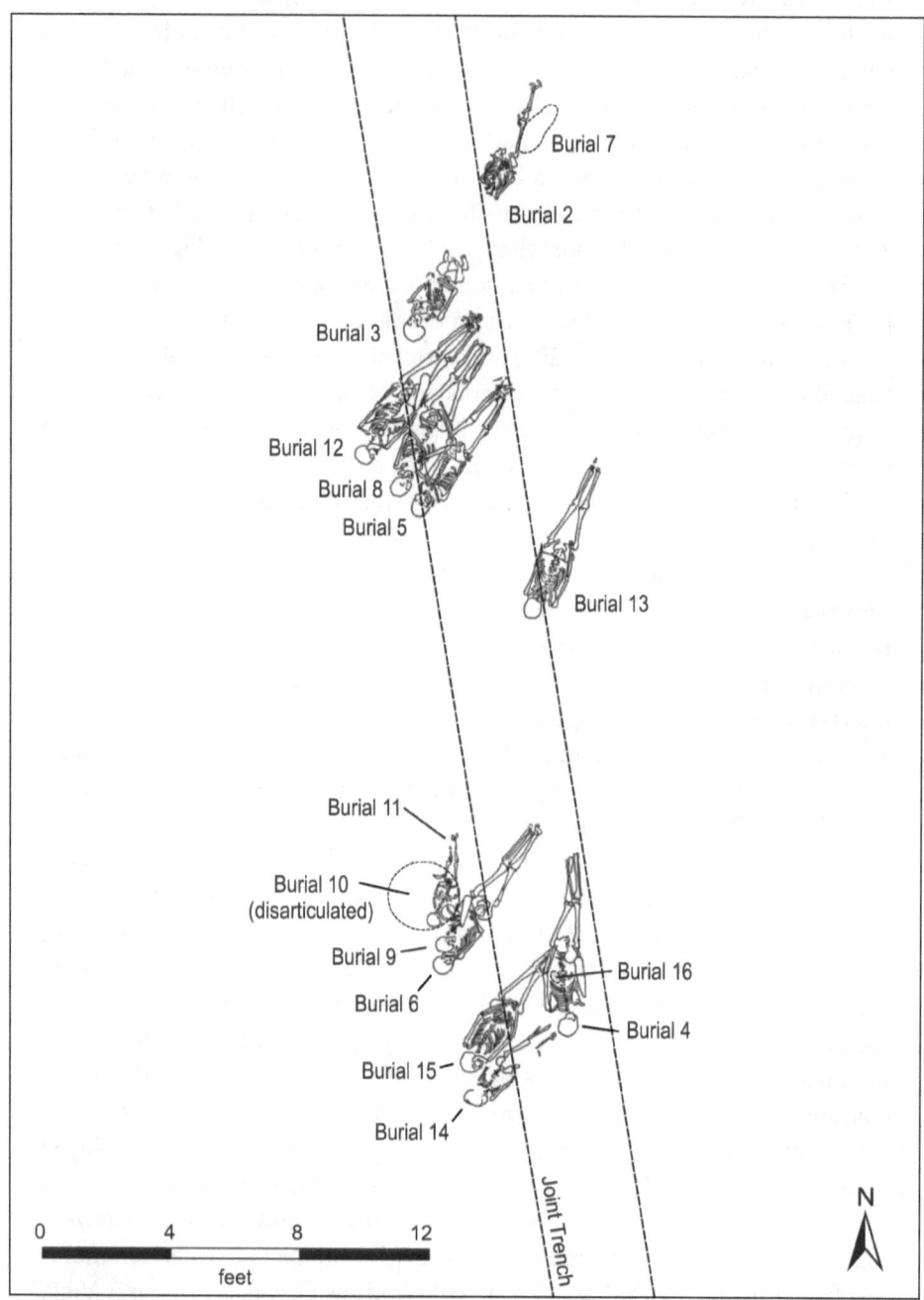

Figure 2.4. Plan map of 2016–18 utility trench excavation, and location and layout of fifteen human burials.

With full tribal support, bioarchaeological and mortuary analyses were conducted that reveal new information about the lives of the fifteen Ohlone ancestors recruited into the Spanish missions. Studies include paleopathology, nonmetric analyses, proteomic sexing of subadults, paleoproteomic analyses of dental calculus as insight into health and disease, analyses to evaluate exposure to heavy metals, chromatographic analyses of plant biochemicals in dental calculus, and stable isotope analyses to reconstruct paleodiet. Funerary offerings, including beads and other objects, were classified using standard typologies and certain samples were submitted for provenance analysis. In the summer of 2022, the Amah Mutsun Tribal Band of Mission San Juan Bautista reburied the skeletal remains of the fifteen individuals, and their belongings that were originally laid to rest with them, at the Sánchez Adobe Park in Pacifica.

Discussion

The primary question of this volume centers on the extent to which Native people were able to maintain aspects of their precontact traditions on the margins of the Spanish mission system. San Pedro y San Pablo is one of only a small number of asistencias to be excavated in California (e.g., Greenwood and Browne 1968), and the site thus offers a fascinating look into the lives of Native people associated with a satellite mission during the early years of colonization in the San Francisco Bay Area. Given that there was no resident missionary, Native people associated with the asistencia likely enjoyed greater freedoms than their compatriots attached to the main mission at San Francisco or to the nearby missions of Santa Clara and Santa Cruz. Such circumstances were undoubtedly preferable for many Native people who were not interested in submitting fully to life under the mission bell. In fact, patterns in the sacramental records—examined in more detail in this volume's penultimate chapter—suggest that whole families became associated with San Pedro y San Pablo during the final years of the eighteenth century.

Using the previous historical and archaeological findings from the Asistencia de San Pedro y San Pablo, discussed above, we can formulate a baseline of information against which to evaluate the results presented in the following chapters. While Mission San Francisco itself has seen only minimal archaeological research (Ambro 2003), major excavations have been conducted within the Native rancheria, or neighborhood, at Mission Santa Clara, with more modest excavations in analogous locations at Missions San José and Santa Cruz (e.g., Allen 1998; Allen et al. 2010; Dadiego et al. 2021; Panich et al. 2014; Panich et al. 2018a; Peelo et al. 2018; Potter et al. 2021b). In addition to the robust datasets from residential areas at these missions, archaeological mitigation at Mission Santa Clara has resulted in multiple bioarchaeological and mortuary studies (Hylkema 1995; Leventhal et al. 2011; Panich 2015; Skowronek and Wizorek 1997). We can use the results of these varied studies to contextualize the following chapters on San Pedro y San Pablo.

Disease

Given the fact that this volume focuses on the asistencia cemetery, it is only natural to examine the health of Native people associated with San Pedro y San Pablo. Milliken (1979:31–33) speculates that an epidemic may have struck the asistencia in 1792, accounting for the sharp increase in burials in that year—nearly a third of all burials recorded for the site. Overall, the demographic data from San Pedro y San Pablo, including the premature deaths of disproportionate numbers of women and children, are in line with the tragic patterns recorded for the main missions. Yet few true epidemics struck Alta California, and the region's abhorrently high death rates can instead be viewed as the result of chronic ailments combined with forced labor, cultural suppression, and poor living conditions at the missions (Jackson 1992; Jones et al. 2021). The data from San Pedro y San Pablo may therefore suggest that Native people associated with the asistencia spent considerable time at the main mission of San Francisco, or perhaps that life at San Pedro y San Pablo was not so idyllic after all.

Unfortunately, the documentary record for the site is nearly silent regarding these questions. Despite the prevalence of disease in explanations for Native population decline in California, the Franciscans themselves inconsistently noted the cause of death for Native people buried in the mission cemeteries. Across the province, in fact, Franciscans typically noted only the causes of extreme or unusual deaths, while others—including illness—were often unremarked upon (Hackel 2012). This pattern may have been exacerbated given the remote location of San Pedro y San Pablo. While a small number of individuals are listed as dying "suddenly," only one individual is noted as being ill, a young man named Josè Manuel who is said to have suffered from an "ayre perlatico," loosely translated as palsy, at the time of his death in 1789 (Early California Population Project 2022: SFD Death# 298). The only other definitive cause of death was for Primo, an Ohlone man mauled by a bear in 1798 (Early California Population Project 2022: SFD Death# 1210).

Metals

Communal and household cooking at California mission sites relied on metal vessels and utensils, typically iron, copper, or copper alloys. For example, large copper vessels were commonly used in the Bay Area missions and have been documented archaeologically at Mission Santa Clara and Mission San José. Similarly, cuprous chocolate pots—*chocolateras*—have been recovered from Native contexts at Mission Santa Clara. Iron implements of various forms, including knives, are also commonly recovered from Native residential areas at Bay Area missions (Graham and Skowronek 2016; Panich et al. 2018; Potter et al. 2021b; Skowronek et al. 2006; Thompson and Galvan 2007). Exposure to heavy metals may have also come through the use or even local manufacture of tin- or lead-glazed ceramics, such as those documented in the 1990 excavations at San Pedro y San Pablo (Costello 1990). Given that Ohlone communities did not traditionally produce pottery, tin-glazed majolica and lead-glazed earthenware ceramics were imported to Alta California from production centers in Mexico. Further, geochemical analysis demonstrates that some lead-glazed earthenware vessels were produced at central California missions, including San Francisco, Santa Clara, and Santa Cruz—all missions where people from the peninsula coast were baptized. Ceramic production in the Bay Area missions, however, did not begin in earnest until the 1790s, likely limiting the period of exposure through manufacturing for Native people associated with the asistencia (Skowronek et al. 2014).

Tobacco

Ohlone people, like other Native Californians, used tobacco regularly. While detailed ethnographic data is lacking for the San Francisco Peninsula, it seems likely that tobacco was used for both recreational and ceremonial purposes. In addition to smoking tobacco leaves, Native Californians formed dried tobacco into cakes that could be eaten, taken as an emetic, or smoked. Regionally, both men and women consumed tobacco, with only minor differences in the context of its use (see overview in Cuthrell et al. 2016). Recent archaeological work has demonstrated the antiquity of tobacco use in the Ohlone culture area. For example, archaeobotanical analysis from a site near Point Año Nuevo, the homeland of some of the Ohlone people associated with San Pedro y San Pablo, revealed the presence of tobacco in samples dating as early as 1000–1300 CE (Cuthrell 2013:328). Stone pipes from a site across the San Francisco Bay, dating to 1305–1415 CE, contained nicotine residues, confirming that tobacco was smoked in precontact times, and nicotine has been recovered from dental calculus samples in the region (Eerkens et al. 2012, 2016).

Tobacco use continued unabated into the colonial period. Spanish missionaries regularly carried tobacco, along with items such as glass beads, to facilitate interactions with Native communities. And records related to imports to Alta California list a variety of tobacco products, from bundles of leaf tobacco to cigars and cigarettes, some of which were undoubtedly distributed to Native people. Documentary evidence from throughout central California also suggests that tobacco was cultivated at many of the Franciscan missions, a notion confirmed by archaeobotanical studies from an assemblage associated with a Native dwelling at Mission Santa Clara. There it seems that Native residents grew and processed domesticated tobacco (*Nicotiana tabacum*), tree tobacco (*Nicotiana glauca*), and at least one other kind of tobacco (either *Nicotiana attenuata, Nicotiana quadrivalvis,* and/or *Nicotiana acuminata*) (Cuthrell et al. 2016). While the presence of tree tobacco in that sample is unusual, these results nonetheless demonstrate that Native people continued to use wild and domesticated tobacco while in residence at colonial sites.

Diet

Prior to colonization, Ohlone communities stewarded a variety of habitats from the Pacific coast into nearby mountain ranges. Acorns were a staple crop by the late precontact period but were used alongside an array of wild plant species, including various grasses and berries. Hunters sought out animals including birds, deer, rabbits, and other small mammals. For communities near the coast, shellfish, various fishes, and sea otters also constituted important dietary contributions (Broughton 1994, 2004; Hylkema 2002:252–254; Lightfoot and Parrish 2009:252–277). Native people living at mission sites were supplied with large quantities of beef, beans, and Euro-American staple grains such as maize, wheat, and barley. These are attested to in the documentary record for every mission site in the region, including the Asistencia de San Pedro y San Pablo. Fruits were an important, but often overlooked, aspect of the mission diet. For example, the orchard at nearby Mission Santa Clara included apple, pear, peach, quince, and pomegranate for the year 1787, just after the founding of San Pedro y San Pablo (Skowronek et al. 2006:131).

Archaeologically, the picture of Native diet at Bay Area mission sites is more varied. Cattle (*Bos taurus*) dominates faunal assemblages from nearly all Mission Period archaeological deposits, with small contributions from other domesticated animals such as chicken and sheep/goat. Closer analysis reveals that Native people also incorporated traditional fauna into their diet, including small mammals, fish, shellfish, several wild bird species, and in some instances, deer and elk (Allen 1998; Allen et al. 2010; Clark et al. 2021; Noe 2023; Panich et al. 2018:23). A similar pattern holds for botanical remains. Archaeobotanical studies from in and around residential structures have confirmed the presence of the Euro-American domesticates listed in the mission records—maize, wheat, beans, barley, and fruits—alongside smaller, yet significant, quantities of culturally meaningful wild plants. Though the quantities differ between particular features, these typically include *Chenopodium*, Asteraceae, and *Quercus* (oak) (Allen et al. 2010; Panich et al. 2018:22–23; Popper 2016; Reddy 2021). The Franciscan missionaries were not astute observers of Native Californian life, but their writings do suggest possible differences in diet by age, namely that older individuals retained more affinity for traditional foods (Geiger and Meighan 1976).

Trade/Connectedness

From their homelands in the San Francisco Bay Area, Ohlone communities were involved in multiple, overlapping regional interaction spheres (Rosenthal 2011). Among the materials that are easiest to track archaeologically are shell beads and obsidian. In precontact times, most shell beads associated with Ohlone sites were crafted from the shells of *Callianax biplicata*, commonly known as Olivella. Isotopic evidence shows that many Olivella beads found locally were produced from shells obtained along the central California coast, but some were traded from as far away as Southern California (Burns et al. 2023; Eerkens et al. 2005). Similar beads were used by Native people associated with the Bay Area missions. At Mission Santa Clara, for example, various excavations have documented Olivella Class A beads, which may have been locally produced, as well as needle-drilled Class H disk beads that were likely produced by Chumash artisans, living along the Santa Barbara Channel, who mass-produced such beads well into the colonial period. Similar small beads produced from the epidermis of red abalone (*Haliotis rufescens*) were likely also traded north from the Santa Barbara Channel. In a sharp contrast to precontact patterns, Bay Area mission sites have also yielded large quantities of clamshell disk beads. These beads were manufactured north of San Francisco Bay and were not commonly used by Ohlone communities prior to the colonial period (Panich 2014; and see Peelo et al. 2018).

Ohlone people also used imported obsidian for the creation of stone tools, such as arrow points. Most of this obsidian came from the large Napa Valley source area, with smaller quantities from the Annadel quarry, both in the Coast Ranges north of San Francisco Bay. Ohlone people also used obsidian that originated at sources in the eastern Sierra Nevada, though those sources seem to have become more restricted after 1000 CE when regional exchange networks shifted with the introduction of the bow and arrow (Jackson and Ericson 1994; Milliken et al. 2007). These same sources continued to be used into the colonial period. While only minimal mission-era obsidian provenance analysis has been conducted for Spanish sites on the San Francisco Peninsula (e.g., Hull and Voss 2016), archaeologists have recently analyzed two large obsidian assemblages—each containing more than a thousand specimens—

from Missions Santa Clara and San José. Material from Napa Valley dominates both assemblages, which also have artifacts manufactured from Annadel obsidian. While Napa Valley and Annadel were the only sources present at Mission San José, approximately 10 percent of the assemblage from Mission Santa Clara originated at sources in the eastern Sierra Nevada (Panich 2016; Panich et al. 2018b).

Conclusion

Archaeological and documentary evidence has revealed a great deal about the lives of Native people who lived and worked at the missions of the greater San Francisco Bay Area. Yet, Native people's continued engagement with the region's broader landscape—including mission outstations such as San Pedro y San Pablo—is a topic that has received comparatively less attention (Byrd et al. 2018; Schneider 2015, 2021; Panich and Schneider 2015). Part of the challenge is methodological: fewer colonial observers were present in the Native hinterlands to leave archival documentation, and such sites often remain in relatively remote areas where they are less impacted by construction (the source of most archaeological information in the region today). Accordingly, research at the Asistencia de San Pedro y San Pablo offers an unparalleled opportunity to examine some of the most important questions in the archaeology of colonial California. The current project also stands as an example of a successful collaboration between the tribal community, county officials, and archaeologists working in both academia and cultural resource management. Such collaborations are without a doubt the future of archaeology in California and elsewhere.

References

Allen, Rebecca
1998   *Native Americans at Mission Santa Cruz, 1791–1834: Interpreting the Archaeological Record.* Perspectives in California Archaeology 5. Institute of Archaeology, University of California, Los Angeles.
2010   Rethinking Mission Land Use and the Archaeological Record in California: An Example from Santa Clara. *Historical Archaeology* 44(2):72–96.
Allen, Rebecca, R. Scott Baxter, Linda J. Hylkema, Clinton M. Blount, and Stella D'Oro
2010   *Uncovering and Interpreting History and Archaeology at Mission Santa Clara: Report on Archaeological Data Recovery at the Leavey School Business, Murguía Parking Lot, and Jesuit Community Residence Project Areas.* Past Forward, Inc., Santa Clara University Archaeology Research Lab, and Albion Environmental,

Inc. Report to Santa Clara University. On file, Department of Anthropology, Santa Clara University.

Alvarado, Juan B.
1839   San Pedro Land Grant. ND 82. Documents Pertaining to the Adjudication of Private Land Claims in California, BANC MSS Land Case Files 1852–1892; BANC MSS C-A 300 FILM, The Bancroft Library, University of California, Berkeley

Ambro, Richard D.
2003   They Danced in the Plaza: The Historical Archaeology of Notre Dame Plaza, Mission San Francisco de Asís (Dolores), 347 Dolores Street, San Francisco, California. Report to Mercy/Charities Housing California, San Francisco. On file, Department of Anthropology, Santa Clara University.

Boylston, Anthea, and Charlotte A. Roberts
1996   The Roman-British Cemetery at Kempston, Bedfordshire. Report on the Human Skeletal Remains. Calvin Well Laboratory, Department of Archaeological Sciences, University of Bradford, Bradford, United Kingdom.

Broughton, Jack M.
1994   Declines in Mammalian Foraging Efficiency During the Late Holocene, San Francisco Bay, California. *Journal of Anthropological Archaeology* 13(4): 371–401.
2004   Prehistoric Human Impacts on California Birds: Evidence from the Emeryville Shellmound Avifauna. *Ornithological Monographs* 78(56): iii–90.

Brown, Alan K.
1975   Pomponio's World. *San Francisco Corral of Westerners Argonaut* 6:1–20.

Buikstra, J. E., and D. H. Ubelaker
1994   Standards for Data Collection from Human Skeletal Remains. Proceedings of a Seminar at the Field Museum of Natural History Arkansas Archaeological Survey Research Series No. 44, Fayetteville.

Burns, Gregory R., Jelmer W. Eerkens, Howard J. Spero, and Jeffrey S. Rosenthal
2023   Isotopic Evidence of Sources for Central California Olivella Beads. *California Archaeology* 15(1): 33–51.

Byrd, Brian F., Shannon DeArmond, Laurel Engbring
2018   Re-Visualizing Indigenous Persistence during Colonization from the Perspective of Traditional Settlements in the San Francisco Bay-Delta Area. *Journal of California and Great Basin Anthropology* 38(2): 163–190.

Campbell, B., K. Brudvik, and B. Vargas
2017   *Sanchez Adobe; Archaeological Testing Report, San Mateo County, California.* Rincon Consultants Project No. 16–03454. On file at the Northwest Information Center, Sonoma State University, California.

Chavez, David, Stephen A. Dietz, and Thomas L. Jackson
1974   *Report of the 1974 Archaeological Excavations at the Sanchez Adobe.* Report to the San Mateo County Department of Parks and Recreation. On file at the Northwest Information Center, Sonoma State University, California.

Clark, Tiffany, Brenna Whellis, and Megan Watson
2021   Vertebrate Fauna and Shellfish Remains. In *575 Benton Street Project Santa*

Clara, California. Volume I: Data Recovery at Site CA-SCL-30H, edited by James M. Potter, Mike Mirro and Brenna Wheelis, 283–312. Technical Report No. 21-099, PaleoWest, Pasadena, California.

Costello, Julia G.
1990 Appendix A: Ceramics. In Draft Report of 1990 Archaeological Investigations, Sanchez Adobe Park Historic District, by Brian P. Wickstrom, Stephen A. Dietz, and Thomas L. Jackson. Report to County of San Mateo. On file, Department of Anthropology, Santa Clara University.

Culp, John
2002 Shell Mounds to Cul-de-Sacs: The Cultural Landscape of San Pedro Valley, Pacifica, California. Master's thesis, Department of Geography, San Francisco State University.

Cuthrell, Rob Q.
2013 An Eco-archaeological Study of Late Holocene Indigenous Foodways and Landscape Management Practices at Quiroste Valley Cultural Preserve, San Mateo County, California. PhD dissertation, Department of Anthropology, University of California, Berkeley.

Cuthrell, Rob Q., Lee M. Panich, and Oliver R. Hegge
2016 Investigating Native Californian Tobacco Use at Mission Santa Clara, California, through Morphometric Analysis of Tobacco (Nicotiana spp.) Seeds. *Journal of Archaeological Science: Reports* 6:451–662.

Dadiego, Danielle L., Alyssa Gelinas, and Tsim D. Schneider
2021 Unpacking the Bead: Exploring a Glass Bead Assemblage from Mission Santa Cruz, California, using LA-ICP-MS. *American Antiquity* 86(2): 413–424.

Dietz, Stephen A.
1979 Report of Archeological Investigations at Sanchez Adobe Park Historic District. Report to the San Mateo County Department of Parks and Recreation. On file at the Northwest Information Center, Sonoma State University, California.

Drake, Robert J.
1952 Samplings in History at the Sanchez Adobe, San Mateo County, California. El Palacio 59(1): 18–29.

Drake, Robert J., and Arnold R. Pilling
1950 Site record for CA-SMA-71/H (41-000074). On file at the Northwest Information Center, Rohnert Park, CA.

Early California Population Project
2022 Edition 1.1. General Editor, Steven W. Hackel. University of California, Riverside and The Huntington Library, Art Museum, and Botanical Gardens, San Marino, California.

Eerkens, J. W., G. S. Herbert, J. S. Rosenthal, and H. J. Spero
2005 Provenience Analysis of Olivella biplicata Shell Beads from the California and Oregon Coast by Stable Isotope Fingerprinting. *Journal of Archaeological Science* 32: 1501–1514.

Eerkens, J., S. Tushingham, K. Lentz, J. Blake, D. Ardura, M. Palazoglu, O. Fiehn
2012 GC/MS analysis of residues reveals nicotine in two late prehistoric pipes from

CA-ALA-554. *Proceedings of the Society for California Archaeology* 26:212–219.

Eerkens, Jelmer W., Shannon Tushingham, Korey J. Brownstein, Ramona Garibay, Katherine Perez, Engel Murga, Phillip Kaijankoski, Jeffrey S. Rosenthal, and David R. Gang

2018   Dental calculus as a source of ancient alkaloids: Detection of nicotine by LC-MS in calculus samples from the Americas. *Journal of Archaeological Science Reports* 18: 509–515.

Geiger, Maynard J., and Clement W. Meighan

1976   *As the Padres Saw Them: California Indian Life and Customs as Reported by the Franciscan Missionaries, 1813–1815.* Santa Barbara Mission Archive-Library, Santa Barbara, California.

Graham, Margaret A., and Russell K. Skowronek

2016   Chocolate on the Borderlands of New Spain. *International Journal of Historical Archaeology* 20:645–665.

Greenwood, Roberta S., and R. O. Browne

1968   The Chapel of Santa Gertrudis. *Pacific Coast Archaeological Society Quarterly* 4(4): 1–60.

Hackel, Steven W.

2012   From Ahogado to Zorrillo: External Causes of Mortality in the California Missions. *The History of the Family* 17(1): 77–104.

Hull, Kathleen L., and Barbara L. Voss

2016   Native Californians at the Presidio of San Francisco: Analysis of Lithic Specimens from El Polín Spring." *International Journal of Historical Archaeology* 20:264–288.

Hylkema, Mark G.

1995   *Archaeological Investigations at the Third Location of Mission Santa Clara de Asís: The Murguía Mission, 1781–1818 (CA-SCL-30/H).* Oakland: California Department of Transportation, District 4, Environmental Planning.

2002   Tidal Marsh, Oak Woodlands, and Cultural Florescence in the Southern San Francisco Bay Region. In *Catalysts to Complexity: Late Holocene Societies of the California Coast*, edited by Jon M. Erlandson and Terry L. Jones, 263–281. Perspectives in California Archaeology, Volume 6. Cotsen Institute of Archaeology, University of California, Los Angeles.

Jackson, Robert H.

1992   The Dynamic of Indian Demographic Collapse in the San Francisco Bay Missions, Alta California, 1776–1840. *American Indian Quarterly* 16(2): 141–156.

Jackson, Robert H., and Edward Castillo

1995   *Indians, Franciscans, and Spanish Colonization: The Impact of the Mission System on California Indians.* University of New Mexico Press, Albuquerque.

Jackson, Thomas L., and Jonathon E. Ericson

1994   Prehistoric Exchange Systems in California. In *Prehistoric Exchange Systems in North America*, edited by Timothy G. Baugh and Jonathon E. Ericson, 385–415. Plenum Press, New York.

Jones, Terry L., Al W. Schwitalla, Marin A. Pilloud, John R. Johnson, Richard R. Paine, and Brian F. Codding
2021   Historic and Bioarchaeological Evidence Supports Late Onset of Post-Columbian Epidemics in Native California. *Proceedings of the National Academy of Sciences* 118(28): e2024802118. https://doi.org/10.1073/pnas.2024802118.

Kováčik, Peter
2017   Macrofloral Analysis of a Sample from Site CA-SMA-71, San Mateo County, California. Report for Rincon Consultants, Inc. PaleoResearch Institue Technical Report 2017–2052. On file, Department of Anthropology, Santa Clara University.

Leventhal, Alan, Diane DiGiuseppe, Melynda Atwood, David Grant, Rosemary Cambra, Charlene Nijmeh, Monica V. Arellano, Sheila Guzman-Schmidt, Gloria E. Gomez, and Norma Sanchez
2011   *Final Report on the Burial and Archaeological Data Recovery Program Conducted on a Portion of the Mission Santa Clara Indian Neophyte Cemetery (1781–1818): Clareño Muwékma Ya Túnneště Nómmo [Where the Clareño Indians are Buried] Site (CA-SCL-30/H), Located in the City of Santa Clara, Santa Clara County, California.* Submitted to Pacific Gas and Electric Company by Ohlone Family Consulting Services.

Lightfoot, Kent G., and Otis Parrish
2009   *California Indians and their Environment: An Introduction.* University of California Press, Berkeley.

Marshall, Christine, E.
1999   ". . . And the Head Shall Remain Uncorrupted": A Taphonomic Analysis of Romano-British Decapitation Burials—unpublished Master of Arts Thesis, Department of Archaeological Science, University of Bradford.

Milliken, Randall
1979   The Mission Outstation of San Pedro and San Pablo. In *Report of Archeological Investigations at Sanchez Adobe Park Historic District* by Stephen A. Dietz, 14–37. Report to the San Mateo County Department of Parks and Recreation. On file at the Northwest Information Center, Sonoma State University, California.
1995   *A Time of Little Choice: The Disintegration of Tribal Culture in the San Francisco Bay Area, 1769–1810.* Ballena Press, Menlo Park, CA.

Milliken, Randall, Laurence H. Shoup, and Beverly R. Ortiz
2009   Ohlone/Costanoan Indians of the San Francisco Peninsula and Their Neighbors, Yesterday and Today. Report to the National Park Service, Golden Gate National Recreation Area, San Francisco.

Milliken, Randall T., Richard T. Fitzgerald, Mark G. Hylkema, Randy Groza, Tom Origer, David G. Bieling, Alan Leventhal, Randy S. Wiberg, Andrew Gottsfield, Donna Gillete, Viviana Bellifemine, Eric Strother, Robert Cartier, and David A. Fredrickson
2007   Punctuated Culture Change in the San Francisco Bay Area. In *California Prehistory: Colonization, Culture, and Complexity*, edited by Terry L. Jones and Kathryn A. Klar, 99–124. Altamira Press, Lanham, MD.

Newell, Quincy D.
2009   Constructing Lives at Mission San Francisco: Native Californians and Hispanic Colonists, 1776–1821. University of New Mexico Press, Albuquerque.
Noe, Sarah J.
2023   Subsistence and Persistence: Indigenous Foodways Within Mission Santa Clara de Asís. *California Archaeology* 15(1): 69–107
Panich, Lee M.
2014   Native American Consumption of Shell and Glass Beads at Mission Santa Clara de Asís. *American Antiquity* 79(4): 730–748.
2015   "Sometimes They Bury the Deceased's Clothes and Trinkets": Indigenous Mortuary Practices at Mission Santa Clara de Asís. *Historical Archaeology* 49(4): 110–129.
2016   Beyond the Colonial Curtain: Investigating Indigenous Use of Obsidian in Spanish California through the pXRF Analysis of Artifacts from Mission Santa Clara. *Journal of Archaeological Science: Reports* 5:521–530.
2020   *Narratives of Persistence: Indigenous Negotiations of Colonialism in Alta and Baja California.* University of Arizona Press, Tucson.
Panich, Lee M., and Tsim D. Schneider
2015   Expanding Mission Archaeology: A Landscape Approach to Indigenous Autonomy in Colonial California. *Journal of Anthropological Archaeology* 40:48–58.
Panich, Lee M., H. Afaghani, and N. Mathwich
2014   Assessing the Diversity of Mission Populations through the Comparison of Native American Residences at Mission Santa Clara de Asis. *International Journal of Historical Archaeology* 18:467–488.
Panich, Lee M., Rebecca Allen, and Andrew Galvan
2018a   The Archaeology of Native American Persistence at Mission San José. *Journal of California and Great Basin Anthropology* 38(1): 11–29.
Panich, Lee M., Ben Griffin, and Tsim D. Schneider
2018b   Native Acquisition of Obsidian in Colonial-Era Central California: Implications from Mission San José. *Journal of Anthropological Archaeology* 50:1–11.
Pastron, Allen, Anna Engberg, and Jason Clairborne
2005   Final Report of Archaeological Investigations at 1335 Adobe Drive, City of Pacifica, San Mateo County. Report to Remax Dolphin Realty. On file at the Northwest Information Center, Sonoma State University, California.
Peelo, Sarah, Linda J. Hylkema, John Ellison, Clinton M. Blount, Mark G. Hylkema, Margie Maher, Tom Garlinghouse, Dustin McKenzie, Stella D'Oro, and Melinda Berge
2018   Persistence in the Indian Ranchería at Mission Santa Clara de Asís. *Journal of California and Great Basin Anthropology* 38(2): 207–234.
Popper, Virginia S.
2016   Change and Persistence: Mission Neophyte Foodways at Selected Colonial Alta California Institutions. *Journal of California and Great Basin Anthropology* 36(1): 5–25.
Potter, James M., Tiffany Clark, and Seetha Reddy
2021a   Subsistence and Ritual: Faunal and Plant Exploitation at the Mission Santa

Clara de Asís Ranchería (CA-SCL-30H). *California Archaeology* 13(2): 203–225.

Potter, James M., Mike Mirro, and Brenna Wheelis
2021b   *575 Benton Street Project Santa Clara, California. Volume I: Data Recovery at Site CA-SCL-30H.* Technical Report No. 21–099, PaleoWest, Pasadena, California. Prepared for Prometheus Real Estate Group, Inc.

Reddy, Seetha N.
2021   Macrobotanical Analysis. In *575 Benton Street Project Santa Clara, California. Volume I: Data Recovery at Site CA-SCL-30H,* edited by James M. Potter, Mike Mirro, and Brenna Wheelis, 399–445. Technical Report No. 21–099, PaleoWest, Pasadena, California.

Rizzo-Martinez, Martin
2022   *We Are Not Animals: Indigenous Politics of Survival, Rebellion, and Reconstruction in Nineteenth-Century California.* University of Nebraska Press, Lincoln.

Rosenthal, Jeffrey S.
2011   The Function of Shell Bead Exchange in Central California. In *Perspectives on Prehistoric Trade and Exchange in California and the Great Basin,* edited by Richard E. Hughes, 83–113. The University of Utah Press, Salt Lake City.

Schneider, Tsim D.
2015   Placing Refuge and the Archaeology of Indigenous Hinterlands in Colonial California. *American Antiquity* 80(4): 695–713.
2021   *The Archaeology of Refuge and Recourse: Coast Miwok Resilience and Indigenous Hinterlands in Colonial California.* University of Arizona Press, Tucson.

Skowronek, Russell K., and Julie C. Wizorek
1997   Archaeology at Santa Clara de Asís: The Slow Rediscovery of a Moveable Mission. *Pacific Coast Archaeological Society Quarterly* 33(3): 54–92.

Skowronek, Russell K., M. James Blackman, and Ronald L. Bishop
2014   *Ceramic Production in Early Hispanic California: Craft, Economy, and Trade on the Frontier of New Spain.* University Press of Florida, Gainesville.

Skowronek, Russell K., Elizabeth Thompson, and Veronica L. Johnson
2006   *Situating Mission Santa Clara de Asís, 1776–1851, Documentary and Material Evidence of Life on the Alta California Frontier: A Timeline.* Academy of American Franciscan History, Berkeley, California.

Thompson, Richard E., and Andrew A. Galvan
2007   Excavations at St. Joséph Catholic Community Rectory, 43148 Mission Boulevard Fremont, California 94539. Report on file at Department of Anthropology, Santa Clara University, Santa Clara, California.

Wickstrom, Brian P., Stephen A. Dietz, and Thomas L. Jackson
1990   Draft Report of 1990 Archaeological Investigations, Sanchez Adobe Park Historic District. Report to County of San Mateo. On file, Department of Anthropology, Santa Clara University.

3

Life and the Biological Consequences therein at the Mission Period Site of Asistencia de San Pedro y San Pablo (CA-SMA-71/H), 1787–1794

ALYSON CAINE, CHRISTOPHER CANZONIERI,
AND CHRISTINE MARSHALL

We focus on demographic and pathological profiles of fifteen individuals recovered at Asistencia de San Pedro y San Pablo, including eight adults and seven nonadults. We compare results to precontact and contact-period archaeological samples in California to highlight the health implications and living conditions during the Mission Period.

Note that, in collaboration with the Most Likely Descendants, we felt it was important to present visual evidence in the form of photographs of particular skeletal pathologies. This allows the interested reader to independently evaluate our interpretations of the pathologies. However, for readers who are sensitive to or prefer not to see images of human skeletal remains, we opted to include the images, not within this chapter, but within an appendix to this book.

Methods

The skeleton provides material evidence of biological and cultural indicators of plastic and fixed identities (Sofaer 2006). Therefore, bioarchaeologists view the skeleton as the embodiment of cultural practices and social identities, wherein intentional and unintentional traces of identity accumulate over an individual's lifetime (Geller 2008; Meskell 1999; Sofaer 2006; Torres-Rouff et al. 2017). Studying human skeletal remains provides insight to differential experiences and the influences of a community and environment on lived experiences. Individuals from San Pedro y San Pablo can elucidate differential experiences influenced by contact with Europeans and differences between Mission sites and Mission outposts.

Standard osteological analysis, following Buikstra and Ubelaker (1994), was conducted by Basin Research Associates, second author Christopher Canzonieri, and recommendations from the most likely descendant community. Alyson Caine and Christine Marshall provided additional expert analysis. Preservation of skeletal elements including cortical bone weathering (Stages 0–5) is recorded following Buikstra and Ubelaker (1994:7, 99).[1] Age-at-death and sex were estimated from features in the skull and pelvic region (Acsádi and Nemeskéri 1970; Brooks and Suchey 1990; Lovejoy 1985; Lovejoy et al. 1985; Lovejoy, Meindl et al. 1985). For age-at-death, standardized age ranges following Boylston and Roberts (1996) were used to categorize individuals (using the same categories given in table 2.1). Proteomic analyses were completed on nonadults with teeth, for which osteological analyses are inconclusive (Cunningham et al. 2016). Those methods and analyses are described further in chapter 4 of this volume, but results are provided here to complete the osteological descriptions. Stature was calculated using metric analyses of long bones following the regression formula presented by Auerbach and Ruff (2010). All measurements are based on the bicondylar length of the femur, except for Burial 6 for which only the tibia was available for stature estimation.

We recorded pathological alterations following protocols outlined by Buikstra and Ubelaker (1994:108). Dental diseases, including periodontal disease following Brothwell (1981), carious lesions, enamel hypoplasia, and periapical lesions were recorded following Buikstra and Ubelaker (1994:54–55). Joint disease, specifically osteoarthritis, was recorded following Rogers and Waldron (1995:44). To diagnosis osteoarthritis, either the presence of eburnation or two of the following criteria were required: (1) marginal osteophyte and/or new bone formation on the joint surface, (2) pitting on the joint surface, and/or (3) alteration in the bony contour of the joint (Rogers and Waldron 1995:44). Trauma was recorded following criteria outlined by Buikstra and Ubelaker (1994:119–120). Infectious diseases were recorded according to protocols for specific (Roberts and Buikstra 2003) and nonspecific infectious diseases (Roberts 2019). In addition to these macroscopic analyses, ancient DNA analysis was completed at the Laboratories for Molecular Anthropol-

---

1   Weathering stages: Stage 0—No sign of cracking or flaking due to weathering; Stage 1—Initial cracking parallel to bone fiber structure; Stage 2—Flaking of outer bone layers; Stage 3—Fibrous, rough texture and remnants of fiber structure; Stage 4 -Deep cracking and coarse, layered fiber structure; and Stage 5—Cancellous bone exposed and bone easily broken.

ogy and Microbiome Research at the University of Oklahoma by Dr. Cara Monroe. Although not further reported in this volume, a vertebral body from Burial 2 was analyzed using qPCR to assess the presence of pathogen DNA, specifically the presence of Mycobacterium tuberculosis, which was not present (Monroe, personal communication).

Asistencia Individuals

A total of fifteen individuals were recovered from CA-SMA-71/H (table 3.1), including two adult males, six adult females, and seven nonadults (<18 years). One individual, Burial 1, although identified during initial monitoring, was not relocated during later excavation. In some instances, burials were identified in association with one another, therefore individuals are described in order in the following paragraphs, but associations are prioritized where present. For example, Burial 7 follows Burial 2 because these two individuals were found in association with one another.

Mortuary Practices

The burials reflect the mortuary practices of the California Mission Period. Burials were primarily on their backs (supine) and oriented northeast to southwest with the skull to the southwest and the arms placed to the side or on the chest. No evidence of coffins, including coffin hardware, wood planks, or mission tiles were recovered. Additionally, no evidence of shrouds exists, although this was a standard burial practice during the Mission Period in California (Panich 2018). An extended interment pattern is more commonly associated with modern burial practices and similar to those recorded at Santa Clara Mission (Skowronek & Wizorek 1997; Panich 2014). The skulls were located to the southwest and faced the east. This differs from the traditional Christian burials where the head was to the west "facing the rising sun" but aligns with Spanish customs where the head faced east (Skowronek & Wizorek 1997; 81). Material culture interred included precontact and historic artifacts signaling the intersection of indigenous and colonial practices. We briefly discuss grave goods recovered from each burial, but for further explanation of artifacts see chapter 5.

Burial 2

Burial 2 was a primary interment recovered in an extended, supine position (i.e., lying on the back with the face up), with the body oriented northeast to southwest. During monitoring the skull was removed by equipment but the cranium was at the southwest end of the burial. Burial 7 intruded on Burial 2

Table 3.1 Summary of demographic profile of the fifteen individuals

Burial #	Sex	Age at Death (yrs)	Associated with Burial	Position	Head Facing	Associated Artifacts
2	Male	9–13	7	Ext Sup	n/a	210 *Olivella* Class A beads, 1 clam bead, 1 glass bead
3	Fem.	45–50	n/a	Ext Sup	NW	2 *Olivella* Class A beads
4	Fem.	50–60	14, 15, 16	Ext Prone	Down	16 *Olivella* Class A beads and a pestle (Type IIb4)
5	Fem.	45–50	8, 12	Ext Sup	North	161 *Olivella* Class A beads and 10 Drawn glass beads
6	Male	18–25	9	Ext Sup	South	9 clamshell disk beads, 49 *Olivella* Class A beads, 1 *Olivella* Class H bead, 27 drawn glass beads, 7 wound glass beads and pestle (Type IIb1a)
7	Ind.	<0.2	2	Sup	n/a	895 clamshell beads and 351 drawn glass beads
8	Male	>45	5, 12	Ext Sup	North	1 clam bead
9	Male	2–2.5	6	Ext Sup	East	1 jet cross, 23 jet beads, 15 clamshell disk beads, 21 *Olivella* Class A beads, 36 *Olivella* Class H beads, 5 *Haliotis* disk beads, 832 drawn glass beads, and 56 wound glass beads
10	Fem.	40–44	n/a	n/a	n/a	None
11	Male	4–8	n/a	Ext Sup	East	1 jet cross, 12 jet beads, 32 clamshell disk beads, 3 *Olivella* Class A beads, 8 *Olivella* Class H beads, 14 *Haliotis* disk beads, 30 drawn glass beads, and 15 wound glass beads
12	Fem	20–25	5, 8	Est Sup	East	237 clamshell disk beads, 504 *Olivella* Class A beads, 2201 drawn glass beads, and a pestle (Type IIb4)
13	Fem	20–24	n/a	Ext Sup	North	445 *Olivella* Class A beads
14	Fem.	5–7	4, 15, 16	Ext Sup	East	None
15	Male	13–17	4, 14, 16	Ext Sup	East	10 bifaces, 2 crystals, 14 whistles (Type FF2), 2 ray barbs, and 1 *Olivella* Class A bead
16	Ind.	<0.2	4, 15, 16	n/a	n/a	None

at the lower limbs suggesting Burial 7 was interred after Burial 2. Burial 2 was approximately 80 percent complete with Stage 4 weathering (deep cracking of cortical surface) across skeletal elements. A number of artifacts were found in association with this individual, including 210 Olivella sp. Class A beads, one glass bead, and one clamshell disk.

Age-at-death of Burial 2 was between nine and thirteen years based on dental eruption and epiphyseal fusion. Proteomic analyses of amelogenin proteins indicate Burial 2 was a male. Dental disease was present in the form of linear enamel hypoplasia (LEH) at the right mandibular and maxillary canine. In total two LEH were present on the maxillary canine and three LEH were present on the mandibular canine. Based on age estimates for dental hypoplasia (Goodman and Rose 1990), the two LEH on the maxillary canine represent periods of stress at 3.36 years and 4.12 years, while the three LEH on the mandibular canine represent periods of stress at 2.17 years, 3.78 years, and 4.11 years. Pathological alterations were observed at the right clavicle, right and left radii, right and left femora, upper ribs, left ilium, and lower thoracic and lumbar vertebrae. Alterations observed in the femora, ribs, ilium, and thoracic and lumbar vertebrae were consistent with tuberculosis.

Changes consistent with tuberculosis included lytic lesions at and destruction of the lower thoracic and lumbar vertebrae, a circular lytic lesion at the left auricular surface of the ilium, morphological changes to ribs bilaterally, and a perpendicular angle at the neck of both femora, coxa vara (for an image of these elements, see appendix figure A.1). Postmortem damage, including heavy erosion of cortical bone, makes it difficult in some places to discern taphonomic from pathological alterations.

Burial 7

Burial 7 was a primary interment recovered in a supine position from southwest to northwest with the skull at the southwest end. Because of postmortem disturbance to the lower limbs, only the upper body was articulated and therefore the position the skull was facing was unknown. Burial 7 intruded on Burial 2 at the lower limbs suggesting Burial 7 was interred after Burial 2. Burial 7 was approximately 75 percent complete with many long bone epiphyses missing along with the hand and foot bones. Weathering of the skeletal elements was Stage 1 (initial cracking of cortical surface). A number of artifacts were found in association with this individual, including 351 white glass beads and 895 clamshell disk beads, which appeared to be strung together around the neck in situ.

Age-at-death of Burial 7 was between forty weeks gestational age and one to two months postpartum based on nonadult metrics, dental development, and epiphyseal fusion. No proteomic analyses to estimate sex were possible for Burial 7 due to a lack of enamel. Because sexually dimorphic features do not present themselves osteologically in nonadults (Cunningham et al. 2016), sex for this individual was indeterminate. No dental or pathological alterations were present in Burial 7.

Burial 3

Burial 3 was a primary interment recovered in an extended, supine position with the body oriented northeast to southwest and the skull facing northwest. Burial 3 was almost complete with postmortem damage at the scapula and hand and foot bones. Monitoring of excavation discovered the burial and resulted in postmortem fracturing at the femora. Weathering of the skeletal elements was Stage 1 (initial cracking of cortical surface). Artifacts were found in association with this individual, including two Olivella spire-lopped, Class A beads.

Burial 3 was a mature adult estimated to have died between the ages of forty-five and fifty based on degeneration of the pubic symphysis and auricular surface in the pelvis. Sex was estimated as female based on morphology of the skull and pelvis. Proteomic analyses of amelogenin proteins confirmed this sex estimation (see chapter 4). Dental disease was present in the form of periapical lesions and periodontal disease. Two periapical lesions were present at the left first maxillary molar at the lingual and buccal surfaces. Periodontal disease ranges from slight (3–4 mm alveolar loss) to severe (>50 percent of root exposed) at the left maxilla. The right maxilla exhibits moderate periodontal disease.

Pathological alterations were present at the right clavicle, a right nonsequenced rib fragment, and right ilium. At the right clavicle there was a healed oblique fracture that shortened the bone at the acromial end. A bone spur was present at the acromial end that was likely a growth in response to a muscle or ligament attachment. The right rib also exhibited a bone spur (possibly a ligament attachment) that was likely a growth in response to trauma at the clavicle. Postmortem fragmentation of the ribs limited our ability to understand the distribution of these changes; however, this change could be related to a fracture of the clavicle during life. The right ilium at the iliac crest exhibited a large notch that altered the morphology of the crest from the midline to the medial aspect, superior to the auricular surface (for an image of this pelvis, see appendix figure A.2). There was a crescent notch in the acetabulum and possible pseudoarthrosis at the medial aspect of the iliac crest. These morphological and possible joint changes could reflect a healed avulsion fracture earlier in life or a congenital alteration.

Burial 4

Burial 4 was a primary interment recovered in an extended, prone position (the only individual buried on their stomach in the sample), with the body oriented north to south and the skull face down. Burial 16 (estimated to be forty weeks to one month at the time of death) was recovered in direct association with Burial 4 from the pelvic region. Two other burials, Burials 14 and 15, were also recovered near Burial 4 but not in direct association. Burial 4 was complete with postmortem damage and loss at the skull, long bones, and ribs. Stage 1 weathering (initial cracking) was present at the cortical bone of most elements preserved. Sixteen Olivella spire-lopped beads (Class A) were recovered with Burial 4. One ground stone pestle (Type IIB4) was also recovered at the left side of the body. One multifaceted black glass bead was found in the burial matrix; however, because of the number of burials in proximity this bead was not definitively associated with Burial 4.

Burial 4 was a mature adult between the ages of forty and fifty years at the time of death based on degenerative changes at the pubic symphysis and auricular surface. Sex was estimated as female based on morphological features of the skull and pelvis. Proteomic analyses of amelogenin proteins confirmed this estimation. Stature for Burial 4 was estimated at 154 cm (5.1 ft) based on the bicondylar length of the femur and tibia (Auerbach and Ruff 2010). Dental disease was present in the form of dental abscesses and severe (>50 percent of root exposed) periodontal disease. Six dental abscesses are present in total. In the maxillary teeth, the buccal surface of the right and left first and second maxillary molars have abscesses. Two mandibular teeth have buccal abscesses, the left first molar and the right second premolar. Pathological alterations were present in the vertebrae and femora. A compression fracture was present at the superior body of the first lumbar vertebra and the superior articular facets have fused to the inferior articular facets of the twelfth thoracic vertebra. There was slight, but bilateral, osteophytic formation at the distal lateral epicondyle of the femora.

Burial 16

Burial 16 was a primary interment found in the pelvic region of Burial 4. Bioturbation disturbed this burial and likely resulted in its poor preservation. The individual was represented by 20 percent of its skeletal elements, including skull fragments, ribs, the left scapula, right humerus, tibia, and fibula, and vertebral bodies and arches. Cortical bone weathering of skeletal elements was Stage 1 (initial cracking of cortical surface). No artifacts were directly associated with Burial 16.

Age-at-death of Burial 16 was between forty weeks to one month based on metric analyses of long bones, epiphyseal fusion rates, and dental development. No proteomic analyses were possible for Burial 16 and because of a lack of sexually dimorphic features observable at this age (Cunningham et al. 2016), sex was indeterminate. No dental disease or pathological alterations were present.

Burial 14

Burial 14 was a primary interment that was recovered in an extended, supine position, with the body oriented northeast to southwest and the skull facing east. The burial was mostly complete with postmortem loss to the ribs, vertebrae, long bones, and hand and foot bones. Cortical bone weathering of skeletal elements was Stage 1 (initial cracking of cortical surface). No artifacts were recovered with Burial 14.

Age-at-death for Burial 14 was between the ages of five and seven years based on metric analyses of long bones, epiphyseal fusion rates, and dental development and eruption. Proteomic analyses of amelogenin proteins indicate Burial 14 was female. Dental disease was present in the form of enamel defects in a variety of teeth. Large smooth pits were present bilaterally on the occlusal surfaces of the maxillary and mandibular first and second molars along with orange/brown staining. The pits ranged from 3.79 mm to 5.30 mm with depths ranging from 0.89 mm to 4.1 mm. Discolored crowns were consistent with these defects reflecting hypomaturation amelogenesis imperfecta (see appendix figure A.3 for an image of these teeth; Kinaston et al. 2019). No other pathological alterations were present.

Burial 15

Burial 15 was a primary interment recovered in an extended, supine position, with the body oriented northeast to southwest and the skull facing east. The burial was complete with postmortem loss of foot bones. Cortical bone weathering of skeletal elements was Stage 2 (flaking of cortical bone). A cache of artifacts were recovered from Burial 15's pelvic region. Nine obsidian projectile point preforms, one chert projectile point preforms, two quartz crystals, fourteen bird bone whistles, two bat ray barbs, and a small, honed stone were recovered with Burial 15. One Olivella spire-lopped bead (Class A) was recovered from the burial matrix of Burial 15 but was not in direct association and therefore could alternatively belong to Burial 14, which was in proximity.

Age-at-death of Burial 15 was between thirteen and seventeen years. Proteomic analyses of amelogenin proteins indicate Burial 15 was male. No dental diseases or pathological alterations were present.

Burial 5

Burial 5 was a primary interment recovered in an extended, supine position, with the body oriented northeast to southwest. Burial 5 was in association with Burials 8 and 12. The burial was mostly complete (75 percent) with postmortem damage at the skull, scapulae, left humerus, radius, ulna, and hand bones, and right ilium. Cortical bone weathering of skeletal elements was Stage 1 (initial cracking). 161 Class A Olivella beads and ten drawn glass beads were recovered with this burial.

Burial 5 was a mature adult between the ages of forty-five and fifty years based on degeneration of the pubic symphysis and auricular surface. Sex was estimated as female based on morphological features of the skull and pelvis. Proteomic analyses of amelogenin proteins confirm female sex estimation. Stature for Burial 5 was estimated at 149 cm (4.9 ft) based on the bicondylar length of the femur and tibia (Auerbach and Ruff 2010). Dental disease was present in the form of slight (3–4 mm alveolar loss) to severe (>50 percent of root exposed) periodontal disease and periapical lesions. Periapical lesions were present at the buccal surface of three maxillary teeth; the right first molar and left second premolar and first molar. No other pathological alterations were present.

Burial 8

Burial 8 was a primary interment recovered in an extended, supine position, with the body oriented northeast to southwest and the skull facing north. The burial was nearly complete with postmortem damage at the scapulae, vertebrae, sacrum, and left pelvis, and postmortem loss of hand and foot bones. Weathering of bone was Stage 1 (initial cracking of cortical surface) with cortical bone well preserved. One clamshell disk bead was recovered from Burial 8.

Age-at-death of Burial 8 was estimated between forty-five and fifty-five years, a mature adult. Sex was estimated as male based on features of the skull and pelvis, which was consistent with proteomic analyses of amelogenin proteins. Stature for Burial 8 was estimated at 162 cm (5.3 ft) based on the bicondylar length of the femur and tibia (Auerbach and Ruff 2010). Dental disease was present in the form of periapical lesions. Two buccal periapical lesions were present at the left and right maxillary first molars. Pathological alterations were present at the vertebrae. Osteophytic formation was present at the first and fifth lumbar vertebrae. The fifth lumbar vertebra exhibited slight compression at the body.

Burial 6

Burial 6 was a primary interment recovered in an extended, supine position, with the body oriented northeast to southwest and the skull facing south. Burial 9 (an infant) was recovered at Burial 6's left side. Burial 6 was complete with postmortem loss of hand and foot bones. Cortical bone weathering of skeletal elements was Stage 0 (no cracking or flaking). Artifacts recovered in association with Burial 6 included one ground stone pestle (Type IIB1a) lying across Burial 6's torso and adjacent to Burial 9, nine clamshell disk beads, forty-nine Olivella spire-lopped Class A beads, one Olivella disk Class H bead, twenty-seven drawn glass beads, and seven wound glass beads.

Burial 6 was a young adult between the ages of eighteen and twenty-five years based on degenerative changes in the pubic symphysis and auricular surface and dental development. Sex was estimated as male based on morphological characteristics of the skull and pelvis. Proteomic analyses of amelogenin proteins indicated Burial 6 was a male. Stature for Burial 6 was estimated at 170 cm (5.6 ft) based on the maximum length of the tibia only because no femora were measurable (Auerbach and Ruff 2010). Slight (3–4 mm alveolar loss) periodontal disease was evident. No other pathological alterations were present.

Burial 9

Burial 9 was a primary interment recovered in an extended, supine position, with the body oriented from the northeast to southwest and the skull facing east. Burial 9 was interred along the left side of Burial 6. Burial 9 was represented by 44 percent of the skeletal elements with almost all bones on the left side missing postmortem. A steel pipe ran along the left side of the body and likely resulted in the postmortem loss on this side of the body. Cortical bone weathering of skeletal elements was Stage 1 (initial cracking). Artifacts recovered from Burial 9 include a cross and various beads. The cross was a Latin Type, made of jet. Twenty-three large multifaceted black beads were present. These black beads and cross may together represent a rosary. There were fifteen clamshell disk beads, 21 Olivella Type A1a, 36 disk beads Type H, 5 *Haliotis* disk beads, 832 drawn glass beads, and 56 wound glass beads.

Age-at-death of Burial 9 was between two and two and a half years (an infant) based on metric analyses of long bones, epiphyseal fusion rates, and dental development. Proteomic analyses of amelogenin proteins indicated Burial 9 was a male. No dental diseases or pathological alterations were present.

Burial 10

Burial 10 was a primary interment previously disturbed by the installation of a steel pipe. No articulations were observed in situ; however, the burial was mostly complete with postmortem loss of cervical and thoracic vertebrae and hand and foot bones. Cortical bone weathering of skeletal elements was Stage 1 (initial cracking). Burial 10 was recovered in proximity to Burials 6, 9, and 11 but no direct associations were present. Artifacts were not recovered with Burial 10.

Burial 10 was a middle adult between the ages of forty and forty-four years based on degenerative changes at the auricular surface. Sex was estimated as female based on features of the skull and pelvis. No proteomic analyses were possible to confirm macroscopic analysis of sex. Stature for Burial 10 was estimated at 156 cm (5.1 ft) based on the bicondylar length of the femur and tibia (Auerbach and Ruff 2010). Dental disease was present in the form of slight (3–4 mm alveolar loss) periodontal disease. No other pathological alterations were present.

Burial 11

Burial 11 was a primary interment recovered in an extended, supine position, with the body oriented north to south and the skull facing east. Most skeletal elements were present with postmortem loss of scapulae, clavicles, sternum, manubrium, and foot bones. Cortical bone weathering of skeletal elements was Stage 1 (initial cracking). Artifacts recovered from Burial 11 included a Latin Type cross made of jet, twelve multifaceted black jet beads, thirty-two clamshell disk beads, three Olivella Type A spire-lopped, eight Type H disk beads, fourteen *Haliotis* disk beads, thirty drawn glass beads, and fifteen wound glass beads. The combination of the Latin Type cross and multifaceted beads could represent a rosary, similar to Burial 9.

Burial 11 was estimated to be between four and eight years of age at the time of death based on metric analyses, epiphyseal fusion rates of long bones, and dental development and eruption. Proteomic analyses of amelogenin proteins indicate Burial 11 was a male. No dental disease or pathological alterations were present.

Burial 12

Burial 12 was a primary interment recovered in an extended, supine position, with the body oriented northeast to southwest and the skull facing east. The burial was complete with postmortem damage at the scapulae, sacrum, and hand and foot bones. Cortical bone weathering of skeletal elements was Stage 1 (initial cracking). Artifacts recovered from Burial 12 included a pestle and various beads. One large, ornate pestle (Type IIB4) was recovered along the lower right arm of Burial 12. A large quantity of beads were recovered, including 2,201 drawn glass beads, 504 Olivella spire-lopped beads, and 237 clamshell disk beads. These beads were recovered around the right arm and in the vicinity of the vertebrae and left ilium.

Burial 12 was a young adult between the ages of twenty and twenty-five years based on degenerative changes at the pubic symphysis and auricular surface. Sex was estimated to be female based on features of the skull and pelvis. Proteomic analysis of amelogenin proteins indicated Burial 12 was a female. Stature for Burial 12 was estimated to be 150 cm (4.9 ft) based on the maximum length of the femur and tibia. Dental disease was present in the form of carious lesions at the left first and second mandibular molars, LEH, and slight (3–4 mm alveolar loss) periodontal disease. LEH were present bilaterally at the mandibular and maxillary canines. One LEH was present at the right maxillary canine, and based on Goodman and Rose (1990), this insult represents a period of stress experienced at 2.6 years. Two LEH were present at the left maxillary canine and represent periods of stress experienced at 1.6 and 2.9 years. One LEH was present bilaterally on the right and left mandibular canines, which represent periods of experienced stress at 3.3 and 3.65 years respectively. No other pathological alterations were present.

Burial 13

Burial 13 was a primary interment that was recovered in an extended, supine position, with the body oriented northeast to southwest and the skull facing north. The burial was complete with postmortem damage at the scapulae, sacrum, pubic symphyses, and hand and foot bones. Cortical bone weathering of skeletal elements was Stage 1 (initial cracking). A total of 445 Olivella Class A spire-lopped beads were recovered near the chin, scapulae, and ribs.

Burial 13 was estimated to be a young adult between the ages of twenty and twenty-four years based on degenerative changes at the auricular surface. Sex was estimated as female based on features of the skull and pelvis. Proteomic analysis of amelogenin proteins indicated Burial 13 was a female. Stature for Burial 13 was estimated to be 156 cm (5.1 ft) based on the bicondylar length of the femur and tibia (Auerbach and Ruff 2010). Dental disease was present in the form of slight (3–4 mm alveolar loss) to severe (>50 percent of root exposed) periodontal disease at the maxillary dentition. No other pathological alterations were present.

Osteological Health within the Mission

Life during the Mission Period is documented by historic and ethnographic accounts; however, life and health at Mission outposts is less understood. Skeletal remains from CA-SMA-71/H can shed light on the demographics and disease profile of individuals from San Pedro y San Pablo exposing experiences during this tumultuous time.

The sample of individuals from the asistencia is small and most are not representative of a complete life at San Pedro y San Pablo. Adults, for example, were living at San Pedro y San Pablo only later in life and likely experienced childhood outside of the Mission system. Therefore, human skeletal remains recovered from the site represent individuals who died at San Pedro y San Pablo and the health profiles of adults may reflect biological consequences before living at San Pedro y San Pablo. On the other hand, nonadults, particularly infants and children, who were likely born at San Pedro y San Pablo, or spent the majority of their years there, will reflect biological consequences of living and dying at San Pedro y San Pablo.

Demographic Profiles

Age-at-death and sex of archaeological samples are useful for understanding differential experiences by age groups and sexes, including morbidity and mortality rates. Age and sex were important factors influencing experience of individuals living at Missions. Age and sex dictated which residential quarters individuals lived in at the Mission with children and unmarried, young women separated from other tribal members (Lightfoot 2005:62). These practices of separation aimed to indoctrinate and subjugate women and children (Lightfoot 2005). Along with differential living practices, age and gender roles influenced the type of work assigned. All individuals regardless of age were expected to perform tasks for the Mission, with work hours ranging from four to nine hours a day (Hackel 2005; Lightfoot 2005:67). Men, generally, performed agricultural tasks while women tended to domestic tasks, including raising children. Life expectancy of individuals living within the Missions is thought to be low, with individuals rarely living past the age of twenty-five (Geiger 1976; Lightfoot 2005:76). Women suffered greater mortality rates during the Mission Period and depopulation has largely been attributed to mortality rates of women. The small sample size (n=15) makes it difficult to draw broad sex-based or age-based conclusions. However, where possible, sex and age-at-death differences were correlated with disease patterns to understand how diseases differentially impacted individuals.

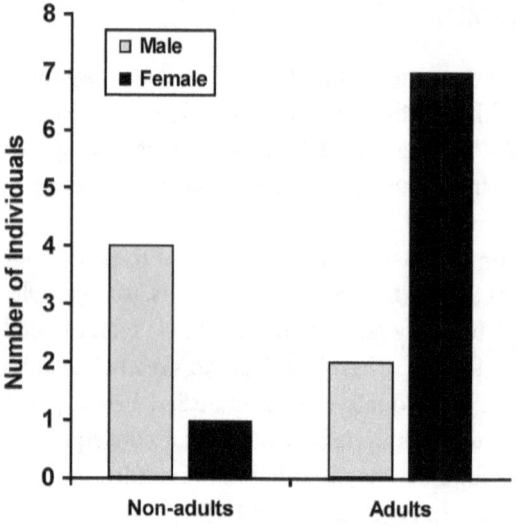

Figure 3.1. Distribution of age-at-death by sex for individuals from CA-SMA-71/H.

Age-at-Death

Of the individuals, all age categories are present except for young/middle adults. From the archaeological sample, 40 percent of individuals are nonadults and the average age-at-death was 25.9 years. The low average age-at-death suggests living conditions at San Pedro y San Pablo were detrimental to the health and lifespan of the people recovered.

Sex

Thirteen of the fifteen individuals have an estimate for sex (all except Burials 7 and 16), based either on osteological and/or proteomic techniques. Overall, the thirteen individuals with sex estimations are evenly split between males (n=6) and females (n=7). However, when age is accounted for, a notable sex-bias is evident in the sample. Seven of the nine adults are female (except Burial 6, a young adult male, and Burial 8, a mature adult male; figure 3.1). By contrast, nonadults are all males with the exception of Burial 14, a female child.

The ratio of adult (over the age of eighteen years at time of death) males to females is 0.67. A Fisher's exact test comparing sex estimates by adult and nonadult age categories was not statistically significant ($p = 0.22$). While not statistically significant, the observed ratio suggests adult females are disproportionally represented in the population at San Pedro y San Pablo. The biased representation of males and females could signal differential susceptibility to disease and/or death. Differences in male and female infant mortality is well documented in archaeological and modern samples (Buonasera et al. 2022; Drevenstedt et al. 2008; Fuse and Crenshaw 2006; McFadden et al. 2022). Studies on historic and archaeological samples with known exposure to crises that impact life expectancy, including slavery, famine, and epidemics, have found that male infants are generally more frail and therefore more susceptible to death (Drevenstedt et al. 2008; Zarulli et al. 2018), including in California archaeological samples (Buonasera et al. 2022). In the case of California archaeological samples, Buonasera and colleagues suggest that differences in male and female infant mortality could be linked to weaning practices for infants. Isotopic analysis of individuals included in their study found male infants recovered from *Síi Túupentak* (CA-ALA-565/H), which was used primarily between 600–150 cal BP, were weaned at approximately 2.3 years whereas female infants were weaned at approximately 3.2 years (Eerkens et al. 2020). These differences in weaning age are thought to be a by-product of differing gender practices with boys learning to hunt at an early age and therefore not in proximity to mothers and the breast milk they provided. However, girls may have received breastmilk longer because of their involvement in gathering and proximity to mother's breastmilk.

Biologically, men and women respond differentially to disease and face different obstacles. For example, pregnancy in women adds new health constraints and potentially impacted individuals, including Burial 4, a mature adult female, who was recovered with Burial 16 who was estimated to have died at birth.

Pathological Alterations

Disease was present in most of the individuals from San Pedro y San Pablo (table 3.2). Dental disease was the most common form of pathological alterations followed by trauma and infectious disease. The majority of individuals exhibiting pathological alterations were adults. These alterations in adults, particularly those reflective of childhood stressors (e.g., LEH), likely reflect stressors before life at San Pedro y San Pablo. On the other hand, the nonadults with pathological alterations, including Burial 2, likely represent stressors experienced while living at San Pedro y San Pablo.

Dental Disease

During the Mission Period, environmental shifts, the introduction of Old-World plants and animals, and the incorporation of Spanish cultural practices resulted in widespread changes to Native peoples' diets (Lightfoot 2005). While dietary shifts characterize the Mission Period, the extent of disuse of Native practices varied by region and Mission (Panich 2018; Panich and Schneider 2015). For individuals from CA-SMA-71/H, a variety of dental

Table 3.2. Pathological alterations present at CA-SMA-71/H by burial

Individual	Dental Disease			Joint Disease	Trauma		Infectious Disease
	Enamel Defect	Periapical Lesion	Periodontal Disease	Carious Lesions	OA	Direct	Indir.	TB
Burial 2	X	—	—	—	—	—	X	X
Burial 3	—	X	X	—	—	X	—	—
Burial 4	—	X	X	—	X	X	—	—
Burial 5	—	X	X	—	—	—	—	—
Burial 6	—	—	X	—	—	—	—	—
Burial 8	—	X	—	—	—	—	—	—
Burial 10	—	—	X	—	—	—	—	—
Burial 12	—	X	X	X	—	—	—	—
Burial 13	—	—	X	—	—	—	—	—
Burial 14	—	X	—	—	—	—	—	—

Note: OA = Osteoarthritis; Indir. = Indirect; TB = Tuberculosis; X = present.

diseases were present, including enamel hypoplasia, periapical lesions, periodontal disease, and carious lesions, which can provide insight to the possible dietary changes.

Enamel hypoplasia is most commonly observed as horizontal lines across the enamel, but can manifest as vertical lines, grooves, and pits, and results from interruptions in the normal formation of enamel (Hu et al. 2007; Kinaston et al. 2019:753). Burial 14 exhibited changes at the enamel that are consistent with amelogenesis imperfecta, reflecting a developmental issue that is distinguished from LEH. Two individuals exhibited LEH on canine dentition, Burials 2 and 12, representing 13.3 percent of the archaeological sample. The presence of LEH in Burial 2 reflects stress to enamel formation that would have happened while living at San Pedro y San Pablo, while the LEH in Burial 12, a young adult, is likely not reflective of life at the asistencia but of a period earlier in life outside the Mission.

Periapical lesions manifest on the mandible or maxilla in the form of a circular hole or sinus, resulting from the accumulation of pus within the tooth socket and its eventual rupturing through the alveolar bone (Kinaston et al. 2019:767). Depending on the infection, acute or chronic, the lesion can be proliferative (bone forming) or destructive (bone removing); however, in dry bone most instances are smaller than 2–3 mm in diameter. Periapical lesions were observed in 26.7 percent of the individuals, often occurring in multiples, with two recorded in Burials 3 and 8, three in Burial 5, and six in Burial 4. Periapical lesions are associated with carious lesions and dental attrition wherein the enamel is worn away or decayed to expose the root of the tooth, leading to infection. Lesions of this sort can manifest quickly or progressively over a long period of time (Kinaston et al. 2019). As periapical lesions were present in many adults from San Pedro y San Pablo (Burials 3, 4, 5, and 8), these infections could represent biological consequences to life at the asistencia.

Periodontal disease is an inflammatory response in the connective tissues that secure teeth in the alveolar sockets. It is triggered by polymicrobial plaque or abrasive effects of calculus (Kinaston et al. 2019:771). Chronic inflammation results in the eventual resorption of the alveolar bone surrounding the teeth. Slight to severe periodontal disease was recorded in six individuals suggesting chronic inflammation, which affected all adults recovered where this could be measured, except for Burial 8, a mature adult male.

Carious lesions are the result of behavioral and biological differences, wherein individuals' diets, labor, and sex hormones drive the prevalence of tooth decay (Lukacs 2008). Two carious lesions were recorded in Burial 12 at the occlusal surface of the mandibular molars representing a 6.7 percent prevalence rate for carious lesions at CA-SMA-71/H. Similar to periapical lesions, carious lesions can manifest quickly or progressively and therefore the presence of carious lesions in a young adult may reflect dietary practices at San Pedro y San Pablo or dietary practices previous to life at the outpost.

Joint Disease

Joint disease, specifically osteoarthritis (OA), is common in modern and ancient populations and results from the breakdown of synovial joint articulations (Lambert and Walker 1991). One individual, Burial 4, a mature adult female, exhibited evidence of joint alterations and evidence of OA. Changes to the distal articular surface of the femur were recorded but the necessary criterion for OA were not present. However, fusion of this individuals' vertebrae was indicative of OA. Burial 3 also exhibited possible pseudoarthrosis at the right acetabulum, which likely was the result of an avulsion fracture to the acetabulum. There were no corresponding changes to the femur, suggesting changes to the joint, if present, were minimal and likely did not impact mobility. OA has been studied in prehistoric samples finding gendered distributions of labor (Cheverko and Bartelink 2017; Walker and Hollimon 1989). Unfortunately, the small sample size of individuals with joint alterations does not permit gendered comparisons.

Trauma

Trauma can result from a variety of mechanisms (Redfern and Roberts 2019:213). Direct trauma includes instances of direct force placed on the bone, which was observed in Burial 4, in the form of a compression fracture at the first lumbar vertebra, and Burial 3 in the form of a healed oblique fracture at the right clavicle. The former, while recorded as trauma, is frequently associated with generalized bone loss, including osteoporosis and osteopenia, which increases susceptibility to compression fractures in vertebral bodies (Brickley 2002). Because of this individual's advanced age-at-death, it is difficult to associate these skeletal alterations directly to life at San Pedro y San Pablo. Indirect trauma results from a force that indirectly impacts bone, for example pulled or strained muscles, which can result in avulsion fractures (Binazzi et al. 1992; Combs 1994; Moeller 2003), like the changes exhibited in Burial 3's right ilium. There were no apparent mobility impacts for Burial 3, but trauma to the femur may have resulted from laborious conditions at San Pedro y San Pablo. Labor practices were generally gendered (Lightfoot 2005:67), but during specific times, including harvests, men and women would complete the same tasks. The presence of trauma, in the form of direct and indirect sources, could reflect practices that exposed individuals to more dangerous activities. In addition to performing more dangerous or strenuous labor, poor nutrition, which can lead to osteopenia and osteoporosis, likely left individuals more susceptible to fracture (Brickley 2002). Trauma from CA-SMA-71/H may reflect labor practices at San Pedro y San Pablo.

Infectious Disease

Infectious diseases can manifest from exposure to specific pathogens, including *Mycobacterium tuberculosis*, or nonspecific pathogens, most commonly *Staphylococcus aureus*, *Streptococcus*, or *Pneumococcus*. Introduction of these pathogens can happen directly by means of a piercing injury (surgical or accidental), direct contact with infection in associated soft tissues, or as a secondary blood-born infection with the generating locus of infection located elsewhere in the body (Roberts 2019). Specific infectious diseases can manifest as proliferative or destructive changes on bone with distributions of lesions that are directly correlated to disease processes, including tuberculosis, leprosy, or syphilis (Roberts 2019:287). Without prior exposure to these bacteria, individuals are prone to fatality. In many instances of contact between European and Indigenous groups, infectious disease is presented as a catalyst for widespread transmission of diseases and death (Jackson 1983, 1994; Jones et al. 2021; Lightfoot 2005; Hackel 2005; Walker et al. 2005); however, bioarchaeological evidence has yet to confirm these hypotheses.

No evidence of nonspecific infection was observed. Specific infectious disease was observed in a nonadult, but no evidence was present in adults. Burial 2 exhibited skeletal alterations consistent with tuberculosis, including Pott's disease or kyphosis of the lower thoracic and lumbar vertebrae. The collapse at the lower thoracic vertebrae from the eleventh thoracic to first lumbar vertebrae (see appendix figure A.1) would have altered this child's mobility and may have resulted in paralysis. The progressed stage of pathological alterations to this individual's vertebral column suggests this individual contracted tuberculosis while living in the Mission system. Alternatively, tuberculosis could have been inactive or latent in this individual and therefore they may not have exhibited any symptoms of tuberculosis or disease upon entering the Mission system, although they could have already contracted tuberculosis. The skeletal alterations in this individual suggest that they eventually experienced symptoms of tuberculosis and could have spread the disease to other individuals while living in proximity to many individuals at San Pedro y San Pablo.

Mycobacterium bacteria come in many different forms but the most common to infect humans is *Mycobacterium tuberculosis* followed by *Mycobacterium bovis*. The transmission of these two diseases differs depending on the bacterium. *Mycobacterium tuberculosis* is generally spread through inhaling infected droplets from other humans. *Mycobacterium bovis* is transmitted by cows to humans either through inhalation of infected droplets or ingesting infected cow by-products, leading to gastrointestinal infections (Roberts and Buikstra 2003:5). Changes to the skeleton in response to tuberculosis include lytic lesions and kyphosis at the thoracic and lumbar vertebrae, lytic lesions in the outer table of the skull, lesions on the ribs, and tubercles at joint surfaces (Roberts and Buikstra 2003:109). To differentiate between bacterium, changes in the ribs have been posited to represent pulmonary infection while changes in the pelvis suggest gastrointestinal infection, although these skeletal alterations are not pathognomic of the respective strains (Roberts and Buikstra 2003:88). Infection by *Mycobacterium bovis* is much more likely to impact the skeleton, particularly nonadults (Roberts and Buikstra 2003:88). Based on this information *Mycobacterium bovis* is posited as the bacterial agent impacting Burial 2. During the use of the Mission outpost, there was potential exposure to infected cows because of the agricultural emphasis of San Pedro y San Pablo (Dietz 1979). The skeletal alterations in Burial 2's pelvic region, including the tubercles at the ilium and changes at the psoas muscle attachment on the femora are consistent with a gastrointestinal infection (see appendix figure A.1). As discussed in chapter 7, cow's milk proteins were found in the dental calculus associated with Burials 5, 6, and 15.

While there was no other evidence of tuberculosis at the site, this does not mean that other individuals were not exposed to or infected with tuberculosis. Skeletal alterations are rare and therefore individuals could have died before manifesting any changes in their skeletons. The presence of probable specific infectious disease (i.e., tuberculosis in Burial 2) suggest individuals were exposed to pathogens but those pathogens may not have been novel for all individuals. The manifestation of tuberculosis requires chronic exposure and rarely impacts bone (Hillson et al. 1998; Roberts and Buikstra 2003). Therefore, the presence of this infectious agent in Burial 2 suggests this bacterium could have been present and circulating in Native groups before and during life at San Pedro y San Pablo. Alternatively, the presence of skeletal alterations could signal Burial 2's resilience in the face of this infectious disease, which frequently results in fatality.

Summary

Epidemics and violence have largely characterized narratives about contacts between Europeans and Native American groups during colonization of North America (Garland et al. 2018; Larsen 2018; Larsen and Milner 1994; Stojanowski 2005; Stojanowski et al. 2007). During California's Mission Period, the depopulation of Native villages is known from archaeological studies and historical documents, with the number of Native individuals significantly reduced by AD 1834 (Arkush 2011; Hackel 2005; Jackson 1994; Jones et al. 2021). Analyses show that while infectious disease was present, there is no clear evidence of an epidemic. From the demographic differences, males and females had different lived experiences at San Pedro y San Pablo, but those differences may be related more to age than sex or gender.

Health Disparities between Precontact and Baptized Native Californians

Paleopathological analysis of ancestral skeletal remains from precontact and contact-period sites has yielded insight into differential experiences of these periods (Jones et al. 2021; Larsen and Milner 1994; Lambert and Walker 1991; Pilloud et al. 2020; Stojanowski 2005). Although the sample from San Pedro y San Pablo is small, contextualizing the demographic profile and pathological alterations with patterns observed in pre- and contact samples enables understanding how health outcomes may have changed within the Mission system. Comparative data for pathological alterations comes from archaeological samples in Central California and coastal Southern California. Previous research has shown regional differences in prevalence of pathological alterations that result from differential responses and buffering to stressors, particularly metabolic disorders (Pilloud et al. 2020; Pilloud and Schwitalla 2020). To maximize comparative datasets, samples from different regions were used; however, where possible the San Francisco Bay Area was prioritized, with the understanding that these results may change as more regional data is obtained.

Demographic Profiles

Temporal studies of average age-at-death of Native Californians show a significant difference between individuals living pre- and post-contact with Europeans (Jones et al. 2021; Schwitalla et al. 2014). Survival analyses support large-scale deaths following occupation by Europeans in 1700, suggesting that persistent contact with Europeans and life at Missions contributed to the spread of more virulent pathogens and earlier death (Jones et al. 2021).

The average age-at-death from CA-SMA-71/H, was 25.9 years, This low average age-at-death is consistent with previously calculated averages for age-at-death of other Mission Period archaeological samples, and archaeological samples experiencing plagues (DeWitte 2014; Jones et al. 2021). As well, this figure of 25.9 years is low in comparison to precontact Californian archaeological samples. There is variation in the average age-at-death across different archaeological sites (Jones et al. 2021), but before 1770, average ages-at-death were systematically over thirty-five years. This difference suggests different stressors and pathogens were impacting the lives of individuals that were either not present or not as severe in precontact time periods. These stressors and pathogens increased mortality rates and shortened the life span of individuals living at San Pedro y San Pablo.

Disproportionate ratios of males to females adversely impact reproduction and the ability of populations to recover from catastrophic events, including migration patterns, epidemics, or food shortages (Lightfoot 2005:75–76). Studies of death records and baptisms within the Mission system have found fluctuations in the ratio of males to females; however, for Mission Dolores, females outnumbered males at an increasing rate from 1796 to 1832 (Jackson 1994). The distribution of the sexes at San Pedro y San Pablo similarly favors females. The ratio of males to females for those over nine years at time of death, .67, is less than the ratio of males to females at Mission Dolores, .94, in 1796. While the sample size from San Pedro y San Pablo is not fully representative of the total population, this ratio is characteristic of sex ratios recorded at other Mission Period sites (Jackson 1994).

Differences in the ratio of males to females has been attributed to differential stressors impacting women and children at Mission Period sites. Women, as discussed, were frequently subjugated and controlled by the Mission system (Lightfoot 2005:61–62). The constriction of women to specific spaces and tasks likely contributed to their poor health. In addition, maternal health likely complicates health outcomes and average life spans expected for women during this time. Childbirth could have been dangerous and potentially life threatening.

Pathological Alterations

Historical and archaeological research on the Mission Period suggests chronic diseases were widespread and readily transmitted between individuals because of overcrowding and poor sanitation of habitation spaces (Lightfoot 2005:76). Epidemics have been posited to explain mass mortality that is documented in death records at Mission sites (Jackson 1983; Jones et al. 2021; Lightfoot 2005); however, limited skeletal evidence corroborates these hypotheses. Here, we compare precontact and contact pathological alterations to understand how rates of disease from the Mission Dolores outpost, San Pedro y San Pablo, contribute to narratives about health during the Mission Period of California.

Dental Disease Differences

The rate of LEH recorded from CA-SMA-71/H is low, in contrast to other contact sites (Bard et al. 1992; Bartelink 2006; Grady et al. 2007; Pilloud 2006). LEH prevalence observed in the sample from San Pedro y San Pablo is closer to rates found in precontact samples. For example, in precontact sites from the San Francisco Bay, CA-ALA-11 and CA-SCL-674, rates of LEH were recorded at 9.3% and 12.9% respectively (Canzonieri and Caine 2023; Grady et al. 2007).

The rate of periapical lesions and abscesses (26.7%), is consistent with rates observed in precontact archaeological samples. For example, CA-ALA-11, CA-SCL-674, and CA-ALA-483, which all date to the Early or Early/Middle Transition period (3050 B.C.E.–A.D. 585) have periapical rates of 39.6%, 35%, and 26.7%, respectively. Bartelink's (2006) analysis of San Francisco Bay hunter-gathers from the Early, Middle, and Late Periods show an increase in rates of periapical lesions from the Early to Late Period (3050 B.C.E.–A.D. 1720); however, these rates are much lower than that reported here, at 3.6%, 4.2%, and 7.8% respectively. Unfortunately, comparative data on periapical lesions from other Mission Period sites are not available. The variability in periapical lesion rates for precontact sites and San Pedro y San Pablo suggests these skeletal alterations result from changes specific to sites and are not reflective of large-scale temporal differences.

While periodontal disease is present in individuals from CA-SMA-71/H, comparative data is not as accessible and therefore is not contextualized within pre- or post-contact samples.

The rate of carious lesions in individuals from CA-SMA-71/H, at 6.7%, is consistent with the rate observed in individuals from CA-ALA-483 (Bard et al. 1992). However, across precontact and contact sites there is a great deal of variability. Bartelink (2006) found low rates of carious lesions in Early, Middle, and Late Period (3050 B.C.E.–A.D. 1720) hunter-gathers from the San Francisco Bay Area, at 1.1%, 2.6%, and 1.4% respectively, while Canzonieri and Caine (2023) observed a rate of 27.5% in individuals from the CA-ALA-11 archaeological sample. Griffin (2014) found similarly low rates of carious lesions, with 2.5% of teeth observed with carious lesions in individuals from CA-CCO-548. In Pilloud's (2006) analysis of individuals from CA-ALA-613/H, 38.5% of the adult sample had carious lesions that dated to the Medieval Climatic Anomaly (A.D. 800–1350), but none were recorded in the adult sample previous to A.D. 800 or after A.D. 1350. South of the San Francisco Bay Area, Walker and Erlandson (1986) found much higher rates of carious lesions in Early to Late Period individuals from CA-SRI-41 and CA-

SRI-2, 80% and 47% respectively. Differences in carious lesions within and between Bay Area and Southern California sites likely results from variable reliance on marine and terrestrial sources. Heavy dental wear has also been posited to explain low prevalence of carious lesions in precontact California archaeological samples (Bartelink 2006; Griffin 2014).

Dental diseases observed in precontact and contact archaeological samples exhibit a high level of variability that is not defined by temporal change (table 3.3). Dietary practices in Native Californians are known to be variable because of seasonal and regional availability of resources, including marine versus terrestrial sources (Bartelink et al. 2020; Eerkens et al. 2013; Walker and Erlandson 1986). This regional variability is reflected in comparisons of dental diseases here; therefore, comparisons of dental diseases alone are not informative of the influence Mission Period practices had on dental health at the asistencia. Contextualization of dental diseases with isotopic analyses (see chapter 6) may highlight specific changes to diet in the Mission Period that correspond to dental disease rates.

While dental diseases are more reflective of regional variability, the presence of LEH, has been interpreted by scholars as evidence of resilience in the skeleton (Wood et al. 1992). Nonspecific stress indicators, like LEH, develop during periods of strain to the body (Kinaston et al. 2019:753). During the Mission Period, the ability of people to survive bouts of stress or strain to their diets was likely hindered by external factors, including malnutrition, laborious activities, overcrowding, and unsanitary living environments. Historic records provide a view into the stressors nonadults may have experienced while living inside and outside of the Mission system, including the stressors associated with weaning. Both individuals recorded with LEH, incurred those skeletal changes around the age of weaning. For Burial 2 (male), for example, weaning is thought to happened around 2.3 years (chapter 6) and LEH onset began as early as 2.17 years. Analyses presented in chapter 11 suggest this individual entered the Mission system as an infant and therefore lived his life within the Mission system.

Alternatively, the onset of LEH in dentition of Burial 12 reflects multiple instances of stress, with the earliest at 1.6 years old and the latest at 3.3 years old. Female infants are thought to be weaned later than males at approximately 3.2 years (chapter 6; see also Eerkens et al. 2020), suggesting that LEH in Burial 12 could reflect weaning but also stress before this, possibly from malnutrition or infection.

While life at San Pedro y San Pablo was difficult, this is not differentially represented in dental diseases between CA-SMA-71/H and other Californian archaeological samples. The distance of the asistencia from Mission Dolores

Table 3.3. Crude prevalence of dental diseases from California Indigenous archaeological samples

Archaeological Site	Time Period	Dental Disease		
		Enamel Hypoplasia	Periapical Lesions	Carious Lesions
CA-SMA-71/H	1787–1794	13.3%	26.7%	6.7%
CA-ALA-613/H (Pilloud 2006)	1890 B.C.–A.D. 800	7.7%	—	0%
	A.D. 800–1350	30.3%	—	38.5%
	A.D. 1350–1760	27.3%	—	0%
CA-ALA-11 (Canzonieri and Caine 2023)	500–210 B.C.	9.3%	39.6%	27.5%
CA-ALA-483 (Bard et al. 1992)	1465–1265 B.C.	—	26.7%	6.7%
CA-SCL-674 (Grady et al. 2007)	500–210 B.C.	12.9%	35%	36%
SF Bay Hunter-Gathers (Bartelink 2006)	>1500–500 B.C	73.3%	3.6%	1.1%
	210 B.C.–A.D. 1010	25.8%	4.2%	2.6%
	A.D. 1210–1720	26.3%	7.8%	1.4%
CA-CCO-548 (Griffin 2014)	2350–1450 B.C.	—	10.7%	2.5%
CA-SRI-2 (Walker and Erlandson 1986)	1820–900 B.C.	—	—	47%
CA-SRI-41 (Walker and Erlandson 1986)	3000–4000 B.C.	—	—	80%

may have buffered individuals, wherein they had greater agency over their diets. Therefore, distance and possible variability in dietary practices may better explain the low rates of dental disease, which are consistent with patterns observed in precontact archaeological samples.

Joint Disease Differences

Oral histories, historic documents, and archaeological evidence of precontact and contact contexts support a sex-linked bias in the distribution of labor, with men performing agricultural and hunting activities and women performing domestic tasks, including child rearing and cooking (Hackel 1997, 2005:285; Lightfoot 2005:67; Walker and Hollimon 1989). Gendered practices have been supported in bioarchaeological studies of joint disease from precontact Native archaeological samples in California (Walker and Hollimon 1989). The lack of skeletal alterations associated with joint disease suggests two possible scenarios. The first is that individuals were not stressing their bodies to the point of alteration. However, the more likely scenario is that the overrepresentation of young adults and nonadults results in a lack of skeletal alterations associated with joint stress. In other words, while individuals may have been exposed to harmful stressors, including laborious daily activities, they are not reflected in their skeletons because individuals died before these practices could alter their skeleton or were lost to the archaeological record. Additionally, stress that impacts soft tissue is lost in the archaeological record and therefore, absence of joint stress in the skeleton may not be indicative of limited performed labor but an absence of evidence. The loss of evidence to the archaeological record is supported by the presence of an avulsion fracture in Burial 3 that suggests adults were experiencing soft tissue trauma, which in the case of this individual also impacted the skeleton.

Trauma Differences

The majority of trauma recorded in Native Californian archaeological samples is related to interpersonal violence resulting in blunt force trauma (Jurmain and Bellifemine 1997; Lambert 1994; 2002; Schwitalla et al. 2014; Walker 1989). High rates of trauma are associated with resource stress or environmental shifts in precontact archaeological samples (Allen et al. 2016; Eerkens et al. 2016; Lambert 2002; Milliken et al. 2007; Schwitalla et al. 2014; Walker 1989). One individual, Burial 3, exhibited trauma at the clavicle that could be attributed to violence; however, it is difficult to differentiate direct (e.g., violence) versus indirect (e.g., accidental falls) fractures in clavicles (Wedel and Galloway 2013:197). Overall the rate of trauma at CA-SMA-71/H is lower than rates observed in precontact sites, where rates of trauma range from 6.7% to 28.2% (Bard et al. 1992; Canzonieri and Caine 2023; Grady et al. 2007; Lambert and Walker 1991; Pilloud 2006). Lower rates of trauma are associated with Historic Period archaeological samples (Pilloud 2006; Schwitalla et al. 2014), which are consistent with the rate of trauma at CA-SMA-71/H. While skeletal evidence of trauma is not prevalent during the Mission Period, historic documents and oral histories suggest a different lived experience. Punishment at Missions has been described as including whipping, use of stocks, leg chains, and other corporal punishment (Hackel 2005:281; Lightfoot 2005:60). While repeated corporal punishment has been identified at other sites globally (Osterholtz 2020), much of the impact to the body results in changes at the soft tissue. Therefore, if corporal punishment was used, the evidence has been lost in the archaeological record. While life at Mission outposts included semi-captive labor, it may have involved less direct oversight and therefore lower levels of punishment because of the distance from the Mission itself.

Infectious Disease Differences

Nonspecific infection, in the form of periostosis and osteomyelitis, are recorded at high rates in Mission Period sites. For example, Pilloud and Schwitalla (2020) found Native Californians from Historic Period San Francisco Bay archaeological sites exhibited periosteal reactions in 22.9% of individuals. A similarly high rate of periosteal reactions, 15%, was observed in Southern California archaeological samples from the Late Period (Lambert and Walker 1991). The absence of periostosis and osteomyelitis in individuals from CA-SMA-71/H suggests individuals were either not experiencing chronic exposure to infectious agents or died before skeletal alterations could manifest. Importantly, the small sample size likely impacts the resultant prevalence of infectious disease, particularly specific infectious diseases that can take months or even years to manifest in the skeleton (Roberts 2019).

While direct evidence of epidemics, in the form of infectious diseases, has not been exhibited in human skeletal remains, ancient DNA (aDNA) analysis has elucidated the history of infectious diseases and provided transmission maps in the Americas (Bos et al. 2014; Brynildsrud et al. 2018; Nelson et al. 2020; Woodman et al. 2019). Studies on aDNA find infectious diseases, including tuberculosis and syphilis (Baker et al. 1988; Bos et al. 2014; Powell and Cook 2005; Roberts and Buikstra 2003), were likely present and circulating in New World communities previous to contact. Genetic evidence also supports the introduction of more virulent strains of tuberculosis brought by European colonizers, which progressively replaced pre-Columbian varieties (Brynildsrud et al. 2018; Woodman et al. 2019). This change in virulency of infectious diseases and increased transmission from living in proximity following contact and during life within the Missions likely led to large-scale deaths in Native communities of California.

Where present, evidence of infectious diseases in Native Californians has been limited and emphasizes venereal syphilis (Walker et al. 2005; Roney 1959). The majority of evidence for syphilis has supported the presence of pathogens previous to the Mission Period, with the reintroduction of more virulent strains during the Mission Period (Walker et al. 2005). Where tuberculosis has been recorded, skeletal alterations include wedging of vertebrae attributed to Pott's disease and thickening of ribs (Roney 1959). The likely presence of tuberculosis is some of the only skeletal evidence of this disease in ancient California. Analysis of aDNA was performed on a vertebra from Burial 2 but was inconclusive for *Mycobacterium tuberculosis*. However, recent studies of aDNA have found that pathological remains are not always repositories for pathogen DNA (Nelson et al. 2020).

Persistence and Resilience at San Pedro y San Pablo

Persistence of traditional practices were seen in the burial practices for individuals recovered from the asistencia. Before and throughout the Mission Period in California, variation has been noted in burial practices, including orientation and grave goods across the state (Panich 2018, 2015). Similar variation was found with burial practices at CA-SMA-71/H. Limited evidence was recovered for coffin or shroud use, but orientation of the burials deviates from Christian practices, which has also been documented in other Mission Period samples (Panich 2018). All but three individuals were provided funerary offerings, with the quantity of grave goods thought to correlate with social status. While not the focus of this chapter, the inclusion of material culture from both precontact and historical periods in many of these mortuary contexts points to further persistence of mortuary practices within the Mission system.

While persistence is evident in the burial practices, resilience was also observed in the individuals themselves. In combination with historical records from the asistencia, osteological analyses highlight the challenges individuals faced at San Pedro y San Pablo and how those challenges varied by status. A common theme for these individuals was the loss of family members within the Mission system (see chapter 11). For many, deaths of family members happened in rapid succession. However, these losses were not described in historical records, leaving gaps in our understanding of how or why people died. The skeletal alterations observed here fill in some of these gaps but show two different experiences of life at San Pedro y San Pablo.

At first glance, the skeletal evidence for disease suggests that most individuals were not exposed to pathogens or other stressors impacting their skeletons, with the exception of dental diseases. The young age of most individuals from this archaeological sample likely influenced the rate of disease observed, particularly the lack of joint disease and traumatic injuries from the site. However, in contrast to other California sites, the absence of disease here more likely reflects differential frailty, or susceptibility to disease and death (Wood et al. 1992). Frailty likely was higher in individuals without evidence of skeletal alterations, leading them to succumb to pathogens more rapidly and therefore not develop skeletal indicators of disease. Differential frailty is supported by the skeletal alterations observed in Burial 2. The necessity of chronic exposure to tuberculosis bacteria for skeletal alterations to manifest suggests Burial 2 was exposed and living with tuberculosis for an extended period of time. Therefore, the presence of tuberculosis could indicate that he had a strong immune system and lower frailty to tuberculosis, which afforded his survival long enough to manifest skeletal alterations. Additionally, long-term experience of tuberculosis suggests he was likely able to spread tuberculosis to others and therefore, individuals without skeletal indicators of disease may reflect individuals with weaker immune systems who were not able to survive as long at San Pedro y San Pablo.

The presence of LEH in Burial 2 and Burial 12 also speaks to differential frailty. LEH reflects response to stress in enamel formation; however, in order for LEH to be present either a decline in stress or recommencing of normal enamel formation is necessary (Kinaston et al. 2019). The presence of LEH in a child and young adult provide different views into experiences for individuals from San Pedro y San Pablo. As discussed previously, Burial 2's skeletal alterations in response to possible tuberculosis along with LEH suggest he was less frail than other children recovered. However, in the case of Burial 12 a young adult, LEH reflects experiences in her childhood and not life at San Pedro y San Pablo. This distinction in age-at-death signals that although Burial 12 was able to survive stressors during childhood, in adulthood she was impacted by internal or external factors that she could not survive, which is supported by the absence of skeletal alterations reflective of adult stress. The necessity for labor and investment in children for religious indoctrination may have resulted in protections for children not afforded to adults. However, changes in Burial 2's mobility while living at San Pedro y San Pablo in response to tuberculosis infection also may have also buffered him from more laborious tasks, enabling longer survival.

Notably, metabolic alterations were not observed in the human skeletal remains from CA-SMA-71/H. Cribra orbitalia (CO) and porotic hyperostosis (PH) have been observed at variable rates in many Indigenous Californian archaeological samples (Bartelink 2006; Bright and Bartelink 2013; Canzonieri and Caine 2023; Grady et al. 2007; Lambert and Walker 1991; Pilloud and Schwitalla 2020; Pilloud et al. 2020; Walker 1986). While CO and PH are not attributable to specific etiologies, they are typically associated with deficiencies of dietary iron due to undernutrition and/or infection (Brickley 2018; Oxenham and Cavill 2010; Walker et al. 2009). Additional factors influencing CO and PH include inheritance (sickle cell anemia and thalassaemia), deficiency in vitamin B12 resulting in megaloblastic anaemia, and/or normal variation across different human groups (Oxenham and Cavill 2010; Stuart-Macadam 1989; Walker et al. 2009; Wapler et al. 2004). The absence of CO and PH in CA-SMA-71/H adults and nonadults could indicate higher levels of stress during childhood and a lower likelihood for survival into adulthood. Similarly, the lack of periosteal reactions in CA-SMA-71/H aligns with higher mortality rates, particularly for children, and has been found for individuals that survived the plague (DeWitte and Wood 2008).

Regional variation in dietary practices, particularly within and between Missions and Mission outposts, suggests individuals from CA-SMA-71/H could have experienced dietary deficiencies while living at San Pedro y San Pablo and prior to entering the Mission system. As discussed in chapter 11, social status and connections of particular families may have afforded certain individuals greater access to resources and could signal lower frailty in childhood, which could be reflected in the absence of LEH. Yet, even some higher status individuals, such as Burial 12, show LEH, suggesting that access to resources may have changed at San Pedro y San Pablo along with susceptibility to death. Likewise, many of the individuals recovered with large quantities of material culture, including Burial 9, and those without material culture, such as Burial 14, exhibited no evidence of pathological alterations. These findings suggest that while status played a role in the burial practices of individuals and may have influenced their experiences within and outside the Mission system, it did not influence their frailty and therefore susceptibility to mortality. Combining the lack of evidence for disease with the incomplete information on cause of death for relatives of individuals recovered from CA-SMA-71/H presented in chapter 11 shows that life in the Mission system was challenging for all individuals regardless of age or social standing.

Conclusions

Human skeletal remains from CA-SMA-71/H highlight a difficult lived experience at San Pedro y San Pablo. The site highlights the regional variability of experiences within the San Francisco Bay Area across prehistoric and historic periods. While the number of individuals is small, results contribute to a growing narrative of the Mission Period, including differences between experiences at Mission sites and outposts such as San Pedro y San Pablo. The Mission Period marks a time of forced assimilation; however, as Panich (2005) points out, missions were primarily "native" spaces with artifacts intimately linked to the Native experience. Therefore, studying these sites, including outposts, presents an opportunity to understand the life histories of Native Californians.

The evidence of specific infectious disease in Burial 2 suggests individuals at San Pedro y San Pablo, and presumably other missions, were in contact with deadly pathogens. However, distinguishing between epidemic and endemic diseases is a persistent issue. One means for addressing this larger debate necessitates more osteological studies. However, this approach also necessitates further disturbance of Native communities and causes additional harm to people today. Archaeological and bioarchaeological studies that work in collaboration with Native communities, especially when human skeletal remains are encountered inadvertently, like this volume exemplifies, present a future that can contribute to research that addresses the trauma inflicted on Native communities of the past while also attending to the pain, concerns, and needs of communities today.

Acknowledgments

We thank Diana Malarchik for reading and providing comments for this chapter.

References

Acsádi, G., and J. Nemeskéri
1970 Determination of Sex and Age from Skeletal Finds. History of Human Life Span and Mortality. Akadémiai Kiadó, Budapest.
Allen, Mark W., Robert Lawrence Bettinger, Brian F. Codding, Terry L. Jones, and Al W. Schwitalla
2016 Resource Scarcity Drives Lethal Aggression among Prehistoric Hunter-Gatherers in Central California. *Proceedings of the National Academy of Sciences* 113(43): 12120–12125.
Arkush, Brooke S.
2011 Native Responses to European Intrusion: Cultural Persistence and Agency among Mission Neophytes in Spanish Colonial Northern California. *Historical Archaeology* 45(4): 62–90.
Auerbach, Benjamin M., and Christopher B. Ruff
2010 Stature Estimation Formulae for Indigenous North American Populations. *American Journal of Physical Anthropology* 141(2): 190–207.
Baker, Brenda J., George J. Armelagos, Marshall Joseph Becker, et al.
1988 The Origin and Antiquity of Syphilis: Paleopathological Diagnosis and Interpretation [and Comments and Reply]. *Current Anthropology* 29(5). JSTOR [University of Chicago Press, Wenner-Gren Foundation for Anthropological Research]: 703–737.
Bard, James C., Colin I. Busby, Michael R. Fong, et al.
1992 CA-ALA-483, Laguna Oaks Project, Pleasanton, Alameda County, California. Archaeological Site Testing Report, Volume 2. Basin Research Associates, INC.
Bartelink, Eric J., Melanie M. Beasley, Jelmer W. Eerkens, et al.
2020 Stable Isotope Evidence of Diet Breadth Expansion and Regional Dietary Variation among Middle-to-Late Holocene Hunter-Gatherers of Central California. *Journal of Archaeological Science: Reports* 29: 102182.

Bartelink, Eric John
2006 Resource Intensification in Pre-Contact Central California: A Bioarchaeological Perspective on Diet and Health Patterns among Hunter-Gatherers from the Lower Sacramento Valley and San Francisco Bay. Texas A&M University.

Binazzi, Roberto, Javier Assiso, Vittorio Vaccari, and Lamberto Felli
1992 Avulsion Fractures of the Scapula: Report of Eight Cases. *The Journal of Trauma* 33(5): 785–789.

Bos, Kirsten I., Kelly M. Harkins, Alexander Herbig, et al.
2014 Pre-Columbian Mycobacterial Genomes Reveal Seals as a Source of New World Human Tuberculosis. *Nature* 514(7523): 494–497.

Boylston, Anthea, and Charlotte A. Roberts
1996 The Roman-British Cemetery at Kempston, Bedfordshire. Report on the Human Skeletal Remains. Calvin Wells Laboratory, Department of Archaeological Sciences, University of Bradford, Bradford.

Brickley, Megan
2002 An Investigation of Historical and Archaeological Evidence for Age-Related Bone Loss and Osteoporosis. *International Journal of Osteoarchaeology* 12(5): 364–371.

Brickley, Megan B.
2018 *Cribra Orbitalia* and Porotic Hyperostosis: A Biological Approach to Diagnosis. *American Journal of Physical Anthropology* 167(4): 896–902.

Bright, Lisa, and Eric J. Bartelink
2013 Health and Nutritional Status at CA-SOL-451 (Encinosa Site): Biological Interpretations and Regional Comparisons. *Pacific Coast Archaeological Society Quarterly* 49(1): 85–104.

Brooks, Sheilagh, and Judy M. Suchey
1990 Skeletal Age Determination Based on the Os Pubis: A Comparison of the Acsádi-Nemeskéri and Suchey-Brooks Methods. *Human Evolution* 5(3): 227–238.

Brothwell, Donald R.
1981 *Digging Up Bones* (3rd ed.). Cornell University Press, Ithaca.

Brynildsrud, Ola B., Caitlin S. Pepperell, Philip Suffys, et al.
2018 Global Expansion of *Mycobacterium Tuberculosis* Lineage 4 Shaped by Colonial Migration and Local Adaptation. *Science Advances* 4(10): eaat5869.

Buikstra, Jane E., and Doug H. Ubelaker (editors)
1994 *Standards for Data Collection from Human Skeletal Remains: Proceedings of a Seminar at the Field Museum of Natural History*. Arkansas Archeological Survey, Fayetteville, AR.

Buonasera, Tammy, Jelmer Eerkens, Brian Byrd, et al.
2022 Sex-Biased Differences in Infant Mortality and Life Expectancy at at Síi Túupentak, an Ancestral Ohlone Village in Central California (ca. 540–145 Cal. BP). Human Biology Open Access Pre-Prints 94.

Canzonieri, Christoper, and Alyson C. Caine
2023 The Burials. In *Data Recovery Excavations at CA-ALA-11/H, An Ancestral Ohlone Shellmound on the Oakland Estuary*, edited by Daniel Shoup and Molly Fierer-Donaldson, 116–224. Archaeological/Historical Consultants, Oakland.

Cheverko, Colleen M., and Eric J. Bartelink
2017   Resource Intensification and Osteoarthritis Patterns: Changes in Activity in the Prehistoric Sacramento-San Joaquin Delta Region. *American Journal of Physical Anthropology* 164(2): 331–342.
Combs, Jan A.
1994   Hip and Pelvis Avulsion Fractures in Adolescents: Proper Diagnosis Improves Compliance. *The Physician and Sportsmedicine* 22(7). Taylor & Francis: 41–49.
Cunningham, Craig, Louise Scheuer, and Sue M. Black
2016   Developmental Juvenile Osteology. Second edition. Amsterdam: Elsevier/AP, Academic Press is an imprint of Elsevier.
DeWitte, S. N., and J. W. Wood
2008   Selectivity of Black Death Mortality with Respect to Preexisting Health. *Proceedings of the National Academy of Sciences* 105(5): 1436–1441.
DeWitte, Sharon N.
2014   Differential Survival among Individuals with Active and Healed Periosteal New Bone Formation. *International Journal of Paleopathology* 7: 38–44.
Dietz, Stephen A.
1979   Report of Archaeological Investigations at Sanchez Adobe Park Historic District. Archaeological Consulting and Research Services, Incorporated.
Drevenstedt, Greg L., Eileen M. Crimmins, Sarinnapha Vasunilashorn, and Caleb E. Finch
2008   The Rise and Fall of Excess Male Infant Mortality. Proceedings of the National Academy of Sciences. 105(13): 5016–5021.
Eerkens, Jelmer W., Eric J. Bartelink, Laura Brink, et al.
2016   Trophy Heads or Ancestor Veneration? A Stable Isotope Perspective on Disassociated and Modified Crania in Precontact Central California. *American Antiquity* 81(1): 114–131.
Eerkens, Jelmer W., Brian F. Byrd, Howard J. Spero, and AnnaMarie K. Fritschi
2013   Stable Isotope Reconstructions of Shellfish Harvesting Seasonality in an Estuarine Environment: Implications for Late Holocene San Francisco Bay Settlement Patterns. *Journal of Archaeological Science* 40(4): 2014–2024.
Eerkens, Jelmer W., Davis Watkins, Samantha Cramer, and Christopher Beckham
2020   Stable Isotope Measures from First and Third Molar Serial Samples. In *Rotohistoric Village Organization and Territorial Maintenance: The Archaeology of Sií Túupentak (CA-ALA-565/H) in the San Francisco Bay Area*, edited by Brian F. Byrd, Laurel Engbring, Michael Darcangelo, and Allika Ruby, 311–330. Center for Archaeological Research at Davis, Davis, CA.
Fuse, Kana, and Edward M. Crenshaw
2006   Gender Imbalance in Infant Mortality: A Cross-National Study of Social Structure and Female Infanticide. *Social Science & Medicine* 62(2): 360–374.
Garland, Carey, Laurie Reitsema, Clark Spencer Larsen, and David Hurst Thomas
2018   Early Life Stress at Mission Santa Catalina de Guale: An Integrative Analysis of Enamel Defects and Dentin Incremental Isotope Variation in Malnutrition. *Bioarchaeology International* 2(2): 75–94.
Geiger, Maynard
1976   As the Padres Saw Them: California Indian Life and Customs as Reported by

the Franciscan Missionaries 1813–1815. The Santa Barbara Bicentennial Historical Series. Santa Barbara Mission Archive Library.

Geller, Pamela L.
2008 Conceiving Sex: Fomenting a Feminist Bioarchaeology. *Journal of Social Archaeology* 8(1): 113–138.

Goodman, Alan H., and Jerome C. Rose
1990 Assessment of Systemic Physiological Perturbations from Dental Enamel Hypoplasias and Associated Histological Structures. *American Journal of Physical Anthropology* 33(S11): 59–110.

Grady, Diane L., Kate A. Latham, and Valerie A. Andrushko
2007 Archaeological Investigations at CA-SCL-674, the Rubino Site, San Jose, Santa Clara County, California, vol.1. Coyote Press.

Griffin, Mark C.
2014 Biocultural Implications of Oral Pathology in an Ancient Central California Population: Oral Pathology in Ancient Central California. *American Journal of Physical Anthropology* 154(2): 171–188.

Hackel, Steven W.
1997 Land, Labor, and Production: The Colonial Economy of Spanish and Mexican California. *California History* 76(2/3). [University of California Press, California Historical Society]: 111–146.

Hackel, Steven W.
2005 Children of Coyote, Missionaries of Saint Francis: Indian-Spanish Relations in Colonial California, 1769–1850. Published for the Omohundro Institute of Early American History and Culture, Williamsburg, Virginia, by the University of North Carolina Press, Chapel Hill.

Hillson, Simon, Caroline Grigson, and Sandra Bond
1998 Dental Defects of Congenital Syphilis. *American Journal of Physical Anthropology*: The Official Publication of the American Association of Physical Anthropologists 107(1). Wiley Online Library: 25–40.

Hu, Jan C.-C., Yong-Hee P. Chun, Turki Al Hazzazzi, and James P. Simmer
2007 Enamel Formation and Amelogenesis Imperfecta. Cells Tissues Organs 186(1): 78–85.

Jackson, Robert H.
1983 Disease and Demographic Patterns at Santa Cruz Mission, Alta California. *Journal of California and Great Basin Anthropology* 5(1/2). JSTOR: 33–57.
1994 Indian Population Decline: The Missions of Northwestern New Spain, 1687–1840. 1st ed. University of New Mexico Press, Albuquerque.

Jones, Terry L., Al W. Schwitalla, Marin A. Pilloud, et al.
2021 Historic and Bioarchaeological Evidence Supports Late Onset of Post-Columbian Epidemics in Native California. *Proceedings of the National Academy of Sciences* 118(28): e2024802118.

Jurmain, Robert, and Viviana Ines Bellifemine
1997 Patterns of Cranial Trauma in a Prehistoric Population from Central California. *International Journal of Osteoarchaeology* 7(1): 43–50.

Kinaston, Rebecca, Anna Willis, Justyna J. Miszkiewicz, Monica Tromp, and Marc F. Oxenham
2019   The Dentition: Development, Disturbances, Disease, Diet, and Chemistry. In *Ortner's Identification of Pathological Conditions in Human Ancestral Remains* (3rd ed.), edited by Jane E. Buikstra, 749–797. Academic Press, San Diego.

Lambert, Patricia M
2002   The Archaeology of War: A North American Perspective. *Journal of Archaeological Research* 10(3): 207–241.

Lambert, Patricia M., and Phillip L. Walker
1991   Physical Anthropological Evidence for the Evolution of Social Complexity in Coastal Southern California. *Antiquity* 65(249). Cambridge University Press: 963–973.

Lambert, Patricia Marie
1994   War and Peace on the Western Front: A Study of Violent Conflict and Its Correlates in Prehistoric Hunter-Gatherer Societies of Coastal Southern California. PhD Thesis, University of California, Santa Barbara.

Larsen, Clark Spencer
2018   The Bioarchaeology of Health Crisis: Infectious Disease in the Past. *Annual Review of Anthropology* 47(1): 295–313.

Larsen, Clark Spencer, and George R. Milner
1994   In the Wake of Contact: Biological Responses to Conquest. Wiley-Blackwell.

Lightfoot, Kent G.
2005   Indians, Missionaries, and Merchants: The Legacy of Colonial Encounters on the California Frontiers. University of California Press, Berkeley.

Lovejoy, C. Owen
1985   Dental Wear in the Libben Population: Its Functional Pattern and Role in the Determination of Adult Skeletal Age at Death. *American Journal of Physical Anthropology* 68(1): 47–56.

Lovejoy, C. Owen, Richard S. Meindl, Robert P. Mensforth, and Thomas J. Barton
1985   Multifactorial Determination of Skeletal Age at Death: A Method and Blind Tests of Its Accuracy. *American Journal of Physical Anthropology* 68(1): 1–14.

Lovejoy, C. Owen, Richard S. Meindl, Thomas R. Pryzbeck, and Robert P. Mensforth
1985   Chronological Metamorphosis of the Auricular Surface of the Ilium: A New Method for the Determination of Adult Skeletal Age at Death. *American Journal of Physical Anthropology* 68(1): 15–28.

Lukacs, John R.
2008   Fertility and Agriculture Accentuate Sex Differences in Dental Caries Rates. *Current Anthropology* 49:901–914.

McFadden, Clare, Brianna Muir, and Marc F. Oxenham
2022   Determinants of Infant Mortality and Representation in Bioarchaeological Samples: A Review. *American Journal of Biological Anthropology* 177(2): 196–206.

Meskell, Lynn
1999   Archaeologies of Social Life: Age, Sex, Class et Cetera in Ancient Egypt. Social Archaeology. Blackwell, Malden, MA.

Milliken, R, RT Fitzgerald, MG Hylkema, et al.
2007 Punctuated Culture Change in San Francisco Bay Area. In *California Prehistory: Colonization, Culture and Complexity*, edited by T. L. Jones and K. A. Klar, 99–123. AltaMira Press, Walnut Creek.

Moeller, James L.
2003 Pelvic and Hip Apophyseal Avulsion Injuries in Young Athletes. *Current Sports Medicine Reports* 2(2). Springer: 110–115.

Nelson, Elizabeth A., Jane E. Buikstra, Alexander Herbig, Tiffiny A. Tung, and Kirsten I. Bos
2020 Advances in the Molecular Detection of Tuberculosis in Pre-Contact Andean South America. *International Journal of Paleopathology* 29. The Paleopathology of Andean South America: 20 Years of Advances and Future Prospects: 128–140.

Osterholtz, Anna
2020 Pain as Power: Torture as a Mechanism for Social Control. In *Purposeful Pain*, 215–231. Springer.

Oxenham, Marc Fredrick, and Ivor Cavill
2010 Porotic Hyperostosis and Cribra Orbitalia: The Erythropoietic Response to Iron-Deficiency Anaemia. Anthropological Science 118(3): 199–200.

Panich, Lee M.
2018 Death, Mourning, and Accommodation in the Missions of Alta California. In *Franciscans and American Indians in Pan-Borderlands Perspective: Adaptation, Negotiation, and Resistance*, edited by J. M. Burns and T. J. Johnson, 251–264. Academy of American Fraciscan History.
2015 "Sometimes They Bury the Deceased's Clothes and Trinkets": Indigenous Mortuary Practices at Mission Santa Clara de Asís. *Historical Archaeology* 49(4): 110–129.

Panich, Lee M., and Tsim D. Schneider
2015 Expanding Mission Archaeology: A Landscape Approach to Indigenous Autonomy in Colonial California. *Journal of Anthropological Archaeology* 40: 48–58.

Pilloud, Marin A.
2006 The Impact of the Medieval Climatic Anomaly in Prehistoric California: A Case Study from Canyon Oaks, CA-ALA-613/H. *Journal of California and Great Basin Anthropology*. JSTOR: 179–192.

Pilloud, Marin A., and Al W. Schwitalla
2020 Re-Evaluating Traditional Markers of Stress in an Archaeological Sample from Central California. *Journal of Archaeological Science* 116: 105102.

Pilloud, Marin A., Al W. Schwitalla, and Kristen A. Broehl
2020 Biological and Cultural Adaptations to Climate Change in Prehistoric Central California. In *The Routledge Handbook of the Bioarchaeology of Climate and Environmental Change*. Routledge.

Powell, Mary Lucas, and Della Collins Cook, eds.
2005 The Myth of Syphilis: The Natural History of Treponematosis in North America. Ripley P. Bullen Series. University Press of Florida, Gainesville.

Redfern, Rebecca, and Charlotte A. Roberts
2019   Trauma. In *Ortner's Identification of Pathological Conditions in Human Skeletal Remains* (3rd ed.), edited by Jane E. Buikstra, 211–284. Elsevier, San Diego.
Roberts, Charlotte A.
2019   Infectious Disease: Introduction, Periostosis, Periostitis, Osteomyelitis, and Septic Arthritis. In *Ortner's Identification of Pathological Conditions in Human Ancestral Remains* (3rd ed.), edited by Jane E. Buikstra, 285–319. Elsevier, San Diego.
Roberts, Charlotte A., and Jane E. Buikstra
2003   The Bioarchaeology of Tuberculosis: A Global View on a Reemerging Disease (1st ed.). Gainesville: University Press of Florida.
Rogers, Juliet, and Tony Waldron
1995   A Field Guide to Joint Disease in Archaeology. John Wiley & Sons.
Roney, James G.
1959   Palaeopathology of a California Archaeological Site. *Bulletin of the History of Medicine* 33(2). Johns Hopkins University Press: 97–109.
Schwitalla, Al W., Terry L. Jones, Marin A. Pilloud, Brian F. Codding, and Randy S. Wiberg
2014   Violence among Foragers: The Bioarchaeological Record from Central California. *Journal of Anthropological Archaeology* 33: 66–83.
Skowronek, Russel K., and Julie C. Wizorek
1997   Archaeology at Santa Clara de Asís: The Slow Rediscovery of a Moveable Mission. *Pacific Coast Archaeological Society Quarterly* 33(3): 54–92.
Sofaer, Joanna R.
2006   The Body as Material Culture: A Theoretical Osteoarchaeology. Topics in Contemporary Archaeology. Cambridge University Press, Cambridge.
Stojanowski, Christopher M.
2005   The Bioarchaeology of Identity in Spanish Colonial Florida: Social and Evolutionary Transformation before, during, and after Demographic Collapse. *American Anthropologist* 107(3): 417–431.
Stojanowski, Christopher M., Clark S. Larsen, Tiffiny A. Tung, and Bonnie G. McEwan
2007   Biological Structure and Health Implications from Tooth Size at Mission San Luis de Apalachee. *American Journal of Physical Anthropology* 132(2): 207–222.
Stuart-Macadam, Patricia L.
1989   Nutritional Deficiency Diseases: A Survey of Scurvy, Rickets, and Iron deficiency Anemia. Reconstruction of Life from the Skeleton: 201–222.
Torres-Rouff, Christina, Kelly J. Knudson, Ramiro Barberena, et al.
2017   Integrating Identities: An Innovative Bioarchaeological and Biogeochemical Approach to Analyzing the Multiplicity of Identities in the Mortuary Record. *Current Anthropology* 58(3): 381–409.
Walker, Philip. L.
1986   Porotic Hyperostosis in a Marine-Dependent California Indian Population. *American Journal of Physical Anthropology* 69(3): 345–354.
Walker, Philip L., and Sandra E. Hollimon
1989   Changes in Osteoarthritis Associated with the Development of a Maritime

Economy among Southern California Indians. *International Journal of Anthropology* 4(3). Springer: 171–183.

Walker, Phillip L.
1989   Cranial Injuries as Evidence of Violence in Prehistoric Southern California. *American Journal of Physical Anthropology* 80(3): 313–323.

Walker, Phillip L., Rhonda R. Bathurst, Rebecca Richman, Thor Gjerdrum, and Valerie A. Andrushko
2009   The Causes of Porotic Hyperostosis and Cribra Orbitalia: A Reappraisal of the Iron-Deficiency-Anemia Hypothesis. *American Journal of Physical Anthropology* 139(2): 109–125.

Walker, Phillip L., and Jon M. Erlandson
1986   Dental Evidence for Prehistoric Dietary Change on the Northern Channel Islands, California. American Antiquity 51(2). Cambridge University Press: 375–383.

Walker, Phillip L., Patricia M. Lambert, Michael Schultz, and Jon M. Erlandson
2005   The Evolution of Treponemal Disease in the Santa Barbara Channel Area of Southern California. In *The Myth of Syphilis: The Natural History of Treponematosis in North America*, 281–305. University of Florida Press, Gainesville.

Wapler, Ulrike, Eric Crubezy, and Michael Schultz
2004   Is Cribra Orbitalia Synonymous with Anemia? Analysis and Interpretation of Cranial Pathology in Sudan. *American Journal of Physical Anthropology*: The Official Publication of the American Association of Physical Anthropologists 123(4): 333–339.

Wedel, Vicki L., and Alison Galloway
2013   Broken Bones: Anthropological Analysis of Blunt Force Trauma. Charles C Thomas Publisher.

Wood, James W., George R. Milner, Henry C. Harpending, et al.
1992   The Osteological Paradox: Problems of Inferring Prehistoric Health from Skeletal Samples [and Comments and Reply]. *Current Anthropology* 33(4): 343–370.

Woodman, Marc, Ilsa Haeusler, and Louis Grandjean
2019   Tuberculosis Genetic Epidemiology: A Latin American Perspective. *Genes* 10(1): 53.

Zarulli, Virginia, Julia A. Barthold Jones, Anna Oksuzyan, et al.
2018   Women Live Longer than Men Even during Severe Famines and Epidemics. *Proceedings of the National Academy of Sciences* 115(4): E832–E840.

4

Proteomic Sex Estimation and Detection of Immune Proteins in Tooth Enamel at the Asistencia de San Pedro y San Pablo (CA-SMA-71/H)

Tammy Buonasera, Diana Malarchik,
Jelmer W. Eerkens, Christopher Canzonieri,
and Glendon Parker

Biological sex plays an important role in the human experience, correlating to lifespan, reproduction, and a wide range of other biological factors. Sex is also fundamental in structuring an array of cultural behaviors, including family relations, community interactions, and economic roles. Sex and socially constructed gender roles would have affected the ways individuals experienced the profound social ruptures and declines in health that accompanied missionization in central California. Although the biological aspects would have remained the same, individuals had to negotiate the transition from the Ohlone worldview about sex, identity, and behavior to the Spanish worldview. As discussed further in chapter 12, there are particular ways that sex (and age) mapped onto the life experience and opportunities individuals had within the Spanish mission system.

To provide more complete and robust sex estimates for skeletal remains that were recovered at the Asistencia de San Pedro y San Pablo (hereafter, simply the asistencia; CA-SMA-71/H) proteomic sex estimation was combined with osteological sex estimation. In total, proteomic sex was established for twelve individuals at the asistencia. Proteomic sex estimation is a relatively new but robust method of sex estimation that relies on differences in the amino acid sequences of X and Y forms of amelogenin protein, which are coded for on the sex chromosomes and expressed in tooth enamel (Parker et al. 2019, 2021). This method uses nano liquid chromatography-tandem mass spectrometry (nano LC-MS/MS) and is a highly sensitive and reliable technique for providing sex estimates for the skeletonized remains of the youngest to the oldest members of a society even when other methods fail due to poor preservation (Buonasera et al. 2020).

An additional benefit of this approach is that results typically provide a rich source of data on the wider enamel proteome. A number of serum proteins are part of the enamel proteome (Gil-Bona and Bidlack 2020; Limeback et al. 1989; Robinson et al. 2003), including serum albumin and immunoglobulin gamma (IgG). These were observed in the enamel of all the individuals in this study. Although we aim to explore these results in greater depth in future research, as part of the results below, we also report on the levels of IgG and C-reactive protein (CRP), two proteins associated with immune function. These proteins may provide a record of stress and disease during the period of tooth formation. As a means of standardizing the analyses (i.e., to account for postdepositional preservation effects), we compare the density of these proteins relative to serum albumin and amelogenin within the same sample.

Immunoglobulins, also known as antibodies, are part of the adaptive, or specific, immune system. They exist as either membrane-bound proteins or are secreted into the blood. There are five main types of immunoglobulins: IgA, IgD, IgE, IgG, and IgM, which differ in their functional location, structure, and specificity for different types of antigens (Schroeder and Cavacini 2010). IgG is the primary immunoglobulin circulating in the blood stream and can be divided into four subtypes: IgG1, IgG2, IgG3, and IgG4, present from highest to lowest concentration (Calonga-Solís et al. 2019).

CRP is associated with inflammation as part of the nonspecific (or innate) immune response and is present in low concentrations. Analyses of blood plasma indicates that total ion intensities for CRP are one to two orders of magnitude lower than IgG, and four or more orders of magnitude lower than serum albumin (Anderson and Anderson 2002). Elevated CRP is associated with chronic inflammation as well as psychosocial stress (Meca et al. 2022; Shenhar-Tsarfaty et al. 2015). Of note, two recent meta-analyses of studies in medical journals find that CRP has a high sensitivity in the screening for pulmonary tuberculosis, particularly in immunocompromised individuals (Meca et al. 2022; Yoon et al. 2017). Beyond this, other studies tie elevated levels of CRP to emotional stress (Johnson et al. 2013) or persistent fear in conflict zones (Shenhar-Tsarfaty et al. 2015).

We argue that persistent, chronic psychosocial stress (in the absence of chronic disease) leads to decreased IgG and elevated CRP. In the current study, we know that Ohlone living through contact and missionization were exposed to both chronic diseases and severe social and emotional stressors. We compare these signals to the pathology data presented in chapter 3.

Methods

Methods follow Parker et al. (2019) with modification in Buonasera et al. (2020). Powdered enamel samples (19.8 to 20.8 mg) from twelve asistencia individuals were demineralized by adding 200 μL of 1.2M hydrochloric acid to 2 mL sample vial with seven 2.8 mM ceramic beads (Omni-International Inc.). Samples were milled for 3 minutes at 7000 rpm in a MagnaLyzer (Roche Inc.), then centrifuged for 5 minutes at 16000 g. After incubation at 56°C, 1200 rpm for 60 minutes, samples were neutralized with 2.0 M ammonium bicarbonate and 0.01% ProteaseMAX (6μL of 0.5% w/v, Promega Inc.) was added to the sample vials along with mass spectrometry grade trypsin (1μL of 0.5μg/μL, Thermo Pierce, Inc). Each sample was incubated at 37°C for 20 hours at 600 rpm. After incubation, the sample vials were centrifuged for 5 minutes and the supernatant was transferred to 0.22μm centrifugal filters and centrifuged for 30 minutes. The filtrate was then transferred to clean Eppendorf® Protein LoBind tubes for ZipTip (Millipore Inc.) to prepare for mass spectrometric analysis. Organic contaminants in aqueous stocks and solutions were removed by prior passage over solid phase extraction (SepPak, C18, Waters Inc.). A sample blank was analyzed along with each batch of samples.

Digested peptides were desalted and concentrated using ZipTip C18 pipette tips (Millipore Inc.) with the eluted material lyophilized and resuspended in 2% (v/v) acetonitrile and 0.1% (v/v) TFA. The peptide concentration was measured using the Pierce™ Quantitative Fluorometric Peptide Assay (Thermo Pierce™) and 1 μg of peptide, or 40 percent of the total sample if the sample was too diluted, was applied to mass spectrometry. The sample was applied to LC-MS/MS on a Thermo Scientific Q Exactive Plus Orbitrap Mass spectrometer in conjunction with a Proxeon Easy-nLC II HPLC (Thermo Scientific) and Proxeon nanospray source. The digested peptides were then loaded a 100 micron x 25 mm Magic C18 100Å 5U reverse phase trap where they were desalted online before being separated using a 75 micron x 150 mm Magic C18 200Å 3U reverse phase column. Peptides were eluted using a 65-minute gradient with a flow rate of 300nl/min. An MS survey scan was obtained for the m/z range 300–1600, MS/MS spectra were acquired using an inclusion list of 28 ions that were subjected to HCD (High Energy Collisional Dissociation). When inclusion list ions were not found, MS/MS was done on other ions in the MS survey scan. An isolation mass window of 1.6

m/z was used for precursor ion selection, and normalized collision energy of 27 percent for fragmentation. A five-second duration was used for the dynamic exclusion. Washes were applied between each sample. After 10 samples a blank run of BSA standards was applied to test for sample-to-sample contamination.

Mass spectrometry datasets (.RAW format) were processed using PEAKS (version 10 Pro) peptide matching software (Bioinformatics Solutions Inc., Waterloo, ON). The FASTA formatted UNIPROT *Homo sapiens* reference protein database (http://www.uniprot.org/proteomes/UP000005640) was modified to include additional FASTA protein entries of peptide sequences from all splice variants associated with AMELX_HUMAN (Q99217-1, -2, -3) and AMELY_HUMAN (Q99218-1, -2) proteins gene products (Salido et al. 1992, Simmer 1995). The reference database was further modified to incorporate a decoy database and was validated in PEAKS™ Software (Zhang et al. 2012). Peptide matching spectral assignment was conducted using default conditions with the following exceptions: error tolerance, precursor mass, 10 ppm, Fragment ion, 0.04 Da., cleavage with trypsin with up to two missed cleavages, and two nonspecific cleavages. The algorithm searched for peptides partially modified by deamidation (NQ), oxidation (MHW), pyroglutamate conversion from glutamate and glutamine, and methionine dioxidation. All peptide assignments were filtered by a 1 percent false discovery rate. Each peptide was quantified by summing the intensity of each signal for the peptide-specific primary precursor mass over charge ratio (m/z). Signals from all peptides specific to either AMELY_HUMAN or AMELX_HUMAN were combined into a single metric (combined intensities [CI] per mg enamel) for each protein. A single unit (1) was added to each measurement to prevent the occurrence of a null signal.

AMELX_HUMAN signals (CI/mg) were log transformed and then solved for Pr(F) using the equation $Pr(F) = 1.0 + (0.059-1.0)/(1+(x/7.54)13.99$ where "x" is the logarithm (base 10) of the AMELX_HUMAN (Parker et al. 2019). Samples with a Pr(F) < 0.5 were considered indeterminate for proteomic sex estimation.

Results

Samples and results are listed in table 4.1, along with quantitative proteomic sex estimates. For enamel samples lacking AMELY_HUMAN we assign a probability of female sex based on the normalized cumulative AMELX_HUMAN signal. In total, seven individuals were male (n=7) and five were female (n=5). Five individuals were non-adults (four males and one female) and the

Table 4.1. Proteomic sex estimation for individuals at San Pedro y San Pablo

Sample	Burial	Age	Tooth	mg	AMELX (CI)	AMELY (CI)	Pr(F)	Sex
TYB 129	2	13–17	LLM3	19.8	2.969E+10	2.987E+09	0.000	M
DM 032	3	45–50	URM3	20.7	6.329E+10	0.000E+00	0.984	F
DM 021	4	50–60	LRM3	20.5	1.785E+11	0.000E+00	0.994	F
DM 022	5	45–50	LLM1	20.6	6.139E+10	0.000E+00	0.984	F
DM 023	6	18–25	LRM1	20.1	4.222E+10	5.603E+09	0.000	M
DM 024	8	46+	LLM1	20.2	8.642E+10	8.666E+09	0.000	M
DM 025	9	2–2.5	dLLM2	20.3	1.669E+10	1.531E+09	0.000	M
TYB 178	11	4–8	M1	20.8	1.694E+08	1.785E+07	0.000	M
DM 027	12	20–25	URM1	20.5	1.276E+10	0.000E+00	0.950	F
DM 028	13	20–24	LRM1	20.8	5.634E+10	0.000E+00	0.982	F
DM 029	14	5–7	ULM3	20.7	4.129E+10	0.000E+00	0.978	F
TYB 179	15	12–13	URM3	20.7	5.061E+08	8.279E+07	0.000	M
DM 033	Blank	13–17	Blank	0	0.000E+00	0.000E+00	–	–
TYB 187	Blank	45–50	Blank	0	0.000E+00	0.000E+00	–	–

youngest was a male infant approximately 2.5 years of age. Seven of the individuals were adults, including three young adults (two males and one female) and four adults who were middle-aged or older (one male and three females). The proteomic sex estimates for the seven adults are 100 percent consistent with prior osteological sex estimations based on pelvic and cranial morphology.

In addition to amelogenin peptides, we also examine summed intensities (total ion count) for specific peptides from the conserved portion of IgG heavy chain (subunits 1–4), C-reactive protein, and serum albumin. Burial 11 enamel was not included in this analysis due to the anomalously low amounts of total peptides and the absence of IgG peptides. The enamel sample for this individual had much lower overall amounts of protein including amelogenin values that were over two orders of magnitude lower than other samples. In fact, without the presence of AMELY peptides, this sample would have been indeterminate for sex estimation based only on the CI of AMELX.

We did not find peptides for IgG or CRP in either of the two sample blanks (DM-033 or TYB-187). However, one peptide for serum albumin was detected in sample blank TYB 187. The intensity of the single ion (3.97×10^5) was more than two orders of magnitude lower than the summed intensity for serum albumin peptides in the lowest intensity sample discussed above (Burial 11) and approximately three to four orders of magnitude lower than all other samples. Table 4.2 gives these results.

We quantified and analyzed levels of IgG in two ways. First, the summed intensities of peptides for the conserved portion of IgG heavy chain (subunits 1–4) were compared to the intensity of all peptides for serum albumin (IgG/SA) (figure 4.1). Summed intensities for IgG were compared in this way because IgG is a serum protein, and albumin is the primary protein present in serum. Further, serum albumin is reliably present in all enamel proteome samples analyzed in this study as well as hundreds of enamel samples that have been analyzed in the laboratories at UC Davis (data not shown). The second way that summed IgG intensities for the conserved portion of IgG heavy chain (subunits 1–4) were compared, was to normalize by sample weight.

As both a ratio of serum albumin, or as normalized intensity by weight, samples from individuals at the asistencia had higher amounts of IgG and CRP than enamel from contemporary military cadets (data not shown). The difference in IgG was significant according to independent t-tests (two tailed, variances not assumed equal) with an alpha of .05. In contrast, amounts of AMELX normalized by sample weight were not statistically different between the two groups. AMELY was not compared because it was not present in many samples. This suggests that individuals at the asistencia were experi-

Table 4.2. Serum albumin, IgG, and C-reactive protein in enamel intensity for individuals at San Pedro y San Pablo

urial	Age (years)	Sex	IgG/mg	IgG/SA	CRP/SA	CRP/mg	Pathologies
	14.5	M	7.56E+07	3.52E-01	5.76E-03	1.24E+06	Dental hypoplasia, vertebral TB possible
	47.5	F	1.32E+07	1.11E-01	0.00E+00	0.00E+00	Dental abscesses, periodontal disease, healed fractures
	55	F	2.64E+07	9.64E-02	0.00E+00	0.00E+00	Dental abscesses, periodontal disease, healed fractures, degenerative knee
	47.5	F	4.01E+07	1.08E-01	1.60E-03	5.96E+05	Dental abscess and periodontal disease
	22	M	3.13E+07	1.45E-01	4.17E-04	8.98E+04	Moderate periodontal disease
	47	M	1.32E+07	1.01E-01	1.05E-03	1.37E+05	Dental abscess, degenerative disc disease
	2.25	M	2.06E+07	2.38E-01	1.26E-02	1.09E+06	None observed
2	23	F	8.48E+06	6.70E-01	3.93E-02	4.97E+05	Dental hypoplasia, slight periodontal disease
3	22.5	F	4.81E+07	1.37E-01	2.21E-03	7.74E+05	Slight periodontal disease
4	6	F	2.49E+07	1.21E-01	1.85E-03	3.81E+05	Dental defects, pit in LRM1
5	12.5	M	1.07E+06	4.86E-02	0.00E+00	0.00E+00	None observed

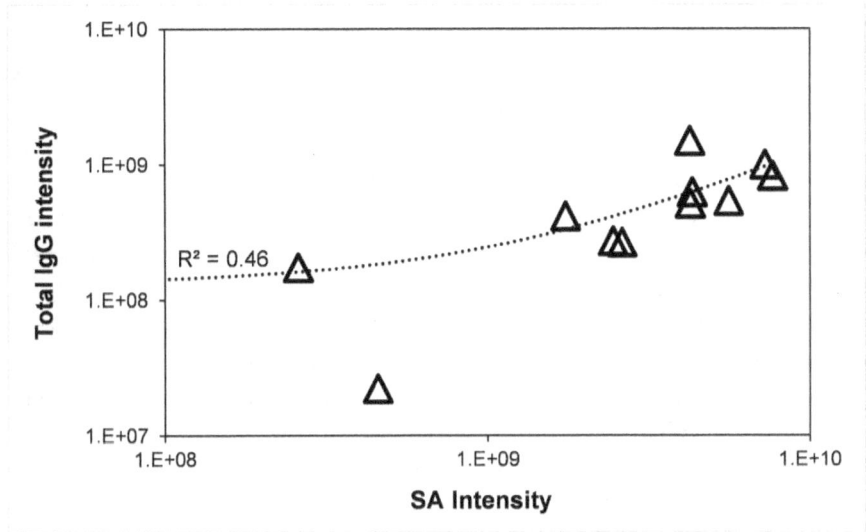

Figure 4.1. Relationship of total IgG peptide signal intensity to SA peptide intensity for tooth enamel from Asistencia San Pedro y San Pablo individuals (CA-SMA-71/H, n=11).

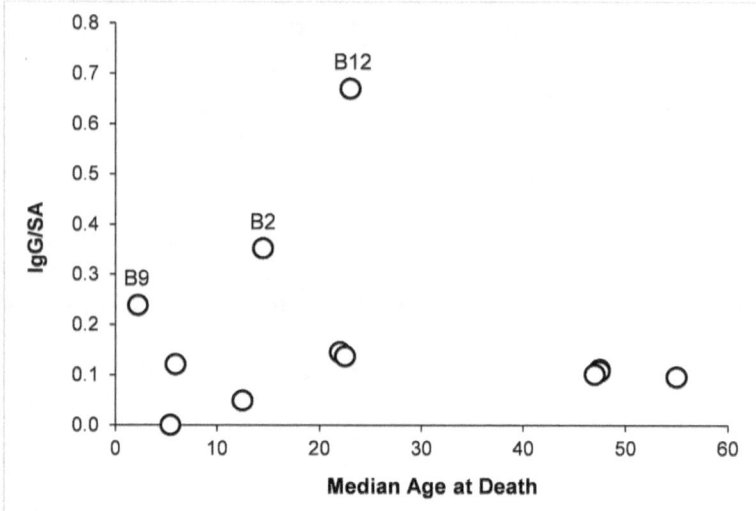

Figure 4.2. Relative IgG levels by age for tooth enamel from Asistencia San Pedro y San Pablo individuals.

encing higher levels of disease and/or stress compared to individuals living in the last two decades. Relative amounts of IgG in individuals at the asistencia are plotted by median age in figure 4.2. The highest relative amounts were observed in enamel from Burials 2, 9, and 12. All of these individuals are children, adolescent, or young adults. By comparison, people who died as older adults have low relative amounts. This finding is consistent with the interpretation that these older Ohlone experienced lower levels of disease and stress during the time their teeth were forming, which, of course, was before the mission system was established.

Within the asistencia enamel samples, intensities of CRP peptides were about two orders of magnitude lower than serum albumin, which is similar to relative concentrations reported in blood serum today (Anderson and Anderson 2002). As shown in table 4.2, CRP was detected in 75 percent (eight of twelve) of the asistencia individuals. As shown, Burials 2, 9, and 12 again stand out with the highest CRP/SA intensities, and individuals over the age of thirty years have lower levels than those who died younger.

As discussed in chapter 3, Burials 2 and 12 each had dental hypoplasias, and Burial 2 also had lesions that were consistent with vertebral tuberculosis. The formation of hypoplasias suggests these individuals experienced significant stress during childhood, enough to affect normal tooth enamel formation. By contrast, no skeletal pathologies were noted in Burial 9. However, this boy, at approximately 2.5 years of age at the time of death, was the youngest

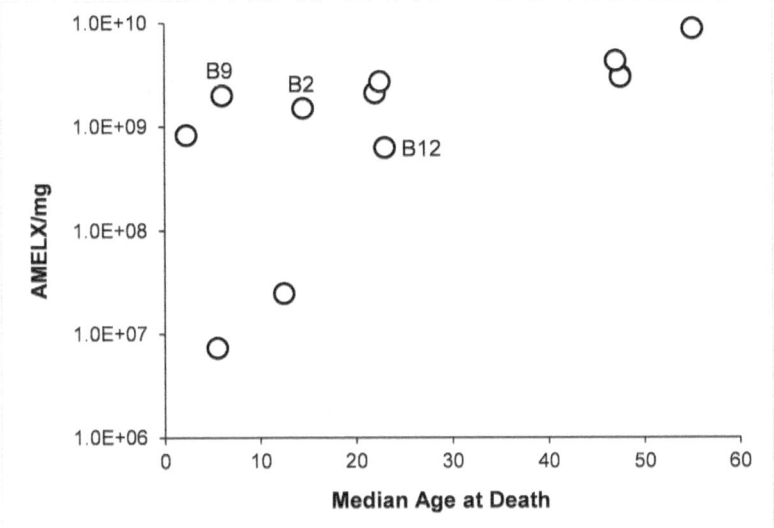

Figure 4.3. Amelogenin X intensities normalized by sample weight (log transformed) for tooth enamel from Asistencia San Pedro y San Pablo individuals.

individual in the enamel proteomic study. As discussed in chapter 11, we believe Burial 9's father died approximately half a year before he died himself. Such trauma, combined perhaps with exposure to diseases that left no marks on the skeleton, could explain the high levels of IgG and CRP.

Finally, figure 4.3 is a plot of AMELX signal normalized by sample weight and plotted by median age. In contrast to IgG and CRP, the highest values are not found in enamel from Burials 2, 9, and 12, but tend to occur among the oldest individuals in the sample who also tended to have lower amounts of IgG and CRP.

Discussion and Conclusions

Proteomic analysis of human tooth enamel was applied to twelve individuals from the Asistencia de San Pedro y San Pablo (CA-SMA-71). Samples were well-preserved, resulting in identification of a wide range of proteins. Each individual produced ample amelogenin peptide fragments and was assigned a probability of female sex. Burial 11 produced a very low signal but was confidently assigned a female probability of zero based on the presence of AMELY peptides. Results indicate seven males and five females. These identifications will contribute to attempts to reconstruct the identities (chapter 11) and gendered life history experiences (chapter 12) of individuals interred at the asistencia.

Beyond sex estimation, proteomic analysis of enamel samples revealed abundant serum proteins, primarily serum albumin and several proteins involved in immune function. Here we analyzed relative intensities of peptides for IgG (a major part of the adaptive immune system) and CRP (a non-specific biomarker of inflammation). Concentrations of serum albumin and IgG were fairly constant across samples prepared by different lab workers, and were not present in blank samples prepared by the same individuals. This suggests that laboratory contamination does not explain their presence. Likewise, there is little correlation between concentrations of amelogenin and these immune-related proteins.

Instead, we propose that serum proteins are incorporated during enamel formation and inform on nutritional or environmental stress, including disease, encountered by individuals during the period of enamel formation. As a result, differences in the relative concentrations of these proteins likely point to differences in how individuals buried at the asistencia experienced chronic infections and/or chronic stress. In this respect, we believe it is telling that individuals who died at a young age, especially those whose teeth were still growing within the mission, show higher levels of IgG and CRP. Three individuals, Burials 2, 9, and 12, stand out in particular. Two of these individuals had dental hypoplasias (Burials 2 and 12), one of whom also had osteological indications of a chronic tuberculosis infection (Burial 2). By contrast, older individuals within the sample (i.e., those dying after age thirty) have lower levels of these proteins. As well, though the data are not included here, levels of IgG and CRP in the enamel of third molars of twenty-first-century military cadets are much lower than levels recorded in the asistencia population.

To our knowledge, this is the first study to compare relative intensities of immune proteins (IgG and CRP) and serum albumin in proteomic extracts of archaeological tooth enamel. In the future, the ability to use tandem mass spectrometry to detect and compare relative amounts of peptides from immune proteins preserved in enamel could provide an important window into health and disease in the past.

References

Anderson, N. Leigh, and Norman G. Anderson
2002 The Human Plasma Proteome: History, Character, and Diagnostic Prospects. *Molecular and Cellular Proteomics* 1: 845–867.
Buonasera, Tammy, Jelmer Eerkens, Alida de Flamingh, Laurel Engbring, Julia Yip, Hongjie Li, Randall Haas, Dianne DiGiuseppe, David Grant, Michelle Salemi, and Charlene Nijmeh
2020 A Comparison of Proteomic, Genomic, and Osteological Methods of Archaeological Sex Estimation. *Scientific Reports* 10(1): 11897.

Calonga-Solís, Verónica, Danielle Malheiros, Marcia Holsbach Beltrame, Luciana de Brito Vargas, Renata Montoro Dourado, Hellen Caroline Issler, Roseli Wassem, Maria Luiza Petzl-Erler, and Danillo G. Augusto
2019   Unveiling the Diversity of Immunoglobulin Heavy Constant Gamma (IGHG) Gene Segments in Brazilian Populations Reveals 28 Novel Alleles and Evidence of Gene Conversion and Natural Selection. *Frontiers in Immunology* 10: 1161.

Gil-Bona, Ana, and Felicitas B. Bidlack
2020   Tooth Enamel and Its Dynamic Protein Matrix. *International Journal of Molecular Sciences* 21:4458.

Johnson, Timothy V., Ammara Abbasi, and Viraj A. Master
2013   Systematic Review of the Evidence of a Relationship Between Chronic Psychosocial Stress and C-Reactive Protein. *Molecular Diagnosis and Therapy* 17:147–164.

Limeback, Hardy, Harry Sakarya, Willa Chu, and Mary Mackinnon
1989   Serum Albumin and Its Acid Hydrolysis Peptides Dominate Preparations of Mineral-Bound Enamel Proteins. *Journal of Bone and Mineral Research* 4: 235–241.

Meca, Andreea-Daniela, Adina Turcu-Stiolica, Maria Bogdan, Mihaela-Simona Subtirelu, Relu Cocoș, Bogdan Silviu Ungureanu, Beatrice Mahler, and Catalina-Gabriela Pisoschi
2022   Screening Performance of C-Reactive Protein for Active Pulmonary Tuberculosis in HIV-Positive Patients: A Systematic Review with a Meta-analysis. *Frontiers in Immunology* 13: 891201.

Parker, Glendon J., Julia M. Yip, Jelmer W. Eerkens, Michelle Salemi, Blythe Durbin-Johnson, Caleb Kiesow, Randall Haas, Jane E. Buikstra, Haagen Klaus, Laura A. Regan, David M. Rocke, and Brett S. Phinney
2019   Sex Estimation Using Sexually Dimorphic Amelogenin Protein Fragments in Human Enamel. *Journal of Archaeological Science* 101: 169–180.

Parker, Glendon J., Tammy Y. Buonasera, Julia M. Yip, Jelmer W. Eerkens, Michelle Salemi, Blythe Durbin-Johnson, Randall Haas, Jane E. Buikstra, Haagen Klaus, David M. Rocke, and Brett S. Phinney
2021   AMELY Deletion Is Not Detected in Systematically Sampled Reference Populations: A Reply to Štamfelj. *Journal of Archaeological Science* 130: 105354.

Robinson, Colin, J. Kirkham, S. J. Brookes, W. A. Bonass, and R. C. Shore
2003   The Chemistry of Enamel Development. *International Journal of Developmental Biology* 39: 145–152.

Salido, Eduardo C., Pauline H. Yen, Kathryn Koprivnikar, Loh-Chung Yu, and Larry J. Shapiro
1992   The Human Enamel Protein Gene Amelogenin Is Expressed from both the X and the Y Chromosomes. *American Journal of Human Genetics* 50: 303–316.

Schroeder Jr., Harry W., and Lisa Cavacini
2010   Structure and Function of Immunoglobulins. *Journal of Allergy and Clinical Immunology* 125:S41–S52.

Shenhar-Tsarfaty, Shani, Nadav Yayon, Nir Waiskopf, Itzhak Shapira, Sharon Toker, David Zaltser, Shlomo Berliner, Ya'acov Ritov, and Hermona Soreq
2015 Fear and C-Reactive Protein Cosynergize Annual Pulse Increases in Healthy Adults. *Proceedings of the National Academy of Sciences* 112:E467–E471.

Simmer, James P.
1994 Alternative Splicing of Amelogenins. *Connective Tissue Research* 32: 131–136.

Yoon, Christina, Lelia H. Chaisson, Sweta M. Patel, I. E. Allen, P. K. Drain, D. Wilson, and A. Cattamanchi
2017 Diagnostic Accuracy of C-Reactive Protein for Active Pulmonary Tuberculosis: A Meta-Analysis. *The International Journal of Tuberculosis and Lung Disease* 21: 1013–1019.

Zhang, Jing, Lei Xin, Baozhen Shan, Weiwu Chen, Mingjie Xie, Denis Yuen, Weiming Zhang, Zefeng Zhang, Gilles A. Lajoie, and Bin Ma
2012 PEAKS DB: De Novo Sequencing Assisted Database Search for Sensitive and Accurate Peptide Identification. *Molecular and Cellular Proteomics* 11(4): M111.010587.

5

San Pedro y San Pablo as a Venue for Cultural Persistence

Mortuary Practices and Exchange Networks on the Margins of the Mission System

Lee M. Panich, Melody Tannam, and Jelmer W. Eerkens

Throughout the North American Borderlands, missionaries from the Franciscan, Jesuit, and Dominican orders established missions in service to the Spanish Crown. Given that these establishments were venues of both strict enculturation programs and high mortality rates, evidence for Native mortuary practices at missions and related sites offer an opportunity to assess processes of negotiation and accommodation on the part of colonists and Native people alike. Expectations about death, burial, and mourning were constantly in tension as different religious orders and the myriad Native groups they sought out each had their own deeply rooted religious beliefs and cultural practices (Blair et al. 2009; Graham 1998; McEwan 2001; Panich 2015). In particular, the presence of funerary offerings in many instances reflects the persistence of Native values within colonial systems, and may also provide evidence for the perpetuation of other important practices, such as technological traditions and regional exchange networks.

The Asistencia de San Pedro y San Pablo was an outstation of Mission San Francisco de Asís, often with a minimal missionary presence. Analyses of mortuary customs at the site therefore provide a unique opportunity to examine these issues on the very margins of the Spanish colonial system in the greater San Francisco Bay region. Such research fits into growing recognition that a full accounting of Native negotiations of missionary colonialism requires looking beyond the mission quadrangles and into the Native landscapes into which colonial outposts were implanted (Byrd et al. 2018; Panich and Schneider 2014; Schneider et al. 2020; Schneider 2021). At the missions themselves, Franciscan accounts from throughout the province of Alta California indicate that the deaths of baptized Native people were supposed to follow contemporary Catholic doctrine, which included a simple burial in church cemeteries without the offering of grave goods (Geiger and Meighan 1976). Taken together, the materials from individual burials at San Pedro y San Pablo, along with other lines of evidence available for the region, demonstrate the different ways that Native people in the greater San Francisco Bay Area accepted, negotiated, and subverted Spanish colonial policies regarding death and mourning. Given the general paucity of published research on mission-period cemetery sites, such a vantage point may also illuminate broader patterns within mission-era California.

Analysis of Burial Associated Belongings

The primary focus here is on burial associated belongings. In precontact times, Native Californian societies laid their loved ones to rest with an array of items that served, at least partially, as markers of the deceased individual's social status. Beads were paramount in this regard, and—depending on the region—included a variety of bead types created from the shells of the olive snail (*Callianax* sp., commonly Olivella) and several species of clam (e.g., *Saxidomus* and *Tivela* sp.). Ornaments and beads manufactured from abalone shell (*Haliotis* sp.) were also common, as were bone tools, flaked stone artifacts, and ground stone implements (Erlandson and Jones 2002; Jones and Klar 2007). That these practices continued in various ways during the colonial period is indisputable. For example, a questionnaire circulated among the Alta California missions in 1813–1815 reveals that Native people throughout the province continued to place objects in the graves of the deceased, often in direct defiance of local Franciscans (Geiger and Meighan 1976). As in precontact times, many of the grave offerings noted by the missionaries focused on shell and glass beads—what Father Gerónimo Boscana at Mission San Juan Capistrano correctly referred to as "bead money" (Johnson 2006:8). As the burials from San Pedro y San Pablo demonstrate, beads were an important part of mortuary practices in the San Francisco Bay region but they were not the only items placed with deceased individuals.

This section is organized by material type, along with the results of standard typological classifications as well as more specialized archaeometric analyses.

Shell, Glass, and Jet Beads

Beads—manufactured from shell, glass, and jet—were the most common category of grave goods among the individuals in this study. Of the fifteen total burials examined, all but three had beads associated with them. Given the close proximity of many of the interments, it possible that some of the smaller bead lots (one or two beads) represent objects that had shifted since deposition, but a full nine of the burials had notable numbers of beads, ranging as high as 2,942 beads per individual. Taken as a whole assemblage, glass beads (n=3,530) outnumber shell beads (n=2,666), though the frequency varied considerably by individual interment, as discussed in the following section. Additionally, thirty-six faceted beads and two crosses made of jet were also placed with the burials.

Shell Beads

The shell beads from the Asistencia de San Pedro y San Pablo resemble those found in mortuary and nonmortuary contexts at other nearby sites associated with the Franciscan mission system, including Missions Santa Clara and Santa Cruz (Allen 1992, 1998; Panich 2014; Peelo et al. 2018). They include Olivella disk beads, spire-lopped Olivella beads, clamshell disk beads, and *Haliotis rufescens* disk beads (figure 5.1) (table 5.1). All classes of shell beads in this study exhibited damage consistent with natural deterioration as well as post-excavation drying and handling. Standard measurements (diameter, thickness, perforation diameter, and weight) were recorded for all Olivella and *Haliotis* disk beads as well as a sample of the clamshell beads. Due to their largely nondiagnostic nature, the spire-lopped Olivella beads were not individually measured beyond that necessary to assign beads to type.

Excavations at San Pedro y San Pablo recovered 1,196 clamshell disk beads (CSDB), of which 829 were complete enough to measure. Archaeologists have classified CSDB in various ways over the years, but researchers in central California have yet to coalesce around a single CSDB typology. This analysis employed the typology published by Von der Porten and colleagues (2014), which is based on an earlier unpublished typology developed by James Bennyhoff and David Frederickson. Their typology separates CSDB into three major types: A1 (small), A2 (medium), and A3 (large), which are distinguished along a gradient of diameter and thickness measurements.

For this assemblage, all complete beads were assigned to subtypes and full CSDB metrics (diameter, thickness, perforation diameter, and weight) were recorded. Fragments were not assigned to subtypes, but visual examination suggests that the overall typological distribution of CSDB fragments mirrors that of the complete beads. As shown in table 5.2, nearly all of the beads in

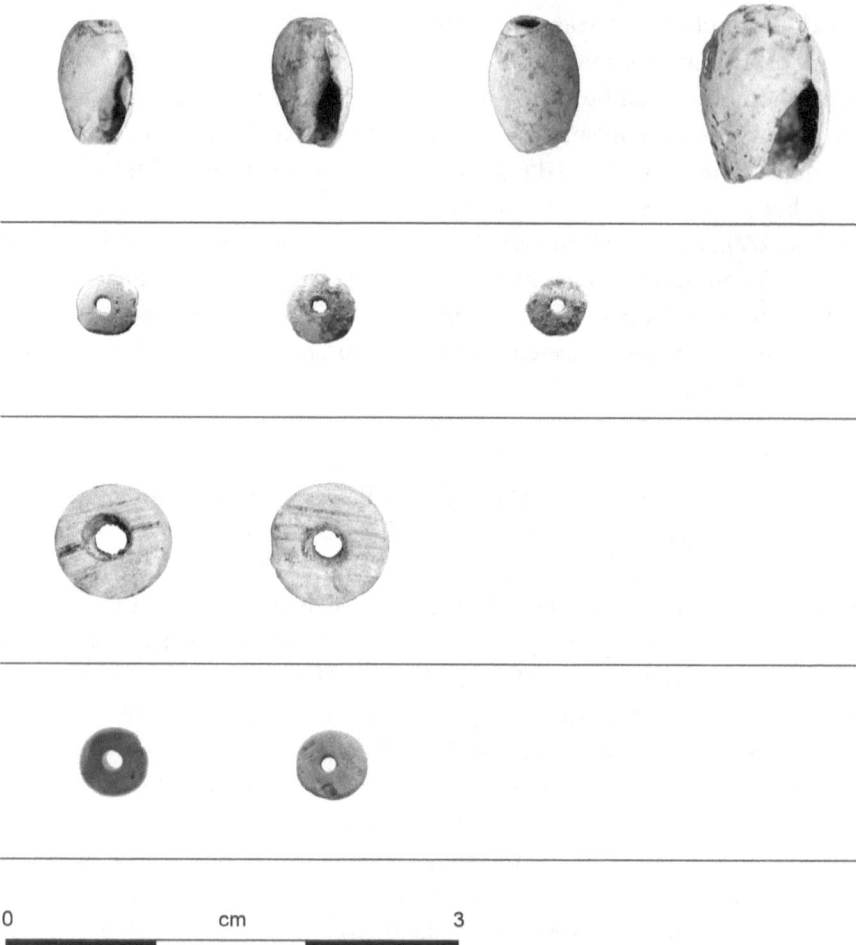

Figure 5.1. Shell beads from San Pedro y San Pablo. *From top to bottom*: Olivella Class A spire lopped beads; Olivella Class H metal drilled disk beads; clamshell disk beads; *Haliotis rufescens* metal drilled disk beads.

this assemblage fall into the small (A1) category, with the majority classified as either A1b or A1c beads. Previous studies suggest that the distinction between A1b and A1c may not be particularly meaningful (Milliken 2005; Von der Porten et al. 2014), and in this assemblage the beads appeared to represent a gradient rather than a clear break between the two subtypes.

The distribution of CSDB subtypes at San Pedro y San Pablo is generally consistent with patterns from other historic-era Indigenous sites in the region, including recent work in the Native Californian *ranchería* at nearby Mission

Table 5.1. Overview of shell beads from San Pedro y San Pablo

Shell material	Generalized bead type	Count	Percent
Clamshell	Disk	1196	44.9
Olivella Class A	Spire-lopped	1406	52.7
Olivella Class H	Metal-drilled disk	45	1.7
Haliotis rufescens	Metal-drilled disk	19	0.7
Total		2666	100

Table 5.2. Distribution of measured clamshell disk dead (CSDB) subtypes

CSDB Type	Diameter Range (mm)	Thickness Range (mm)	Count	Percent
A1a	3–5	1–2	103	12.4
A1b	5–7	1–4	504	60.8
A1c	7–8.5	2–6	214	25.8
A1d	3–6	3–5	3	0.4
A2a	8.5–12.5	2–6	5	0.6
Total			829	100

Santa Clara (e.g., Panich 2021). Though not all projects there have used the same typology for CSDBs, reported diameter measurements offer a point of comparison. For example, CSDBs from likely early burials in the cemetery associated with the third mission complex at Santa Clara (ca. 1784–1818) had an average diameter of 6.55 mm, whereas CSDB lots from *ranchería* contexts dating to the entire Mission Period exhibited average diameters between roughly 6.0 and 7.5 mm (Hylkema 1995; Panich 2014). At San Pedro y San Pablo, the average diameter of all measured CSDBs was 6.23 mm. However, diameter (and therefore subtype) differ dramatically between individual burials. Of the two burials with the largest numbers of CSDBs, Burial 7 (n=895) had an average diameter of 6.66 mm whereas Burial 12 (n=237) had an average diameter of only 5.39 mm. This clustering of diameters demonstrates that Native people intentionally grouped beads by size as they formed particular strands of beads.

The CSDBs at San Pedro y San Pablo are also interesting given the chronology and tribal makeup of the site. Previous research on shell bead manufacture and exchange suggests that most CSDBs were produced north of San Francisco Bay, in a broad area stretching from Point Reyes to the eastern slopes of the Coast Ranges. Importantly, CSDBs are not present in appreciable quantities in precontact Ohlone sites on the San Francisco Bay Peninsula or adjacent inland areas along the bay shore (Milliken et al. 2007; Rosenthal

2011). As noted above, quantities of CSBDs have been reported from what were likely early burials in the third mission cemetery at Mission Santa Clara, and their presence at the Asistencia de San Pedro y San Pablo is further evidence of changing patterns of shell bead conveyance and acquisition in the colonial period (Hylkema and Allen 2010; Panich 2014).

The Olivella shell beads recovered from San Pedro y San Pablo constitute two broad categories, Class A spire-lopped beads and Class H wall disks. Most Olivella shell beads in central California were manufactured with *Callianax biplicata* (formerly *Olivella biplicata*) shells. Beads were analyzed according to the typology developed by Bennyhoff and Hughes (1987) and updated by Milliken and Schwitalla (2012).

A total of 1,133 complete Class A spire-lopped Olivella beads were present in the assemblage, along with approximately 273 fragments. Class A Olivella beads consist of nearly whole shells, the spires of which have been removed. The beads in this assemblage fall predominantly in the A1a (small-sized) category with maximum shell body diameters between 3 and 6.5 mm (n=847). A notable quantity (n=255) of medium-sized A1b beads (6.5–9.5 mm diameter) were also present, as well as 11 A1c (large, 9.5–15 mm diameter) beads. Twenty A4 wall punched beads were identified, but given their poor preservation it is possible that the holes in the shell walls are naturally occurring or the result of post-depositional damage. Class A bead fragments were not typed. At nearby Mission Santa Clara, similar beads have been reported for nearly all archaeological projects (Allen et al. 2010; Hylkema 1995; Panich 2014, 2021; Peelo et al. 2018; Skowronek and Wizorek 1997). Despite their presence at colonial-era archaeological sites, Class A Olivella beads are not considered to be chronologically diagnostic in central California (Bennyhoff and Hughes 1987; Milliken and Schwitalla 2012).

Beads created from the wall of the Olivella shell, however, have more interpretive potential. Of the historic-era varieties, Class H Olivella wall disks—small, circular beads with cylindrical apertures drilled with metal needles—are the most common (Bennyhoff and Hughes 1987; Milliken and Schwitalla 2012). Analysts sort Class H beads into subtypes based on size and the degree of edge grinding, which is thought to have decreased over the course of the Mission Period. This chronology is based on seriated bead lots from Southern California, where fully ground H1a beads date to the early Mission Period (1770–1800) and partially ground H1b beads date to the late Mission Period (1800–1816). Later beads include H2 (1816–1834) and H3 (1834–1900) beads, which exhibit little to no edge grinding, respectfully. In the assemblage from the Asistencia de San Pedro y San Pablo, a total of 45 H1a beads were present. Though some analysts question whether the Class H chrono-

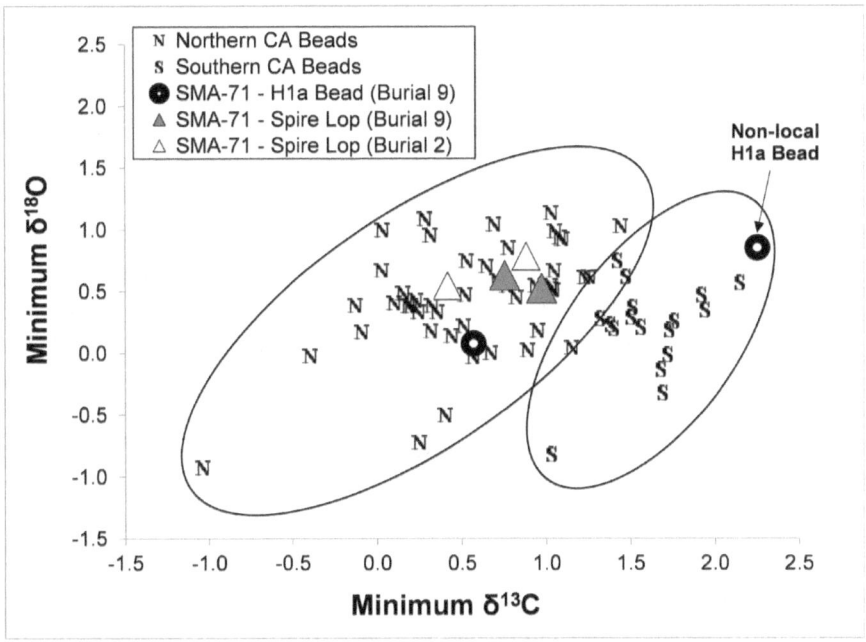

Figure 5.2. Comparison of isotopic analysis of selected Olivella beads from San Pedro y San Pablo to values of Olivella beads from Northern (N) and Southern (S) California.

logical sequence applies in the greater San Francisco Bay region (e.g., Peelo et al. 2018), the fact that all the beads from San Pedro y San Pablo are classed as H1a, combined with the timing of the cemetery's use between 1787 and 1800, fits squarely within the accepted Olivella bead chronology developed in Southern California.

To trace provenance, six Olivella beads from San Pedro y San Pablo were analyzed for carbon and oxygen stable isotopes following methods presented in Eerkens et al. (2005) and Burns et al. (2023) (figure 5.2). The sample included four Class A spired lopped beads (two each from Burial 2 and Burial 9) as well as two H1a needle-drilled disk beads from Burial 9. Results show that five beads from San Pedro y San Pablo clustered with beads characteristic of a Northern California signature (i.e., with water conditions found north of Point Conception). Only one bead, an H1a bead from Burial 9, clearly clusters with beads exhibiting a Southern California signature. These results generally fit with the emerging picture of Olivella bead production and exchange in central California. In previous studies, Class A spire-lopped beads from sites in the greater San Francisco Bay Area tend to cluster with other Northern California bead types, regardless of temporal placement. This is not surprising given that spire-lopped beads have been in use for thousands of years, require little to no specialized production, and Olivella shells are naturally abundant throughout the California Coast. The small number of analyses of colonial-era, Class H Olivella disk beads present a more complex picture. Most of those analyzed thus far—primarily drawn from Mission Santa Clara—can be linked to Southern California (Burns 2019; Eerkens et al. 2005). How such exotic items traveled up the coast during the colonial period is unknown, but most contextual evidence suggest that they moved from person-to-person through traditional Native Californian trading networks. In any case, the presence of a single locally produced Class H bead from San Pedro y San Pablo may correspond to the apparent production of such beads at Mission Santa Cruz, on the Pacific coast, and possibly at Mission Santa Clara further inland (Allen 1992; Peelo et al. 2018).

The San Pedro y San Pablo bead assemblage also contained nineteen red abalone (*Haliotis rufescens*) epidermis disk beads, with small cylindrical perforations exhibiting diameters consistent with drilling by metal needles. *Haliotis rufescens* epidermis disk beads originated in the late precontact period in the Santa Barbara Channel region, with Santa Rosa Island as a likely production center. They are common in many historic-period contexts in Southern California and into the Central Valley (King 2011). While not found in abundant quantities at colonial-era sites in central California, *Haliotis* epidermis beads are present in shell bead assemblages from previous archaeological investigations at nearby Mission Santa Clara, including the cemetery associated with the third mission complex (Hylkema 1995; Leventhal et al. 2011) and other areas of the Native American *ranchería* (Allen et al. 2010; Panich 2014, 2021; Peelo et al. 2018). It is possible that these beads were conveyed northward along the same networks as Class H Olivella disk beads.

Glass Beads

The individuals at San Pedro y San Pablo were interred with a wide variety of glass beads. The most common types have been identified at nearby mission sites (e.g., Allen 1998; Dadiego et al. 2021; Panich 2014; Panich et al. 2018a), but some are unusual for the region. Here, we relied on the basic classificatory system developed by Kidd and Kidd (2012) and expanded by Karklins (2012), which assigns beads to types through a primary consideration of manufacturing method, but also shape, size, color, and diaphaneity. Drawn beads—which are made by drawing molten glass into a rod and then chopping it into small segments—are categorized two ways: by the number of glass layers and by the presence or absence of rounding by reheating. Nearly all of the drawn beads in this assemblage have heat-rounded ends and are either simple (i.e., monochrome) or compound beads: Types IIa and IVa, respectively. Wound beads

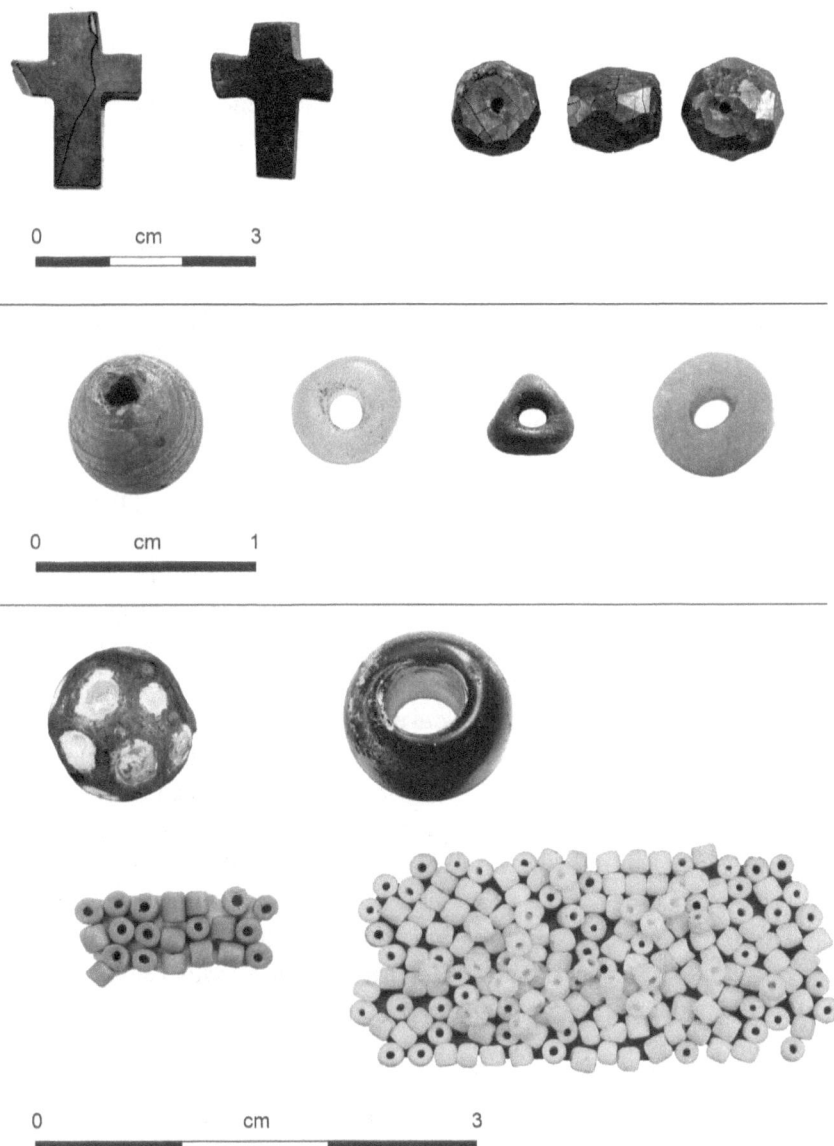

Figure 5.3. Jet and glass beads from San Pedro y San Pablo. *Top row, left to right:* Jet crosses and jet faceted beads (Burials 9 and 11). *Middle row, left to right:* Blue wound bead, Kidd and Kidd Type WIb13 (Burial 11); Colorless drawn bead, Kidd and Kidd Type IIa (no exact color match) / Meighan Type 442 (Burial 9); Brown triangular bead, Kidd and Kidd Type WIc (no exact match) / Meighan Type 120 (Burial 9); Aqua drawn bead, Kidd and Kidd Type IIa37 (Burial 5). *Bottom section, clockwise from top left:* Compound "eye bead," Kidd and Kidd Type IIg1 (Burial 11); Blue wound bead, Kidd and Kidd Type WIb15 (Burial 6); Compound white drawn beads, Kidd and Kidd Type IVa11 (Burial 7); Light blue drawn beads, Kidd and Kidd Type IIa47 (Burial 11).

(Class W), in contrast, are made by winding molten glass around a mandrel and are typically less common in California colonial-era sites (Karklins 2012; Kidd and Kidd 2012). In most cases, beads were identifiable to specific varieties. For certain bead varieties not included in the Kidd and Kidd typology, the California glass bead typology originally created by Clement Meighan (2024) was consulted instead.

Table 5.3 provides an overview of the glass beads from San Pedro y San Pablo (figure 5.3). By far, the largest category was Type IIa drawn beads, which were dominated by very small yellowish beads (IIa17, n=1440) as well as larger black (IIa7, n=764) and aqua blue (IIa43, n=793) varieties. In contrast, there were only 363 Type IVa compound beads, all of which are what are known colloquially as white-on-white beads. This is surprising given that such beads are among the most prevalent glass beads at other colonial-period sites occupied by Native people in central California (e.g., Panich 2014; Panich et al. 2018a; Silliman 2004). Also missing are the common red-on-green beads—Kidd and Kidd types IVa5, IVa6, or IVa7, also known as "greenhearts"—which have been documented at nearly all colonial-era Native sites throughout the region. While the sample from San Pedro y San Pablo is too small to make definitive conclusions, it may be that there was a chronological element to the distribution of the common white-on-white and red-on-green glass beads. At nearby Mission Santa Clara, for example, the documentary evidence suggests it was not until 1795 that the Franciscans there began explicitly ordering white beads from suppliers in New Spain (Panich 2014:737). As noted in table 5.3, the glass bead assemblage from San Pedro y San Pablo also included some relatively rare examples, such as an "eye bead" as well as several wound beads that had no exact matches in the Kidd and Kidd (2012) typology. For these less common beads, concordance information in Meighan's California glass bead typology places most in the early colonial period (Meighan 2024).

A sample of twenty-five white-on-white glass beads (variety IVa11) were part of a study that compared the chemical composition of similar beads from three sites where Native people lived in central California. Analysis was conducted via laser ablation-inductively coupled plasma-mass spectrometry (LA-ICP-MS) at the Field Museum, and the full results are provided elsewhere (Panich et al. 2022). Two findings are of particular interest here. One is that the beads from San Pedro y San Pablo are all consistent with the general chronological trends in the chemical composition white glass beads—related to the use of different elements as opacifiers—documented at other nearby sites, such as Mission Santa Cruz, as well as other regions of North America (Dadiego et al. 2021). The beads, in other words, securely correspond to the use of the site as an outstation for Mission San Francisco. More surprising is

Table 5.3. Glass beads from San Pedro y San Pablo

Type	Description	Color*	Count	Comments
Ia13	Drawn, simple	Light blue	7	Not exact Kidd & Kidd match
Ia18	Drawn, simple	Blue	2	—
IIa	Drawn, simple	Colorless	1	No Kidd & Kidd match; Meighan Type 442
IIa7	Drawn, simple	Black	764	—
IIa14	Drawn, simple	White	1	—
IIa17	Drawn, simple	Yellow	1440	—
IIa21	Drawn, simple	Citron	1	—
IIa24	Drawn, simple	Green	5	—
IIa37	Drawn, simple	Aqua	10	—
IIa43	Drawn, simple	Aqua	793	—
IIa45	Drawn, simple	Blue	1	—
IIa47	Drawn, simple	Light blue	60	—
IIa53	Drawn, simple	Dark blue	1	—
IIa54	Drawn, simple	Dark blue	1	—
IIg1	Drawn, complex	Black/white	1	Eye bead. Meighan Type 15
IIIa4	Drawn, compound	Red/blue	2	—
IVa11	Drawn, compound	White/white	363	—
WIb11	Wound, simple	Aqua	34	—
WIb12	Wound, simple	Blue	1	—
WIb13	Wound, simple	Blue	13	—
WIb15	Wound, simple	Blue	1	—
WIb16	Wound, simple	Blue	4	—
WIc	Wound, simple	Red	5	No Kidd & Kidd match
WIc	Wound, simple	Brown	5	No Kidd & Kidd match; Meighan Type 120
WIc11	Wound, simple	Blue	4	Small version of Meighan Type 125
WII	Wound, shaped	Red	6	No Kidd & Kidd match; Meighan Type 128
WII	Wound, shaped	Green	2	No Kidd & Kidd match; Similar to Meighan Type 128
WII	Wound, shaped	Brown	1	No Kidd & Kidd match; Similar to Meighan Type 128
WIIIb	Wound, complex	Red	1	Meighan Type 17
Total			3530	

the finding that the group of beads from San Pedro y San Pablo—all of which were associated with Burial 7—exhibited a distinct chemical composition when compared to the same variety of beads from the other study sites, likely reflecting subtle differences in the recipe for the base glass used to manufacture the beads. This suggests that the white-on-white beads from San Pedro y San Pablo remained together all the way from their manufacture in Venice through to their final deposition with an Ohlone child in coastal California (Panich et al. 2022:127–128).

Jet Beads and Crosses

A number of jet artifacts were associated with burials at San Pedro y San Pablo (see figure 5.3). Jet is a type of fossilized wood, similar in appearance to coal, that has been used for jewelry and other purposes for thousands of years. Though jet was used by Ancestral Puebloans in the American Southwest, the objects from San Pedro y San Pablo were likely European in origin. Throughout medieval Europe, jet was particularly popular for religious jewelry, including crosses and rosary beads (Muller 1980). Whitby jet from England is of particularly high quality and is perhaps the most well-known source today. Yet Spain also has a major deposit in the Asturias region, and jet—or *azabache*—has long been used for the production of beads and other objects of adornment in Spain (Menéndez 2019). The peak of the Spanish jet industry was in the sixteenth century, with a particular association with religion and mourning (Ward 2008:307–308). A number of different types of jet objects were imported from Spain to the Americas beginning in the mid-sixteenth century (Francis 2009:114).

The jet objects from San Pedro y San Pablo include two jet crosses and thirty-six faceted jet beads. Though each object was individually carved, they display general consistency of form. Most of the beads are approximately spherical, measuring 11–12 mm in diameter and between 14 and 16 mm in length. Perforations are small, about 2mm. The number of facets ranges between 25 and 30. The crosses measure between 22 and 24 mm along the long axis and 18 and 19 mm on the shorter axis. They are about 7.5 mm thick. The perforations run through the long axis of the cross and measure roughly 2.5 mm in diameter. All of the artifacts display pronounced cracking, which worsened in the time between excavation and reburial. This may suggest that the material is "soft jet," which would correspond to the presumed Spanish source of the objects (Francis 2009:113). The association of the beads with crosses of the same material points toward their use in rosaries. Though the number of jet beads found associated with each jet cross (twenty-three with Burial 9 and twelve with Burial 11) does not directly correspond to that use, it is worth noting that many rosaries employ beads of different sizes and that those burials also included a range of other shell and glass beads.

No other examples of jet beads or crosses could be found in the literature on Spanish colonial California. In the American Southeast—the Spanish colony of La Florida—archaeological and documentary evidence suggest that faceted jet beads were popular from the mid-seventeenth century through the end of the eighteenth century at a range of Spanish missions and other sites (Deagan 1987:182–183; Francis 2009:114). For example, faceted jet beads similar in shape to those from San Pedro y San Pablo—but smaller in size—have been recovered from Native burials at Mission Santa Catalina de Guale in present-day Georgia (Blair et al. 2009). Given the generally early dates for the importation and use of jet objects elsewhere in New Spain, the jet beads and crosses from San Pedro y San Pablo correspond to the known use of the outstation's cemetery in the late eighteenth century. And as the only jet artifacts yet recorded at a colonial-era Native Californian site they add intriguing detail to the importance of the asistencia and the Ohlone families who lived there.

Flaked Stone

Flaked stone objects were rare among the burials from San Pedro y San Pablo. However, one individual (Burial 15, discussed in more detail below) was laid to rest with a bundle of materials that included ten flaked stone tools of various forms and sizes, as noted in table 5.4. These range from large bifaces between 6.75 and 10 cm in length to somewhat smaller point blanks or roughouts. Among the finished points are two with triangular blades and contracting stems, measuring between 5.9 and 8.1 cm in length. Two other finished points are lanceolate in form, one of which exhibits fine serrations and measures nearly 10 cm in length, what would likely be called an Excelsior point in more ancient assemblages. Indeed, the finished points—both stemmed and lanceolate—fit most closely with the Coastal Contracting Stem Cluster as defined by Justice (2002). Interestingly, these large points are anachronistic for the Mission Period, generally dating to hundreds, if not thousands, of years earlier. In contrast, nearly all projectile points from nearby mission sites are small, arrow-sized points (Panich et al. 2021).

In terms of material, one projectile point was black Monterey Chert, and the other nine stone tools were obsidian. Based on XRF analysis, the majority of the obsidian artifacts (n=7) originated at the Napa Valley source, near St. Helena, California. One each was from Bodie Hills and Mono Glass Mountain, both in the eastern Sierra Nevada (see table 5.4). Obsidian hydration analysis revealed that the group of flaked stone objects was of a mixed age,

Table 5.4. Results of specialized obsidian studies of flaked stone tools from Burial 15

Cat. Number	Description	Obsidian Source[a]	Hydration Band[b] (μm)	EHT[c] Adjusted Age (ybp)
B15-1	Lanceolate point, serrated	Napa Valley	1.05	240
B15-2	Lanceolate point	Bodie Hills	2, 3.4	884, 2454
B15-3	Biface	Napa Valley	2.8	1670
B15-4	Point blank or rough out	Napa Valley	1.8	676
B15-5	Point fragment, serrated	Napa Valley	Diffuse	n/a
B15-6	Contracting stem point	Napa Valley	1.05	240
B15-7	Triangular point	Mono Glass Mountain	3.3	Unknown[d]
B15-8	Biface	Napa Valley	1.07	244
B15-9	Contracting stem point	Monterey Chert	n/a	n/a
B15-10	Point blank or rough out	Napa Valley	3.0	1381

Notes: [a]Obsidian provenance analysis was conducted via XRF by Richard Hughes.
[b]Obsidian hydration analysis was conducted by Origer's Obsidian Lab in 2020.
[c]The effective hydration temperature (EHT) was estimated by the lab based on the location of San Pedro y San Pablo.
[d]No source specific hydration rate has been developed for Mono Glass Mountain.

with some likely created during the colonial period while others exhibited significant antiquity more closely matching their typology. At San Pedro y San Pablo, both of the obsidian artifacts that originated in the eastern Sierra Nevada exhibit hydration readings that point toward their manufacture in precontact times. Thus, it is likely that they were heirlooms or recycled from earlier sites. The Napa Valley specimens suggest a combination of extant exchange networks, recycling, and possibly heirlooming.

Generally speaking, these patterns correspond to recent research on flaked stone tools at other colonial-era sites in the San Francisco Bay Area. There, Native people continued to use a mix of locally available cherts as well as obsidians from more distant sources. At Mission Santa Cruz, for example, an early study revealed that Native residents relied on a combination of Monterey Chert as well as obsidian from Napa Valley and eastern Sierra Nevada sources such as Bodie Hills (Allen 1998:82). Likewise, recent XRF analysis of more than a thousand obsidian artifacts from Mission Santa Clara confirmed Napa Valley as the most common source but also revealed the presence of smaller quantities of obsidian from Bodie Hills and other sources in the eastern Sierra Nevada (Panich 2016). A similar XRF study at Mission San José found that Napa Valley was also the most prevalent source in use at that site, but noted a total absence of obsidian from the eastern Sierra Nevada (Panich

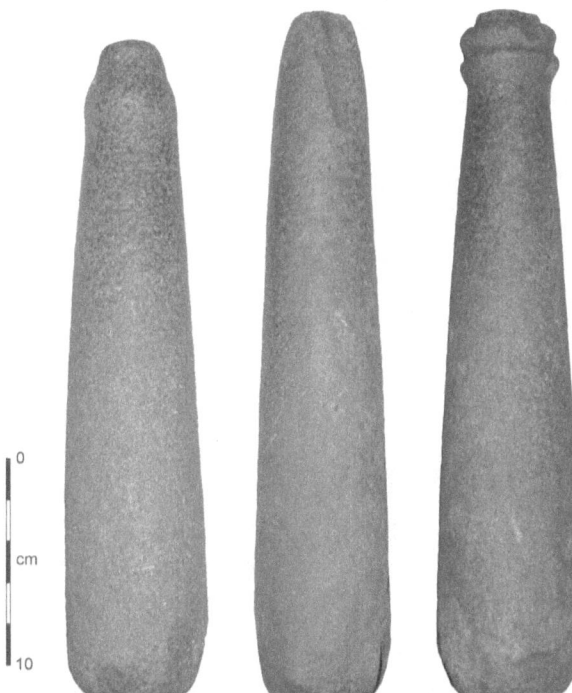

Figure 5.4. Pestles from San Pedro y San Pablo. *Left to right*: single flanged, tapering, double flanged.

et al. 2018b). Obsidian hydration studies from colonial-era sites in the San Francisco Bay Area are rarer. At Mission San José and Rancho Petaluma—where the largest studies have been conducted—hydration analysis returned a range of readings that suggested both the continuation of Native trade networks during the colonial period as well as the recycling of some obsidian materials from older archaeological sites (Panich et al. 2018b; Silliman 2005; and see Hull and Voss 2016).

Ground Stone

Three burials contained complete ground stone pestles, which were typed using Beardsley's (1954) classification system (figure 5.4). These included two large pestles with double-flanged handles (Type IIB4) and a single tapering pestle (Type IIB1a). All three are presumed to have been manufactured in the greater San Francisco Bay region. In contrast to shell and glass beads, pestles have not been noted among the mortuary assemblages from contemporary cemeteries at the main mission sites in Alta California. One imported ground stone artifact—a fragment of a basalt tripod metate—was noted during monitoring and was not directly associated with burials (figure 5.5). Simi-

Figure 5.5. Basalt metate, likely of Mexican origin, found during construction monitoring at San Pedro y San Pablo.

lar metates have been found at nearby missions and are assumed to have been imported from what is today Mexico (e.g., Peelo et al. 2018:216–217). As an exploratory exercise, we used an Olympus Vanta portable x-ray fluorescence spectrometer to conduct a preliminary geochemical analysis of the metate from San Pedro y San Pablo and two fragments from similar metates from Mission Santa Clara. All three appear to be similar in origin, though we do not have source material for comparison (cf. Burg et al. 2021).

Specific Mortuary Assemblages

As the previous section attests, specific classes of artifacts found in mortuary contexts can offer wide-ranging insights into the persistence of specific

Table 5.5. Funerary offerings by burial number

Burial #	2	3	4	5	6	7	8	9	10	11	12	13	14	15	16
Beads[a]															
Clamshell disk beads	1	0	0	0	9	895	1	15	0	32	237	0	0	0	0
Olivella Class A beads	210	2	16	161	49	0	0	21	0	3	504	445	0	1	0
Olivella Class H disks	0	0	0	0	1	0	0	36	0	8	0	0	0	0	0
Haliotis disks	0	0	0	0	0	0	0	5	0	14	0	0	0	0	0
Drawn glass beads	1	0	0	10	27	351	0	832	0	30	2201	0	0	0	0
Wound glass beads	0	0	0	0	7	0	0	56	0	15	0	0	0	0	0
Jet beads	0	0	1	0	0	0	0	23	0	12	0	0	0	0	0
Bead Total	**212**	**2**	**17**	**171**	**93**	**1246**	**1**	**988**	**0**	**114**	**2942**	**445**	**0**	**1**	**0**
Other Materials															
Jet crosses	0	0	0	0	0	0	0	1	0	1	0	0	0	0	0
Pestles	0	0	1	0	1	0	0	0	0	0	1	0	0	0	0
Flaked Stone Tools	0	0	0	0	0	0	0	0	0	0	0	0	0	10	0
Bird Bone Tubes	0	0	0	0	0	0	0	0	0	0	0	0	0	14	0

Note: [a]Includes fragments.

technologies and exchange networks, as well as the integration of new materials into familiar practices. But by separating funerary offerings, analysts may inadvertently miss connections that tie different materials together and the meaning that may have adhered to them. In this section, we briefly discuss some of the individual burial assemblages from San Pedro y San Pablo (table 5.5).

Perhaps the most striking burial assemblage from San Pedro y San Pablo was Burial 15 (figure 5.6). As discussed in more detail elsewhere in this volume, osteological analysis and proteomic sex estimation indicate that this individual was a young man who died between the ages of thirteen and seventeen. Based on examination of mission death records, this burial matches a young Ohlone man named Tarsi, who was baptized in the summer of 1791 and given the Spanish name Aparicio (SFD Baptism 963). He was around thirteen years old when he died in early 1792 (SFD Death 398a). Though his tribal origin is unclear from the documents—his parents were listed simply as gentiles, meaning that they remained unbaptized—the belongings with which he was buried suggest that he had important connections in the Native world.

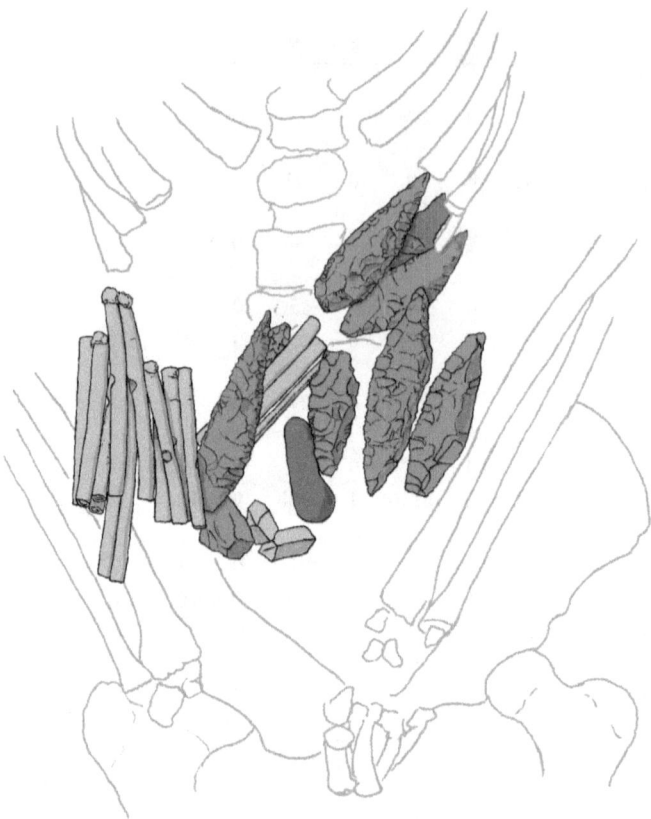

Figure 5.6. Drawing of bundle of belongings found with Burial 15. Materials pictured include bird bone whistles (*left*), a polished stone (*center*), quartz crystals (*lower center*), obsidian projectile points and bifaces (*center and right*), and a chert projectile point (*far right*).

Excavators encountered a range of objects that appear to have been placed in a bundle or bag on the young man's abdomen. The contents included: fourteen bird bone whistles or tubes (all Gifford Type FF2); nine obsidian tools (a mix of large projectile points and bifaces) and one chert projectile point; two quartz crystals; two bat ray barbs; one polished stone; and a single Olivella A1a spire-lopped bead. As noted above, the specific types of stone tools associated with Burial 15 are largely anachronistic for the Mission Period even as obsidian hydration analysis demonstrates that they represent a mix of ancient and contemporaneous production.

Two burials stood out due to the inclusion of jet artifacts, which are unique in archaeological contexts from colonial California. The individuals—Burials

9 and 11—seem to have been interred around the same time. Burial 9 was a boy who died between his second and third birthday, whereas Burial 11 was a slightly older boy, between the ages of four and eight. Both were interred with jet crosses and quantities of faceted jet beads, shell beads, and glass beads. Though Burial 9 had a much larger overall quantity of beads, they each had very diverse bead lots—and both appear to be from elite lineages based on our analysis of the death records for San Pedro y San Pablo (chapter 11). If our identifications are correct, a Ssatumnumo Captain named Cancégmne was the maternal grandfather of the younger boy, Burial 9, while the older boy—Burial 11—was Burial 9's paternal uncle. Burial 7, another child, also was also accompanied by a large quantity of beads, though they were more typologically restricted. These included 895 clamshell disk beads and 351 white-on-white glass beads. This burial assemblage represented approximately three-quarters of the CSDBs and over 95 percent of the white-on-white glass beads from the project, with the latter beads exhibiting the unique chemical signature discussed above (and see Panich et al. 2022).

The burials with pestles are all interesting in their own right. Burial 12, for example, was laid to rest with a large pestle exhibiting a double-flanged handle (Type IIB4) as well as an array of shell and glass beads, some 2,942 in all or almost half of the total bead assemblage. Based on our analysis of the sacramental records, Burial 12 appears to be Jagessém, who was the daughter of Cancégmne, the Ssatumnumo Captain and the aunt of Burial 9. Burial 4, a mature female, also contained a double-flanged pestle (Type IIB4) but only had one jet bead, which may have been intrusive. Two aspects of this burial stand out: she was buried in an extended prone (face down) position and approximately 45 degrees off the typical northeast-southwest orientation of the others in the cemetery. It is possible that Burial 4 is associated with Burial 16, who was estimated to be post-40 weeks of gestational age or a newborn. The third burial to include a pestle (Type IIB1a) was a young adult male—Burial 6—which is another seemingly uncommon pattern. This individual was also buried with a modest number of shell and glass beads. Based on the sacramental records, this individual appears to be the brother of Burial 11 and the father of Burial 9, the two boys buried with jet beads.

Other Lines of Evidence for San Pedro y San Pablo

As noted in chapter 1, the Native people buried at San Pedro y San Pablo were all associated with Mission San Francisco de Asís. They hailed from a range of tribal communities within what is today considered Ohlone territory, with most having ties to the Pacific coast south of the asistencia. The relatively circumscribed homelands for those buried at the site allows us to contextualize their mortuary practices within regional archaeological, historical, and ethnographic information.

Generally speaking, archaeological data indicate that most Ohlone communities buried their dead, though cremations did occur (Panich 2015:113–115). Grave goods were commonly included in late period burials throughout the region. Though the coast of the San Francisco Peninsula is underrepresented in regional archaeology, broader research syntheses suggest that patterns of burial assemblages—including both the type and quantity of materials—seem to have shifted dramatically beginning about two hundred years before the arrival of the Spanish (Hylkema 2002; Milliken et al. 2007). As noted in the previous section, Ohlone individuals and others from neighboring tribal communities continued to bury their loved ones with grave goods throughout the entirety of the Mission Period, as demonstrated by the presence of beads and other materials associated with burials in cemeteries at Mission Santa Clara spanning the period of ca. 1781–1851 (Hylkema 1995; Leventhal et al. 2011; Skowronek and Wizorek 1997).

The ethnographic and historical records provide further detail. In November 1814, the Franciscans at Mission San Francisco de Asís, Fathers Ramón Abella and Juan Sainz de Lucio, remarked that among the mission's Native population, "the effects belonging to the deceased are, as a rule, burned or are placed with him in such a way that no one will make use of anything which had come into contact with the dead person" (Geiger and Meighan 1976:120). Though this account postdates the use of the cemetery at San Pedro y San Pablo, the description likely applied to most of the Ohlone communities who were associated with both sites. A century later, Alfred Kroeber (1925:469) came to a similar conclusion regarding the importance of funerary offerings among the Ohlone: "The property of the dead was thoroughly destroyed, the reason alleged being that the deceased would then be no longer remembered."

The question remains, however, about whether the perpetuation of traditional mortuary practices by Ohlone people in the missions was carried on clandestinely or if it was perhaps tolerated by certain Franciscans, despite the fact that it contravened the Catholic doctrine of the time. One potential clue comes from an episode at Mission San Francisco de Asís in which two Ohlone individuals were whipped for loudly mourning the death of their relatives, a common component of Native Californian funerary practices (Newell 2009:155). That this punishment took place in 1797—during the period of use of the cemetery at San Pedro y San Pablo—suggests that the Ohlone community would have been keenly aware of the Franciscans' attitudes toward traditional mourning practices. Yet, the Franciscans often acknowledged the difficulty of controlling the beliefs of Native people. The accounts from 1814 from Mission San Francisco also admit that "there are many, however, even the majority who return from the countryside where they have been with the pagans such as their parents who hold on to the old practices" (Geiger and Meighan 1976:51).

Given what we know about Native life at San Pedro y San Pablo, there is little doubt that the site's occupants had ample opportunity to interact with their kin who continued to live outside of the mission system. At Mission San Francisco, Native people regularly used the policy of *paseo*, which offered approved leaves from the mission at certain times of year, to remain connected to a range of people and places out of earshot of the mission bells (Newell 2009). In particular, it appears that Native people from Mission San Francisco regularly fled the mission—often by manipulating the policy of paseo—to return to their ancestral homelands where they could die and be mourned in traditional ways. The Asistencia de San Pedro y San Pablo may have been something of a middle ground. It did not have a full-time missionary presence, even during the peak years of its operation, and there is no indication that Native people associated with the outstation lived directly on-site as they would have at Mission San Francisco proper (Newell 2009:169–173). Therefore, it would not be surprising if Native people viewed San Pedro y San Pablo as a locale where they could practice at least some mortuary practices without interference from the Franciscans.

Discussion and Conclusions

The study of Ohlone burials from the Asistencia de San Pedro y San Pablo illuminates many aspects of the lives of Native people caught up in the Franciscan mission system of Alta California. In addition to the demographic and health information explored in other chapters, the analysis of belongings buried with individuals at the site offers important insights into Native mortuary practices during the colonial period and provides the basis for further inferences about the persistence of exchange networks and technological traditions. While the asistencia was an outpost of Mission San Francisco de Asís—and church death records suggest that all those buried at San Pedro y San Pablo had been baptized—the site did not have a permanent missionary presence. The information presented in this chapter expands our understanding of how Ohlone people, like other Native Californians, continued many aspects of their traditional mortuary practices and exchange networks at the margins of the Spanish colonial system.

In aggregate, the types and quantities of grave goods at San Pedro y San

Pablo do not differ dramatically from those noted from colonial-era Native burials elsewhere in the province. Archaeological documentation from mission cemeteries in Alta California indicates that baptized Native people regularly interred their dead with quantities of shell and glass beads, in addition to other materials. From north to south, such evidence has been documented at Missions San Francisco Solano, San José, Santa Clara, Soledad, San Gabriel, and San Diego (Carrico 2014; Dietler et al. 2019; Howard 1972; Hylkema 1995; Panich 2018; Skowronek 1998; Skowronek and Wizorek 1997; Treganza 1956). One possible exception is Mission La Purísima. There, only one burial out of more than fifty excavated at the second site of Mission La Purísima (ca. 1812–1834) had associated beads; the others completely lacked funerary offerings (Humphrey 1965; Walker et al. 1988). Still, given the widespread geographic distribution of these practices, one wonders whether certain Franciscans tolerated the continued practice of burying deceased individuals with various types of belongings—a pattern of accommodation that is also hinted at in the documentary record (Panich 2018).

Outside of the mission compounds, unbaptized Native people and those fleeing or on leave from the missions continued to practice traditional mortuary practices—and integrated Euro-American goods into them—throughout the colonial period and beyond. Burial records from Mission Santa Clara, for example, list dozens of baptized individuals who were cremated in their ancestral villages in contradiction of mission policies (Panich 2015). Archaeological examples of such activities are relatively rare in the Bay Area proper, but Native burials in greater central California have yielded mission-era glass beads in several geographic contexts (e.g., Hildebrand et al. 1991; Schneider et al. 2014; Wiberg 2005). Further afield, projects in Southern California have documented historic-era Native cemeteries outside of missions or other colonial centers that included an array of grave goods including both Native-made and introduced goods (e.g., Gamble 2008; Reddy and Douglass 2016). Though many were not excavated to today's standards, Native cemeteries throughout the San Joaquin Valley and adjacent areas likewise provide evidence that funerary offerings remained a critical component of Native Californian mortuary practices throughout the early and middle nineteenth century even as flows of shell and glass beads, among other objects, shifted throughout the colonial period (see overview in Panich and Schneider 2015).

San Pedro y San Pablo also fits within emerging understandings of persistent exchange networks in the greater San Francisco Bay region. Archaeological work at Mission San Francisco de Asís—the most closely related mission site—has not (yet) focused on Native cemeteries or residential areas, which is perhaps not surprising given its urban setting (but see Ambro 2003). However, decades of research at nearby Mission Santa Clara and smaller projects at Mission San José have revealed comparable assemblages of shell and glass beads, flaked stone tools, ground stone tools, and other objects such as bone tubes and bat ray barbs from residential contexts, as well as significant quantities of shell and glass beads from mortuary contexts at two separate mission cemeteries at Santa Clara (Hylkema 1995; Panich 2014, 2016; Panich et al. 2018a, 2018b; Peelo et al. 2018; Potter et al. 2021; Skowronek and Wizorek 1997). In some ways, then, the findings from San Pedro y San Pablo help to fill in the evidentiary gaps left by the lack of archaeological evidence for Native lifeways at Mission San Francisco. Given that baptized Native people from that mission comprised the resident population at San Pedro y San Pablo, it is clear that they too had access to obsidian and other stone tool materials, obtained shell beads from diverse sources, and incorporated glass—and, in this case, jet—beads into the same types of cultural traditions.

As a mission outstation, the Asistencia de San Pedro y San Pablo offers a relatively rare look into the cultural persistence of Native people living on the margins of the mission system. Based on the evidence from the site and comparisons to nearby missions, it seems clear that Native people throughout the region maintained their mortuary practices and exchange networks despite the pressures of colonialism. But the evidence from San Pedro y San Pablo also offers insight about individual Ohlone people, some of whom—as evidenced by the exceedingly rare jet beads and crosses—may have had complex relationships with the Franciscans. Others were buried with items, like large ground stone pestles or the unique assemblage from Burial 15, that have not been documented in cemetery contexts at other mission sites. It may be, then, that the asistencia offered an intermediate space where Native people could die and be mourned without the full intrusion of colonial policies implemented by the Franciscans. Instead, the evidence from the Asistencia de San Pedro y San Pablo adds to a growing corpus of information regarding persistence of Native cultural traditions across the broader colonial-period landscape in Alta California.

Acknowledgments

We thank the Amah Mutsun Tribal Band of Mission San Juan Bautista for their support of these analyses. A number of individuals contributed to the research synthesized here. Chris Canzonieri provided key contextual information. Laure Dussubieux of the Field Museum conducted the LA-ICP-MS analysis of the glass beads. Shell isotope analyses were conducted by Miro Joyal and Howard Spero at the University of California Davis. Alison Sheridan provided information on the jet artifacts. Richard Hughes conducted the XRF analysis of obsidian artifacts, and the obsidian hydration dating was performed by Tom Origer and Associates. Portions of the specialized studies were funded by separate National Science Foundation grants to Panich (BCS 1559666) and Eerkens (BCS 1220048).

References

Allen, Rebecca
1992 The Use of Shellfish and Shell Beads at Santa Cruz Mission. *Pacific Coast Archaeological Society Quarterly* 28(2):18–34.
1998 *Native Americans at Mission Santa Cruz, 1791–1834: Interpreting the Archaeological Record.* Perspectives in California Archaeology Vol. 5. Institute of Archaeology, University of California, Los Angeles.

Allen, Rebecca, R. Scott Baxter, Linda Hylkema, Clinton Blount, and Stella D'Oro
2010 *Uncovering and Interpreting History and Archaeology at Mission Santa Clara.* Report to Santa Clara University, Santa Clara, California, from Past Forward, Inc., Garden Valley, Santa Clara University Archaeology Research Lab, and Albion Environmental, Inc., Santa Cruz, California.

Ambro, Richard D.
2003 They Danced in the Plaza: The Historical Archaeology of Notre Dame Plaza, Mission San Francisco de Asís (Dolores), 347 Dolores Street, San Francisco, California. Report to Mercy/Charities Housing California, San Francisco.

Beardsley, Richard K.
1954 Temporal and Areal Relationships in Central California Archaeology. *Reports of the University of California Archaeological Survey,* 24. University of California, Berkeley.

Bennyhoff, James A., and Richard E. Hughes
1987 *Shell Bead and Ornament Exchange Networks Between California and the Western Great Basin.* Anthropological Papers of the American Museum of Natural History, Volume 64, Part 2, New York.

Blair, Elliot H., Lorann S. A. Pendleton, and Peter Francis Jr.
2009 *The Beads of St. Catherine's Island.* American Museum of Natural History Anthropological Papers, Number 89. New York.

Burg, Marieka Brouwer, Tawny L. B. Tibbits, and Eleanor Harrison-Buck
2021 Advances in Geochemical Sourcing of Granite Ground Stone. *Advances in Archaeological Practice* 9(4):338–353.

Burns, Gregory R.
2019 Evolution of Shell Bead Money in Central California: An Isotopic Approach. PhD dissertation, University of California, Davis.

Burns, Gregory R., Jelmer W. Eerkens, Howard J. Spero, and Jeffrey S. Rosenthal
2023 Isotopic Evidence of Sources for Central California Olivella Beads. *California Archaeology* 15(1):33–51.

Byrd, Brian F., Shannon DeArmond, and Laurel Engbring
2018   Re-visualizing Indigenous Persistence during Colonization from the Perspective of Traditional Settlements in the San Francisco Bay-Delta Area. *Journal of California and Great Basin Anthropology* 38(2):163–190.
Carrico, Richard L.
2014   Remnants Pulled from the Fire: Report on the 1989 Spring-Summer Mission San Diego de Alcalá Archaeological Excavations. Manuscript on file with Richard Carrico.
Dadiego, Danielle L., Alyssa Gelinas, and Tsim D. Schneider
2021   Unpacking the Bead: Exploring a Glass Bead Assemblage from Mission Santa Cruz, California, Using LA-ICP-MS. *American Antiquity* 86(2):413–424.
Deagan, Kathleen
1987   Artifacts of the Spanish Colonies of Florida and the Caribbean, 1500–1820. Volume 1. Ceramics, Glassware, and Beads. Smithsonian Institution Press, Washington, DC.
Dietler, John, Heather Gibson, and Alyssa Newcomb
2019   The Lost San Gabriel Mission Cemetery. Addendum Report: Archaeological Monitoring for the San Gabriel Trench Grade Separation Project, San Gabriel, Los Angeles County, California. Report to the San Gabriel Valley Council of Governments. SWCA Environmental Consultants, Pasadena.
Eerkens, Jelmer W., Gregory S. Herbert, Jeffrey S. Rosenthal, and Howard J. Spero
2005   Provenance Analysis of *Olivella biplicata* Shell Beads from the California and Oregon Coast by Stable Isotope Fingerprinting. *Journal of Archaeological Science* 32: 1501–1514.
Erlandson, Jon M., and Terry L. Jones, eds.
2002   *Catalysts to Complexity: Late Holocene Societies of the California Coast*. Perspectives in California Archaeology, Volume 6. Cotsen Institute of Archaeology, University of California Los Angeles.
Francis, Peter, Jr.
2009   Imported Beads Made from Organic Materials. In *The Beads of St. Catherine's Island*, by Elliot H. Blair, Lorann S. A. Pendleton, and Peter Francis Jr., 113–116. American Museum of Natural History Anthropological Papers, Number 89. New York.
Gamble, Lynn H.
2008   *The Chumash World at European Contact: Power, Trade, and Feasting among Complex Hunter-Gatherers*. University of California Press, Berkeley.
Geiger, Maynard J., and Clement W. Meighan, eds.
1976   *As the Padres Saw Them: California Indian Life and Customs as Reported by the Franciscan Missionaries, 1813–1815*. Santa Barbara Mission Archive Library, Santa Barbara, CA.
Graham, Elizabeth
1998   Mission Archaeology. *Annual Review of Anthropology* 27:25–62.
Hildebrandt, William R., Kenneth R. Bethard, and David Boe
1991   Archaeological Investigations at CA-SCL-714/H: A Protohistoric Cemetery

Area near Gilroy, California. Report on file at the Northwest Information Center, Sonoma State University.

Howard, Donald M.
1972 Archaeological Investigation at Misión Nuestra Señora de La Soledad, MNT-233–Monterey County, California. *Monterey County Archaeological Society Quarterly* 1(3):1–10.

Hull, Kathleen L., and Barbara L. Voss
2016 Native Californians at the Presidio of San Francisco: Analysis of Lithic Specimens from El Polín Spring. *International Journal of Historical Archaeology* 20(2):264–288.

Humphrey, Richard
1965 The La Purísima Mission Cemetery. *Annual Reports of the University of California Archaeological Survey* 7:179–192. Los Angeles, CA.

Hylkema, Mark G.
1995 *Archaeological Investigations at the Third Location of Mission Santa Clara de Asís: The Murguía Mission, 1781–1818 (CA-SCL-30/H)*. California Department of Transportation, District 4, Environmental Planning, Oakland.
2002 Tidal Marsh, Oak Woodlands, and Cultural Florescence in the Southern San Francisco Bay Region. In *Catalysts to Complexity: Late Holocene Societies of the California Coast*, edited by Jon M. Erlandson and Terry L. Jones, 263–281. Perspectives in California Archaeology, Volume 6. Cotsen Institute of Archaeology, University of California Los Angeles.

Hylkema, Mark G., and Rebecca Allen
2009 Archaeological Investigations at the Third Mission Site, Santa Clara University, and a Comparison of Shell Bead Assemblages with Recent Mission-Era Findings. *Society for California Archaeology Proceedings* 21:28–35.

Johnson, John R.
2006 The Various Chinigchinich Manuscripts of Father Gerónimo Boscana. In *San Diego, Alta California, and the Borderlands:* Proceedings of the 23rd Annual Conference of the California Mission Studies Association, Mission San Diego de Alcalá, February 17–19, 2006, eds. R. M. Beebe and R. M. Senkewicz, 1–19. California Mission Studies Association, Santa Clara.

Jones, Terry L., and Kathryn A. Klar, eds.
2007 *California Prehistory: Colonization, Culture, and Complexity*. Altamira Press, Lanham, MD.

Justice, Noel D.
2002 *Stone Age Spear and Arrow Points of the California and the Great Basin*. Indiana University Press, Bloomington.

Karklins, Karlis
2012 Guide to the Description and Classification of Glass Beads Found in the Americas. *Beads: Journal of the Society of Bead Researchers* 24:62–90. Originally published 1982, Parks Canada, History and Archaeology 59:83–117.

Kidd, Kenneth E., and Martha Ann Kidd
2012 A Classification System for Glass Beads for the Use of Field Archaeologists. *Beads: Journal of the Society of Bead Researchers* 24:39–61. Originally pub-

lished 1970, Canadian Historic Sites, Occasional Papers in Archaeology and History 1:45–89.

King, Chester
2011   *Overview of the History of American Indians in the Santa Monica Mountains.* Report to the National Park Service Pacific West Region, Santa Monica Mountains National Recreation Area, but Topanga Anthropological Consultants, Topanga, CA.

Kroeber, Alfred L.
1925   *Handbook of the Indians of California.* Bureau of American Ethnology Bulletin, No. 78. Smithsonian Institution, Washington, DC.

Leventhal, Alan, Diane DiGiuseppe, Melynda Atwood, David Grant, Rosemary Cambra, Charlene Nijmeh, Monica V. Arellano, Sheila Guzman-Schmidt, Gloria E. Gomez, and Norma Sanchez
2011   *Final Report on the Burial and Archaeological Data Recovery Program Conducted on a Portion of the Mission Santa Clara Indian Neophyte Cemetery (1781–1818): Clareño Muwékma Ya Túnneöte Nómmo [Where the Clareño Indians are Buried] Site (CA-SCL-30/H), Located in the City of Santa Clara, Santa Clara County, California.* Report to Pacific Gas and Electric Company by Ohlone Family Consulting Services. Available at the Northwest Information Center, Sonoma State University, Rohnert Park, California.

McEwan, Bonnie G.
2001   The Spiritual Conquest of La Florida. *American Anthropologist* 103(3):633–644.

Meighan, Clement W.
2024   *Glass Trade Beads in California*, ed. Elliot Blair. BAR Publishing, Oxford.

Menéndez Menéndez, Andrea
2019   Aproximación histórica y tipológica al uso del azabache, y otros materiales afines, durante la época romana y la Tardoantigüedad en la península ibérica. *Nailos, Estudios Interdisciplinares de Arqueología* 6:123–203.

Milliken, Randall T.
2005   Shell Beads. In *Final Report: Archaeological Evaluation and Mitigative Data Recovery at CA-YOL069, Madison Aggregate Plant, Yolo County, California,* by Randy S. Wiberg, 6-1–6-19. Report to Solano Concrete Company, Inc. by Holman and Associates. Available at the Northwest Information Center, Sonoma State University, Rohnert Park, California.

Milliken, Randall T., and Al W. Schwitalla
2012   *California and Great Basin Olivella Shell Bead Guide.* Left Coast Press, Walnut Creek, California.

Milliken, Randall T., Richard T. Fitzgerald, Mark G. Hylkema, Randy Groza, Tom Origer, David G. Bieling, Alan Leventhal, Randy S. Wiberg, Andrew Gottsfield, Donna Gillete, Viviana Bellifemine, Eric Strother, Robert Cartier, and David A. Fredrickson
2007   Punctuated Culture Change in the San Francisco Bay Area. In *California Prehistory: Colonization, Culture, and Complexity*, edited by Terry L. Jones and Kathryn A. Klar, 99–124. Altamira Press, Lanham, MD.

Muller, Helen
1980 *Jet Jewellery and Ornaments*. Shire Publications, Princes Risborough, Buckinghamshire.

Newell, Quincy D.
2009 *Constructing Lives at Mission San Francisco: Native Californians and Hispanic Colonists, 1776–1821*. University of New Mexico Press, Albuquerque.

Panich, Lee M.
2014 Native American Consumption of Shell and Glass Beads at Mission Santa Clara de Asís. *American Antiquity* 79(4):730–748.
2015 "Sometimes They Bury the Deceased's Clothes and Trinkets": Indigenous Mortuary Practices at Mission Santa Clara de Asís. *Historical Archaeology* 49(4):110–129.
2016 Beyond the Colonial Curtain: Investigating Indigenous Use of Obsidian in Spanish California through the pXRF Analysis of Artifacts from Mission Santa Clara. *Journal of Archaeological Science: Reports* 5:521–530.
2018 Death, Mourning, and Accommodation in the Missions of Alta California. In *Franciscans and American Indians in Pan-Borderlands Perspective: Adaptation, Negotiation, and Resistance*, edited by Jeffrey M. Burns and Timothy J. Johnson, 251–264. American Academy of Franciscan History, Oceanside, CA.
2021 Glass Beads, Shell Beads, and Shell Ornaments. In, *575 Benton Street Project, Santa Clara California. Volume 1: Data Recovery at Site CA-SCL-30H*, edited by James M. Potter, Mike Mirro, and Brenna Wheelis, 374–398. Report to Prometheus Real Estate Group, Inc. Paleowest, Walnut Creek, CA.

Panich, Lee M., and Tsim D. Schneider, eds.
2014 *Indigenous Landscapes and Spanish Missions: New Perspectives from Archaeology and Ethnohistory*. University of Arizona Press, Tucson.

Panich, Lee M., and Tsim D. Schneider
2015 Expanding Mission Archaeology: A Landscape Approach to Indigenous Autonomy in Colonial California. *Journal of Anthropological Archaeology* 40:48–58.

Panich, Lee M., Rebecca Allen, and Andrew Galvan
2018a The Archaeology of Native American Persistence at Mission San José. *Journal of California and Great Basin Anthropology* 38(1):11–29.

Panich, Lee M., Ben Griffin, and Tsim D. Schneider
2018b Native Acquisition of Obsidian in Colonial-Era Central California: Implications from Mission San José. *Journal of Anthropological Archaeology* 50:1–11.

Panich, Lee M., Mark Hylkema, and Tsim D. Schneider
2021 Points of Contention: Tradition, Resistance, and Arrow Points in the California Missions. *Journal of Anthropological Archaeology* 64: 101366.

Panich, Lee M., Laure Dussubieux, Tsim D. Schneider, Christopher Canzonieri, Irenne Zwierlein, Christopher Zimmer, and Michelle Zimmer
2022 Compositional Analysis of Compound Drawn White Glass Beads from Colonial California: Implications for Chronology and Dispersal. In *The Elemental Analysis of Glass Beads: Technology, Chronology, and Exchange*, edited by Laure

Dussubieux and Heather Walder, 119–136. Studies in Archaeological Sciences, Vol. 8. Leuven University Press, Leuven.

Peelo, Sarah, Linda Hylkema, John Ellison, Clinton Blount, Mark Hylkema, Margie Maher, Tom Garlinghouse, Dustin McKenzie, Stella D'Oro, and Melinda Berge
2018   Persistence in the Indian *Ranchería* at Mission Santa Clara de Asís. *Journal of California and Great Basin Anthropology* 38(2):207–234.

Potter, James M., Mike Mirro, and Brenna Wheelis, eds.
2021   *575 Benton Street Project, Santa Clara California. Volume 1: Data Recovery at Site CA-SCL-30H.* Report to Prometheus Real Estate Group, Inc. Paleowest, Walnut Creek, CA.

Reddy, Seetha N., and John G. Douglass, eds.
2016   *People in a Changing Land: The Archaeology and History of the Ballona in Los Angeles, California. Volume 3: Material Culture and Subsistence Practices.* Technical Series 94. Statistical Research, Inc., Tucson.

Rosenthal, Jeffrey S.
2011   The Function of Shell Bead Exchange in Central California, in *Perspectives on Prehistoric Trade and Exchange in California and the Great Basin*, edited by R. E. Hughes, 83–113. University of Utah Press, Salt Lake City.

Schneider, Tsim D.
2021   *The Archaeology of Refuge and Recourse: Coast Miwok Resilience and Indigenous Hinterlands in Colonial California.* University of Arizona Press, Tucson.

Schneider, Tsim D., Khal Schneider, and Lee M. Panich
2020   Scaling Invisible Walls: Reasserting Indigenous Persistence in Mission-Era California. *The Public Historian* 42(2):97–120.

Schneider, Tsim D., John Holson, Lori D. Hager, Samantha S. Schell, and Lucian N. Schrader
2014   Obsidian Production and Mortuary Practices at CA-NAP-399, Napa Valley: Inferences from AMS Radiocarbon Assays. *California Archaeology* 6(2):191–218.

Silliman, Stephen W.
2004   *Lost Laborers in Colonial California: Native Americans and the Archaeology of Rancho Petaluma.* University of Arizona Press, Tucson.
2005   Obsidian Studies and the Archaeology of 19th-Century California. *Journal of Field Archaeology* 30:75–94.

Skowronek, Russell K.
1998   Sifting the Evidence: Perceptions of Life at the Ohlone (Costanoan) Missions of Alta California. *Ethnohistory* 45:675–708.

Skowronek, Russell K., and Julie C. Wizorek
1997   Archaeology at Santa Clara de Asís: The Slow Rediscovery of a Moveable Mission. *Pacific Coast Archaeological Society Quarterly* 33(3):54–92.

Treganza, Adan E.
1956   Sonoma Mission: An Archaeological Reconstruction of the Mission San Francisco de Solano Quadrangle. *Kroeber Anthropological Society Papers* 14:1–18.

Von der Porten, Peter, Katherine Dixon, and Alex DeGeorgey
2014   Seriation of Clam Shell Disk Beads in Central California. *Proceedings of the Society for California Archaeology* 28:267–281.

Walker, Phillip L., John R. Johnson, and Patricia M. Lambert
1988   Age and Sex Biases in the Preservation of Human Skeletal Remains. *American Journal of Physical Anthropology* 76:183–188.

Ward, Gerald W.R., ed.
2008   *The Grove Encyclopedia of Materials and Techniques in Art*. Oxford University Press, Oxford.

Wiberg, Randy S.
2005   Final Report: Archaeological Evaluation and Mitigative Data Recovery at CA-YOL069, Madison Aggregate Plant, Yolo County, California. Report to Solano Concrete Company, Inc.

6

Dietary Persistence and Change in California's Mission Period

Stable Isotope Evidence from Tooth and Bone from Asistencia de San Pedro y San Pablo (CA-SMA-71/H)

JELMER W. EERKENS, CHRISTOPHER CANZONIERI,
AND JASON MISZANIEC

Food is an important way that people express identity in contemporary cultures around the world (Fischler 1988; Montanari 2006). Therefore, food was surely an important component of identity expression for Native people within the California Mission system (Dietler 2007; Popper 2016; Reddy 2015). Preparing and consuming traditional foods would not only have served as an expression of a non-European Native identity vis-à-vis the Spanish diet, but likely as a means to express tribal identity within the multi-ethnic community within a particular mission.

Historical records are one means to examine diet within the California missions. Of course, such records were written from the perspective of eighteenth-century Spanish colonists, and as such, are subject to particular biases. Nonetheless, these records indicate that diet consisted of a range of livestock (e.g., sheep, cows, pigs, chickens) and agricultural products (e.g., wheat, barley, maize, beans, grapes, peaches, squash, melons), with little mention of traditional foods (Geiger and Meighan 1976; Webb 1983).

Archaeological investigations represent an alternative way to examine food practices. Under the assumption that they represent the by-products of food preparation and consumption, identification of animal bones and/or charred paleobotanical remains in archaeological sites has been an important approach. For example, recent analyses of macrobotanical remains from flotation samples suggests many traditional food preparation activities continued within the missions. While European foods were consumed mainly within the more public spaces of mission buildings, traditional hunted and gathered foods are especially prominent within spaces associated with Indigenous domiciles (Noe 2023; Popper 2016; Reddy 2015). Similarly, archaeologists also examine of dental microwear (e.g., El-Zaatari et al. 2010; Grine et al. 2012; Scott et al. 2005; Schmidt et al. 2015) and analyze starch grains, phytoliths, and other dietary remains preserved in dental calculus (Dudgeon et al. 2014; Mickleburgh et al. 2012; Poulson et al. 2013; Scott et al. 2012) to reconstruct ancient diets. However, to our knowledge, the latter approaches have not been applied to California Mission contexts.

Stable isotope analysis of bones and teeth provides another archaeological approach to trace paleodiet (Ambrose et al. 2003; Price et al. 2002; Schoeninger et al. 1983; Schwarcz et al. 1985; Van der Merwe et al. 1982; Vogel and Van der Merwe, 1977; Wright 2005). Because foods vary in their underlying stable isotopic composition, and are used to grow skeletal tissues, stable isotope signatures of foods become embedded in bones and teeth. By measuring stable isotope signatures in bones and teeth, we can work backward to estimate the types of foods an individual ate. Tracing out the diets of individuals, we can then examine dietary variation within communities, for example, among males vs. females, wealthy vs. non-wealthy, old vs. young, or local vs. foreigner (as determined by osteological and/or archaeometric techniques).

Bone is a constantly remodeling tissue even into late adult years, which is how a bone heals following a fracture (unlike a tooth). The turnover rate of bone depends on age (bone in younger individuals turns over faster) and the particular bone (dense bones such as femurs turn over more slowly). The rate of complete turnover is estimated at between five and twenty years for bone (Hedges et al. 2007; Manolagas 2000). In this respect, bone can represent dietary behaviors averaged over the last half to two decades of life.

By contrast, some tissues, such as teeth, do not remodel and form in layers, much like tree rings. Such tissues allow us to examine dietary patterns earlier in life, and to examine dietary change for a particular person across windows of time those tissues grew. For example, a permanent first molar (M1) begins forming around the time of birth and continues growing until between nine and ten years of age (Hillson 1996). Currently, archaeologists are able to extract tissues from growth layers within M1s that represent approximately 0.5 to 1-year intervals. Similarly, a permanent M3 starts forming around age seven to ten and continues growing until age eighteen to twenty-five, and current sampling strategies allow us to estimate diet at about 0.8 to 1.5 year intervals. By examining growth layers in paired M1 and M3 teeth from the same person, we can reconstruct a dietary life history for the first two decades of life, with bone providing an estimate on the final five to twenty years before death.

This is the approach followed in this chapter. Many individuals buried at the asistencia were born before and outside of the Mission system. Tissues that grew within that context (e.g., early growing teeth) should record the isotopic signature of their traditional diet. Later, after these individuals entered the mission, they may have shifted their diets to include domesticated animals and crops. Bone, a constantly remodeling tissue, ought to record some component of this transition, though depending on how many years they were in the mission before dying, this could be time-averaged with some of the bone that formed before missionization. More informative are dental tissues that were still forming at the time of death, since they represent a shorter amount of time (e.g., 0.5–1 years for an M1 layer), and should reflect a greater component of the Mission diet. In this respect, the studies below reflect the degree to which an individual, on average, shifted the isotopic composition of their diet within the Mission system compared to pre-mission times. The study provides an independent evaluation on the persistence, or not, of a traditional diet within the California Mission systems in the San Francisco Bay Area.

Isotopic Model

Carbon, nitrogen, and sulfur are major components of the organic component of bone and teeth, including collagen. In humans, the C, N, and S necessary for tissue synthesis are derived entirely from consumed foods. Following digestion, the body routes these elements via the blood system to sites of bone and tooth construction (or repair in the case of bone). Because underlying food sources can vary in their C, N, and S composition, measuring these elements in human skeletal tissues can provide information on the diet of an individual at the time those skeletal tissues were forming.

The ratio of carbon isotopes ($^{13}C/^{12}C$, expressed as $\delta^{13}C$, see below) is often used to provide an estimate of the consumption of C_3 vs. C_4 plants. The majority of plants around the world are C_3 plants, producing a three-carbon molecule during the fixation of atmospheric carbon. This method of photosynthesis discriminates against the heavier ^{13}C, resulting in $\delta^{13}C$ values between −30‰ and −22‰ (Cerling et al. 1998; Ehleringer et al. 1993; Farquhar et al. 1989). Major domesticates used by the Spanish, including wheat, barley, beans, and most fruits, fall into the C_3 category. By contrast, a small number of plants produce a four-carbon molecule (C_4) and produce tissues with $\delta^{13}C$ values typically between −16‰ and −10‰. In central California, there are few native C_4 plants (Cloern et al. 2002), and none were important dietary staples prior to contact (Bartelink 2006, 2009). However, maize is an important C_4 plant that was imported from Mexico and grown within the mission system. As well, millet and sugar cane are C_4 plants that were occasionally grown in historic contexts. In this regard, because nearly all traditional California dietary plants are C_3, marked increases in $\delta^{13}C$ after missionization could be indicative of a transition from native plants to maize.

In contrast to terrestrial systems, carbon enters marine environments mainly through exchange with atmospheric CO_2 and through photosynthesizing phytoplankton (Boutton 1991). $\delta^{13}C$ values of biologically available carbon in marine environments can overlap with those of C_4 plants. However, when C isotopes are combined with N and S, it is possible to distinguish the two. Marine organisms are heavier (less negative) in $\delta^{13}C$ (Bartelink 2009; Schoeninger et al. 1983; Schwarcz and Schoeninger 1991).

Nitrogen isotopes ($^{15}N/^{14}N$, expressed as $\delta^{15}N$) provide an indicator of the trophic level of dietary proteins. Nitrogen enters biological systems either through atmospheric fixation by soil bacteria or through physical processes (e.g., lightning strikes). Nitrates and nitrites are then taken up by plants and converted into various biomolecular compounds, especially proteins. Animals access nitrogen through the consumption of protein-containing tissues, such as plants or animal meat. Following digestion, animals differentially excrete the lighter ^{14}N in the formation of urea and retain the heavier ^{15}N for tissue synthesis. As a result, $\delta^{15}N$ increases by about 3–4‰ with each trophic level (Ambrose 1986, 1991; DeNiro and Epstein 1981; Minagawa and Wada 1984; Schoeninger 1984). Carbon has a similar trophic effect, but much smaller in magnitude, typically 0.5 to 1‰ for each trophic level. In aquatic environments, baseline $\delta^{15}N$ at the bottom of the food pyramid is typically higher than the bottom in terrestrial systems, and there are usually more trophic levels. As a result, aquatic environments generally have greater enrichment of ^{15}N toward the top of the food chain, especially for benthic consumers (e.g., large fish, predatory birds, and aquatic mammals; Croteau et al. 2005; Schoeninger 1995; Vander Zanden et al. 2011).

A difference also exists in wild versus fertilized plants. Because nitrogen (as well as other essential nutrients such as phosphorus) are often limiting factors in plant growth, providing artificial sources of these nutrients increases plant productivity. The source of nitrogen in fertilizers is typically animal dung and food refuse, which will be elevated in $\delta^{15}N$ relative to atmospheric sources (Szpak et al. 2012). Therefore, plants grown in fertilized fields will be higher in $\delta^{15}N$, and often slightly higher in $\delta^{13}C$ as well. Furthermore, animals fed plant products from fertilized fields will also be elevated in these isotopic signatures relative to wild animals or domesticated animals eating wild browse such as bunchgrasses. In short, fertilizing fields raises the baseline $\delta^{15}N$ in trophic systems.

Sulfur is present in various forms (e.g., sulfates, sulfides) in soils. It is taken up by plants from the soil and passed up the food chain to animals and humans (Richards et al. 2003). As a result, the ratio of sulfur isotopes ($^{34}S/^{32}S$, expressed as $\delta^{34}S$) can vary between soils derived from different geological formation across a region, and may also contrast with sulfur in marine environments. While marine sulfur has a relatively constant $\delta^{34}S$ value of 21.0 ± 0.2‰, terrestrial environments are usually much lower and have a much greater range of variation, occasionally extending below 0‰. Sulfur is essential in the formation of the amino acid methionine, which is present in small amounts in collagen. Because of the greater sample size required for mass spectrometry analysis (10mg collagen vs. 1mg for $\delta^{13}C$ and $\delta^{15}N$ combined), and the small size of dentinal serial samples, in this study, $\delta^{34}S$ was only measured in bone collagen.

In terrestrial systems in central California, there are essentially three trophic levels: plants (producers), herbivores (primary consumers), and carnivores (secondary and tertiary consumers).

Together, $\delta^{13}C$, $\delta^{15}N$, and $\delta^{34}S$ can discriminate the importance of foods from different environments and trophic levels (Froehle et al. 2009, 2010). In this paper we are particularly interested in examining the role of marine resources (higher $\delta^{13}C$, $\delta^{15}N$, and $\delta^{34}S$), terrestrial game (lower $\delta^{13}C$ and $\delta^{34}S$, and higher $\delta^{15}N$), C_3 terrestrial plants (lower $\delta^{13}C$, $\delta^{15}N$, and $\delta^{34}S$), and C_4 terrestrial plants (higher $\delta^{13}C$, and lower $\delta^{15}N$ and $\delta^{34}S$) in the diets of people and animals within the Mission system. Further, we aim to examine the importance of such resources by age and sex, how the Mission Period samples compare to pre-contact individuals and Euro-Americans from the mid-1800s, and how dental tissues that formed prior to establishment of the mission system within in a person contrast with tissues that likely formed after they started living within the mission. Together, these comparisons should inform on the degree of dietary change within the mission at the scale of the individual.

A long history of research in western North America shows that the isotopic composition of pre-contact diets varied mainly by region and environment (e.g., Eerkens et al. 2022). Figure 6.1 shows a general model for $\delta^{13}C$ and $\delta^{15}N$, based on empirical data from California generated in the UC Davis Archaeometry lab. Ellipses represent the approximate isotopic range of diets dominated by foods from different ecological contexts. Of course, humans are omnivores and incorporate foods from a range of environmental sources.

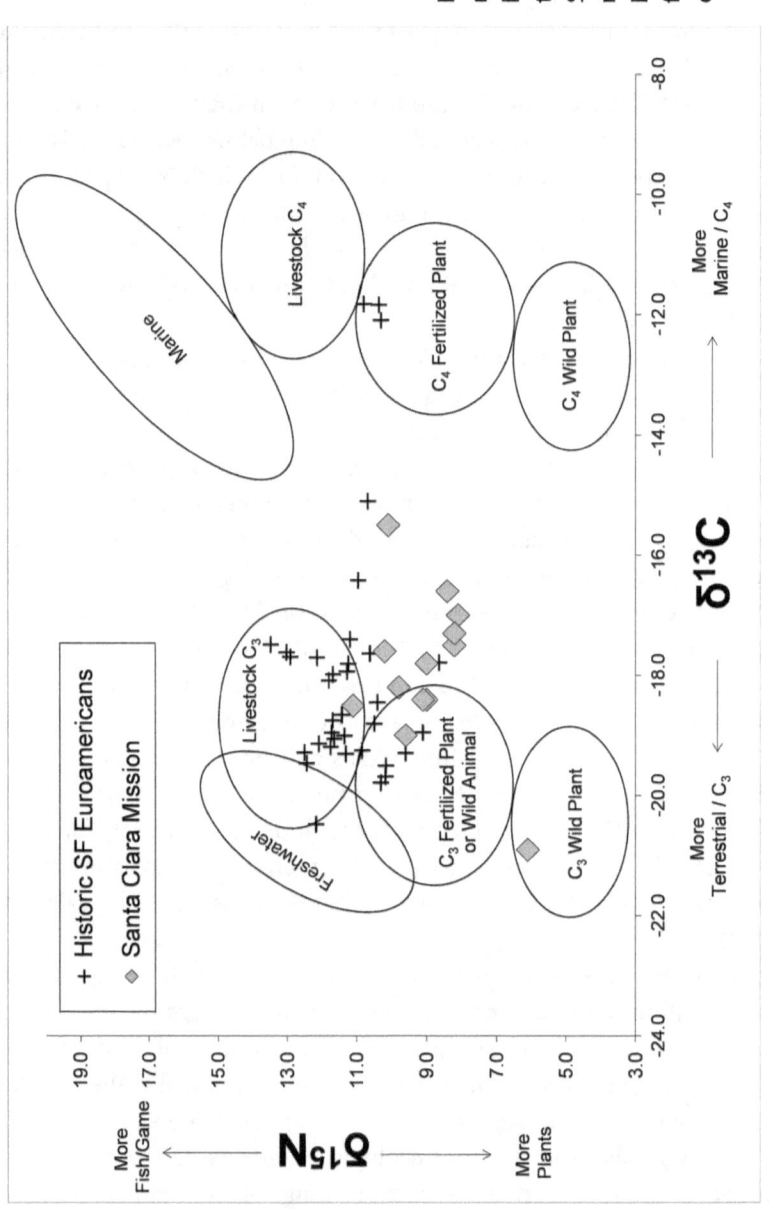

Figure 6.1. Isotopic model and previous human C and N isotopes from Mission Santa Clara and late nineteenth-century Euro-Americans from the San Francisco Bay area.

Thus, there are often multiple ways to achieve the final empirical values in $\delta^{13}C$ and $\delta^{15}N$ recorded for an individual. Intermediary values between the ellipses likely represent people who consumed foods from more than one source, creating an average between ellipses. Over these ellipses, we have plotted empirical data from historic-period Euro-Americans buried in the city of San Francisco (unpublished data collected by Eerkens and colleagues), as well as a sample of native people buried at Mission Santa Clara (data from Bartelink 2011).

As shown in figure 6.1, the majority of Euro-Americans buried in San Francisco were consuming C_3 plant products (e.g., bread made from wheat or barley), likely from fertilized fields, as well as animals raised on C_3 plants (e.g., cows, pigs, chickens) and/or their by-products (e.g., milk, eggs). Three individuals, however, plot far to the right, within the range expected of C_4 plants. Likely these three individuals were consuming high amounts of maize, maize-based products, or animals raised on maize. As well, some Euro-Americans fall more in the center of the plot, suggesting they mixed varying amounts of C_4 plant products, or perhaps marine foods.

By contrast, all but one of the individuals buried at the Santa Clara Mission are lower in $\delta^{15}N$ and somewhat higher in $\delta^{13}C$ than Euro-Americans. This would be consistent with greater amounts of wild animals or plants, as well as higher amounts of maize. However, one Santa Clara Mission individual shows a diet dominated by C_3 wild plants, similar to data from precontact individuals from interior areas of central California. Perhaps this person had recently entered the mission before dying, or refused foods that other Native people living at the mission ate, retaining an isotopic signature that represented a traditional diet.

Isotope Methods

We analyzed one bone sample from each of the fifteen individuals in this study. All samples produced enough collagen to measure $\delta^{13}C$ and $\delta^{15}N$, and fourteen bone samples yielded sufficient collagen to measure $\delta^{34}S$. In addition, 209 age-controlled isotopic measurements were made on 23 teeth from 13 individuals (Burials 7 and 16, both infants, did not have teeth). The isotopic data from teeth allow us to estimate diet earlier in people's lives.

To provide baseline data for the human bone isotope analyses, we also present stable isotope data from twenty-two unmodified faunal remains from the site, representing both domestic livestock and poultry and native species. These bones were recovered during excavations by Stephen Dietz in the 1970s and early 1990s (Dietz 1979; Wickstrom et al. 1990), not in the cemetery where the burials discussed below were found, but further to the east in areas thought to represent granaries. We also analyzed a small fragment from a bird-bone whistle that was included in the grave of Burial 15 (depicted in figure 5.6 in the previous chapter), though the species is unknown.

For additional details on methods, the reader is referred to Eerkens and colleagues (2013) for bone, and Eerkens and colleagues (2011) for teeth. In short, this approach involves cleaning samples of visible surface contamination such as soil, and removing the outer layer of bone or tooth by drilling exposed surfaces with a diamond bit. Cementum and enamel are also removed for teeth, leaving only dentin. Samples are then sonicated in deionized H_2O, demineralized in a solution of 0.5M hydrochloric acid (HCl), and soaked in 0.125M NaOH (sodium hydroxide) to remove humic acids. Collagen is then solubilized in slightly acidic pH3 water within an oven set at 70°–90°C, separated from any material that does not solubilize, and freeze-dried. $\delta^{13}C$, $\delta^{15}N$, and $\delta^{34}S$ are measured by continuous-flow mass spectrometry alongside a series of standards. Instrument precisions are 0.1‰ for $\delta^{13}C$, 0.2‰ for $\delta^{15}N$, and 0.4‰ for $\delta^{34}S$.

Results

Mission records indicate that the majority of individuals buried at the asistencia were from communities on the west side of the San Francisco Peninsula near the Pacific Ocean (chapter 2). Traditional foods in these communities emphasize resources from marine environments, including plants (kelp, seaweed), shellfish (e.g., mussel, clam), fish (e.g., herring, surfperch), birds (e.g., cormorant, coot), and marine mammals (e.g., otter, sea lion). As well, access to the coastal plain and interior hills provided a range of terrestrial foods from C_3 food webs, including acorns, manzanita, grass seeds, hares, rabbits, deer, and elk. Research at other Bay Area sites shows that individuals within a community often varied in the importance of one or the other environment to their overall dietary composition (Beasley et al. 2013; Eerkens et al. 2013; Goring et al. 2020). Thus, we expect some variation along a marine-C_3 terrestrial continuum for individuals from Asistencia de San Pedro y San Pablo.

What Did Fauna Eat?

Table 6.1 shows isotopic results from asistencia faunal samples, including introduced domesticated animals (cow, horse, goat, sheep, chicken), native species (bear, goose, cottontail, hare, sea mammals), and species that could be native or introduced (canids). As shown, these samples cover a wide range of isotopic values, with $\delta^{13}C$ varying between -23.6‰ and -9.9‰ and $\delta^{15}N$

Table 6.1. Results of stable isotope analyses from faunal remains

Scientific Name	Common Name	δ^{13}C	δ^{15}N	δ^{34}S	%C	%N	C/N	%S
Bos taurus	Cow	-21.2	5.8	16.4	49%	17%	3.3	.18%
Bos taurus	Cow	-20.8	6.5	8.5	34%	11%	3.4	.18%
Bos taurus	Cow	-21.3	6.4	4.9	35%	12%	3.4	.19%
Bos taurus	Cow	-18	8.7	15.8	35%	12%	3.3	.18%
Bos taurus	Cow	-21.1	7.7	14.5	34%	12%	3.2	.19%
Equus sp.	Horse	-20.8	5.9	—	30%	9%	3.8	—
Capra sp.	Goat	-20.5	7.7	—	38%	13%	3.4	—
Ovis sp.	Sheep	-21.6	10.7	—	38%	12%	3.7	—
Gallus gallus domesticus	Chicken	-17.8	9.9	—	46%	16%	3.4	—
Gallus gallus domesticus	Chicken	-11.8	8.9	—	43%	15%	3.4	—
Canis sp.	Canid	-20.2	10	—	32%	11%	3.4	—
Canis sp.	Canid	-20.2	10.2	—	45%	14%	3.7	—
Ursus sp.	Bear	-20.1	6.1	—	56%	20%	3.3	—
Sylvilagus sp.	Cottontail	-21.3	6.4	—	34%	12%	3.3	—
Sylvilagus sp.	Cottontail	-22.4	5.1	—	46%	16%	3.4	—
Lepus sp.	Hare	-22.2	10.6	—	56%	19%	3.4	—
Enhydra lutris	Sea Otter	-11.1	15.5	—	34%	12%	3.4	—
Zalophus sp.	Sea Lion	-9.9	19.2	—	38%	12%	3.6	—
Branta sp.	Goose	-15.4	5.3	—	34%	12%	3.3	—
Branta sp.	Goose	-15.5	5.9	—	48%	17%	3.4	—
Branta sp.	Goose	-23.6	6.6	—	40%	14%	3.3	—
Aves	Bird-bone whistle	-21.3	7.7	—	43%	14%	3.6	—

between 5.1‰ and 19.2‰. This range is about five times greater than the range of bone collagen values in humans buried at the site (see below). Collagen quality control measures are presented at the right as percent carbon, percent nitrogen, C/N ratios, and percent sulfur. The reported values are within the ranges expected of well-preserved collagen (Ambrose 1986; DeNiro 1985; Guiry and Szpak 2021).

Figure 6.2 plots the faunal values over the ellipses shown in figure 6.1. We plot introduced species as solid symbols, native species as open symbols, and birds as hatched symbols. Native species generally fall where we expect them. Thus, the sea mammals fall within the marine ellipse, the bear is within the C_3 wild plant ellipse, and two of the three leporids have low δ^{13}C and δ^{15}N indicating a C_3 plant-based diet. As well, the three geese are all low in $\delta^{15}N$, but quite variable in $\delta^{13}C$, a pattern we have documented among precontact geese at a site further inland (Su et al. 2023). On the other hand, the only hare included in the study is higher in $\delta^{15}N$ than expected, suggesting it may have been eating plants from a fertilized field. Perhaps it foraged in gardens maintained at the asistencia.

Figure 6.2 also reveals information about domesticated animals presumably kept at the asistencia. The two chickens show contrasting diets, with one falling within the fertilized C_4 plant ellipse, suggesting it was raised predominantly on maize, and the other falling between the C_3 and C_4 ellipses, suggesting a mix of grains or plants from these two groups (though it is closer to the C_3 ellipse). The single horse, the single goat, and five of the six cows fall within the C_3 wild plant ellipse, suggesting these animals grazed mainly on wild native vegetation. One cow, however, is slightly elevated in $\delta^{13}C$ and $\delta^{15}N$, suggesting it ate significant amounts of fertilized crops, such as oats or alfalfa, likely mixed with some maize judging by the slightly elevated $\delta^{13}C$ value. Likewise, the sheep displays an isotopic signature in line with fertilized C_3 crops rather than wild vegetation.

The two canids fall within the wild animal ellipse and are lower in $\delta^{15}N$ than expected for carnivores eating domesticated animals. This suggests they are either wild coyotes, domesticated dogs eating large amounts of wild animals (such as leporids), or dogs eating mostly C_3 crop products (such as bread). Finally, the single bird-bone whistle also falls within the range of an animal eating mostly terrestrial C_3 plants. Although no diagnostic features are present on the bone to estimate species, the isotopic data rule out marine birds as a source for the whistle.

What Did Humans Eat?

Table 6.2 presents bone collagen data from the Asistencia de San Pedro y San Pablo humans. If plotted in figure 6.1, these values would fall in the center of the graph, between the wild-animal-dominated and marine-dominated ellipses, suggesting a mixed terrestrial-marine diet. There are many different dietary combinations that could lead to a similar outcome, such as a mixture of C_3 and C_4 plants from fertilized fields. In this respect, the sulfur isotope data are particularly valuable. The higher $\delta^{34}S$ values, and positive correlation between $\delta^{34}S$ and $\delta^{13}C$ are most consistent with significant input of marine-derived protein.

When comparing the six adult females (Burials 3, 4, 5, 10, 12, and 13) against the two adult males (Burials 6 and 8), the males are slightly elevated in both $\delta^{13}C$ (-15.8‰ vs. -16.6‰) vs. and $\delta^{15}N$ (12.7‰ vs. 11.1‰), but slightly

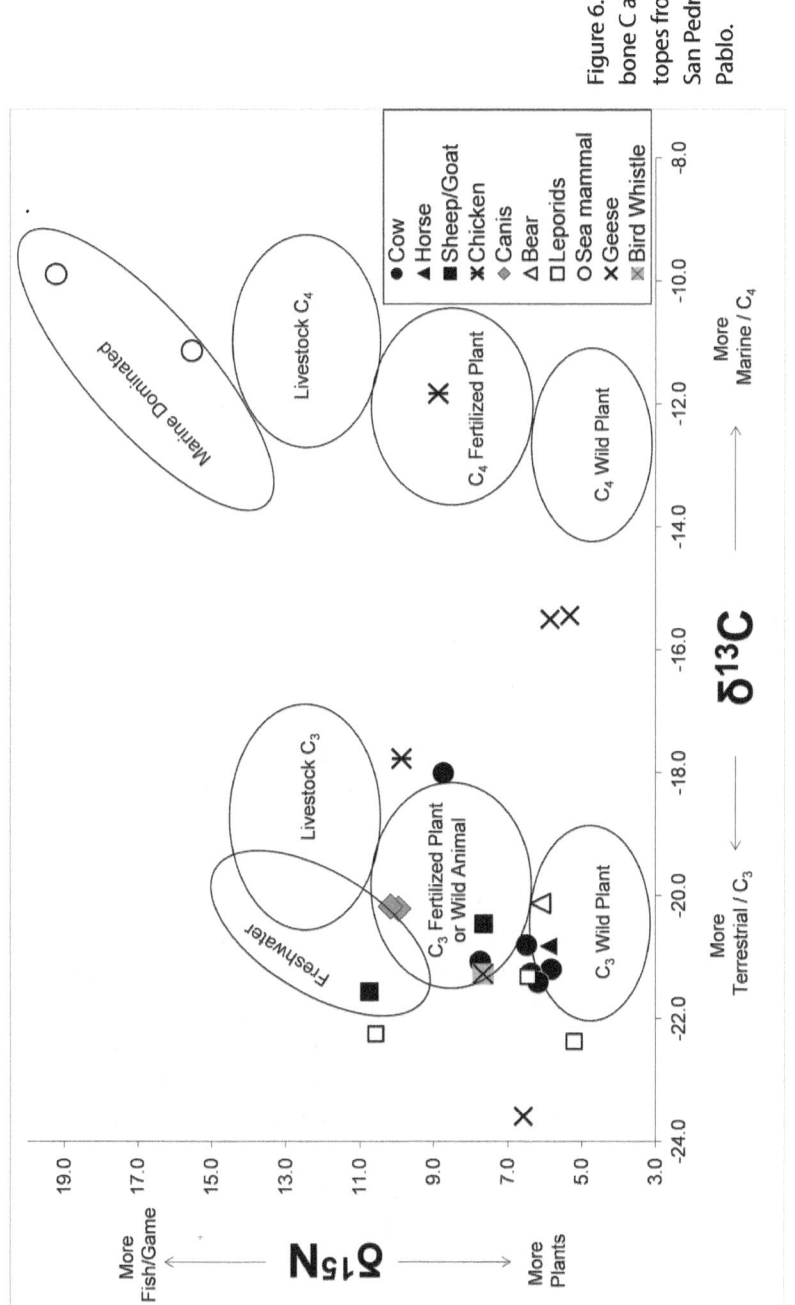

Figure 6.2. Animal bone C and N isotopes from Asistencia San Pedro y San Pablo.

Table 6.2. Bone collagen isotopes from San Pedro y San Pablo humans

Burial #	Age at Death	Sex	δ^{13}C	δ^{15}N	δ^{34}S	%C	%N	C/N	%S
2	Adol	Male	-16.8	11.7	13.8	26%	9%	3.4	0.15%
3	Mat A	Female	-17.4	10	9.9	28%	10%	3.3	0.15%
4	Mat A	Female	-16.4	11.3	14.1	36%	13%	3.3	0.20%
5	Mat A	Female	-16.6	11	11.8	42%	15%	3.3	0.23%
6	Yng A	Male	-16.4	12.5	12.7	41%	15%	3.3	0.23%
7	Infant	Indet.	-15.7	12.9	13.6	43%	15%	3.3	0.23%
8	Mat A	Male	-15.2	12.9	10	31%	11%	3.3	0.17%
9	Infant	Male	-17.6	11.5	13.5	33%	12%	3.2	0.19%
10	Mid A	Female	-17.2	11.2		20%	7%	3.3	
11	Child	Male	-17	12.2	12.8	43%	15%	3.3	0.22%
12	Yng A	Female	-16.7	11	13.5	44%	15%	3.4	0.22%
13	Yng A	Female	-15.6	11.9	13.7	41%	15%	3.3	0.22%
14	Child	Female	-16.2	10.6	12.9	44%	16%	3.3	0.22%
15	Adol	Male	-16.1	10.8	12.4	41%	15%	3.3	0.22%
16	Infant	Indet.	-15.7	10.9	13.9	42%	15%	3.3	0.22%

Note: Infant = 0–3 year; Child = 4–12 years; Adol. = Adolescent (13–17 years); Mat A = Mature Adult (ca. 46+ years); Mid A = Middle-Aged Adult (ca. 36–45 years); Yng A = Young Adult (ca. 18–25 years).

lower in δ^{34}S (11.3‰ vs. 12.6‰). The sample size is small, making interpretations of such comparisons subject to sampling biases. However, as much of the bone collagen signal for these adults will represent pre-contact period diets, it suggests males were consuming more high trophic–level marine foods (e.g., large fish vs. shellfish) and less terrestrial plant foods, relative to females. Higher levels of meat and/or fish consumption for males is a pattern documented at other pre-contact period sites in California (Eerkens et al. 2020, 2023).

In addition to the bone collagen, we also analyzed δ^{13}C and δ^{15}N in serial samples of teeth. For older individuals, these teeth would have formed before they entered the mission system, thereby representing their traditional diet. For some younger individuals, whose teeth were still growing at or shortly before the time of death, this will represent diet within the mission. Table 6.3 presents dentinal collage values for different age ranges for each individual. Burials 7 and 16 are not included in table 6.3 because they died as infants and did not have teeth.

From the tooth serial samples, we can construct something akin to a dietary life history for each individual. Figure 6.3 plots four such isotopic biographies for Burials 2 (upper left quadrat), 6 (upper right), 8 (lower left), and 13 (lower right). Within each quadrat, approximate age is plotted along the

Table 6.3. Age of weaning estimates, and $\delta^{13}C$ and $\delta^{15}N$ values across different life history windows

Burial #	Wean Age	Weaning Food		Age 4–6.9 years		Age 7–9.5 years		Age 9.5–12.9 years		Age 13–16.9 years		Age 17–21.5 years		Mission Diet	
		$\delta^{13}C$	$\delta^{15}N$	$\delta^{13}C$	$\delta^{15}N$	$\delta^{13}C$	$\delta^{15}N$	$\delta^{13}C$	$\delta^{15}N$	$\delta^{13}C$	$\delta^{15}N$	$\delta^{13}C$	$\delta^{15}N$	$\delta^{13}C$	$\delta^{15}N$
2	2	-14.8	12.5	-15.4	12.5	-15.6	12.5	-15.9	12.7	—	—	—	—	-15.6	12.8
3	N/A	—	—	-16.5	12	-16.4	11.7	-15.9	11.5	-15.4	12.8	-16.5	11.9	—	—
4	<2.9	-15.1	13.7	-15.1	14.1	-15.4	13.5	-15.8	13.2	-15.3	13.7	-15.4	13.4	—	—
5	2.2	-16.3	11.3	-16.7	11.4	-16.3	12.4	-16.1	12	-16.2	11.8	-16.9	11.3	—	—
6	3.4	-16.4	11.4	-15.9	12	-15.8	13.1	-15.9	13.3	-15.8	13.4	-16.5	12.3	-16.8	11.9
8	2.1	-15	14.2	-14.3	14.5	-14.3	14.9	-14.4	14.2	-13.9	15.1	-14.3	15.2	—	—
9	Not	—	—	—	—	—	—	—	—	—	—	—	—	-17.3	13.3
10	2.6	-16.6	11.7	-15.4	13.6	-16	13.2	-16.8	10.8	-17	10.7	-16.5	12.9	—	—
11	N/A	—	—	-18	12.7	—	—	—	—	—	—	v	—	-18.2	12.6
12	1.5	-16	13.7	-15.8	13	-15.7	12.8	-15.3	13.4	-16.3	12.6	—	—	-16.7	13
13	2.1	-15.9	13.5	-15.7	13.5	-16.1	12.8	-15.5	12.9	-15.3	14	-15.7	13.7	-16	12
14	N/A	—	—	-15.5	13.6	-15.4	13.8	-15.5	13.7	-15.9	13.5	—	—	-15.9	13.5
15	3.2	-16.5	10.9	-16.5	11	-17.3	11.1	-16.2	13.2	-16.1	12.4	—	—	-17.3	11.1

Note. Not = Not yet weaned at death.

x-axis, with $\delta^{15}N$ plotted as circles in the upper half of the quadrat and $\delta^{13}C$ as triangles in the lower half. Bone collagen values are plotted as X marks on the right of each age series. Marked changes in isotopic values are likely to correspond to behavioral changes for an individual. For example, weaning is typically represented by a marked decrease in $\delta^{15}N$, that is, a drop in trophic level, in the early growing sections of the permanent M1 (see Eerkens et al. 2011). All four individuals in figure 6.3 show this drop in $\delta^{15}N$ across the early growing tooth sections. Assuming the terminal point of the drop marks the cessation of breastmilk, we can then estimate an age of weaning. Table 6.3 presents age of weaning estimates for all individuals with relatively complete M1 teeth. For a few individuals, such as Burials 3, 11, and 14, we did not have enough in-tact serial sections to generate an age at weaning estimate, due either to occlusal wear that removed the earliest-forming sections or because of poor preservation. As well, Burial 9 appears to have died before being weaned.

Other shifts in isotopic values may correspond to changes in residence location. For example, marked changes in $\delta^{13}C$ may correspond to residential moves to areas with greater (higher $\delta^{13}C$) or less (lower $\delta^{13}C$) access to marine foods. For example, male Burial 8 (lower left quadrant in figure 6.3), shows a marked increase and then decrease in $\delta^{13}C$ (and $\delta^{15}N$) between the ages of fourteen and twenty-one, suggesting he ate significantly more marine foods during this window in his life. Because he died as a mature adult in his fifties, this dietary shift would have occurred in the 1740s or 1750s, before missions were established in Northern California. Thus, rather than a dietary shift associated with a move into the missions, this may reflect instead a residential move associated with his marriage. For example, he may have married a woman living in a different village that was closer to the Pacific Ocean with greater access to marine foods around age fourteen, spent a number of years there, perhaps performing bride service or until after his first child was born, and then moved back to his natal village.

By contrast, Burial 2, who was likely born and lived his entire life within the mission, shows little change in $\delta^{13}C$ after he was weaned. The lack of major shifts in $\delta^{13}C$ is consistent with a single place of residence, and indicates a consistent and stable amount of marine and/or maize in his diet.

Burials 6 and 13 were both young adults at death, with the former displaying still-growing M3 roots, and the latter just-completed M3 roots at the time of death. As shown in figure 6.3, both individuals show significant shifts in diet in late teenage years, marked by decreases in both $\delta^{13}C$ and $\delta^{15}N$. Burial 6 is tentatively identified as an individual baptized at age fifteen and dying at age seventeen (see chapter 11). The decrease in $\delta^{13}C$ and $\delta^{15}N$ beginning around age fourteen for Burial 6 accords well with the timing of his baptism,

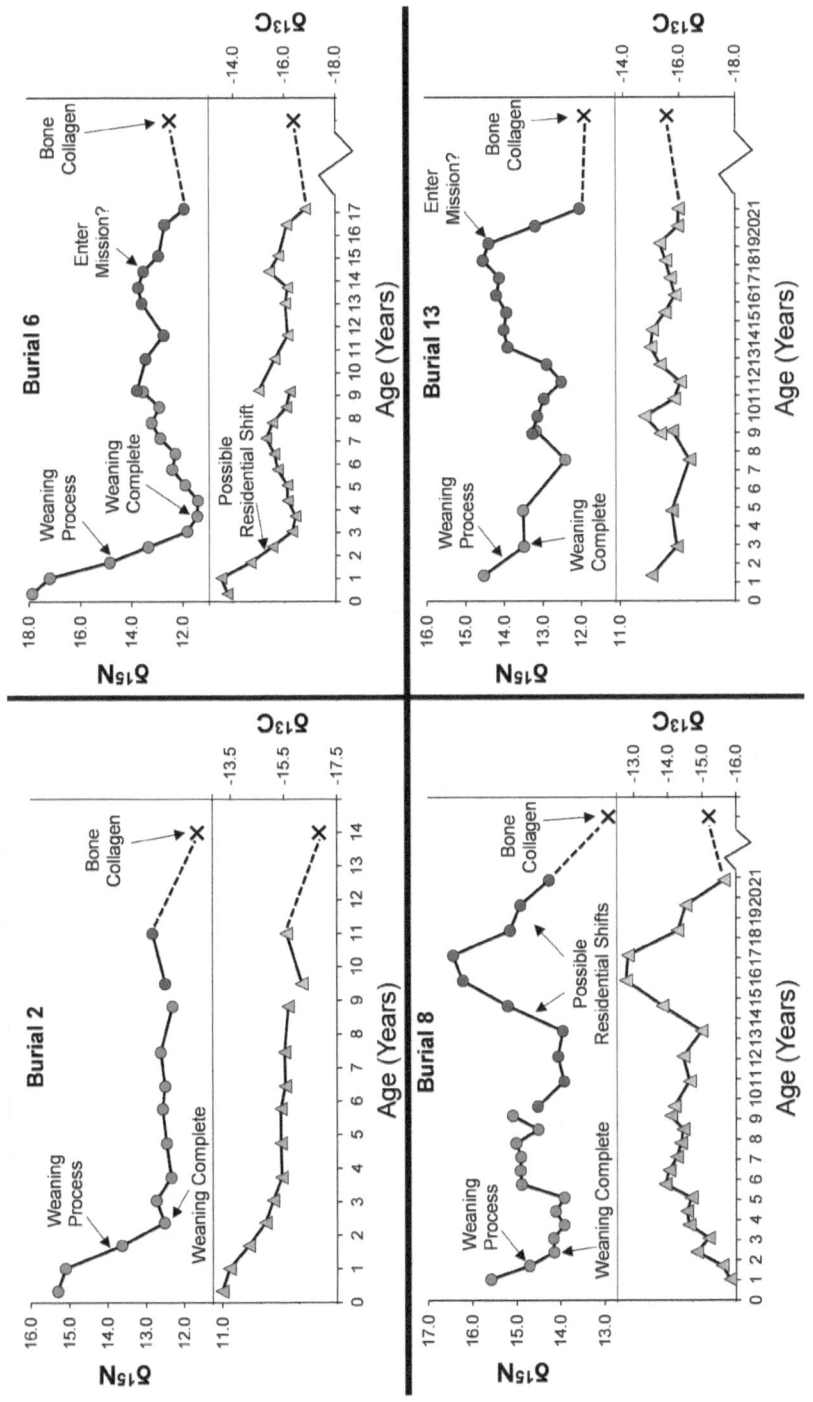

Figure 6.3. Isotopic life histories for Burials 2, 6, 8, and 13.

both two to three years before his death, and could be associated with a dietary shift when he entered the mission. Likewise, the decrease in $\delta^{13}C$, and especially $\delta^{15}N$, for Burial 13 around age nineteen, approximately two to four years before her death, would also accord with a residential move to the mission and a transition to a more mission-based diet with less marine and more plant-derived foods.

Using this approach, we were able to derive an isotopic estimate for the "Mission Diet" for seven individuals who had still-growing or just-completed teeth at the time of death. Collagen extracted from the terminal sections of these teeth should represent $\delta^{13}C$ and $\delta^{15}N$ dietary composition close to the time of death, in other words, that while within the mission system. These estimates are given in the final column of table 6.3.

Establishing the Mission Period diet for individuals allows us to compare pre- and post-mission dietary composition for a subset of the individuals in the study. Figure 6.4 plots the mission diets of six adults as large triangles (with the burial number inside the triangle). Small triangles, connected by a line, represent what we estimate their isotopic composition was before entering the mission. The pre-mission diet reflects diet at approximately nine to thirteen years of age, again based on dentinal collage values. The trajectory of the connecting line thus indicates directional change in the diet of these six individuals from their traditional to mission diet.

As shown in figure 6.4, for all six adult individuals, the Mission Period diet is lower in $\delta^{13}C$ (an average of 0.7‰ lower), and for five of six lower in $\delta^{15}N$ (an average of 0.8‰ lower). This shift is consistent with a decrease in marine food, and an increase in plant-derived foods and/or domesticated animals raised on C_3 plants.

The two infants, Burials 7 and 16, are plotted as square symbols in figure 6.4. Assuming the infants were stillborn, or had not been breastfeeding for very long before their deaths, the bone collagen isotopic values should correlate with the diet of their mothers, most likely while in the mission. As shown, the isotopic values fall close to other adults, suggesting mothers of the infants were eating a mixed diet, most likely a combination of marine and terrestrial-based foods.

Figure 6.4 plots also the two children, Burials 9 and 11, as diamonds. Proteomic analyses in chapter 4 indicate both are male. These boys stand somewhat apart isotopically from the adults. The low $\delta^{13}C$ values, paired with still relatively high $\delta^{15}N$, place both boys within the "livestock C_3 dominated" ellipse. Marine foods seem to have played only a small role in their diets.

Interestingly, comparison of the pre- to post-contact isotopic data show that the pre-contact pattern of adult males having higher $\delta^{13}C$ and $\delta^{15}N$ than

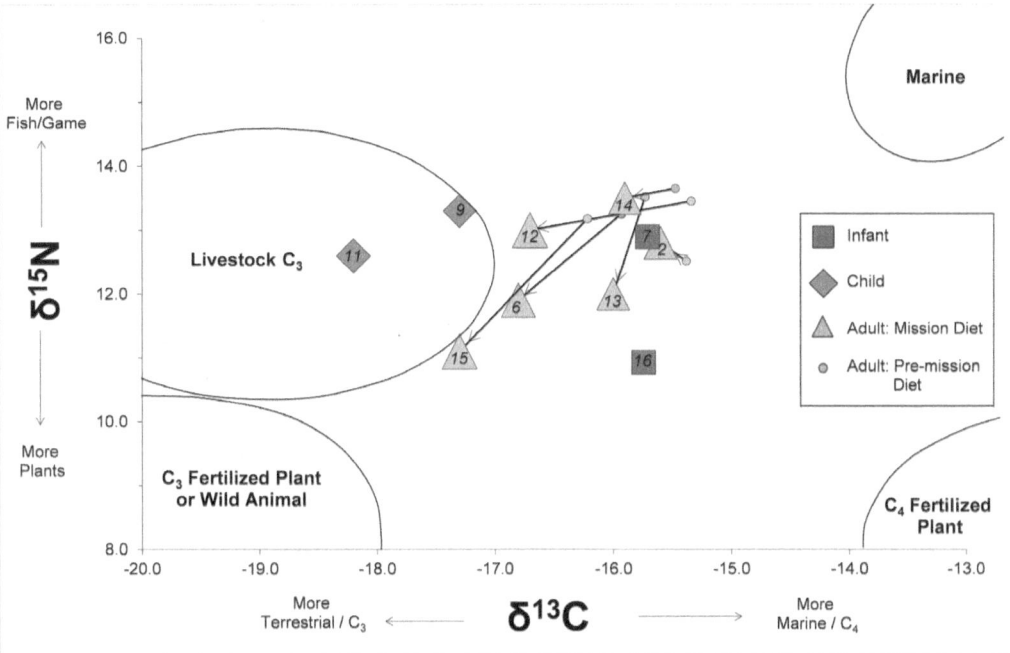

Figure 6.4. Comparison of isotopic composition of precontact (circles) and Mission Period diets for older individual (triangles) who were born outside the mission but had forming or recently formed dental tissues at the time of death (trailing lines show directional change in diet across the temporal transition), two children (diamonds), and two infants (squares).

females, is reversed in the Mission Period. We are limited to just three males (Burials 2, 6, and 15) and three females (Burials 12, 13, and 14) for such a comparison, but Mission Period female $\delta^{13}C$ is 0.4‰ higher (-16.2‰ vs. -16.6‰) and $\delta^{15}N$ is 0.9‰ higher (12.8‰ vs. 11.9‰) than males. This pattern is reinforced by the two infants, whose bone collagen values likely reflect the mother's mission diet, who are both higher in $\delta^{13}C$ relative to the male adults. Overall, this suggests that within the mission, females were eating more higher-trophic level foods, perhaps in the form of greater proportion of marine food. As well, this suggests that male diets were more dynamic across the pre-contact vs. Mission Period transition, while female diets were more stable.

Conclusions

Stable isotope data from teeth and bone provide insight into pre–Mission Period diets, and for some individuals, how that changed after entering the mission. Results indicate that marine foods were important in the diets of most individuals who were buried at the asistencia, both before and during the Mission Period. The highest $\delta^{13}C$ and $\delta^{34}S$ values among the individuals indicate marine foods may have contributed over 50 percent of the protein in a year in the pre-mission time period, while the lowest pre-contact values indicate about 25 percent in a year, with an average near 35 percent. Here, marine foods could come from both the Pacific coast as well as the San Francisco Bay, though given the proximity of the coast, the former seems more likely.

This finding contrasts with individuals buried at Mission Santa Clara. As shown in figure 6.1, bone collagen at this more inland location is generally lower for $\delta^{13}C$ (on average by 1.5‰) and $\delta^{15}N$ (on average by 2.5‰) compared to those from Asistencia de San Pedro y San Pablo. Not surprisingly, this indicates that individuals in the interior in Santa Clara Valley had much less access to marine foods, even from San Francisco Bay, and were probably eating higher amounts of plant-derived foods, much from fertilized fields, and likely included some C_4 foods (i.e., maize).

Within the Asistencia de San Pedro y San Pablo sample, we examined in detail six younger adults who were born before the mission system started, and thus had recorded a traditional dietary signal in their earlier growing dental tissues. These individuals died at the mission while some teeth were still growing, therein also recording their diet from the Mission Period, and allowing a comparison of diet across this transition. For these individuals, the pre-mission diets fall along the axis between the "marine-dominated" and "C_3 wild plant dominated" ellipses, suggesting a mix of plants and marine animals (including shellfish) in the traditional diet. Notably, isotopic values do not overlap data at pre-contact sites in modern-day San Francisco (e.g., CA-SFR-191; unpublished data in possession of the author which show much higher $\delta^{13}C$ and $\delta^{15}N$ values), nor with data from pre-contact sites in San Jose and the Santa Clara Valley (e.g., CA-SCL-128 and -287 which show much lower $\delta^{13}C$ and $\delta^{15}N$ values; Bartelink 2014; Greenwald et al. 2016). Instead, they closely match isotopic data from other pre-contact individuals from the central part of the San Francisco Peninsula (e.g., CA-SMA-78 and -160; see Goring et al. 2020). From these findings, we suggest the people buried at the asistencia were likely native to the central peninsular area, and not from more distant or inland localities.

Change across the pre-contact to Mission Period indicates a reduction in both marine foods (as indicated by lower $\delta^{13}C$) and trophic position (as indicated by lower $\delta^{15}N$). Using the simple linear mixing model proposed by Bartelink (2006), the 0.7‰ decrease in $\delta^{13}C$ corresponds to an average absolute reduction by about 5 percent in marine-derived protein within the Mission Period, or from about 35 percent to 30 percent. Similarly, assuming a 4‰ difference between trophic levels, the 0.8‰ decrease in $\delta^{15}N$ corresponds to a relative increase in plant protein by about 15–25 percent compared to animal sources of protein, depending somewhat on the precise original mixture of foods. The direction of this dietary shift is toward isotopic data observed among many nineteenth-century Euro-Americans from San Francisco (figure 6.1). However, asistencia diets are still distinct isotopically from the latter. In particular, the lower $\delta^{15}N$ values among Native people, relative to Euro-Americans, suggests the former were eating more plant-derived foods and less meat than the latter.

Male diets seem to have been more dynamic across the pre-contact to Mission Period transition, while female diets were more stable. The sample sizes are small, but this may indicate more of a persistence of traditional diet among females, versus a greater change for males. Indeed, the two younger children (Burials 9 and 11), both males, stand apart from all the other individuals. These two children seem to have adopted a more Euro-American-like diet, with apparently little seafood, little to no maize, and more terrestrial animal foods than other Native people within the asistencia.

Finally, the data from faunal remains provide insight into foddering of domesticated animals within the asistencia. Most animals seem to have been eating wild C_3 foods, likely grasses and other shrubs that grew naturally in the region. However, one chicken was fed primarily maize, while a second chicken and one cow seem to have been eating at least some maize as well.

In short, isotopic data indicate that diets for Native people within the asistencia incorporated a greater proportion of plant products, likely plants from fertilized fields, and greater amounts of terrestrial (versus marine) animals, compared to their traditional diets. Yet, people still ate a significant number of traditional foods, especially those from marine environments, that set them apart from nineteenth-century Euro-Americans and from Native people at Mission Santa Clara. In this respect, both persistence of some traditional foods, especially among women, as well as incorporation of new mission food products, especially among male children, seems to have characterized dietary patterns for individuals who were buried at Asistencia de San Pedro y San Pablo.

Acknowledgments

We thank Madisen Webb and Nikki Karapanos who helped process the bone and tooth samples, the late Dwight Simons who identified some of the faunal remains, and the UC Davis Stable Isotope Facility for assistance in analyzing collagen samples. Funding for some of the isotopic analyses comes from a grant from the National Science Foundation (BCS 2021256).

References

Ambrose, Stanley H.
1986   Stable Carbon and Nitrogen Isotope Analysis of Human and Animal Diet in Africa. *Journal of Human Evolution* 15:707–731.
1991   Effects of Diet, Climate and Physiology on Nitrogen Isotope Abundances in Terrestrial Foodwebs. *Journal of Archaeological Science* 18:293–317.
Ambrose, Stanley, Jane Buikstra, and Harold W. Krueger
2003   Status and Gender Differences in Diet at Mound 72, Cahokia, Revealed by Isotopic Analysis of Bone. *Journal of Anthropological Archaeology* 22:217–226.
Bartelink, Eric J.
2006   Resource Intensification in Pre-Contact Central California: A Bioarchaeological Perspective on Diet and Health Patterns among Hunter-Gatherers from the Lower Sacramento Valley and San Francisco Bay. Unpublished PhD Dissertation, Department of Anthropology, Texas A&M University.
2009   Late Holocene Dietary Change in the San Francisco Bay Area: Stable Isotope Evidence for an Expansion in Diet Breadth. *California Archaeology* 1:227–252.
2011   Dietary Patterns at Mission Santa Clara De Asís (CA-SCL-30/H): Stable Isotope Analysis of an Ohlone Neophyte Cemetery Sample, 1781–1818. In *Final Report on the Burial and Archaeological Data Recovery Program Conducted on a Portion of a Mission Santa Clara Indian Neophyte Cemetery (1781–1818): Clareño Muwékma Ya Túnneŝte Nómmo [Where the Indians are Buried] Site (CA-SCL-30/H), Located in the City of Santa Clara, Santa Clara County, California*, edited by Leventhal A. et al., 1–10.
2014   Stable Isotope Analysis and Paleodiet of an Ancestral Ohlone Human Burial from Róokoš Tiwoo Koro'Ayttakiš (Tule Elk Leg Woman) from Thámien Rúmmey-Tka [Thámien (Guadalupe) River Site] (CA-SCL-128), Santa Clara County, California. Report prepared for Alan Leventhal, San Jose State University. 1–11.
Beasley M. M., A. M. Martinez, D. D. Simons, E. J. Bartelink
2013   Paleodietary Analysis of a San Francisco Bay Area Shellmound: Stable Carbon and Nitrogen Isotope Analysis of Late Holocene Humans from the Ellis Landing Site (CA-CCO-295). *Journal of Archaeological Science* 40:2084–2094.
Boutton, Thomas W.
1991   Stable Carbon Isotope Ratios of Natural Materials: II. Atmospheric, Terrestrial, Marine, and Freshwater Environments. In *Carbon Isotope Techniques*, edited by David C. Coleman and Brian Fry, 173–185. Academic Press, San Diego.
Cerling, Thure E., James R. Ehleringer, and John M. Harris
1998   Carbon Dioxide Starvation, the Development of C_4 Ecosystems and Mammalian Evolution. *Proceedings of the Royal Society of London B* 353:159–171.

Cloern, James E., Elizabeth A. Canuel, and David Harris
2002 Stable Carbon and Nitrogen Isotope Composition of Aquatic and Terrestrial Plants of the San Francisco Bay Estuarine System. *Limnology and Oceanography* 47:713–729.

Croteau, Marie-Noële, Samuel N. Luoma, and Robin A. Stewart
2005 Trophic Transfer of Metals along Freshwater Food Webs: Evidence of Cadmium Biomagnification in Nature. *Limnology and Oceanography* 50: 1511–1519.

DeNiro, Michael J.
1985 Postmortem Preservation and Alteration of In Vivo Bone-Collagen Isotope Ratios in Relation to Paleodietary Reconstruction. *Nature* 317: 806–809.

DeNiro, Michael J., and Samuel Epstein
1981 Influence of Diet on the Distribution of Nitrogen Isotopes in Animals. *Geochimica et Cosmochimica Acta* 45:341–351.

Dietler, Michael
2007 Culinary Encounters: Food Identity, and Colonialism. In *The Archaeology of Food and Identity*, edited by K. Twiss, 218–242. Southern Illinois University Press, Carbondale.

Dietz, Steven A. (editor), with M. Bredemeyer, R. Milliken, D. Simons, and L. White
1979 Report of Archaeological Investigations at Sanchez Adobe Park Historic District. Report prepared for the County of San Mateo, California.

Dudgeon, John V., and Monica Tromp
2014 Diet, Geography and Drinking Water in Polynesia: Microfossil Research from Archaeological Human Dental Calculus, Rapa Nui (Easter Island). *International Journal of Osteoarchaeology* 24:634–648.

Eerkens, J. W., A. G. Berget, and E. J. Bartelink
2011 Estimating Weaning and Early Childhood Diet from Serial Micro-Samples of Dentin Collagen. *Journal of Archaeological Science* 38: 3101–3111.

Eerkens, Jelmer W., Madeline Mackie, and Eric J. Bartelink
2013 Brackish Water Foraging and Isotopic Landscapes in Central California: Dietary Reconstruction in a Late Holocene Hunter-Gatherer Population in Suisun Marsh. *Journal of Archaeological Science* 40:3270–3281.

Eerkens, J. W., E. J. Bartelink, S. Talcott, and B. E. Hull
2020 The Evolution of Male and Female Diets: Stable Isotope Insights on the Intensification Process in Central California. In *Cowboy Ecologist: Essays in Honor of Robert L. Bettinger*, edited by R. S. Bakhtiary, T. L. Jones, and M. G. Delacorte, 271–287. Center for Archaeological Research at Davis, Davis, CA.

Eerkens, Jelmer W., Bryna Hull, Jessica Morales, Tom Little Bear Nason, Barry Price, Candice Ralston, Seetha Reddy, Ann Marie Sayer, Kanyon Sayer-Roods, and Fred Sogovia
2022 The Role of Marine Foods in Ancient Diets across a Coastal to Inland Transect of Monterey County, California. *Journal of California and Great Basin Anthropology* 42:159–176.

Eerkens, Jelmer W., A. Tichinin, N. Karapanos, A. Campbell-Grey, A. M. Firenzi, E. J. Bartelink, A. M. Leventhal, M. V. Arellano, and B. DeOrnellas
2023   Contrasting Male and Female Dietary Life Histories: A Case Study at an Ancestral Muwekma Ohlone Heritage Site in San Jose, California. *Human Biology* 94: in press.

Ehleringer, James R., Anthony E. Hall, and Graham D. Farquhar
1993   *Stable Isotopes and Plant Carbon-Water Relations*. Academic Press, New York.

El-Zaatari, Sireen
2010   Occlusal Microwear Texture Analysis and the Diets of Historical/Prehistoric Hunter-Gatherers. *International Journal of Osteoarchaeology* 20:67–87.

Farquhar, Graham D., James R. Ehleringer, and Kerry T. Hubick
1989   Carbon Isotope Discrimination and Photosynthesis. *Annual Review of Plant Physiology and Plant Molecular Biology* 40:503–537.

Fischler, Claude
1988   Food, Self, and Identity. *Social Science Information* 27(2): 275–292.

Froehle, Andrew W., Corina M. Kellner, and Margaret J. Schoeninger
2009   A Three-Variable Analysis of Carbon and Nitrogen Isotope Values Discriminates between Dietary Energy and Protein Sources in Prehistoric Humans. *American Journal of Physical Anthropology* 48:130.

Froehle, Andrew W., Corina M. Kellner, and Margaret J. Schoeninger
2010   FOCUS: Effect of Diet and Protein Source on Carbon Stable Isotope Ratios in Collagen: Follow up to Warinner and Tuross (2009). *Journal of Archaeological Science* 37:2662–2670.

Geiger, Maynard J., and Clement W. Meighan.
1976   *As The Padres Saw Them: California Indian Life and Customs as Reported by the Franciscan Missions, 1813–1815*. Santa Barbara Mission Archive Library, Santa Barbara.

Goring, D., J. W. Eerkens, C. Canzonieri, I. Zwierlein, M. Zimmer, and E. J. Bartelink.
2020   Insights into Intragroup Variation in Precontact Paleodiet: A Middle Period Example from San Mateo County. *Proceedings of the Society for California Archaeology* 34:1–14.

Greenwald A. M., J. W. Eerkens, E. J. Bartelink, A. Leventhal, and R. Cambra
2016   Stable Isotope Evidence of Episodic Access to Marine Resources at CA-SCL-287. In *Reconstructing Lifeways in Ancient California: Stable Isotope Evidence of Foraging Behavior, Life History Strategies, and Kinship Patterns*, edited by A. M. Greenwald and G. R. Burns, 59–71. CARD Publication No. 18, UC Davis.

Greenwald, Alexandra M.
2017   Isotopic Reconstruction of Weaning Age and Childhood Diet Among Ancient California Foragers: Life History Strategies and Implications for Demographics, Resource Intensification, and Social Organization. PhD Dissertation. Department of Anthropology, University of California Davis.

Grine, Frederick E., Matt Sponheimer, Peter S. Ungar, Julia Lee-Thorp, and Mark F. Teaford
2012   Dental Microwear and Stable Isotopes Inform the Paleoecology of Extinct Hominins. *American Journal of Physical Anthropology* 148:285–317.

Guiry, Erik J., and Paul Szpak
2021   Improved Quality Control Criteria for Stable Carbon and Nitrogen Isotope Measurements of Ancient Bone Collagen. *Journal of Archaeological Science* 132: 105416.

Hedges, Robert E. M., John G. Clement, C. David L. Thomas, and Tamsin C. O'Connell
2007   Collagen Turnover in the Adult Femoral Mid-Shaft: Modeled from Anthropogenic Radiocarbon Tracer Measurements. *American Journal of Physical Anthropology* 133:808–816.

Hillson, Simon
1996   *Dental Anthropology.* Cambridge University Press, Cambridge.

Noe, Sarah J.
2023   Subsistence and Persistence: Indigenous Foodways Within Mission Santa Clara de Asís. *California Archaeology* 1–39.

Manolagas, Stavros C.
2000   Birth and Death of Bone Cells: Basic Regulatory Mechanisms and Implications for the Pathogenesis and Treatment of Osteoporosis. *Endocrinology Reviews* 21:115–137.

Mickleburgh, Hayley L., and Jaime R. Pagán-Jiménez
2012   New Insights into the Consumption of Maize and Other Food Plants in the Pre-Columbian Caribbean from Starch Grains Trapped in Human Dental Calculus. *Journal of Archaeological Science* 39:2468–2478.

Minagawa, Masao, and Eitaro Wada
1984   Step-Wise Enrichment of ^{15}N Along Food Chains: Further Evidence and the Relationship between δ^{15}N and Animal Age. *Geochimica et Cosmochimica Acta* 48:1135–1140.

Montanari, Massimo
2006   *Food Is Culture.* Columbia University Press.

Popper, Virginia S.
2016   Change and Persistence: Mission Neophyte Foodways at Selected Colonial Alta California Institutions. *Journal of California and Great Basin Anthropology* 36: 5–25.

Poulson, Simon R., Susan C. Kuzminsky, G. Richard Scott, Vivien G. Standen, Bernardo Arriaza, Ivan Muñoz, and Lindsay Dorio
2013   Paleodiet in Northern Chile Through the Holocene: Extremely Heavy δ^{15}N Values in Dental Calculus Suggest a Guano-Derived Signature? *Journal of Archaeological Science* 40:4576–4585.

Price, T. Douglas, James H. Burton, and R. Alexander Bentley
2002   The Characterization of Biologically Available Strontium Isotope Ratios for the Study of Prehistoric Migration. *Archaeometry* 44:117–135.

Reddy, Seetha N.
2015   Feeding Family and Ancestors: Persistence of Traditional Native American Lifeways During the Mission Period in Coastal Southern California. *Journal of Anthropological Archaeology* 37: 48–66.

Richards, Michael P., Ben T. Fuller, Matt Sponheimer, Todd Robinson, and Linda Ayliffe
2003   Sulphur Isotopes in Palaeodietary Studies: A Review and Results from a Con-

trolled Feeding Experiment. *International Journal of Osteoarchaeology* 13:37–45.

Schmidt, Christopher W., Jeremy J. Beach, Jacqueline I. McKinley, and Jacqueline T. Eng
2015   Distinguishing Dietary Indicators of Pastoralists and Agriculturists via Dental Microwear Texture Analysis. *Surface Topography: Metrology and Properties* 4: 014008.

Schoeninger, Margaret J.
1984   Nitrogen and Carbon Isotopic Composition of Bone Collagen from Marine and Terrestrial Animals. *Geochimica et Cosmochimica Acta* 48:625–639.
1995   Stable Isotope Studies in Human Evolution. *Evolutionary Anthropology* 4:83–98.

Schoeninger, Margaret J., Michael J. DeNiro, and Henrik Tauber
1983   Stable Nitrogen Isotope Ratios of Bone Collagen Reflect Marine and Terrestrial Components of Prehistoric Human Diet. *Science* 220 (4604):1381–1383.

Schwarcz, Henry P., Jerry Melbye, M. Anne Katzenberg, and Martin Knyf
1985   Stable Isotopes in Human Skeletons of Southern Ontario: Reconstructing Palaeodiet. *Journal of Archaeological Science* 12:187–206.

Schwarcz, Henry P., and Margaret J. Schoeninger
1991   Stable Isotope Analyses in Human Nutritional Ecology. *Yearbook of Physical Anthropology* 34:283–321.

Scott, G. Richard, and Simon R. Poulson
2012   Stable Carbon and Nitrogen Isotopes of Human Dental Calculus: A Potentially New Non-Destructive Proxy for Paleodietary Analysis. *Journal of Archaeological Science* 39:1388–1393.

Scott, Robert S., Peter S. Ungar, Torbjorn S. Bergstrom, Christopher A. Brown, Frederick E. Grine, Mark F. Teaford, and Alan Walker
2005   Dental Microwear Texture Analysis Shows Within-Species Diet Variability in Fossil Hominins. *Nature* 436(7051): 693.

Szpak, Paul, Jean-François Millaire, Christine D. White, and Fred J. Longstaffe
2012   Influence of Seabird Guano and Camelid Dung Fertilization on the Nitrogen Isotopic Composition of Field-Grown Maize (Zea mays). *Journal of Archaeological Science* 39:3721–3740.

Van der Merwe, Nikolaas J.
1982   Carbon Isotopes, Photosynthesis, and Archaeology: Different Pathways of Photosynthesis Cause Characteristic Changes in Carbon Isotope Ratios that Make Possible the Study of Prehistoric Human Diets. *American Scientist* 70(6): 596–606.

Vander Zanden, M. Jake, Vadeboncoeur, Yvonne, Chandra, Sudeep
2011   Fish Reliance on Littoral Benthic Resources and the Distribution of Primary Production in Lakes. *Ecosystems* 14: 894–903.

Vogel, J. C., and Nikolaas J. Van Der Merwe
1977   Isotopic Evidence for Early Maize Cultivation in New York State. *American Antiquity* 42:238–242.

Webb, Edith B.
1983   *Indian Life at the Old Missions.* University of Nebraska Press.
Wickstrom, Brian P., Stephen A. Dietz, and Thomas L. Jackson
1990   Archaeological Investigations Sanchez Adobe Park Historic District. Report prepared for the County of San Mateo, California.
Wright, Lori E.
2005   Identifying Immigrants to Tikal, Guatemala: Defining Local Variability in Strontium Isotope Ratios of Human Tooth Enamel. *Journal of Archaeological Science* 32:555–566.
Yiran Su, Jill S. Eubanks, Jelmer W. Eerkens, and Ramona Garibay
2023   Foraging Adaptation of Birds and Humans During the Medieval Climatic Anomaly: Stable Isotope Analysis of Avian Species from CA-ALA-554. *Proceedings of the Society for California Archaeology* 36:1–12.

7

Proteomic Analysis of Dental Calculus as Insight into Mission Period Diets in California

Kyle Burk, Glendon Parker, Jelmer W. Eerkens,
Christopher Canzonieri, Christopher Zimmer,
Monica V. Arellano, and Alan Leventhal

One of the key questions in the archaeology of colonialism in California is the extent to which Native people accepted introduced cultural practices, such as religion, technology, and diet, or continued traditional practices. This is especially pertinent for studies of Spanish missions and related sites, where colonial authorities sought to control the daily lives of Native people. Historical sources, such as mission records and diaries of Spanish fathers, provide one perspective on life in the mission. Research in the mid-1900s tended to emphasize such sources in dietary reconstruction (e.g., Geiger and Meighan 1976; Webb 1952).

More recent research recognizes that the Spanish may not have observed all traditional behaviors and that historical sources likely include particular biases, especially those of omission. As a result, much recent work emphasizes archaeological sources of data to provide an alternative perspective (e.g., Allen 1998; Kiel 2016; Noe 2023 Popper 2016; Reddy 2015). Although archaeology is subject to many of its own biases, they are different in nature than those provided in written historical sources. Together with still other perspectives (i.e., ethnographic, oral history), we can provide a more complete picture of dietary and other behaviors within the missions.

This chapter attempts to provide a modern archaeometric perspective on diet for individuals buried at the Asistencia de San Pedro y San Pablo. We focus on biomolecular signatures, fragments of proteins (peptides), preserved in dental calculus. These signatures are used to estimate the original food (or non-food) source. Because such studies have never been conducted in California before, we contextualize the results by comparing the asistencia individuals to a set of samples from precontact San Francisco Bay area. Doing so, we can estimate how diet may have changed from pre-mission to the Mission Period.

If peptides matching a known introduced species, such as cattle, were to be found in the asistencia Mission Period set but not the precontact set, it would provide support for the consumption of an introduced species, and hence a change in dietary practices. Likewise, if peptides matching a native species were found in both sample sets, it would suggest continuation of traditional dietary practices within the Mission system. However, as we note below, proteomic baseline data are not available for all species, especially many native Californian ones, and many species share ranges of protein sequence, making discrimination challenging. Thus, tracing the sources of peptide fragments requires caution in interpretation.

Dental Calculus

Dental plaque biofilm often accumulates within regions in the oral cavity that are relatively sheltered from the disruptive forces attendant to chewing, and is classified according to its position above or below the gingival margin (Marsh 2004). Plaque formation begins with salivary proteins adhering to the surface of teeth, forming a substrate that is colonized by a multitude of bacterial species; the complex interactions of which result in the development of an extracellular matrix (Marsh 2004; Warinner et al. 2015). This porous matrix is a scaffold for a wide range of macromolecules including bacterial proteins, polysaccharides, and extracellular DNA, and is both generated and maintained by the complementary biochemical processes of the disparate bacterial species living within the biofilm (Marsh 2004; Warinner et al. 2015).

Over time, calcium phosphate ions will periodically precipitate within both the plaque matrix as well as within some of the bacteria, resulting in a mineralized structure that itself serves as a surface upon which more plaque may develop, and the mineralization cycle repeats (Aghanashini et al. 2016, 42–50; Marsh 2004). A given specimen of calculus therefore represents a temporally ordered sequence of successive calcification events, each of which may trap and preserve host cellular material, as well as that from bacterial, viral, fungal, dietary, and environmental sources (Fagernäs et al. 2020; Warinner et al. 2014, 2015).

Preservation and Identification of Biomolecules

Calcified plaque is resistant to interference from microbes, enzymes, and non-acidic conditions, and can therefore preserve the structure of macromolecules trapped within it. These biomolecules can then be identified if subjected to modern analytical methods. Microscopic examination of dental calculus is effective in dietary reconstruction by identification of certain microfossils, such as starch or phytolith granules (Warinner et al. 2015) if they retain enough morphological differences between species or genera of interest.

However, many dietary constituents do not leave such traces, and as such their identification lies primarily in the realm of ancient DNA or protein analysis. Demineralization followed by specialized genomic or proteomic workflows can allow bioinformatic searches of DNA sequencing or mass spectrometry data against databases of reference sequences, thereby enabling identification of preserved biomolecules, providing information about an individual's life history, including host disease state or diet (Fagernäs et al. 2020; Sawafuji et al. 2020; Warinner et al. 2014).

Optimized genomic and proteomic workflows involve steps that render them incompatible with one another, and while experimentation has shown that is possible to collect both genomic and proteomic data from the same sample, the concessions made in experimental design to facilitate combined DNA and protein extraction seem to come at the cost of DNA yield and protein diversity (Fagernäs et al. 2020). This potential bias to data yield is not inherently prohibitive because dietary biomolecules are present at far lower abundance in dental calculus samples than are residua from host or oral microbiome sources (Warinner et al. 2014). An experiment aimed specifically at elucidating dietary composition from dental calculus may be better served by focusing solely on one class of biomolecule for optimized extraction. Given that proteins are more robust than DNA, and present at much higher copy number, a proteomic workflow was selected for the sample set described below.

Proteomic Context

Every species on Earth uses some subset of the same twenty amino acids to synthesize the proteins coded for in its genetic sequence. Akin to DNA, the "sense" of a protein is given not by an individual molecule—be it nucleotide or peptide—but by the sequence in which several such molecules are arranged. Sets of three nucleotides "code" for single amino acids, strings of which, covalently bonded to one another, form the primary structure of a protein. The sequence of amino acids in a protein therefore carries a degree of specificity to the organism whose genes coded for it. Many proteins are essential to basic biological necessities (such as carrying oxygen to muscles, or gene transcription), and may vary little if at all between species. However, because genetic variation between organisms tends to correspond to evolutionary distance (i.e., the number of generations elapsed since they last had a common ancestor), to the degree that distinguishing protein sequences are preserved in a sample, proteomic analysis is capable of phylogenetic discrimination.

Because dietary constituents were unknown, and because the proteins preserved in the dental calculus were expected to be degraded, the workflow was designed as a "shotgun proteomics" project. In brief, proteins encapsulated in calculus were solubilized by mechanical milling in acid, then digested with trypsin, and injected onto a liquid chromatography instrument coupled to a tandem mass spectrometer (LC-MS/MS). In this setup, peptides are separated by relative hydrophobicity, ionized, then fragmented, yielding predictable peptide fragments of around ten to twenty amino acids long. The resultant fragmentation spectra are compared to expected peptide sequences from a reference protein database for specific foodstuffs using bioinformatic software (Steen and Mann 2004). Sequences/spectra reported by the software were considered for comparison and validation (discussed more in the "analysis" section below) if they passed the standard quality threshold of 1 percent false discovery rate (FDR) (Eng et al. 2011).

Samples

This study focuses on dental calculus removed from the teeth of nine individuals from the Asistencia de San Pedro y San Pablo (see table 7.1). Because plaque accumulates over time, the sample is biased toward older individuals from the site, those who lived long enough to form substantial calculus deposits. Several of the infants and younger children did not contain calculus and could not be included in the study. Together, the sample represents six adult females (four older adults and two younger adults) and three males (one older adult, one younger adult, and one adolescent).

For context and comparison, dental calculus was also analyzed using the same methodology from eleven precontact individuals, six from CA-ALA-329 (dating 2,500 to 200 years ago) and five from CA-SFR-191 (dating 1,400 to 700 years ago). These precontact samples were analyzed with permission from Most Likely Descendant groups, the Muwekma Ohlone and Ramona Garibay (Him'Ren Ohlone), respectively. This enabled comparison of proteomic species searches between precontact and Mission Period sample

Table 7.1. Individuals and samples included in calculus proteomic study

Bur. #	Sex	Age at Death (yrs)	Calculus Weight	Tooth Associated
3	Fem.	45–50	17.3 mg	ULM3
4	Fem.	40–50	0.9 mg	Upper M3
5	Fem.	45–50	1.0 mg	LLM1
6	Male	18–25	8.1 mg	LLC + ULM1 + LLI2 (mixed)
8	Male	>45	5.0 mg	LRM2
10	Fem.	40–44	0.6 mg	LRM1
12	Fem.	20–25	0.8 mg	URM1
13	Fem.	20–24	6.5 mg	URC
15	Male	13–17	2.7 mg	Lower Incisor

sets to investigate change in dietary composition between time periods, as well as, in the case of species thought to have been introduced by the Spanish settlers, to provide a rough validation of such species.

Methods

Samples were processed using a method previously optimized for use on tooth enamel (Parker et al. 2018). Each sample was weighed into a milling tube containing seven ceramic beads and 200 uL of 1.2 M HCl. Tubes were milled in an Omni-International bead beater, centrifuged, and subject to reduction via addition of 6 uL of 0.5 M Dithiothreitol (DTT) at 56 C for 60 minutes. Alkylation was performed with addition of 12 uL of 0.5 M Iodoacetamide (IAA) and incubation for 60 minutes in the dark at room temperature, and the reaction was quenched with addition of 12 uL of 0.5 M DTT. Proteins were digested via sequencing grade trypsin and protease max for 20 hours at 600 RPM, then desalted and concentrated using Pierce C18 tips before separation by liquid chromatography and data acquisition using an Orbitrap Fusion Lumos Tribrid instrument.

LC-MS/MS data was processed first using the global proteome machine (GPM) to identify bacterial species from peptide sequences present in the calculus samples. Any bacterial species found in the samples that could be attributed to environmental contamination were eliminated from consideration as contributors to the oral milieu during the life of the individual. Two such environmental contaminant bacterial species, as well as several other non-eukaryotic species including normal human oral flora and potential pathogens were selected based on their presence in the GPM data for use as a comparator to potential dietary species in the data analysis stage using PEAKs xPRO bioinformatic software.

The bulk of the data analysis was conducted using search function results for all proteomes searched in PEAKs. These results were from a module designed to associate unassigned but high de novo scoring spectra to the database search results (Chen et al. 2020), with mass tolerances for combinations of over three hundred naturally occurring post-translational modifications. For this project, 3 PTMs per peptide were considered, with carbamidomethylation of Cysteine residues accounted as a fixed modification. Proteins matching sheep keratin and porcine trypsin were discounted, as porcine trypsin was used as the protease in this experiment, and both are represented in the common Repository of Adventitious Proteins (The Global Proteome Machine 2014).

Species Search Strategy

Identifying species based on peptide sequences was challenging for four main reasons, points we elaborate on below. First, proteins derived from plants and animals comprise only a minor component of calculus, with the majority representing bacterial species and humans (presumably from the host). Isolating the former from the latter was computationally and analytically challenging. Second, only certain types of animal proteins were recovered, principally collagen. Because collagen proteins are common across animal species, and are functionally important in animal survival, there are relatively few amino acid substitutions that distinguish collagen of one species from another (Richter et al. 2022). Third, due to computational and time limitations, it was necessary to limit the search to peptides associated with key species of interest, rather than all species present in global databases. Fourth, complete proteomes for many taxa that would have been of interest anthropologically are not available. This is especially true for species that are not economically important today. As a result, we had to either use closely related "stand-in" species for the species of interest. For example, we used quinoa (*Chenopodium quinoa*) and introduced wine grape (*Vitis vinifera*), for which proteomes do exist, as stand-ins for the native goosefoot (*Chenopodium californicum*) and native grape (*Vitis californica*), for which they do not.

For this study, we limited the search to two broad categories. First, we generated a list of species endemic to California and known to be important in precontact diets based on ethnographic and archaeological data. Second, we created a list of species that were introduced post-contact and are known to be important in Mission Period diets based on historical documents. The decision to restrict the species searched to a small subset of potential candidates (foregoing, for example, barley, spinach, rabbit, and many bird species) was made to provide reasonable analysis time. We chose goosefoot and grape, as discussed above. As well, we chose *Quercus lobata* (valley oak) as a stand-in for all acorns, recognizing that coastal oak groves will be dominated by other species (for which no proteomes exist), and *Oncorhynchus gorbuscha* (pink salmon) as a stand-in for all salmon, though chinook are dominant in most California environments. In the final analysis, *Enhydra lutris kenyoni* (sea otter), *Apis cerana* (honeybee), and *Brassica oleracea* (wild cabbage) were chosen due to their presence in an initial undirected GPM search result. *Fasciola hepatica* (liver fluke) was also chosen due to the initial GPM result, though as a substitute for the GPM reported species *Fasciola gigantica* (giant liver fluke), for which there was no proteome available. *Cervus canadensis* (elk), *Odocoileus virginianis* (deer), and *Mytilus californianus* (marine mussel) were included in the search as they are known components of Native diets.

Bos taurus (cow), *Sus scrofa* (pig), *Ovis aries* (sheep), *Capra hircus* (goat), *Vitis vinifera* (grape), *Zea mays* (maize), and *Gallus gallus* (chicken) were also chosen to represent common introduced species. In the course of data comparison and sequence refinement of the PEAKs search results, we also added *Castor canadensis* (beaver) and *Punica granatum* (pomegranate). While not considered as a distinct dietary contributor, the proteome of *Lupinus albus* (white lupin) was also searched—this was used to filter out ambiguous sequences from pomegranate that could not be distinguished from native lupine. PEAKs Xpro software was used to identify peptides within calculus samples, and all reference proteomes were obtained in FASTA format from NCBI.gov.

Phylogeny Refinement

As mentioned, a number of challenges complicated assignment of recovered peptide sequences to distinct dietary sources. There was no proteome available for several species of interest. Consequently, no sequences were available for to search within the bioinformatic software for direct peptide evidence of native Californian bighorn sheep, nor for pronghorn antelope, either of which could have served as a "competitor" proteomes for domesticated sheep and goat. By Occam's razor, it is easier to assign species in the precontact data set. Thus, a match to artiodactyl likely represents a small number of possibilities (pronghorn, elk, or deer), but a much larger set including both native and introduced species in the Mission data set.

Because the proteomes searched in PEAKs represent only a fraction of all available proteomes—which itself represents only a fraction of the species diversity on the planet—there remained a need to determine what other species ought to be considered before assigning a given result as a dietary contributor. Because species contain many overlapping protein sequences, the determination of species candidacy was made on the basis of parsimony. This was achieved by taking validated spectra/sequence candidates from the PEAKs comparative database search which appeared unique to a single species (or to a set of two closely related species in the case of *Capra hircus* and *Ovis aries*, or *Cervus canadensis* and *Odocoileus virginianis*) and applying those sequences to the Basic Local Alignment Search Tool (BLAST) in both NCBI and Uniprot databases. We only accepted species that were common between the two analyses as candidates for a given peptide sequence. Accepted peptide sequences were then assigned so as to be accounted for by the minimum number of geographically feasible species, and reported at the highest level of resolution supported (i.e., family, genus, or species). For example, while a peptide sequence matching more generally bird, but also Burmese python and Chinese alligator, given the geographic context, the avian designation is the most likely.

Although we argue that species selection by sequence parsimony is the most reasonable means of discriminating a dietary component's presence or absence, it is difficult to assign a metric that establishes the quantity or intensity of such a signal. A summative ion current "signal" metric risks overestimating those dietary constituents whose sequences were most convincing by parsimony. We report a more conservative measure when comparing differential dietary "contributions" to each sample, the simple raw count of the number of distinct ions (ionized peptides) that made up the sequences parsimoniously classified.

Results

The twenty candidate floral/faunal proteomes yielded only a small number of sufficiently distinctive spectral matches to be carried forward for sequence validation. Of those that did, almost all were faunal in origin. Most floral species—including *Quercus lobata*, consumption of which (in the form of acorns) is attested to in anthropological sources (Popper 2016)—could not be resolved to peptide sequences with better matching to fragmentation spectra than the bacterial or human proteomes. Those peptides that were confidently distinguished nonetheless tended to correspond to the same class of protein or to overlap in sequence with one another. For validation, therefore, in accordance with the principle of parsimony, any overlapping sequences assigned to the same protein were combined, and the "total" peptide sequence was validated by cross-reference in NCBI and Uniprot Blast tools.

The majority of peptides supporting the presence of deer and elk in the diet could not be resolved from one another in the fragmentation comparison in PEAKs software, though in the validation step, deer was slightly more supported in the precontact calculus samples. Neither was outperformed by the pronghorn antelope sequence.

Peptides matching pig, goat, sheep, and grape were identified in the precontact sample set. While the sequences for pig clustered at the validation stage with beaver by parsimony, the two peptides matching grape and several matching sheep or goat remained distinguished. Proteomes from native Californian grape (*Vitis californica*) and sheep (*Ovis canadensis* or close relative) were not available to attempt to refine the level of specificity, so any occurrence of peptides from these species in the Mission Period dataset contains an inherent ambiguity (i.e., could be native, could be introduced). In the precontact dataset, these must match related species not present in the selected proteome search.

Three peptides matching the pomegranate proteome were identified in the precontact set, but as this was geographically impossible, the assignment was discounted in favor of parsimonious assignment of two of those peptides to grape. The remaining peptide—given that the range of possible species candidates could not be narrowed beyond geographic context—was identified simply as an ambiguous plant sequence. For pomegranate in the Mission Period dataset, one peptide sequence overlapped with that identified in the precontact set, but there were sufficient additional peptides to indicate parsimonious association of the sequences with pomegranate.

Mission Period Samples

Forty-two peptides representing ten of the twenty candidate floral and faunal proteomes were compiled into twenty-three sequences prior to cross-referencing NCBI and Uniprot BLAST results. Comparison of all species candidates that could account for those sequences, when grouped parsimoniously, indicated support for the presence of several sources in the plaque matrix.

Table 7.2 summarizes results. Deer (*Cervus canadensis* / *Odocoileus virginianis*), or a closely related species, was found in two of nine individuals. Otter (*Enhydra lutris kenyoni*), mink (*Neovison vison*), or a closely related species was found in eight of nine individuals. Huchen / Salmon (*Salmo* / *Huchen* / *Oncorhynchus*), or a closely related species, was found in one of nine individuals. Cow (*Bos taurus*), or a closely related species, was found in three of nine individuals. Fowl of indeterminate species was found in three of nine individuals. Beaver (*Castor canadensis*), or a closely related species,

Table 7.2. Proteomic results from Mission Period human dental calculus at the asistencia

Bur.	Sex / Age	Deer	Otter	Fish	Cow	Parasite/Bacteria	Fowl	Beaver	Pome-granate
3	F / 45–50	—	—	—	—	—	—	2	1
4	F / 40–50	7	3	—	—	—	1	8	—
5	F / 45–50	—	1	v	1	—	—	2	3
6	M / 18–25	—	1	—	6	1	1	3	3
8	M / >45	8	3	1	—	—	1	7	1
10	F / 40–44	—	1	—	—	—	—	—	—
12	F / 20–25	—	2	—	—	—	—	1	—
13	F / 20–24	—	1	—	1	—	—	2	1
15	M / 13–17	—	1	—	—	—	—	—	—

Note: Cells indicate the number of peptides supporting a given species determination. The symbol "—" indicates no peptides found.

was found in seven of nine individuals. Pomegranate (*Punica granatum*), or a closely related species, was found in five of nine individuals. A parasite that inhabits large ruminant animals (*Fasciola hepatica*), or an unrelated bacteria, was found in two of nine individuals.

For every faunal species excepting *Bos taurus*, it was distinctive peptides of collagen that identified the species, and for four of seven faunal species collagen was the only identified protein. In the case of *Bos taurus*, no collagen proteins were identified—the identified proteins instead consisted of an albumin precursor (in Burial 6 only) and beta-lactoglobulin isoform (a whey protein of milk).

Precontact Period Samples

Thirty-one peptides representing eight of the twenty candidate floral and faunal proteomes were compiled into sixteen sequences prior to cross-referencing NCBI and Uniprot BLAST results. Comparison of all species candidates that could account for those sequences, when grouped parsimoniously, indicated support for the presence of several sources in the plaque matrix.

Table 7.3 summarizes results. Elk or deer (*Cervus canadensis* / *Odocoileus virginianis*), or a closely related species, was found in five of eleven individuals. Otter (*Enhydra lutris kenyoni*), mink (*Neovison vison*), or another closely related species, was found in ten of eleven individuals. Beaver (*Castor canadensis*), or a closely related species, was found in eight of eleven individuals. Native sheep/goat (*Capra hircus* / *Ovis aries*), or closely related species, was found in three of eleven individuals. Native grape (*Vitis vinifera*), or a closely related species, was found in two of eleven individuals. An unresolved native plant was found in four of eleven individuals.

As with the asistencia samples, collagen was again the most common protein identified in every faunal candidate. In two of four faunal species, collagen was the only identified protein.

Discussion

Consistent with previous studies on biomolecule yield from dental calculus, the vast majority of residual proteins in this study were associated with bacterial or human sources (Palmer et al. 2021; Warinner et al. 2014). A total of 3,522 human peptides were identified in the Mission dataset, and 2,398 in the precontact dataset. Only a very small number identified as deriving from animal or vegetal sources, and of those the majority were animal collagen protein—23/42 in the Mission dataset and 25/31 in the precontact dataset. Given the range of overlap between the collagen sequences of the larger mam-

Table 7.3. Proteomic results from precontact-period human dental calculus

Site/ Individual	Sex / Age	Arch Period	Deer	Otter/ Mink	Sheep/ Goat	Beaver	Grape	Plant
ALA-329 Bur 102	M / 21–30	MP	1	6	—	1	1	—
ALA-329 Bur 64	M / 30–39	LP2	—	1	—	3	—	—
ALA-329 Bur 74	F / 35–44	LP1	4	7	—	8	—	—
ALA-329 Bur 110	M / 30–35	LP1	—	1	—	2	—	—
ALA-329 Bur 263	F / 25+	MP	—	1	—	—	—	1
ALA-329 Bur 251	F / 25–35	MP	—	1	—	3	—	—
SFR-191 Bur 18.1	M / 35–45	MP	—	1	1	3	—	1
SFR-191 Bur 17.3	M / 30–40	MP	1	4	1	3	1	1
SFR-191 Bur 17.5A	Ind / 25–45	MP	—	—	—	—	—	—
SFR-191 Bur 17.9	F / 35–40	MP	2	1	—	2	—	1
SFR-191 Bur 17.10	Ind / 15–18	MP	1	3	1	—	—	—

Notes: Cells indicate the number of peptides supporting a given species determination which were derived from the individuals calculus dataset. The symbol "—" indicates no peptides found. Ind = Indeterminate sex; MP = Middle Period (ca. 2500–965 cal BP); LP1 = Late Phase 1 (ca. 685–430 cal BP); LP2 = Late Phase 2 (ca. 430–180 cal BP).

mals searched in this dataset, the determination of direct peptide evidence for consumption of a single, parsimonious species, should not be construed as unambiguous evidence of absence of other species also included in the study. For example, no unique peptides were found that correlate to bovine meat, while peptide evidence was found for deer and goat/sheep meat. However, there is much sequence overlap between bovine, deer, and sheep collagen, and anthropological records indicate widespread consumption both of cattle and other imported livestock within the missions (Allen 2010; Schneider et al. 2020).

A surprising result is the number of precontact individuals with apparent evidence for sheep/goat specific peptide signals. While California does have native bighorn sheep (*Ovis canadensis*), today they are restricted to desert locations in the eastern part of the state, including in the Sierra Nevada, and are not known from the western part of the state. Some historic records suggest native sheep may have existed in the coast range, including around San Francisco Bay (Wagner et al. 1938), yet zooarchaeological studies do not support this finding. It is unlikely that bighorn meat was commonly carried from the Sierra Nevada, across the valley to the San Francisco Bay area. Most likely, then, the presence of "sheep/goat" peptides in precontact calculus samples represents the consumption of a different native animal, one that is not present in proteomic databases, but that overlaps in its peptide sequence with sheep/goat collagen.

By contrast, peptide signals for fowl and possible parasitic infection are easily resolvable from the other mammals and plants, but lack close comparators at the level of a proteome search that would render them unique to a species. For example, fowl collagen could have come from chickens raised in the Mission but could equally have come from native birds hunted for meat such as goose or duck. As mentioned above, the peptide sequence itself is common across a wide swathe of the animal kingdom and resolvable to avian origin in this context only because of geographical constraint. The lack of confident assignments to *Quercus lobata* (well-attested to in the literature as a component of traditional diet), or *Zea mays* and *Triticum aestivum* (both common cultivars among the Missions), are more surprising. It is possible that peptides unique to these species do not survive well or are not readily recovered. Additional study will be necessary to resolve this question.

The peptide sequence matching the liver fluke (*Fasciola hepatica*) proteome in one individual in the asistencia dataset (Burial 6) is reported more as a point of interest rather than to assert clear parasitic infection, given the lack of species resolution. No such peptides were observed in the precontact dataset. While just a single observation, this result could be suggestive of the coincidence of parasitic infection associated with introduced ruminant species.

Overall, there does appear to be a shift in dietary trends between the precontact and Mission Periods. While evidence of fruit consumption is poorly represented in both data sets, there is strong evidence for the incorporation of imported fruit into Mission dietary practices. Grape proteins found in the precontact dataset were supplanted by pomegranate peptides present in just over half of samples in the Mission set. Moreover, the Mission samples show evidence of limited dairy consumption, with the majority of peptide evidence limited to a single young male adult, and only sparsely represented in two other individuals, one older female and one younger adolescent male. These findings broadly corroborate anthropological reports of Mission residents incorporating domesticated animal products and cultivated fruit into their diets, as well as the absence of widespread dairying—as cattle were reportedly used primarily for meat and leather rather than milk among the Native population (Allen 2010; Arkush 2011; Popper 2016). The sample size is small, but it may be noteworthy that two of the four younger individuals included in the dataset have evidence for milk consumption, while only one of the five older adults do. Taking bovine and pomegranate peptides as rough indicators of imported nutrition sources, these peptides represented a larger proportion of the total peptides identified in the younger individuals than their older counterparts. Together, these findings are consistent with greater dietary change, or greater experimentation with nontraditional dietary items, among the younger individuals within the asistencia population.

If peptides for wild deer serve as a proxy for larger game hunting in general, the decrease (though not elimination) in prevalence of unique deer sequences among members of the Mission Period dataset compared to their precontact cohort suggests greater reliance of domesticated animal sources of protein within the Missions. Both Mission Period individuals with evidence of deer consumption were older adults. Indeed, both these individuals had over twice as many peptides in their datasets relative to others (excepting one individual), with the majority of those peptides representing traditional sources of nutrition, including the only instance of fish peptide in the dataset (likely salmon, given the geographic context). Again, this is consistent with older individuals continuing more of a traditional diet, though it is also possible that peptide signals were preserved in their calculus from a time before they entered the Mission.

By the same token, the prevalence of otter/mink and beaver in both the precontact and Mission Period samples, even among some of the younger individuals in the latter group, provides evidence for continuation of some traditional dietary patterns cross-generationally. Moreover, by dint of the natural habitats of otter, mink, and beaver, their prevalence in the calculus data also support conclusions made elsewhere in the anthropological literature (Panich 2016; Schneider et al. 2020) that far from being held to a single geographic locale as intended by the principles of the Franciscan program of *reduccion*, Native people within the missions were commonly engaged in traffic outside the walls of the compounds.

It is possible that such peregrinations might have been more the province of the younger individuals. For example, the list of artifacts associated with each grave indicates by far the greatest prevalence of Olivella and clam beads among the younger individuals. Given that these artifacts are well represented in the ethnographic and archaeological record as important items in trading networks (Panich 2016), the gravesite context could suggest that it was the younger adults who were more heavily involved in these trade networks. Such trading could dovetail with hunting of smaller game including otter/mink and beaver, and fishing.

Beaver and otter pelts were particularly important trade items during the Mission Period in California, for example, traded by Spanish crown to China in exchange for mercury that was then used in mining activities (Hackell 1997; Ogden 1975). Within the missions, baptized individuals were encouraged to obtain these items by hunting or trapping. It seems likely that while the Spanish crown desired the pelts, Native people could retain the meat for consumption. The prevalence of beaver and otter collagen within the calculus of baptized individuals at the asistencia may represent such activities. Although only some individuals may have hunted or trapped such animals, widespread sharing of meat among the baptized may explain why nearly all the asistencia individuals display such evidence in their calculus.

Conclusions

Results from this exploratory study add new information about diets for Native people recruited into the mission system, relative to diets in precontact time periods from San Francisco region, assuming the majority of peptides recovered from the Asistencia de San Pedro y San Pablo sample were deposited after entrance into the missions. The sample size is clearly small, and additional analogous studies at other mission sites would help evaluate how widespread the patterns documented here were. Yet even with the limited scope of the current studies, it is clear that some aspects of diet changed, while others continued.

In terms of change, three individuals seem to have incorporated cow, and more specifically cow's milk, into their diet. This suggests a willingness or encouragement to substitute domesticated animal protein for some traditional game. It is of particular interest that two of these individuals, Burials 6 and 15, were younger males at the time of death (eighteen to twenty-five and thirteen to seventeen years, respectively). This matches results from the stable isotope studies (see chapter 6), where younger male individuals had divergent diets compared to older adults, especially with regard to the protein component of the diet. This suggests greater dietary exploration and/or change among younger individuals within the mission system. The presence of peptides matching liver fluke in Burial 6 also suggests that zoonotic pathogens may have been introduced by the Spanish, which then spread to the Native population vis-à-vis food sources.

Along these lines, results also hint at a reduction in the prevalence of deer relative to the precontact samples. Only two individuals (of nine), Burials 4 and 8, both older adults at the time of death, have evidence for deer, while five of eleven precontact samples have peptides consistent with deer. In this regard, it appears that cow, and perhaps sheep and goat, may have substituted as a source of meat for many individuals. At the same time, both of the individuals who do, have large numbers of deer peptides (and no distinguishing cow peptides). If the quantity of peptides is an indication of the importance of a food item in the diet, it may suggest that when people ate deer, they ate large amounts of it, foregoing domesticated animals.

The presence of peptides consistent with pomegranate also hint at dietary change within the population. In contrast to cow, peptides from pomegranate occur more widely throughout the population, including younger and older individuals. Perhaps pomegranate more easily substituted for other naturally occurring fruit plants within the traditional diet.

While some peptides are consistent with dietary change, others indicate a continuance of traditional food practices. Peptides associated with otter and beaver were widespread in both precontact and the mission individuals, while fowl was found in three and fish in one Mission Period individual (Burial 8). This indicates that small game hunting continued on a significant scale, and perhaps fishing and fowling as well, among the baptized population.

As mentioned, it remains to be seen how widespread these dietary changes were among baptized individuals within the mission system. This will require similar studies among other mission populations in Northern California. Working and living at an asistencia, rather than a mission, it is possible that the individuals here may have had particular freedoms that others within the mission system may not have had. This may have included time to hunt or fish and continue traditional foodways. As well, as discussed in the chapter examining grave goods, individuals may have had access to trading networks wherein traditional food items could have moved. All of this may have allowed Native residents of the asistencia more freedom in choosing their diets than those who lived at the associated Mission San Francisco de Asis.

References

Aghanashini, Suchetha, Bhavana Puvvalla, Darshan B. Mundinamane, S. M. Apoorva, Divya Bhat, and Manjari Lalwani
2016   A Comprehensive Review on Dental Calculus. *Journal of Health Sciences and Research* 7(2): 42–50.

Allen, Rebecca
1998   *Native Americans at Mission Santa Cruz, 1791–1834.* Perspectives in California Archaeology, Vol. 5, Institute of Archaeology, University of California, Los Angeles.
2010   Alta California Missions and the Pre-1849 Transformation of Coastal Lands. *Historical Archaeology* 44(3): 69–80.

Arkush, Brooke S.
2011   Native Responses to European Intrusion: Cultural Persistence and Agency among Mission Neophytes in Spanish Colonial Northern California. *Historical Archaeology* 45(4): 62–90.

Chen, Chen, Jie Hou, John J. Tanner, and Jianlin Cheng
2020   Bioinformatics Methods for Mass Spectrometry-Based Proteomics Data Analysis. *International Journal of Molecular Sciences* 21(8): 2873. doi:10.3390/ijms21082873

Eng, Jimmy K., Brian C. Searle, Karl R. Clauser, and David L. Tabb
2011   A Face in the Crowd: Recognizing Peptides through Database Search. *Molecular and Cellular Proteomics* 10(11): R111.009522. https://doi.org/10.1074/mcp.R111.009522

Fagernäs, Zandra, Maite I. García-Collado, Jessica Hendy, Courtney A. Hofman, Camilla Speller, Irina Velsko, and Christina Warinner
2020   A Unified Protocol for Simultaneous Extraction of DNA and Proteins from Archaeological Dental Calculus. *Journal of Archaeological Science* 118:105135. https://doi.org/10.1016/j.jas.2020.105135

Geiger, Maynard J., and Clement W. Meighan
1976   *As the Padres Saw Them: California Indian Life and Customs as Reported by the Franciscan Missions, 1813–1815.* Santa Barbara Mission Archive Library, Santa Barbara.

The Global Proteome Machine
2014   cRAP Protein Sequences. https://www.thegpm.org/crap/, accessed June 22, 2023.

Hackell, Steven W.
1997   Land, Labor, and Production: The Colonial Economy of Spanish and Mexican California. *California History* 76:111–146.

Kiel, Lindsay
2016   The Complexities of Neophyte Diet: An Analysis of Faunal Remains from Feature 157 at Mission Santa Clara de Asís. Unpublished MA thesis. University of Idaho.

Marsh, P. D.
2004   Dental Plaque as a Microbial Biofilm. *Caries Research* 38(3): 204–211.

Noe, Sarah J.
2023   Subsistence and Persistence: Indigenous Foodways within Mission Santa Clara de Asís. *California Archaeology* 15:69–107.

Ogden, Adele
1975   *The California Sea Otter Trade, 1784–1848.* University of California Press.

Palmer, Karren S., Cheryl A. Makarewicz, Alexey A. Tishkin, Svetlana S. Tur, Amartuvshin Chunag, Erdenebaatar Diimajav, Bayarsaikhan Jamsranjav, and Michael Buckley
2021   Comparing the Use of Magnetic Beads with Ultrafiltration for Ancient Dental Calculus Proteomics. *Journal of Proteome Research* 20(3): 1689–1704.

Panich, Lee M.
2016   After Saint Serra: Unearthing Indigenous Histories at the California Missions. *Journal of Social Archaeology* 16:238–258.

Parker, Glendon J., Julia M. Yip, Jelmer W. Eerkens, Michelle Salemi, Blythe Durbin-Johnson, Caleb Kiesow, Randall Haas, Jane E. Buikstra, Haagen Klaus, Laura A. Regan, David M. Rocke, and Brett S. Phinney
2018   Sex Estimation Using Sexually Dimorphic Amelogenin Protein Fragments in Human Enamel. *Journal of Archaeological Science* 101: 169–180.

Popper, Virginia S.
2016   Change and Persistence: Mission Neophyte Foodways at Selected Colonial Alta California Institutions. *Journal of California and Great Basin Anthropology* 36: 5–25.

Reddy, Seetha N.
2015   Feeding Family and Ancestors: Persistence of Traditional Native American Lifeways during the Mission Period in Coastal Southern California. *Journal of Anthropological Archaeology* 37: 48–66.

Richter, Kristine Korzow, Maria C. Codlin, Melina Seabrook, and Christina Warinner
2022   A Primer for ZooMS Applications in Archaeology. *Proceedings of the National Academy of Sciences of the United States of America* 119(20): e2109323119. DOI:10.1073/pnas.2109323119.

Sawafuji, Rikai, Aiko Saso, Wataru Suda, Masahira Hattori, and Shintaroh Ueda
2020   Ancient DNA Analysis of Food Remains in Human Dental Calculus from the Edo Period, Japan. *PLOS ONE* 15(3): e0226654.

Schneider, Tsim D., Khal Schneider, and Lee M. Panich
2020   Scaling Invisible Walls. *The Public Historian* 42(4): 97–120. DOI:10.1525/tph.2020.42.4.97.

Steen, Hanno, and Matthias Mann
2004   The ABC's (and XYZ's) of Peptide Sequencing. *Molecular Cell Biology* 5(9): 699–711.

Wagner, H. R., Pedro Fages, and Herbert Ingram Priestley
1938   A Historical, Political, and Natural Description of California. *The Hispanic American Historical Review* 18(2): 205.

Warinner, Christina, João F. Matias Rodrigues, Rounak Vyas, Christian Trachsel, Natallia Shved, Jonas Grossmann, Anita Radini, Y. Hancock, Raul Y. Tito, Sarah Fiddyment, Camilla Speller, Jessica Hendy, Sophy Charlton, Hans Ulrich Luder, Domingo C Salazar-García, Elisabeth Eppler, Roger Seiler, Lars H. Hansen, José Alfredo Samaniego Castruita, Simon Barkow-Oesterreicher, Kai Yik Teoh, Christian D. Kelstrup, Jesper V. Olsen, Paolo Nanni, Toshihisa Kawai, Eske Willerslev, Christian von Mering, Cecil M. Lewis, Matthew J. Collins, M. Thomas P. Gilbert, Frank Rühli, and Enrico Cappellini
2014   Pathogens and Host Immunity in the Ancient Human Oral Cavity. *Nature Genetics* 46(4): 336–344.

Warinner, Christina, Camilla Speller, and Matthew J. Collins
2015   A New Era in Palaeomicrobiology: Prospects for Ancient Dental Calculus as a Long Term Record of the Human Oral Microbiome. *Philosophical Transactions of the Royal Society of London. Series B, Biological Sciences* 370(1660). http://dx.doi.org/10.1098/rstb.2013.0376

Webb, Edith B.
1983   *Indian Life at the Old Missions.* University of Nebraska Press.

8

Biochemical Ethnobotany of Ohlone Plant Use during the Mission Period

Mario Zimmermann, Shannon Tushingham,
Anna Berim, and David R. Gang

The Mission Period represents an era of unprecedented change in the lifeways of Native Californians. Accompanying militarized expeditionary forces, Franciscan friars founded missions along the coast of Alta and Baja California throughout the late eighteenth and early nineteenth centuries. In their attempt to evangelize local communities, Franciscans disrupted settlement patterns, forced conversion to Catholicism, and implemented Western education. In the past, historical treatments of this period were dominated by narratives of assimilation and loss, where neophytes largely abandoned their way of life once integrated into the Spanish colonial system (Hackel 2005; Milliken 1995). Without dismissing the transformative and devastating impacts of missionization and colonization, more recent approaches highlight the agency of Native Californians and provide a more nuanced understanding of colonial entanglements during this period. Archaeological studies of residences at Mission and non-Mission sites testify to a variety of responses by Native Californians, and processes of persistence, hybridity, and resistance, depending on their geographic and social circumstances (e.g., Byrd et al. 2018; Jones et al. 2022; Panich et al. 2018; Panich and Schneider 2015; Reddy 2015; Silliman 2015).

In this chapter we contribute to this discourse by considering Native ethnobotanical practices and consumption patterns through the Mission Period, with a focus on psychoactive plants and "non-dietary" substances. We conduct a biochemical analysis of residue extracted from dental calculus samples from individual burials from the Asistencia de San Pedro y San Pablo, a satellite or "sub-mission" connected to Mission San Francisco de Asis established in 1786 at Pruristac, an Ohlone village near present-day Pacifica, California.

Our analysis involves an Ultra Performance Liquid Chromatography-Mass Spectrometry (UPLC-MS)–based metabolomics approach that can help discriminate various compounds, mostly associated with plants, and provides insights into the consumption practices of men and women of different ages and status categories through this critical period. While we paid particular attention to tobacco biomarkers such as nicotine and cotinine, the recovery of several thousand unidentified chromatographic signals also allows us to examine the ingestion of xenobiotics on a broader level. Our data indicate that tobacco consumption remained consistent with patterns observed for precontact populations from the same area. By comparison, sex biases related to other non-dietary products increased. Metabolomic fingerprints also confirms the presence of one individual with a set of vastly different compounds, also identified by a unique set of grave goods, suggesting a link between higher status and consumption of xenobiotic substances. New substances were also incorporated into the diet of some individuals; the presence of caffeine in some samples likely is associated with imported cacao or chocolate consumption.

More Than Food: Plants and Medicines in California

Plants are fundamentally connected to Native Californian lifeways and culture. While much attention is typically given to their dietary contribution—nuts, seeds, and greens provided sustenance for generations—plants were also important for ceremonial and medicinal purposes, as raw materials for tools, houses, watercraft, and baskets, to mention just a few examples. No less than 265 species of medicinal plants were used by Native Californians prior to the Mission Period (McBride et al. 2020; Mead 1972). Medicinal expertise was used to treat an array of illnesses by applying leaves or herbal mixtures directly to wounds, by ingesting as liquid decoctions, chewing or eating, and smoking. Whenever written documents or oral histories are unavailable, the ability to trace these products and practices over archaeological time spans is dependent on whether there is an associated complex of material culture, archaeobotanical remains, or residues that preserve with artifacts or alongside human remains.

For Tobacco (*Nicotiana* sp.) we can count on all three. Ethnographic and ethnohistoric accounts indicate the widespread importance of sacred tobacco among hunting, gathering, and fishing communities in western North America. For example, among the Ohlone and their neighbors in the San Francisco Bay Area smoked tobacco (*Nicotiana* sp.) in pipes, but also chewed or ate it combined with lime (e.g., Harrington 1932; Kroeber 1941). The importance of tobacco in antiquity is reflected in studies confirming its use via (1) Residue analysis of clay and stone pipes—Though relatively rare, these artifacts and corresponding residue analyses indicate a smoking tradition of at least 1,100 years of antiquity in California and 1,600 years in northern Washington state, well outside of its native range (Damitio et al. 2021; Tushingham and Eerkens 2016; Tushingham et al. 2013, 2018). (2) Archaeobotanical identification—While exceedingly small, charred tobacco seeds have been recovered in Mission Period sites in California to as early as 12,300 years before present (Cuthrell et al. 2016; Duke et al. 2022). (3) The extraction of residues from dental calculus samples corresponding to ancestral Ohlone burials offers a window into the underlying social factors that are associated with non-dietary substance consumption on the individual level (Eerkens et al. 2018; Tushingham et al., 2020; Zimmermann et al., in press).

Medicinal Practices, Sacred Tobacco, and Colonialism

Examining ethnobotanical compilations and firsthand accounts from Native and Euro-American observers, McBride et al. (2020) show that processes of persistence were not unique to dietary resources. Frequent shortages in medical supplies led mission staff to consult with knowledgeable baptized individuals about the availability of local medicines. About one-third of the plants used to treat illnesses during the Mission Period had already been part of California's ethnopharmacopoeia before contact. McBride et al. (2020) also point out that this proportion increased significantly after secularization in the 1830s. One of the traditional medicines that persisted over time is tobacco with both wild and domesticated species being listed (McBride et al. 2020: Table 3).

The case of tobacco and its role in the colonial Americas and Enlightenment-era Europe is intriguing in its complexity. Although Columbus and his sailors were baffled when being offered cigars during their first encounters (Díaz del Castillo 2007[1568]), tobacco soon established a following among settlers in the New World as well as countries across Europe, Asia, and Africa (Goodman 1993). While usage initially followed Native American tradition in its focus on ceremony and medicine, historians credit the rise of recreational smoking to falling prices in the eighteenth century (Matthee 1995:45–46). Nonetheless, use of tobacco had become a contested matter as even high-ranking church officials could not agree on a unified stance. Roughly a century after its introduction to Europeans, Urban VII issued the first anti-smoking edict in 1590. Anyone who "took tobacco in the porchway of or inside a church, whether by chewing it, smoking it with a pipe, or sniffing it in powdered form through the nose" would risk excommunication. The law remained on the books in various forms until 1724, when Pope Benedict XIII, a smoker himself, repealed it (Corti 1932).

In California, missionaries did not always agree with their spiritual leaders. The friars exercised a certain degree of autonomy and enforced either stricter or more lax rules. Winter (2000:34) relates that tobacco formed part of clandestine activities conducted by Native peoples. However, he also mentions that local communities convinced Father Junípero Serra to include tobacco among the species grown at the Mission Carmel garden. The same Franciscan friar had already reported previously that local Native communities started requesting tobacco rather than glass beads as trade gifts soon after Spanish arrival. The account books of several mission settlements provide testimony to the massive scale achieved by tobacco imports from New Spain over the late eighteenth and early nineteenth centuries (Cuthrell et al. 2016). Ethnohistoric reports also indicate that tobacco was part of gender-specific taboos connected to the birth of children. To guarantee their well-being, incumbent fathers desisted temporarily from both hunting and tobacco consumption (Newell 2008). On the opposite end of normativity, mortuary ceremonies very much relied on tobacco in honoring the dead (Fages and Priestley 1919).

The ambivalence toward tobacco was somewhat similar among physicians. While tobacco was celebrated as a panacea shortly after its arrival in Europe, by the seventeenth century mistrust had grown notably. With opinions split, tobacco remained featured in reference works such as Wesley's "Primitive Physick" through the eighteenth and into the nineteenth century (Charlton 2004). For New Spain, Hernández de Toledo describes its use as an expectorant and anti-asthmatic, stimulant, analgesic, and soporific. The same royal physician, however, also warns against abuse as overdoses might lead to liver tremors, cachexia, and dropsy (de Micheli and Izaguirre-Ávila 2005).

Despite the recognition of its potential deleterious effects, the Spanish Crown ratified the creation of the Royal New Hispanic Tobacconist in 1765. This state monopoly controlled the entire agro-industrial enterprise surrounding tobacco all the way from cultivation in designated fields, to factory processing in Mexico City and six other towns, to sales in *estanquillos* all around New Spain. The products switching hands included cigars and cigarettes as well as cut and ground tobacco for pipe smoking and snuffing. During the decades leading up to Mexican Independence, the *Estanco* or Royal Tobacconist accounted for about 20 percent of all the revenues New Spain ceded to the Crown, including the silver trade (Suárez Argüello 2011). Recreational consumption had reached this massive scale among others due to tobacco's acceptance across large sectors of society. With both slaves and masters, as well as women and men partaking, Ortiz (1963) argues that tobacco had become "the most democratic of all vices."

Approach

The opportunity to study dental calculus associated with some of the inhabitants of the asistencia allows us to approach the subject of non-dietary use of plants, and, more specifically, medicinal and mind-altering substance use on an individual level. Dental calculus or mineralized plaque accumulates throughout the mouth naturally and incorporates microscopic and chemical residues of a broad array of products ingested by humans. Regarding the former, it has been proven that these archives extend even to hominid ancestors (Hardy et al. 2012). Diagnostic chemical markers, on the other hand, have so far only been detected in samples of individuals up to 4,500 years old (Moonkham 2023). Even though biomarkers such as nicotine might not preserve as long as starch granules or phytoliths, lists of unidentified chemical features summing thousands of elements hold considerable potential for the reconstruction of human ingestion. Similar metabolomic datasets from European and Native American populations have shown associations between residue signatures and pathological profiles, thus opening a door for the deep-time study of ethnopharmacological practices (Velsko et al. 2017; Zimmermann et al., in press).

It stands to mention that biomarker-focused studies have until recently dominated organic residue analysis. The reliance on gas chromatography-mass spectrometry (GC-MS) platforms also brought about a focus on primary metabolites such as proteins and lipids, which are imperative for an organism's growth and reproduction. More recently, UPLC-MS systems have been employed by cross-disciplinary teams with anthropological research foci. These platforms were developed as an innovation in the field of chemical profiling and allow comprehensive characterization of a broader suite of molecules including secondary metabolites. These molecules fulfill ecological functions such as defense and signaling for fully developed organisms. Given their specificity, secondary metabolites are often exclusive to relatively small taxonomic groups compared to the virtual omnipresence and thus low diagnostic potential of primary metabolites. A particular class of secondary metabolites with great cultural significance are alkaloids, which feature substances like nicotine, caffeine, morphine, cocaine, and psilocybin.

As the individuals at the asistencia lived only around 235 years ago, we were optimistic about the potential to recover biomarkers that had not undergone major processes of degradation. We scanned our UPLC-MS profiles for nicotine (a biomarker of tobacco), scopolamine and atropine (datura), caffeine (cacao, coffee), and morphine (laudanum) (table 8.1). We considered adding tartaric acid to this list to serve as a biomarker for grapes, as wine production was an important economic activity in colonial California. However, the data produced by the corresponding chemical standard behaves very differently from the above-mentioned alkaloids under our current protocols, which made it impossible to reliably detect its signal. Moreover, a recent review of wine residue research identified significant shortfalls related to the use of tartaric acid as a biomarker (Drieu et al., 2020). The compound is present in a rather large array of fruits and thus can be easily introduced into the matrix of porous archaeological materials through environmental contamination. Its water solubility also poses problems in terms of conservation over archaeological time spans.

In addition to scanning for secondary metabolites of cultural significance, we also pursued an untargeted approach exploring possible associations between the comprehensive signal lists and the demographic and pathological data available for the burial collection. The corresponding Partial Least Square–Discriminant Analyses (PLSDA) allowed us to examine the role of biocultural factors such as sex, age, and health with regard to the consumption of non-dietary substances at the asistencia.

Materials

This study is based on the analysis of sixteen dental calculus samples corresponding to ten individuals. In other words, for half of the individuals more than one sample was available for residue extraction. Generally, calculus material was gathered in complementary fashion from anterior (incisors and canines) and posterior (premolars and molars), as well as maxillary (upper jaw) and mandibular (lower jaw) teeth. Dental calculus sample weight ranged from 1 to 37.3 mg (table 8.1).

UPLC-MS Analysis

The UPLC-MS protocol was identical to the protocol published by Eerkens et al. (2018). Chemical residues were extracted by immersing the dental calculus samples in 0.5 mL of a solution of acetonitrile, 2-propanol, and water [3:2:2] followed by 10 minutes of sonication. The supernatants were transferred to a second microvial, lyophilized, and eventually resuspended in 0.05 mL of a 1:1 solution of acetonitrile and water spiked with 0.1% formic acid. Chemical standards for nicotine, arbutin, caffeine, theobromine, theophyl-

Table 8.1. Biomarker data from dental calculus samples

Burial	Sex	Age	Tooth	Wt. (mg)	Nicotine	Caffeine
2	M	13–17	M^2	6.4	-	-
3	F	40–45	I	4.6	+	+
			RM^3	37.3	~	+
4	F	50–60	LC^0	1.6	~	~
			RM^3	9.3	~	~
6	M	18–25	LI^1	8.7	~	-
			RM^1	1.6	-	+
8	M	46+	RC^0	2.7	+	-
			LPM^1	2.9	-	+
			RM^3	7.8	-	+
10	F	40–44	LM^3	19.1	-	-
11	M	4–8	RI^1	7.1	+	-
			LM^1	6.3	~	-
12	F	20–25	I^0	1.3	+	-
13	F	20–24	RI^1	2.5	~	-
15	M	13–17	LI^2	1	+	+

Notes: Within cells "+" = confirmed presence, "~" = unconfirmed presence, "-" = absence. "Tooth" column: "L" left; "R" right; "M" molar; "I" incisor; "C" canine; superscript numbers refer to tooth position (e.g., "RI^1" right first incisor). Nico. = Nicotine, Caff. = Caffeine, Scop. = Scopolamine, Atro. = Atropine, Mor. = Morphine.

line, morphine, and ephedrine were included in the analysis batch to allow for biomarker identification. Analysis was conducted on a Waters Acquity UPLC system with photodiode array (PDA) detection ranging between 210 and 400 nm and a total analysis time of 16 minutes. Progenesis QI as well as TargetLynx software were used for raw data processing.

Data Processing

Multivariate approaches such as untargeted metabolomics benefit notably from the filtering of noise-inducing variables. For this analysis, we first reduced the list of all detected chemical features by those signals accounted for in solvent blanks. To remain under consideration, a given signal had to feature at least one calculus sample with an abundance value ten times stronger than the maximum observed among the blanks. Afterward, we standardized the area values for all peaks by sample weight and eliminated all signals with a coefficient of variation (CV) below 100. This filter removes a significant number of shared chemical features associated with the human oral metabolome

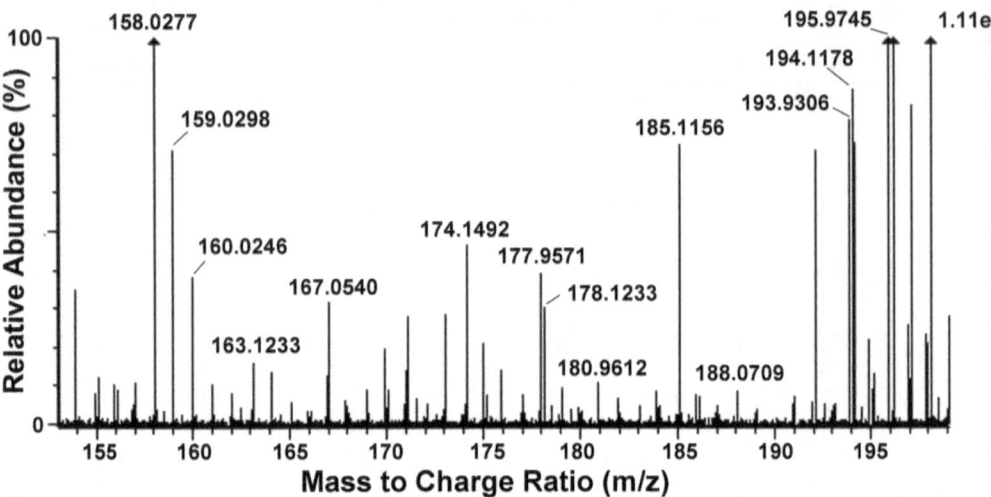

Figure 8.1. Mass spectrum of calculus from Burial 11's right lower first incisor, featuring nicotine signal (163.12 m/z).

and thus increases the spread between cases. A third step involved cutting records indicative of instrument noise at the start and end of the retention time sequence, which led to a short list of 109 chemical features comprised in an interval ranging from 1.62 to 7.97 min.

The availability of multiple samples for most of the individuals (table 8.1) allowed for two sets of comparisons between chemical residue and bioarchaeological data. Provenience variables such as anterior vs. posterior position, and mandibular vs. maxillary row were examined on a per-specimen basis. In turn, demographic (sex; age) and pathological (abscesses; periodontitis) data were contrasted by individual. For the latter assays, the highest abundance value among samples belonging to the same individual was retained for each chemical feature on the short list. We conducted principal component analysis (PCA) for specimen-based tests, and partial least squares–discriminant analysis (PLSDA) for visualizing patterns among individual burials.

Results

We initiated our analysis examining presence/absence data for the abovementioned biomarkers. Similar to precontact populations from the same area (Eerkens et al. 2018; Tushingham et al. 2020), a significant proportion (n=5) of the 16 samples yielded confirmed nicotine signals. Positive cases correspond to Burials 3, 8, 11, 12, and 15, and thus feature both sexes as well as all available age groups except for middle-aged adults. In addition, we detected peaks that match nicotine standards in both retention time and molecular mass (± 5 ppm) in six additional samples yet did not attain abundance values significantly above background noise levels (figure 8.1).

We detected caffeine in a similar number of cases (n=6) but without a complete overlap in the corresponding individuals. For this biomarker, samples from Burials 3, 6, 8, and 15 tested positive (see table 8.1). A higher number of confirmed cases associated with a lower number of burials indicates that caffeine samples yielded repetitive positives twice (i.e., multiple teeth from the same individual). Caffeine detection remains unconfirmed for both samples associated with Burial 4. Again, both women and men are represented, and while neither children nor middle-aged adults do, juveniles as well as young and old adults figure among the caffeine-positive individuals. The biomarkers for datura (scopolamine and atropine), opium-based products (morphine) were absent from the asistencia samples, and are therefore not listed in table 8.1. This confirms the negative results of previous studies as none of these substances has been detected in extracts derived from dental calculus samples recovered from historic populations.

After biomarker analysis, we proceeded with multivariate statistics on other compounds, many unidentified. This lack of identification is not uncommon in UPLC-MS-based analyses. Despite relatively low mass error ranges for m/z peaks, the sheer number of detected signals as well as the continuing difficulties in standardizing output data across instrument systems and laboratories often cause results to acquire an aggregate rather than a diagnostic character. Nonetheless, specimen-based PCA had the objective of examining possible differences in residue deposits between anterior and posterior teeth. Similar to previous studies conducted in Native Californian populations, we did not observe consistent patterning characterizing either group. The evaluation of associations between chemical residues and demographic variables relied on PLSDA performed on the condensed per-individual dataset. Figure 8.2 does not present evidence for a clear clustering of burials among age groups. However, accounting for a dominant percentage of all variation (86 percent), Component 1 separates Burial 15 from all other individuals. Similarly, representing only 11 percent of overall variation, Component 2 leads to a split of two young adults and two older adults from the remaining individuals (Burials 4, 8, 12, and 13). The cluster with negative Component 2 scores features all age groups that are part of this study.

The panorama appears to be more significant with respect to sex. Despite a slight decrease in impact, Component 1 again accounts for most of the variation (77 percent). Component 2 essentially doubled its associated percentage

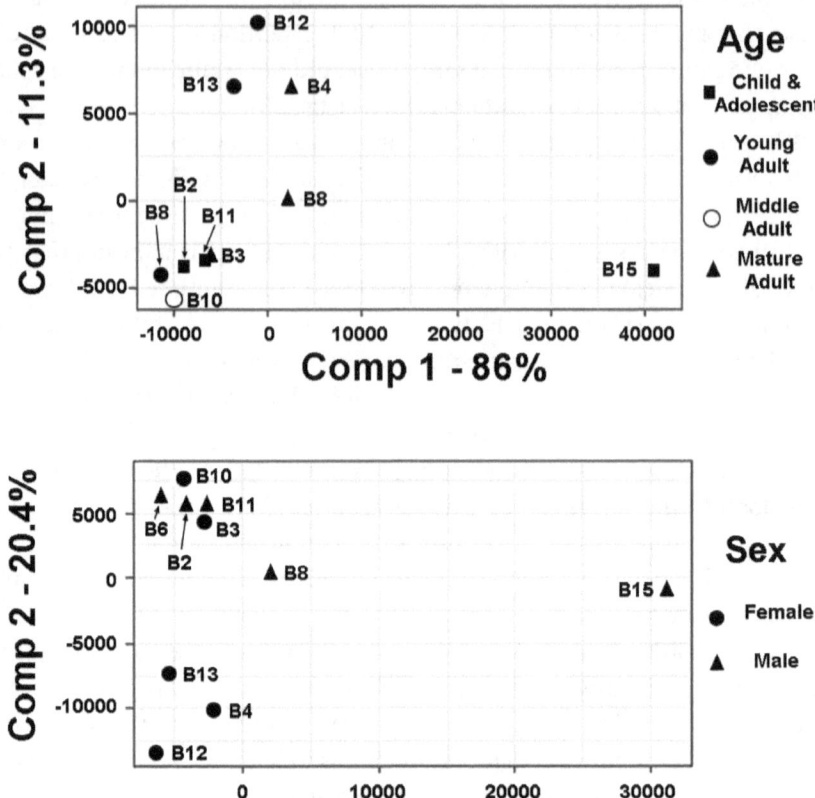

Figure 8.2. Partial least squares–discriminant analysis (PLSDA) for visualizing patterns among individual burials, by age (*top*), and sex (*bottom*).

(20 percent). Like the previous category, Component 1 only sets Burial 15 apart from all other individuals, while Component 2 exhibits a strong sorting for males. All individuals in this group produced either zero or positive values for this dimension. Female burials are split; some score positively and others negatively on Component 2.

A look at the loading plot for the PLSDA associating metabolomic data and sex estimates shows that both components are disproportionately impacted by single chemical features (figure 8.3). The outlier status of Burial 15 is intimately related to a molecule with a retention time of 7.36 min and a mass-charge ratio of 244. Component 2, on the other hand, grants significant weight to a substance eluting at 6.40 min with 233 m/z. Its association with negative Component 2 values indicates that the other male individuals, with

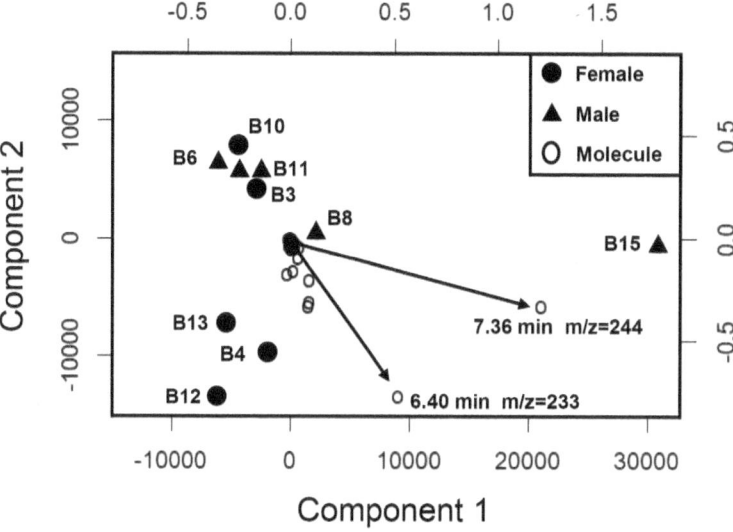

Figure 8.3. Loading plot for Residues-Sex PLSDA.

exclusively positive Component 2 values, did not partake in the consumption of this substance.

Unfortunately, PLSDA relating chemical residues data with oral pathological conditions such as abscesses and periodontitis did not provide clear associations. Even though the asistencia burials again split into clusters, these conglomerates were composed of individuals with different degrees of severity in diseases of the mouth. Nonetheless, it is important to stress that Burial 15 forms an outlier in every single multivariate analysis for the asistencia population, independent of the association with either demographic or pathological information.

Discussion

Winter (2000) provides a detailed panorama of (proto)historic tobacco consumption in central California, both among Native groups on the coast as well as the interior. While the plant does not appear to have been cultivated in the area but only gathered from wild stands, he reports on several distinct modes of consumption including smoking, chewing, snuffing, eating, and drinking. Even though the author underscores tobacco's role in several ceremonies, he also mentions its use as a medicine. This information is particularly relevant in finding an explanation for the nicotine positives detected in samples originating from children and juvenile individuals. It is possible these community members were not ingesting tobacco for its stimulant, but maybe its emetic, anti-parasitic, or other health-benefiting properties. Interestingly, Burk et al. (this volume) identify proteomic signatures associated with liver fluke (*Fasciola* sp.), a common helminth among pastoralist societies, in at least one individual.

Recent ethnopharmacological research in areas with a deep-time history of medicinal tobacco usage provides additional insights. In the Peruvian Amazon, for example, liquid preparations for either nasal, oral, or topical applications is the most common mode of preparation for tobacco remedies. While a local healer stresses that a certain level of physical strength among patients is required to prevent harm, he also acknowledges that children above the age of five years old are generally eligible for infusion-based treatments (Berlowitz et al. 2020). Similarly, Roulette et al. (2014) observes that tobacco and cannabis consumers among Central African hunter-gatherers are significantly less affected by parasitic infections than other community members who do not smoke. Here, worm burden was specifically low among young adult males and those men of senior age (Roulette et al. 2014).

According to ethnographic records, however, children were not regular tobacco users (e.g., Harrington 1932:13). If indeed outside of the norm, could it be that these children and adolescents were given tobacco as treatment for illnesses or European-introduced diseases that were so common at this time? The sacred nature of tobacco to Native Californians seems especially relevant to this discussion. While today commercial tobacco use is widely understood as a harmful, recreational habit, tobacco was widely viewed as a powerful substance that connected people with ceremony and a spiritual world (Harrington 1932; Panich et al. 2018). In other words, tobacco was more than "medicine" in the western sense of the word. Given the chaos of the times, these aspects of tobacco likely held deep meaning for the Native people who lived and died at the asistencia.

A topic that remains actively under research is the association of *Nicotiana* residues with either domesticated or wild tobacco plants. In other words, at the moment we cannot say whether people were growing Aztec (*N. rustica*) or trade tobacco (*N. tabacum*) in gardens, or if they collected it in the wild while on *paseo*. Archaeological research at contemporary settlements such as Mission San Jose demonstrates that baptized individuals enjoyed a certain degree of autonomy with regard to practices considered vices by friars even within their supervised quarters. Panich et al. (2018) argue that small, unperforated *teja* disks found in significant numbers in an adobe structure were dice used in gambling. The same site produced incised bird bone tubes (Panich et al. 2018: Figure 6) whose stylistic and formal attributes suggest they were pieces of compound pipes. More importantly, macrobotanical research conducted at Mission Santa Clara yielded direct evidence for tobacco cultivation in colonial California. Applying linear discriminant analysis to the morphometric features recorded in an assemblage of over 1,400 tobacco seeds, Cuthrell et al. (2016) demonstrate that nearly 70 percent belong to two introduced species: tree tobacco (*N. glauca*) and trade tobacco (*N. tabacum*). It is thus not unreasonable to assume that tobacco was predominantly grown at the asistencia too. In this case, children would have been intimately familiar with the plant given it was their responsibility to clear mission gardens and safeguard crops from birds (Cook 1943).

Similar to the question marks behind the specific identification of domesticated vs. wild tobacco species, the caffeine positives detected in several of the individuals prompts inquiry into their source. During the late eighteenth and early nineteenth centuries, four major caffeine-producing plants were present in North America: cacao (*Theobroma cacao*), yaupon holly (*Ilex vomitoria*), coffee (*Coffea arabica*), and tea (*Camellia sinensis*). The first two are native to the Americas yet neither species grew naturally in California. Yaupon holly along the coasts of the southeastern United States was used by local communities to brew an infusion later coined "Black Drink," and seemingly traded in precontact times as far as the area occupied by the Mississippian culture (King et al. 2017). Cacao was intensively grown throughout Mesoamerica and had acquired currency status during the Mexica's (formerly Aztec) reign of central Mexico. Chemical residue studies have demonstrated that its trade extended at least into the current southwestern United States (Crown et al. 2015). Coffee and tea, on the other hand, were brought to the Americas as part of the Columbian exchange. Due to political turmoil, the late eighteenth century saw a notable increase in the consumption of the former at expense of the latter, especially in the English-speaking realm.

Compiling evidence for the northern borderlands of New Spain, Graham and Skowronek (2016) emphasize the purposeful imports of cacao by settlers, the military, and the clergy alike to serve as gift for local Native people. In the San Francisco Bay Area, more specifically, Mission Santa Clara alone imported around 3.3 metric tons over the span of thirty-five years. At the same time, at the Santa Barbara Presidio coffee was acquired via shipments that sum slightly less than 1 kg, while its soldiers ordered over 600 kg of cacao (Graham and Skowronek 2016). It is especially interesting that a Mesoamerican-style metate was recovered at Asistencia de San Pedro y San Pablo and "chocolate pot" vessels have been identified in archaeological studies at Mission Santa Clara. In sum, while molecular distinction remains unresolved, the artifactual evidence and historical records suggests that cacao is the likeliest source of caffeine residues. Future residue studies may consider directly targeting secondary metabolites associated with cinnamon, since it was an ingredient often used in traditional chocolate consumption (and often mass imported with chocolate and sugar during this period) (Graham and Skowronek 2016).

In addition to the biomarker data, the untargeted metabolomic analysis yielded results that merit further consideration. First, figure 8.3 indicates that sex-related differences in residue profiles can be driven by a rather small set of molecules. For the asistencia, it appears that a single substance accounts for an important split within the community. None of the male individuals seems to have partaken in its consumption. Among women, some did, and others did not. While we acknowledge the reduced size of our study population, this sort of panorama is typical of gendered foods or activities (see chapter 12). For colonial-era California, basketry production is a likely candidate. The crafting of baskets was a female domain in which many but not all women participated. And while it is not per se classified as an activity of consumption, Native cultures throughout North America used not only hands but also teeth in manipulating raw materials to prepare and process plant fibers. O'Neale (1932) recorded basketry traditions specifically for the San Francisco Bay Area and Grant (2010) observed associated oral pathologies such as patterns of slanted tooth wear. Thus, there is a strong likelihood that the constant presence of plant fibers in the mouths of women led to the deposition of distinct yet traceable non-dietary residues.

Last, the untargeted metabolomics approach also produced further evidence as to the anomalous character of Burial 15. This teenage boy or young man is distinguished by a set of mortuary offerings that differed significantly from all other burials (chapter 5). The residues extracted from his dental calculus deposits further place him as an outlier. In fact, our results suggest differences in substance consumption substantial enough to achieve the degree of impact observed in every single one of the multivariate statistical analyses we conducted. Given the lack of pathological markers for a chronic or long-term condition, this could have resulted from a specialized diet, unique from all other individuals in the study. This coincides with data from baptismal records for an individual who may have been a recent arrival to Asistencia de San Pedro y San Pablo before passing away after only four months at the asistencia (see details in chapter 11).

Conclusion

The metabolomic analysis of dental calculus belonging to the baptized inhabitants of the asistencia provide additional archaeological evidence for the persistence of Native Californian traditions in the face of colonization and missionization. We detected nicotine residues in samples belonging to men and women, as well as children and adults. This suggests that tobacco consumption was widespread and at least tolerated by the community's religious leaders. We agree with Panich et al. (2018) by stating that the continued use of tobacco as medicine and/or ceremonial paraphernalia helped Native members of mission communities maintain elements of precontact social identity. The significant proportion of caffeine-positive individuals is a testimony to the early adoption of an imported substance, most likely cacao originating from Mesoamerica, given the widespread and enthusiastic use if this beverage by Spanish colonists (Graham and Skowronek 2016). Native Californians were probably exposed to chocolate traditions by sharing close quarters with Franciscan friars and other members of settler communities. Ultimately, this study provided further proof that residue profiles contain culturally relevant information beyond the presence or absence of known biomarkers. As a whole, the metabolomic data from the site opens a window onto sex-biased behavior and in-group/out-group and status dynamics among Native Californian during the colonial period.

References

Berlowitz, Ilana, Ernesto García Torres, Heinrich Walt, Ursula Wolf, Caroline Maake, and Chantal Martin-Soelch
2020   "Tobacco Is the Chief Medicinal Plant in My Work": Therapeutic Uses of Tobacco in Peruvian Amazonian Medicine Exemplified by the Work of a Maestro Tabaquero. *Frontiers in Pharmacology* 11:1–14.
Byrd, Brian F., Shannon Dearmond, and Laurel Engbring
2018   Re-visualizing Indigenous Persistence during Colonization from the Perspective of Traditional Settlements in the San Francisco Bay-Delta Area. *Journal of California and Great Basin Anthropology* 38(2):163–190.
Charlton, Anne
2004   Medicinal Uses of Tobacco in History. *Journal of the Royal Society of Medicine* 97:292–296.
Cook, S. F.
1943   The Indian Versus the Spanish Mission. *Ibero-Americana* 21:1–194.
Corti, Egon Caesar
1932   *A History of Smoking*. Harcourt, New York.
Crown, Patricia L., Jiyan Gu, W. Jeffrey Hurst, Timothy J. Ward, Ardith D. Bravenec, Syed Ali, Laura Kebert, Marlaina Berch, Erin Redman, Patrick D. Lyons, Jamie Merewether, David A. Phillips, Lori S. Reed, and Kyle Woodson
2015   Ritual Drinks in the Pre-Hispanic US Southwest and Mexican Northwest. *Proceedings of the National Academy of Sciences* 112:11436–11442.

Cuthrell, Rob Q., Lee M. Panich, and Oliver R. Hegge
2016   Investigating Native Californian Tobacco Use at Mission Santa Clara, California, through Morphometric Analysis of Tobacco (*Nicotiana* spp.) Seeds. *Journal of Archaeological Science: Reports* 6:451–462.

Damitio, William J., Shannon Tushingham, Korey J. Brownstein, R. G. Matson, and David R. Gang
2021   The Evolution of Smoking and Intoxicant Plant Use in Ancient Northwestern North America. *American Antiquity* 86(4):715–733.

Díaz del Castillo, Bernal
2007   *Historia Verdadera de la Conquista de la Nueva España*. Editorial Porrúa, Mexico City.

Drieu, Léa, Maxime Rageot, Nathan Wales, Ben Stern, Jasmine Lundy, Maximilian Zerrer, Isabella Gaffney, Manon Bondetti, Cynthianne Spiteri, Jane Thomas-Oates, and Oliver E. Craig
2020   Is It Possible to Identify Ancient Wine Production Using Biomolecular Approaches? *Science and Technology of Archaeological Research* 6:16–29.

Duke, Daron, Eric Wohlgemuth, Karen R. Adams, Angela Armstrong-Ingram, Sarah K. Rice, and D. Craig Young
2022   Earliest Evidence for Human Use of Tobacco in the Pleistocene Americas. *Nature Human Behavior* 6:183–192.

Eerkens, Jelmer W., Shannon Tushingham, Korey J. Brownstein, Ramona Garibay, Katherine Perez, Engel Murga, Phil Kaijankoski, Jeffrey S. Rosenthal, and David R. Gang
2018   Dental Calculus as a Source of Ancient Alkaloids: Detection of Nicotine by LC-MS in Calculus Samples from the Americas. *Journal of Archaeological Science: Reports* 18:509–515.

Fages, Pedro, and Herbert J. Priestley
1919   An Historical, Political, and Natural Description of California. *The Catholic Historic Review* 4:486–509.

Goodman, Jordan
1993   *Tobacco in History*. Routledge, London.

Graham, Margaret A., and Russell K. Skowronek
2016   Chocolate on the Borderlands of New Spain. *International Journal of Historical Archaeology* 20:645–665.

Grant, David
2010   Native Americans in the San Francisco Bay Area: Patterns in Ancient Teeth, Palimpsests of Behavior. Unpublished MA thesis. Department of Anthropology, San Jose State University.

Hackel, Steven W.
2005   *Children of the Coyote, Missionaries of Saint Francis: Indian–Spanish Relations in Colonial California, 1769-1850*. University of North Carolina Press, Chapel Hill.

Hardy, Karen, Stephen Buckley, Matthew J. Collins, Almudena Estalrrich, Don Brothwell, Les Copeland, Antonio García-Tabernero, Samuel García-Vargas, Marco De La Rasilla, Carles Lalueza-Fox, Rosa Huguet, Markus Bastir, David Santamaría, Marco Madella, Julie Wilson, Ángel Fernández Cortés, and Antonio Rosas
2012   Neanderthal Medics? Evidence for Food, Cooking, and Medicinal Plants Entrapped in Dental Calculus. *Naturwissenschaften* 99:617–626.

Harrington, John P.
1932   Tobacco among the Karuk Indians of California. *Bureau of American Ethnology Bulletin* 94:1–284.

Jones, Terry L., William R. Hildebrandt, Eric Wohlgemuth, and Brian F. Codding
2022   Postcontact Cultural Perseverance on the Central California Coast: Sedentism and Maritime Intensification. *American Antiquity* 87:505–522.

King, Adam, Terry G. Powis, Kong F. Cheong, and Nilesh W. Gaikwad
2017   Cautionary Tales on the Identification of Caffeinated Beverages in North America. *Journal of Archaeological Science* 85:30–40.

Kroeber, Alfred L.
1941   Culture Element Distributions XV: Salt, Dogs, Tobacco. *Anthropological Records* 6:1–20.

Matthee, Rudi
1995   Exotic Substances: The Introduction and Global Spread of Tobacco, Coffee, Cocoa, Tea, and Distilled Liquor, Sixteenth to Eighteenth Centuries. In *Drugs and Narcotics in History*, edited by Roy Porter and Mikuláš Teich, 24–51. Cambridge University Press, Cambridge.

McBride, Joe Rayl, Rita Yolanda Cavero, Anna Liisa Cheshire, María Isabel Calvo, and Deborah Lea McBride
2020   Exchange of Medicinal Plant Information in California Missions. *Journal of Ethnobiology and Ethnomedicine* 16:1–36.

Mead, George R.
1972   The Ethnobotany of the California Indians: A Compendium of the Plants, Their Users, and Their Uses. Museum of Anthropology, University of Northern Colorado, Greeley.

de Micheli, Alfredo, and Raúl Izaguirre-Ávila
2005   Taboco y Tabaquismo en la Historia de México y de Europa. *Revista de Investigacion Clinica* 57:608–613.

Milliken, Randall
1995   *A Time of Little Choice: The Disintegration of Tribal Culture in the San Francisco Bay Area 1769–1810*. Ballena Press, Ramona.

Moonkham, Piyawit
2023   Community Based Archaeology: Social Space, Plant Use, and Heterarchy in Thailand. Unpublished PhD dissertation. Department of Anthropology, Washington State University.

Newell, Quincy D.
2008   The Varieties of Religious Experience: Baptized Indians at Mission San Francisco de Asís, 1776–1821. *American Indian Quarterly* 32:412–442.

O'Neale, Lila M.
1932   *Yurok-Karok Basket Weavers.* Phoebe A. Hearst Museum of Anthropology, Berkeley.

Ortiz, Fernando
1963   *Contrapunteo Cubano del Tabaco y el Azúcar.* Consejo Nacional de Cultura, La Habana.

Panich, Lee M., and Tsim D. Schneider
2015   Expanding Mission Archaeology: A Landscape Approach to Indigenous Autonomy in Colonial California. *Journal of Anthropological Archaeology* 40:48–58.

Panich, Lee M., Rebecca Allen, and Andrew Galvan
2018   The Archaeology of Native American Persistence at Mission San José. *Journal of California and Great Basin Anthropology* 38:11–29.

Reddy, Seetha N.
2015   Feeding Family and Ancestors: Persistence of Traditional Native American Lifeways during the Mission Period in Coastal Southern California. *Journal of Anthropological Archaeology* 37:48–66.

Robinson, David W., Kelly Brown, Moira McMenemy, Lynn Dennany, Matthew J. Baker, Pamela Allan, Caroline Cartwright, Julienne Bernard, Fraser Sturt, Elena Kotoula, Christopher Jazwa, Kristina M. Gill, Patrick Randolph-Quinney, Thomas Ash, Clare Bedford, Devlin Gandy, Matthew Armstrong, James Miles, and David Haviland
2020   Datura Quids at Pinwheel Cave, California, Provide Unambiguous Confirmation of the Ingestion of Hallucinogens at a Rock Art Site. *Proceedings of the National Academy of Sciences* 117:31026–31037.

Roulette, Casey J., Hayley Mann, Brian M. Kemp, Mark Remiker, Jennifer W. Roulette, Barry S. Hewlett, Mirdad Kazanji, Sébastien Breurec, Didier Monchy, Roger J. Sullivan, and Edward H. Hagen
2014   Tobacco Use vs. Helminths in Congo Basin Hunter-Gatherers: Self-Medication in Humans? *Evolution and Human Behavior* 35:397–407.

Silliman, Stephen W.
2015   A Requiem for Hybridity? The Problem with Frankensteins, Purees, and Mules. *Journal of Social Archaeology* 15:277–298.

Suárez Argüello, Clara Elena
2011   De Mercado Libre a Monopolio Estatal: La Producción Tabacalera en Nueva España, 1760–1800. In *Caminos y Mercados de México*, edited by Janet Long Towell and Amalia Attolini Lecón, 411–432. UNAM–INAH, Mexico City.

Tushingham, Shannon, Dominique Ardura, J. W. Jelmer W. Eerkens, Mine Palazoglu, Sevini Shahbaz, and Oliver Fiehn
2013   Hunter-Gatherer Tobacco Smoking: Earliest Evidence from the Pacific Northwest Coast of North America. *Journal of Archaeological Science* 40(2):1397–1407.

Tushingham, Shannon, and Jelmer W. Eerkens
2016   Hunter-Gatherer Tobacco Smoking in Ancient North America: Current Chemical Evidence and a Framework for Future Studies. In *Perspectives on the*

Archaeology of Pipes, Tobacco and other Smoke Plants in the Ancient Americas, edited by Elizabeth Bollwerk and Shannon Tushingham, 211–230. Springer, New York.

Tushingham, Shannon, Jelmer W. Eerkens, Anna Berim, Korey J. Brownstein, and David R. Gang

2020 Age and Gender Dynamics of Tobacco Use: Residue Analysis of Dental Calculus and Archaeological Pipes. In *Protohistoric Village Organization and Territorial Maintenance: The Archaeology of Síi Túupentak (CA-ALA-565/H) in the San Francisco Bay Area.* Center for Archaeological Research at Davis Publication Number 20, edited by Brian F. Byrd, Laurel Engbring, Michael Darcangelo, and Allika Ruby, 345–358. Center for Archaeological Research at Davis, Davis.

Tushingham, Shannon, Charles M. Snyder, Korey J. Brownstein, William J. Damitio, and David R. Gang

2018 Biomolecular Archaeology Reveals Ancient Origins of Indigenous Tobacco Smoking in North American Plateau. *Proceedings of the National Academy of Sciences* 115:11742–11747.

Velsko, Irina M., Katherine A. Overmyer, Camilla Speller, Lauren Klaus, Matthew J. Collins, Louise Loe, Laurent A. F. Frantz, Krithivasan Sankaranarayanan, Cecil M. Lewis, Juan Bautista Rodriguez Martinez, Eros Chaves, Joshua J. Coon, Greger Larson, and Christina Warinner

2017 The Dental Calculus Metabolome in Modern and Historic Samples. *Metabolomics* 13:1–17.

Winter, Joseph C.

2000 *Tobacco Use by Native North Americans: Sacred Smoke and Silent Killer.* University of Oklahoma Press, Norman.

Zimmermann, Mario, Brian Byrd, Laurel Engbring, Jelmer Eerkens, Monica Arellano, Alan Leventhal, Dave Grant, Diane DiGiuseppe, Elisabeth Mabie, Anna Berim, David Gang, and Shannon Tushingham

i.p. Disease and Healing in Ancient Societies: Dental Calculus Residues and Skeletal Pathology Data Indicate Age and Sex-Biased Medicinal Practices among Native Californians. *Human Biology.* In Press.

9

Examining Heavy Metal Exposure at Asistencia de San Pedro y San Pablo during the Mission Period in Northern California

Diana Malarchik, Jelmer W. Eerkens,
Christopher Canzonieri, Christopher Zimmer,
Tanya M. Smith, Christine Austin, and Austin Cole

The Spanish introduced agriculture, a range of new foodstuffs and material technologies to the Native people of California, including inhabitants of Asistencia de San Pedro y San Pablo (CA-SMA-71/H; hereafter referred to simply as the asistencia). Records specifically mention corn, beans, peas, wheat, asparagus, rosemary, barley, peach and quince trees, and grape vineyards. While historic records provide information about the types of foods grown, they often fail to account for the manners in which many foods were prepared, cooked, and served.

Changes in heavy metal exposure from precontact to the Mission Period can point to cultural changes in food preparation. For example, it is known that copper pots and iron grills were often used to prepare Spanish food and drink across the mission system (Popper, 2016; Simmons and Turley, 1980). Whether these were used at specific Northern Californian missions is less well known.

We hypothesize that use of metal tools, especially as part of cooking, and new food types, exposed Native communities to higher levels of copper and zinc compared to precontact individuals. Furthermore, we hypothesize that the introduction of agriculture and domesticated cattle exposed individuals to elevated levels of iron and zinc through red meat consumption. As foods consumed are incorporated into hard tissues of the body, these dietary practices can be reflected in the chemical signatures preserved in bones and teeth. Dental enamel is of particular interest because it mineralizes in layers during childhood and does not remodel during life, and thus records exposure during childhood years within the growth layers. Furthermore, because some metals can be absorbed into subsurface enamel after formation, enamel may also record adult exposures if metals are consistently present in the mouth. Together, this allows a unique opportunity to use dentition to study heavy metal exposure across a population. We test these hypotheses with data from the asistencia population.

Essential Metals in Dental Enamel

Copper, zinc, and iron are present throughout the human body as well as within the oral cavity. Copper and zinc have been studied in modern populations to determine changes in the acidity of the oral cavity and their effect on dental caries (Khan et al., 2020). The majority of zinc accumulates in dental enamel just after eruption (Cuellar-Rivas and Pustovrh-Ramos, 2015; Khan et al., 2020; Klimuszko et al., 2018). Metalloproteinases, specifically enamelysin, are created in enamel during the maturation process of each tooth. After eruption, these proteinases bind to calcium and zinc within the oral cavity. Through this protein-binding mechanism zinc is retained in dental enamel, with an average concentration between 115 and 215 µg/g in modern populations (Cuellar-Rivas and Pustovrh-Ramos, 2015; Kamenov et al., 2018; Khan et al., 2020; Klimuszko et al., 2018).

The introduction of copper into dental enamel is less understood. There is no strong consensus on in vitro changes that raise levels of copper in dental enamel. Copper creates a protective phosphate phase on the surface of the tooth, which inhibits demineralization of enamel, and can prevent dental caries (Khan et al., 2020; Klimuszko et al., 2018). Some studies suggest that increasing dietary copper by 2–6 µg/g during pregnancy and early childhood will increase copper in dental enamel and decrease rates of caries (Klimuszko et al., 2018).

Iron exposure has been the subject of both clinical and archaeological studies due to its widespread use in antiquity. Iron uptake in dental enamel occurs both during in vitro and in vivo conditions. During in vitro development, iron is not incorporated into the hydroxyapatite crystals of dental enamel, but rather is absorbed on the surface of the enamel. During life, iron in enamel is taken in as a trivalent iron compound, meaning that iron is not a part of the mineral component of teeth (Bauminger et al., 1985). Modern teeth show iron concentrations that range from 10 to 50µg/g in enamel (Williams and Siegele, 2014). Archaeological teeth show that there often is post-depositional uptake of iron, but typically constrained to the first 100µm of exposed enamel.

Interestingly, both iron-rich and low-iron soil show similar uptakes in archaeological dentition (Williams and Siegele, 2014), such that different soil conditions do not affect iron concentrations in archaeological teeth.

While the diagenetic processes of heavy metals are not fully understood, potential change can be accounted for in concordance for how each metal should be taken in by enamel. Recent studies show that the highest levels of zinc are contained in the outmost enamel (Dean et al., 2019; Smith et al., 2022). Most zinc is retained in enamel after eruption, which suggests low effects of diagenesis after burial as there would be few, if any metalloproteases left to bind zinc from the soil environment (Cuellar-Rivas and Pustovrh-Ramos, 2015; Khan et al., 2020; Klimuszko et al., 2018). Potential for copper absorption after burial also seems relatively low, as copper absorption in enamel notably increases when copper is introduced during mineralization but is not significantly absorbed after this stage, suggesting a time restriction to increasing copper levels (Klimuszko et al., 2018). While iron shows uptake after deposition, normally constrained to 100um in depth, such iron is removed during sample preparation as the outer layer of enamel is drilled away before powder is collected.

Heavy Metals

Wide-scale industrialization in the eighteenth and nineteenth centuries (lead piping, lead glazed pottery, and lead based paints) along with new medicinal practices (mercurial cures) increased human exposure to lead and mercury in many places around the world. Clinically, exposure to lead during childhood impairs the ability to control emotions and create complex interpersonal relationships, regulate aggression, and has recently shown connection to behaviors associated with autism and attention deficit disorder (Gump et al., 2017). High exposure to mercury during pregnancy has been linked to cerebral palsy, blindness, deafness, cerebral ataxia, and impaired physical growth in offspring (Acosta-Saavedra et al., 2011). High heavy metal exposure is known to be more prevalent in mid-nineteenth-century to early twentieth-century United States Euro-American populations (Budd et al., 1998; Martínez-García et al., 2005).

Copper, iron, and zinc are among the list of essential nutrients required by humans for a range of physiological processes. Copper is required for growth and development (Gaetke and Chow, 2003), and is used by enzymes during cellular respiration, antioxidant defense, and connective tissue formation (Ellingsen et al., 2015). Copper is present in both water and food, with high amounts found in oysters, animal liver, legumes, grains, and dried fruit

(Gaetke and Chow, 2003). Zinc is a protein inhibitor of serine protease, an enzyme that cleaves peptide bonds in proteins and is necessary throughout the body (Klimuszko et al., 2018; Sandstead, 2015). Insufficient zinc leads to oxidative stress, lessened resistance to infections, decreased fertility, and decreased growth and development (Sandstead, 2015). Zinc also has a role in the formation of dental calculus, inhibiting the formation of hydroxyapatite, and is incorporated in calcium triphosphate, a major mineral of teeth (Martin et al., 2007). While zinc and copper are necessary throughout the body, they have an inverse relationship. As the level of zinc within the body rises, the level of copper reduces, and vice versa (Klimuszko et al., 2018). This counter relationship increases chances of toxicity in the body of either element when the other metal is below the normal range necessary for physiological processes.

Iron is a biological catalyst and is the dominant metal in the human body. Specific biological functions where iron is needed include oxygen transport, electron transfers, and DNA synthesis (Ponka et al., 2015). While copper exposure decreases absorption of zinc, it has the opposite effect on iron, where it increases absorption (Konikowska and Mandecka, 2018). While copper, zinc, and iron are used through the body in a wide range of biological functions, health problems can occur when the levels of each of these metals is either too low or too high.

Metal Toxicity

Because they are essential, the human body has evolved to regulate copper, iron, and zinc, and toxicity is reached only with intense and extended exposure. For example, necessary daily amounts of copper for an adult range from 1 to 100 mg per day, while copper toxicity starts at 6000 mg and lethal doses at 9000 to 11,000 mg (Collins and Klevay, 2011). Clinical symptoms can manifest at levels as low as 1,000 mg of copper present in blood levels (Collins and Klevay, 2011; Fraga and Oteiza, 2002; Gaetke and Chow, 2003; Nriagu, 2007). Common symptoms of copper poisoning include lethargy, nausea, liver problems, and disruptions to renal functions (Gaetke and Chow, 2003).

Zinc and iron toxicity operate in a similar manner to copper. Both require high exposure and affect overall liver and kidney health. Recommended daily levels for zinc in adults is 15 mg, with symptoms of toxicity manifesting at levels of 1,000–2,000 mg (Agnew and Slesinger, 2022). As zinc accumulates, a person typically experiences stomach pains and diarrhea, and with more severe exposure, vomiting, nausea, pulmonary edema, and liver damage that can be fatal (Nriagu, 2007). The average amount of iron required for adults is approximately 20 mg/kg, with moderate toxicity appearing at levels from 20 to 60mg/kg, and severe symptoms and mortality occurring at levels exceeding 60mg/kg (Yuen and Becker, 2022). High amounts of iron affect the liver and heart, and lead to hormone abnormalities and immune system dysfunction (Fraga and Oteiza, 2002; Ponka et al., 2015).

Though exposure to metals would need to be severe and prolonged to increase morbidity and mortality, increased exposure to copper, iron, and zinc can speak to overall health at both the individual and group level. Examining exposure to these elements, in comparison to precontact periods, can provide important context on the life experience of Native people living within the mission system.

Exposure to metals can be expressed in three ways within the tooth enamel. First, exposure could be during childhood, perhaps in time-restricted windows relating to particular behaviors (e.g., consumption of metal-containing medicines during illnesses). For such exposure, we expect to either see high levels throughout the enamel, if exposure was constant, or see bands of higher exposure within the enamel along expected growth axes, surrounded by lower-density bands, if exposure was periodic. Second, exposure could be primarily after enamel formation but within the lifespan of an individual. If such metals are within items placed in the mouth, such as food or medicine, metals could be absorbed on the surface and into the subsurface enamel through biochemical processes similar to those involved in fluoride incorporation. If so, we should see a band of high density on the outer surfaces of teeth, with thinner or nonexistent bands on the occlusal surfaces where the layer of higher-density metal would be actively ground away (as is the case for naturally occurring zinc, e.g., Dean et al., 2019). Third, exposure could be post-depositional as metals from soil absorb into the tooth through chemical processes after death. Post-depositional changes would affect exposed dentin as well as enamel.

Materials and Methods

We analyzed first and third molar enamel from individuals representing three different time periods, precontact, Mission Period, and nineteenth-century historic, within the San Francisco Bay. Three individuals from CA-SFR-191 represent the precontact period, dating between 700 and 1500 calBP. We use these individuals to represent a baseline of heavy metal exposure in ancestral Ohlone lifeways prior to missionization. These samples were analyzed with permission from the Native American Most Likely Descendant (MLD) at the site. Five individuals from the asistencia represent the Mission Period sample. The historic sample is comprised of three individuals from Yerba Buena Cemetery and one from City Cemetery within San Francisco City. These historic Euro-American burials date to the second half of the nineteenth century, with Yerba Buena representing 1850–1870 and City Cemetery dating to 1870–1900. The goal is to show how heavy metal exposure changed on the San Francisco Peninsula from precontact to Mission Period for Native Americans, and then into the Historic Period for Euro-Americans for comparison.

Because some individuals in the asistencia population were born before establishment of the missions, and likely developed their teeth under precontact lifeways, while others were likely born and lived their entire lives within the mission, we expect differences in the expression of heavy metals with ontogenetic age.

Bulk Heavy Metal Analysis

Each third molar was sectioned into vertical halves using a Isomet low-speed saw, with a complete crown to root segment. Enamel from one halved section of each third molar was removed using a Foredom drill with a stainless-steel bit. The powdered enamel was submitted for Inductively Coupled Plasma-Mass Spectrometry (ICP-MS) analysis at the UC Davis Interdisciplinary Center for Plasma Mass Spectrometry. Approximately 30 mg of powdered enamel was placed in 500μL (microliters) 50% nitric acid (HNO_3) and heated for fifteen minutes at 95C and allowed to cool. Then in five-minute increments for a total of twenty-five minutes, a total of 500μL of 30% hydrogen peroxide (H_2O_2) was added to each sample, followed by an additional thirty minutes of heating (55 minutes total) to digest the sample. Samples were then cooled and brought up with MilliQ Water until they were 1.5mL. Blanks were made for control. Sample blanks consisting of 30μL MilliQ Water, laboratory control standards, a heavy metal standard, and 125μL100ppm gold (Au) were prepared with the samples in a similar fashion. After trial runs, samples were diluted in MilliQ Water by a factor of 25 to bring element concentrations into the measurable range on the Agilent Technologies 7500ce ICP quadrupole mass spectrometer. The results of the heavy metal analysis provide elemental concentrations for thirty-four elements. Here, we focus on Cu, Fe, Hg, Pb, and Zn.

Laser Ablation-Inductively Coupled Plasma-Mass Spectrometry Imaging

While the dissolution analyses above determine "bulk" concentrations in enamel, Laser Ablation-Inductively Coupled Plasma-Mass Spectrometry (LA-ICP-MS) determines elemental distributions within a tooth in situ at a finer spatial scale (Hare et al., 2011; Kangas et al., 2004; Smith et al., 2021). Following the histological preparation methods of Smith et al. (2021), LA-ICP-MS maps of first molars of Burials 2, 11, and 14 were prepared according to methods first detailed in Hare et al. (2011). The laser aerosolizes a small amount of the tooth, which is transported to the ICP-MS where the particles are volatized, atomized, and ionized in high temperature plasma and measured by the mass spectrometer (Smith et al., 2021). A resulting two-dimensional concentration map for each tooth section shows relative concentrations of Ca-normalized elements within the cross section, blues representing low levels and reds for higher levels. For this study, only Cu, Zn, and Pb are considered. The goal is to examine how copper and zinc are distributed within a tooth, that is, in a manner consistent with in vivo absorption, exposure after tooth formation but before death, or post-depositional contamination.

Results

Results for the two sets of analyses, bulk enamel vs. LA-ICP-MS on tooth cross sections, are presented in the following section. Where possible, we also compare to data from modern dental studies (Abdullah et al., 2012; Kamenov et al., 2018).

Changes in Metal Concentrations in the California Mission Period

Comparing concentrations of trace elements shows patterns of metal exposure that appear to co-occur with cultural shifts (table 9.1). While most elements were roughly comparable in concentration (Ag, Al, As, B, Ba, Be, Ca, Cd, Co, Cr, Cs, Ga, H, K, Li, Mg, Mn, Na, Ni, P, Sb, Se, Si, Sn, Sr, Ti, U, and V) among all the tooth samples, copper, iron, zinc, lead, and mercury separate the three San Francisco populations. In particular, precontact Ohlone (CA-SFR-191) show relatively low concentrations of all heavy metals; Mission Period Ohlone show high levels of iron, zinc, and especially copper; and historic samples are elevated in zinc and iron, but are especially elevated in lead and mercury. The last row in table 9.1 shows average values from professionally extracted adult dentition from Europe, the Caribbean, and Africa, and North, South, and Central America (see Abdullah et al., 2012; Kamenov et al., 2018).

Focusing on the asistencia samples, there are distinct patterns that suggest an increase in heavy metal exposure during the years of M3 crown development. Because they were not yet adults at the time of death, Burials 2 and 14 would have been forming their third molar crowns during Spanish missionization. Likewise, Burial 6, at eighteen to twenty-five years old at the time of death, may have been recruited into the mission while his third molars were

Table 9.1. Results from bulk heavy metal analysis for each individual in parts per million, as well as an average of published averages from modern teeth

Burial	Sex	Age	Tooth	Cu	Fe	Zn	Hg	Pb
SFR-191 B3	Indeterminate	16–19	LLM3	1.8	117	777	0.5	0.7
SFR-191 B17.2	Indeterminate	15–20	LLM3	1.5	188	997	5.8	2.4
SFR-191 18.1	Male	35–45	LLM3	218	617	997	0.6	1.1
Sánchez Adobe B2	Male	13–17	URM3	8.4	865	1333	0.5	1.4
Sánchez Adobe B3	Female	45+	LRM3	133	960	1600	3.4	2
Sánchez Adobe B6	Male	18–25	URM3	142	562	1045	2.2	1.9
Sánchez Adobe B8	Male	45+	ULM3	64.1	1151	1934	0.5	11.9
Sánchez Adobe B14	Female	5–7	ULM3	7.8	1253	1046	0.6	3.4
Yerba Buena B1	Male	20–35	LLM3	13.1	1255	1714	198	281
Yerba Buena B3	Male	30–39	ULM3	9.2	2127	1597	10.8	488
Yerba Buena B4	Indeterminate	35+	LLM3	4.9	1484	1000	142	264
Baker Beach B1	Female	30–40	URM3	5.6	485	1098	573	371
Published Averages	-	-	-	3.6	15	215	1.5	6.6

still growing. By contrast, as older adults at the time of death, Burials 3 and 8 formed their third molars prior to missionization.

As shown in table 9.1, bulk M3 enamel in the asistencia individuals is generally higher in Cu, Fe, and Zn than precontact Ohlone individuals from CA-SFR-191, but equal (and low) in Hg and Pb. Burial 6 has the highest level of Cu and Burial 14 the highest concentration of Fe of all the asistencia individuals in this study, which could represent in vivo exposure. Yet, Burial 2, a teenage male, and Burial 14 show relatively low levels of Cu. Interestingly, the two older individuals, Burial 3 (female) and Burial 8 (male), also have high levels of Cu.

With completely formed third molars at the time of Spanish contact there must be another explanation for this high amount of copper, iron, and zinc. Burials 3 and 8 were both older adults (45+) both with dental wear and periodontal disease, and periapical lesions in Burial 3. Perhaps dental wear and cracks in the enamel allowed copper, iron, and zinc a route into the tooth where it was later collected during our analysis. Higher rates of copper in the oral environment has been linked to a decrease in caries (Khan et al., 2020), suggesting a role played in remineralization of dentition, which could also provide an explanation for increased levels in older individuals.

Copper is the metal that sets the Mission Period samples apart, with higher amounts of variation and overall exposure. It should be noted that the individual represented by SFR-191–18.1 has extremely high concentrations of both copper and iron (table 9.1). Box and whisker plots (figure 9.1) reflect these higher levels through lengthened third and fourth quartiles yet retain a very low mean reflective of the other two precontact Ohlone. While it is not known how this individual was exposed to these metals during life, it may be due to their high status. Burial goods with SFR-191 Burial 18.1 included a number of unusual items such as mica pendants, and a large number of shell beads, marking this grave as a person of importance. Their high levels of metal might be representative of behaviors associated with their high status, such as use of body paints. Though SFR-191 Burial 18.1 is an outlier, the changes in copper, iron, and zinc in Mission Period Ohlone are still noteworthy.

Overall the increase in metal exposure in all samples demonstrates a specific change that came with Spanish missions. Historic period samples demonstrate increased exposure to additional heavy metals (figure 9.1). While both historic and Mission Period samples contain higher amounts of zinc and iron, historic San Franciscans are unique in their lead and mercury exposure. While this exposure is explained through the use of lead in industrialization and mercury in cosmetics and medicines, we do not see these cultural behaviors in the Mission Period. Many other elements, such as calcium, highlight the similarities seen across the three time periods with heavy metal exposure. To further examine exposure to heavy metals, we undertook LA-ICP-MS analysis of a small sample of teeth from the asistencia.

LA-ICP-MS and Elemental Distribution within a Tooth

To better understand the distribution of heavy metals within teeth, LA-ICP-MS imaging was used to examine lead, copper, and zinc ratios (relative to calcium) in first molars of three individuals. Unfortunately, we were unable to analyze iron in a similar manner. These images represent varying concentrations of elements over a cross section. All three individuals died at young ages, with Burial 11 (a male child) and Burial 14 (a female child) dying before their first molar roots completed growing. As a result, if heavy metal concentrations in the teeth represent in vivo behavior of the individual, it should

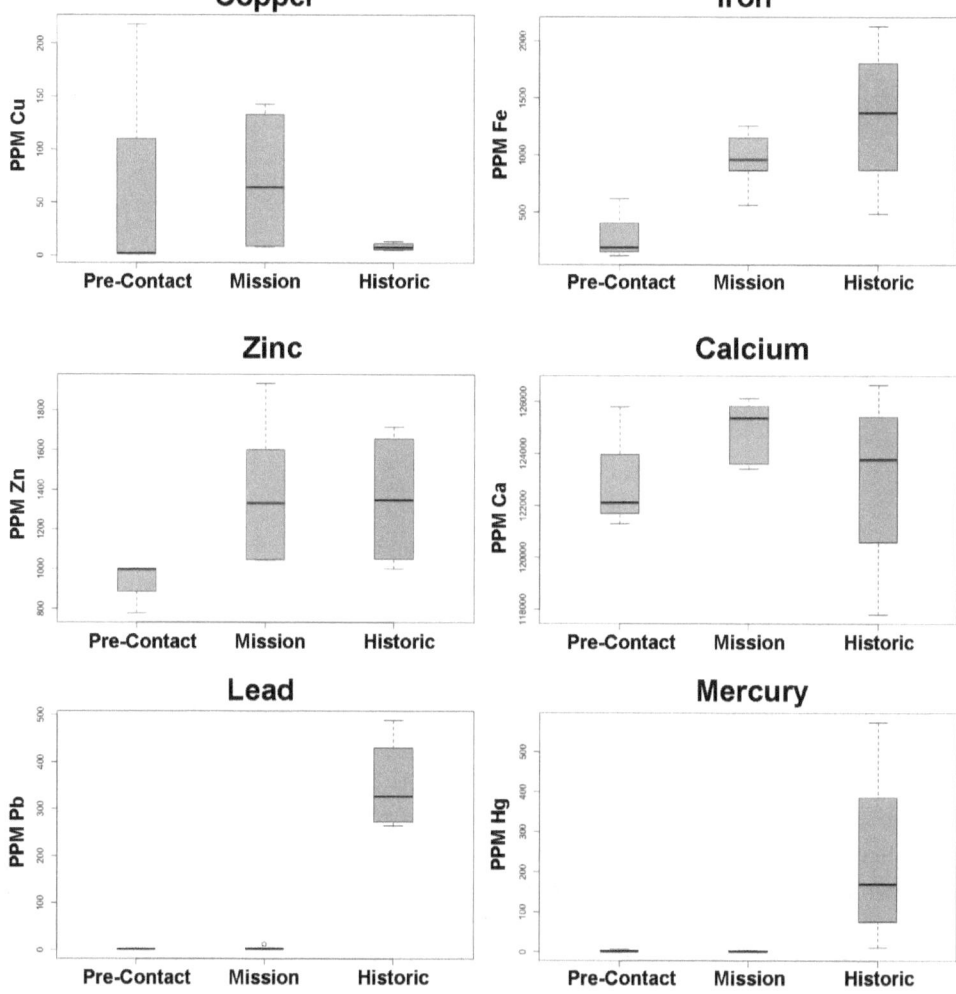

Figure 9.1. Box and whisker plots showing metal levels in parts per million for copper (*top left*), iron (*top right*), zinc (*middle left*), calcium (*middle right*), lead (*bottom left*), and mercury (*bottom right*) by time period.

correspond to periods of time they were participating in the mission system (i.e., in the several years before death). Differences in how different metals enter into dental tissues can be seen by comparing lead, zinc, and copper concentrations along the enamel surface, the occlusal surface, and the pulp cavity.

The accumulation of lead within dental tissues often occurs during dental development (Budd et al., 1998; Smith et al. 2018). While post-depositional lead accumulation can take place, enamel is often well-regarded for its resis-

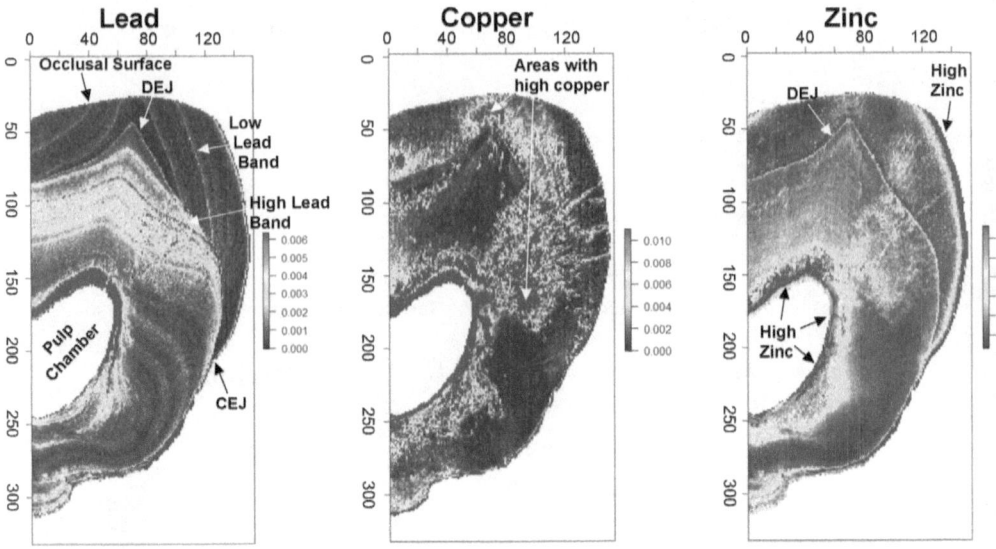

Figure 9.2. LA-ICP-MS maps showing lead, copper, and zinc concentrations, relative to ^{43}Ca for Burial 2 first molar.

tance to diagenetic changes. Dentin, though, due to its higher organic content, is more susceptible to changes after death (Hillson, 1996). All concentration maps show increases and decreases in lead along growth lines, which support the interpretation that these changes in lead occurred in vivo rather than being the result of post-depositional effects.

The three burials from the asistencia show mild exposure to lead, with higher exposure occurring after the weaning period and toward the end of crown completion. Dentin in Burials 2 and 11 show distinct bands of higher and lower lead, suggesting increased exposure came as these individuals shifted from breastfeeding to eating adult foodstuffs around the ages of two to four years (see chapter 6). Burial 14 is more interesting as she has a large hypoplasia that appears at approximately six months of age. This individual may have been weaned early and underwent further stressors during the short time her tooth developed. Though lead levels seem to have increased during dentinogenesis for these individuals, their overall levels are minimal when compared to historic Euro-American samples.

As mentioned, most zinc enters the crystalline structure of enamel after eruption (Cuellar-Rivas and Pustovrh-Ramos, 2015; Khan et al., 2020; Klimuszko et al., 2018). This is evident in the first molar for Burial 2, shown in figure 9.2. Zinc concentrations in Burial 2 (thirteen- to seventeen-year-old male) show the highest concentrations (red colors) along the non-occlusal enamel outer surface and pulp cavity. The area of high zinc concentration,

Examining Heavy Metal Exposure · 187

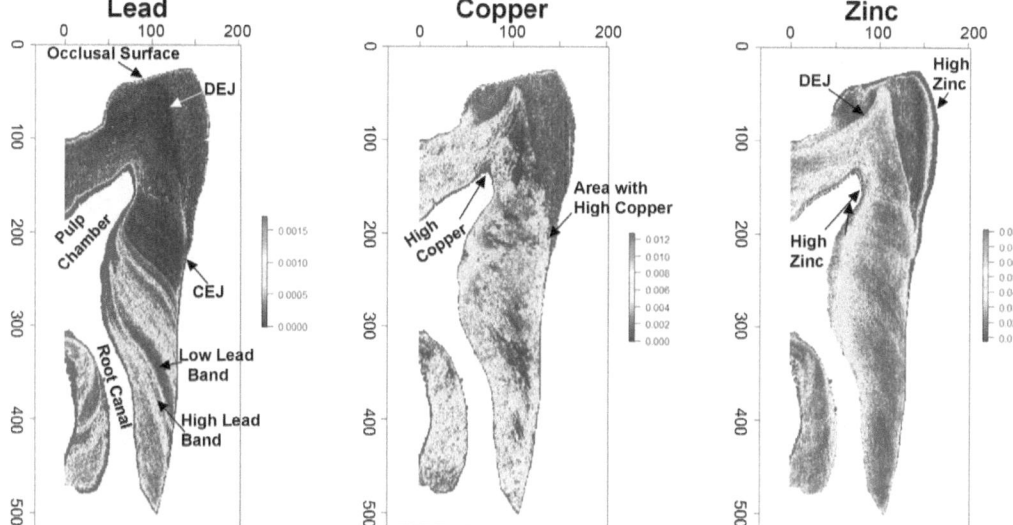

Figure 9.3. LA-ICP-MS maps showing lead, copper, and zinc concentrations, relative to ^{43}Ca for Burial 14 first molar.

however, has been removed along the occlusal surface, likely due to wear. For a color heat map of figure 9.2, please refer to the online version of this chapter. For an image of the original tooth cross section, see the book appendix, figure A.4.

Due to the wear found on Burial 14 (see figure 9.3), the layer of high Zn along the exposed enamel, which mirrors much of what is seen on Burial 2, is likely due to diagenesis. For an image of the original tooth cross section, see the book appendix, figure A.5. For a color heat map of figure 9.3, refer to the online version of this chapter.

By contrast, in Burial 11 (see figure 9.4), there is no or very minimal occlusal wear, resulting in a more even layer of high Zn all along the outer surface of the enamel. For an image of the original tooth cross section, see the book appendix, figure A.6. A color heat map is available in the online version of this chapter.

In short, the maps indicate that Zn in the oral cavity (for enamel), or in the blood (for the circumpulpal dentin lining the pulp cavity), was absorbed through chemical reactions into dental tissues, *after* enamel formation. Dentin is somewhat affected in vivo, as the circumpupal later is accreted slowly throughout life, which is what ultimately leads to the narrowing of the pupal cavity. Some of this Zn is then lost through occlusal wear. At the same time, figures 9.2–9.4 also show distinctive variation in Zn concentration along growth lines, especially in the dentin, resulting in a banded appearance. Most

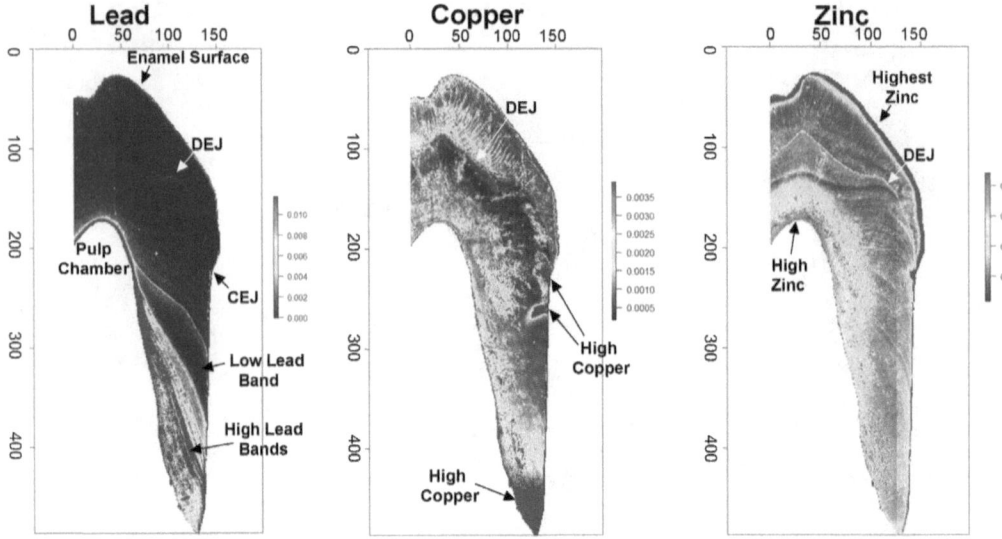

Figure 9.4. LA-ICP-MS maps showing lead, copper, and zinc concentrations, relative to ^{43}Ca for Burial 11 first molar.

of this Zn was not deposited during exposure in the oral cavity since much of this tissue formed prior to tooth eruption, particularly in Burial 2 and 11. Instead, such Zn must have been deposited during tissue formation as exposure to Zn shifted between higher and lower values in vivo. These banded lines show that zinc exposure was not continual during childhood, but recorded periods of higher and lower exposure. Finally, Zn is not higher in the final layer of growth (e.g., Burial 14 and 11) where the dentin was exposed to soil. This suggests that Zn was not absorbed after burial from the soil.

Less is known about the pattern of copper absorption into dental enamel, though higher levels of dietary copper during pregnancy and early childhood, which correlate to times of enamel mineralization, have been shown to increase levels in enamel (Klimuszko et al., 2018). Levels of copper in the individuals depicted in figures 9.2–9.4 are highest along the exposed walls of the pulp cavity, which could indicate transfer from blood or other soft tissue in vivo but after tissue formation for enamel or within dentin with the accretion of the circumpupal layer. There are also layers of higher concentrations of copper along growth lines in Burial 2, which would be consistent with copper being deposited into teeth as enamel is forming, prior to tooth eruption.

At the same time, copper concentrations are much more heterogeneous within both enamel and dentin, showing areas of higher density that do not correspond to growth layers. The larger area of copper in Burial 2 seems to be following cracks from the enamel surface down into the deeper enamel and dentin. This pattern is not seen in Burials 11 and 14, supporting the idea of post-depositional changes when enamel is damaged. As well, some areas of high copper correspond to areas of the tooth that were most exposed to soil (e.g., Burial 11 and 14 apical root dentin). Such copper was most likely deposited post-depositionally and is not reflective of events during life.

In short, these heat maps indicate that the highest concentrations of zinc in enamel correspond to in vivo transfer from the oral cavity onto the enamel surface, which is then removed by occlusal wear. Evidence for post-depositional absorption of zinc only appears in small patches. Evidence in Burial 11 also indicates that copper could have been absorbed in vivo, creating bands of higher and lower concentrations. However, evidence is also consistent with most copper being absorbed post-depositionally, especially into dentin.

Discussion

As described in several chapters of this volume, Ohlone who lived during the Mission Period saw rapid changes in many facets of daily life. As we show above, asistencia individuals have higher copper, iron, and zinc relative to precontact Ohlone, and higher copper relative to historic burials, which we interpret as markers of behavioral change across the precontact to historic periods. We hypothesize that changes in diet and cooking methods within the mission are responsible for these observations.

In many California Missions, ceramics and metal appliances were used to prepare food. The first major ceramic production site at Mission San Francisco dates to 1794 and at Mission Santa Clara to 1795 (Skowronek et al., 2009). Local production was necessary to meet mission demand, as transporting ceramics across California was expensive and resulted in high loss of product (i.e., through breakage). Indeed, approximately one hundred stoneware pottery sherds were recovered during excavations in the Mission Period levels at the asistencia (Dietz, 1979). Along with these fragments, two "pinch pots" were recovered, suggesting that ceramics were made locally at the mission outpost (Dietz, 1979). Only two fragments of majolica, a Spanish style of pottery, were recovered. These fragments were associated with the late eighteenth-century Mexican Complex. The blue and white intricately glazed pottery were rare at the asistencia, and likely were for display or decoration only (Dietz, 1979). In short, while present, ceramic sherds were uncommon at the asistencia (CA-SMA-71/H), which suggests that ceramic use was not widespread.

The low number of ceramic sherds, along with the lack of glazes, likely explain the low levels of lead in the bulk enamel samples from individuals studied here. These Ohlone died before the Northern California forges responsible for much of the Mission Period pottery production were constructed in 1794 and 1795 (Skowronek et al., 2009).

Though ceramic sherds were uncommon at the asistencia, many metal artifacts were recovered from the strata associated with the Mission Period. While most were unidentifiable metal fragments (Dietz, 1979), large numbers of metal cooking and food storage tools have been recovered from other missions throughout California and the American Southwest (Simmons and Turley, 1980). These implements were used to prepare a wide range of new foodstuffs. For example, *posole*, a Mexican-style soup made of dried maize and a staple in many Spanish missions, required long cook times in metal cauldrons, often made of copper (Popper, 2016; Skowronek et al., 2009). The dish is traditionally prepared with ancho or guajillo peppers, which have a tomato-like acidity. Long cook times in conjuncture with an acidic foodstuff creates an environment where copper and other metals leach out of the cauldron, into the food, and into the people consuming the food. At the nearby Mission Santa Cruz the Ohlone were served *posole* "from two large cauldrons, by means of a copper ladle" and distributed "in a *cora* (a small kind of basket), from which they ate with a shell or the fingers" (Harrison, 1892, p. 47; Popper, 2016). This account shows use of new metal implements in food preparation (mostly by the Spanish), but also continued use of traditional consumption utensils (shells), and does not mention ceramics.

Various drinks were also prepared in metal vessels. For example, copper pitchers, called chocolateras, have been found at other mission sites in California (Simmons and Turley, 1980). These copper pitchers are known for making both hot chocolate beverages, common among the Spanish, and *atole*, a Mexican hot-drink made from corn masa (Popper, 2016). Beverages cooked in copper, bronze, or brass pitchers provide another vector for the introduction of copper and zinc to the Mission Period Ohlone. Negatively charged organic acids in these foods and drinks cause metals from vessel surfaces to dissolve into the food or beverage, providing a vehicle for entry into the human body.

Exposure to increased amounts of iron in Mission Period Ohlone may have resulted from a number of processes. Blacksmithing was a cornerstone of Spanish life during the Mission Period, where everything from tools, horseshoes, religious imagery, and cookware were produced within Mission sites in California and the American Southwest (Simmons and Turley, 1980). Spanish iron cookware such as *comales de fierro*, a type of iron griddle, have been uncovered at many mission sites in western North America. For example, excavations at San Sabá in Texas revealed ninety-three *comales* used by the local Native population to prepare food (Simmons and Turley, 1980). These griddles were simple rectangular sheets of iron, sometimes containing a copper plate within. Leaching of iron into foods may have occurred in small but consistent amounts relative to precontact exposure, but did not result in toxic doses within the missions. Clinical studies show that foods prepared in cast iron pans can decrease the incidence of anemia in preschool-aged children (Sharma et al., 2021).

Alongside changes in food preparation and serving, new foodstuffs with higher concentrations of certain metals may also have contributed to increased zinc, copper, and iron. During the first year of Spanish occupation, 1769, beans, corn, and wheat were planted on land within the outpost. The following five years brought efforts that added peach and quince trees, a grape vineyard, additional crops of barely, maize, wheat, and corn and fenced areas for livestock, presumably cattle and horses (Dietz, 1979).

Data presented above show that zinc in precontact Ohlone was already elevated in comparison to the average in modern populations (table 9.1). Traditional Ohlone foods on the San Francisco Peninsula included a number of high-zinc traditional foods, especially mussel and oyster. For example, oysters have up to 120 mg/100 mg when freshly harvested (Scherz and Kirchhoff, 2006). As shown above, while levels among the precontact individuals started high, levels of zinc were even higher in Mission Period individuals, suggesting the introduction of even more zinc-rich foods or the use of brass (an alloy of copper and zinc) vessels. Red meat, particularly beef, and dairy products are high in zinc and were introduced to the Ohlone in the mission. Clinical studies have shown that meat-heavy diets, especially beef, allow for increased zinc absorption and retention (Kristensen et al., 2006). Other studies show an association between increased zinc and increased iron absorption which could also explain patterns seen in the Mission Period Ohlone (Hunt et al., 1995; Johnson and Walker, 1992).

Conclusion

The Mission Period brought significant change to the daily lives of Ohlone, including in food preparation and diet. Copper and iron were commonly used to prepare and store food, including cauldrons, pitchers, and griddles, and represent a likely pathway for increased exposure to these metals. Trace amounts of zinc and other metals in these tools may also have contributed to increased exposure to other elements. We argue that changes in cooking implements (brass), as well as diet, including the addition of beef and dairy, is a likely mechanism to explain the higher zinc levels in dental enamel. While analysis of trace elements highlights changes, particularly to cooking and diet, Ohlone still kept many traditional practices as exemplified by their continued use of basketry and shell utensils.

By contrast, lead exposure in the asistencia population is similar to precontact individuals and suggests that ceramics, specifically lead glazed ceramics, were not used extensively within the asistencia. The lack of extensive ceramic sherds, especially glazed, recovered from archaeological work at the outpost is consistent with the low levels of lead in enamel, suggesting traditional practices continued, including traditional eating practices with shells and baskets. Similarly, low levels of mercury suggest that Spanish use of mercurial treatments of disease were not prevalent, and that traditional healing continued in large part among the Ohlone population.

Heavy metal analysis points to different aspects of the complex changes that came with Spanish missionization in Northern California. Behavioral changes, specifically those that reflect changes in food and cooking, can be seen in heavy metal exposure in Mission Period Ohlone. While copper, iron, and zinc point to the adoption of Spanish customs, low concentrations of lead and mercury, similar to precontact period levels, provide support that the intensive industrialization seen in the historic samples had not yet occurred.

References

Abdullah, Maryam M., Agnes R. Ly, Wendy A. Goldberg, K. Alison Clarke-Stewart, John V. Dudgeon, Christopher G. Mull, Tony J. Chan, Erin E. Kent, Andrew Z. Mason, and Jonathon E. Ericson
2012 Heavy Metal in Children's Tooth Enamel: Related to Autism and Disruptive Behaviors? *Journal of Autism and Developmental Disorders* 42: 929–936.

Acosta-Saavedra, Leonor C., Ma Elena Moreno, Theresia Rodríguez-Kessler, Ana Luna, Rocío Gomez, Daniela Arias-Salvatierra, and Emma S. Calderon-Aranda
2011 Environmental Exposure to Lead and Mercury in Mexican Children: A Real Health Problem. *Toxicology Mechanisms and Methods* 21: 656–666.

Agnew, Ulrika M., and Todd L. Slesinger
2022 Zinc Toxicity. StatPearls Publishing, Treasure Island, FL.

Bauminger, E., S. Ofer, I. Gedalia, G. Horowitz, and I. Mayer
1985 Iron Uptake by Teeth and Bones: A Mossbauer Effect Study. *Calcified Tissue International* 37: 386–389.

Budd, P., J. Montgomery, A. Cox, P. Krause, B. Barreiro, and R. G. Thomas
1998 The Distribution of Lead Within Ancient and Modern Human Teeth: Implications for Long-Term and Historical Exposure Monitoring. *Science of The Total Environment* 220: 121–136.

Collins, James F., and Leslie M. Klevay
2011   Copper. *Advances in Nutrition* 2: 520–522.
Cuéllar-Rivas, Estefanía, and María Carolina Pustovrh-Ramos
2015   El Papel de la Enamelisina (mmp-20) en el Desarrollo Dentario: Revisión Sistemática. *Revista Facultad de Odontología Universidad de Antioquia* 27: Article 1. https://doi.org/10.17533/udea.rfo.v27n1a8
Dean, M. Christopher, Kathryn M. Spiers, Jan Garrevoet, and Adeline Le Cabec
2019   Synchrotron X-ray Fluorescence Mapping of Ca, Sr and Zn at the Neonatal Line in Human Deciduous Teeth Reflects Changing Perinatal Physiology. *Archives of Oral Biology* 104: 90–102.
Dietz, Stephen A.
1979   Report of Archeological Investigations at Sanchez Adobe Park Historic District. Report to the San Mateo County Department of Parks and Recreation. On file at the Northwest Information Center, Sonoma State University, California.
Ellingsen, D. G., L. B. Moller, and J. Aaseth
2015   Copper. In *Handbook on the Toxicology of Metals: Vol. II*, edited by G. F. Nordberg, B. A. Fowler, and M. Nordberg, 765–786. Elsevier and Academic Press, Amsterdam.
Fraga, Cesar G., and Patricia I. Oteiza
2002   Iron Toxicity and Antioxidant Nutrients. *Toxicology* 180: 23–32.
Gaetke, Lisa M., and Ching Kuang Chow
2003   Copper Toxicity, Oxidative Stress, and Antioxidant Nutrients. *Toxicology* 189: 147–163.
Gump, Brooks B., Matthew J. Dykas, James A. MacKenzie, Amy K. Dumas, Bryce Hruska, Craig K. Ewart, Patrick J. Parsons, Christopher D. Palmer, and Kestutis Bendinskas
2017   Background Lead and Mercury Exposures: Psychological and Behavioral Problems in Children. *Environmental Research* 158: 576–582.
Hare, Dominic, Christine Austin, Philip Doble, and Manish Arora
2011   Elemental Bio-Imaging of Trace Elements in Teeth Using Laser Ablation-Inductively Coupled Plasma-Mass Spectrometry. *Journal of Dentistry* 39: 397–403.
Harrison, E. S.
1892   *History of Santa Cruz County, California*. Pacific Press Co., San Francisco.
Hillson, S.
1996   *Dental Anthropology*. Cambridge University Press.
Hunt, Janet R., Sandra K. Gallagher, L. K. Johnson, and Glenn I. Lykken
1995   High- Versus Low-Meat Diets: Effects on Zinc Absorption, Iron Status, and Calcium, Copper, Iron, Magnesium, Manganese, Nitrogen, Phosphorus, and Zinc Balance in Postmenopausal Women. *American Journal of Clinical Nutrition* 62: 621–632.
Johnson, Jan M., and Paul M. Walker
1992   Zinc and Iron Utilization in Young Women Consuming a Beef-Based Diet. *Journal of the American Dietetic Association* 92: 1474–1478.

Kamenov, George D., Ellen M. Lofaro, Gennifer Goad, and John Krigbaum
2018   Trace Elements in Modern and Archaeological Human Teeth: Implications for Human Metal Exposure and Enamel Diagenetic Changes. *Journal of Archaeological Science* 99: 27–34.

Kangas, Aapo T., Alistair R. Evans, Irma Thesleff, and Jukka Jernvall
2004   Nonindependence of Mammalian Dental Characters. *Nature* 432(7014): 211–214.

Khan, Ambar, Basavaraj Patthi, Ashish Singla, Ravneet Malhi, Divyangi Goel, and Monika Kumari
2020   The Role of Copper and Zinc in the Prevention of Dental Caries-A Systematic Review. *Journal of Indian Association of Public Health Dentistry* 18: 4–12.

Klimuszko, Elzbieta, Karolina Orywal, Teresa Sierpinska, Jarosław Sidun, and Maria Golebiewska
2018   The Evaluation of Zinc and Copper Content in Tooth Enamel Without any Pathological Changes: An *In Vitro* Study. *International Journal of Nanomedicine* 13: 1257–1264.

Konikowska, Klaudia, and Anna Mandecka
2018   Trace Elements in Human Nutrition. In *Recent Advances in Trace Elements*, edited by Katarzyna Chojnacka, Agnieszka Saeid, 339–372. John Wiley and Sons, Ltd.

Kristensen, Mette Bach, Ole Hels, Catrine M. Morberg, Jens Marving, Susanne Büge, and Inge Tetens
2006   Total Zinc Absorption in Young Women, but Not Fractional Zinc Absorption, Differs between Vegetarian and Meat-Based Diets with Equal Phytic Acid Content. *British Journal of Nutrition* 95: 963–967.

Martin, Ronald R., Steven J. Naftel, Andrew J. Nelson, and William D. Sapp III
2007   Comparison of the Distributions of Bromine, Lead, and Zinc in Tooth and Bone from an Ancient Peruvian Burial Site by X-ray Fluorescence. *Canadian Journal of Chemistry,* 85: 831–836.

Martínez-García, M. J., J. M. Moreno, J. Moreno-Clavel, N. Vergara, A. García-Sánchez, A. Guillamón, M. Portí, and S. Moreno-Grau
2005   Heavy Metals in Human Bones in Different Historical Epochs. *Science of The Total Environment* 348: 51–72.

Nriagu, J.
2007   Zinc Toxicity in Humans. School of Public Health, University of Michigan.

Ponka, P., M. Tenenbein, and J. W. Eaton
2015   Iron. In *Handbook on the Toxicology of Metals: Vol. II*, edited by G. F. Nordberg, B. A. Fowler, and M. Nordberg, 879–902. Elsevier and Academic Press, Amsterdam.

Popper, Virginia
2016   Change and Persistence: Mission Neophyte Foodways at Selected Colonial Alta California Institutions. *Journal of California and Great Basin Anthropology* 36: 5–25.

Sandstead, H. H.
2015   Zinc. In *Handbook on the Toxicology of Metals: Vol. II*, edited by G. F. Nordberg, B. A. Fowler, and M. Nordberg, 1369–1385. Elsevier and Academic Press, Amsterdam.

Scherz, Heimo, and Eva Kirchhoff
2006   Trace Elements in Foods: Zinc Contents of Raw Foods—A Comparison of Data Originating from Different Geographical Regions of the World. *Journal of Food Composition and Analysis* 19: 420–433.

Sharma, Shally, Ritika Khandelwal, Kapil Yadav, Gomathi Ramaswamy, and Kashish Vohra
2021   Effect of Cooking Food in Iron-Containing Cookware on Increase in Blood Hemoglobin Level and Iron Content of the Food: A Systematic Review. *Nepal Journal of Epidemiology* 11: 994–1005.

Simmons, Marc, and Frank Turley
1980   *Southwestern Colonial Ironwork: The Spanish Blacksmithing Tradition.* Museum of New Mexico Press.

Skowronek, Russell K., M. James Blackman, and Ronald L. Bishop
2009   Locally-Made or Imported? Identifying Ceramic Composition Variation in the San Francisco Presidio Jurisdiction. *Historical Archaeology* 43: 1–21.

Smith, Tanya M., Christine Austin, Janaína N. Ávila, Wendy Dirks, Daniel R. Green, Ian S. Williams, and Manish Arora
2022   Permanent Signatures of Birth and Nursing Initiation are Chemically Recorded in Teeth. *Journal of Archaeological Science* 140: 105564.

Smith, Tanya M., Luisa Cook, Wendy Dirks, Daniel R. Green, and Christine Austin
2021   Teeth Reveal Juvenile Diet, Health and Neurotoxicant Exposure Retrospectively: What Biological Rhythms and Chemical Records Tell Us. *BioEssays* 43: 2000298.

Williams, A. M. M., and R. Siegele
2014   Iron Deposition in Modern and Archaeological Teeth. *Nuclear Instruments and Methods in Physics Research Section B: Beam Interactions with Materials and Atoms* 335: 19–23.

Yuen, H.-W., and W. Becker
2022   *Iron Toxicity.* StatPearls Publishing, Treasure Island, FL.

10

Dental Biodistance and Kinship at Asistencia de San Pedro y San Pablo

Kristen A. Broehl-Droke

This chapter explores dental metric variation at the Asistencia de San Pedro y San Pablo (CA-SMA-71/H) and what it reveals about potential biological relations among the Ohlone ancestors who were buried there. The small sample of skeletal individuals (n = 15) from the asistencia were studied following the wishes of the Amah Mutsun Tribal Band of Mission San Juan Bautista, the state-assigned most likely descendants (MLD). This study analyzes dental remains using a biological distance (biodistance) approach.

As is common in archaeological contexts, several of the excavated individuals were missing teeth due to taphonomic processes or age or had moderate to severe dental wear that precluded measurements of the enamel. These factors left just eleven individuals for dental analysis. Still, even with this small sample, the data provide an important opportunity to explore degrees of biological relatedness among a mission-era group in central California and evaluate the role of biological affinity in burial practices.

Biodistance Analysis and Kinship

Biodistance analysis is the use of dental or skeletal traits for estimating genetic relationships between populations or individuals (Stojanowski and Schillaci 2006). Such methods have been used worldwide to explore migration patterns and gene flow by comparing phenotypic variance between archaeological populations (e.g., Blom et al. 1998; McIlvaine et al. 2014; O'Donnell and Schillaci 2021; Suchey 1975). Studies suggest that the dental and skeletal variants targeted in biodistance studies are largely selectively neutral (e.g., Rathmann et al. 2017), so that gene flow and genetic drift are the primary determinants of trait frequencies rather than similarities in environment. Populations with more similarities in frequencies, therefore, are assumed to have diverged more recently while differing phenotypic frequencies indicate the populations are more distantly related. While the targeted traits are complex, prior studies of heritability as well as comparisons between genetic and phenotypic datasets show that dental phenotypes are under enough genetic control to successfully act as proxies for underlying genetic information (Dempsey and Townsend 2001; Hanihara and Ishida 2005; Hubbard et al. 2015; Irish et al. 2020; Paul and Stojanowski 2017; Paul et al. 2020; Rathmann et al. 2017; Stojanowski et al. 2017; Townsend and Brown 1978). In short, dental phenotypic similarity indicates a higher likelihood for genetic closeness.

Due to the small sample at CA-SMA-71/H, population-level comparisons are not the aim of this study. Instead, analyses were applied within the site to assess intragroup patterns of phenotypic variation. Still, the assumptions outlined above, particularly that similar phenotypes correspond with closer genetic relatedness, remain true (Stojanowski and Schillaci 2006). It is important to note that dental phenotypes cannot positively tell us whether individuals are close biological kin but can be useful in estimating relative degree of relatedness (Stojanowski and Schillaci 2006). In other words, biodistance analysis does not necessarily tell us whether two individuals are siblings or a parent-child pair but can tell us whether certain individuals are more or less likely to share close genetic relationships to each other as compared to the other individuals in the sample.

Studies of biological distance at other sites in North and South America have successfully used hard-tissue phenotypes to estimate relatedness at the intra-site level, between individuals, usually by comparing patterns of relatedness with archaeologically defined patterns. For example, Stojanowski and Schillaci (2006) found phenotypic differences between people buried in the eastern versus western parts of the Archaic Windover Pond site in Florida, while Howell and Kintigh (1996) found that dental variation was unevenly distributed between cemetery groups at the Zuni site of Hawikku in New Mexico. Potentially relevant to the current research are kinship studies of Native populations subjected to the Spanish missionization system. Stojanowski (2005) showed the deceased from San Pedro y San Pablo de Patale mission in Florida tended to phenotypically cluster by row, and within-burial-row tooth size variability was lower than between-row variability. This suggests that individuals buried within the same row tended to share closer genetic relationships than individuals from differing contexts. Similarly, Jacobi (2000) identified morphological and metric differences based on burial location within the Tipu Mayan cemetery affiliated with a Spanish colonial church in Belize, also demonstrating the role of kinship in burial practices. Besides bio-spatial cemetery structures, features such as similar grave inclusions, burial orientation, and multiple burials have marked kinship in archaeological populations worldwide (e.g., Gomes et al. 2020; Meyer et al. 2012; Paul et al. 2013).

These studies show the potential for genetic relatedness, and hence kinship, to impose structure on ancient cemeteries. Because kinship is an important social category that impacts human behavior, burial of individuals according to kin relations can be a way to reaffirm and perpetuate family connections beyond life (Johnson and Paul 2016; Paul et al. 2013). It is important to note that biological relationships are not the only factor societies use to construct kinship (Hill et al. 2011; Johnson and Paul 2016; Pilloud and Larsen 2011), so a lack of concordance between biological and contextual data does not mean the cemetery lacks kin structuring. Still, the presence of identifiable phenetic patterning can elucidate cases when biological genealogies are imbued with a broader cultural significance in defining family relationships, and thus provide insight into identity formation processes and social memory in past groups (Johnson and Paul 2016).

At the asistencia, there were several individuals who appeared to share a grave, including Individuals 6 and 11, Individuals 8 and 12, and Individuals 14 and 15. Given the role kinship can play in mortuary practices, site archaeologists suggested there may be familial relations between individuals buried together or close to one another. This chapter uses biodistance analysis to test the hypothesis that multiple burials are an expression of a shared identity constructed around biological kinship.

Methods

A series of metric traits were observed on all permanent teeth from CA-SMA--71/H. Nonmetric data were also collected from the dentition, but because of missing data, odontometric variables are the focus for this study. Eleven individuals had observable measurements. Age and sex estimates for the eleven individuals, based on a mixture of osteological and proteomic analyses (chapters 3 and 4), include one female child (Burial 14), two male children (Burials 2 and 11), one adolescent male (Burial 15), two young adult females (Burials 12 and 13), one young adult male (Burial 6), one middle adult female (Burial 10), two old adult females (Burials 3 and 5), and one old adult male (Burial 8). Due to the young ages of several individuals, some data were recorded on teeth that had not fully erupted because their crowns were formed.

Odontometric variables were collected using Hillson-Fitzgerald dental calipers (Hillson et al. 2005) and included the maximum mesiodistal and buccolingual crown diameters as well as landmark-based mesiodistal and buccolingual diameters at the cementoenamel junction (CEJ; Hillson et al. 2005; Moorrees and Reed 1964). Although all data were collected on both the left and right sides of the dental arcade, the left side was selected for analysis, with the right antimere used as a substitute when dimensions on the left were impacted by wear, pathology, or taphonomy (Pilloud and Kenyhercz 2016).

Biodistance Cluster Analyses

Biodistance analyses were completed using RStudio (Posit team 2022) for R (R Core Team 2021). Prior to distance analyses, datasets must be reduced to fewer variables that show the greatest canalization and least missing data. Only variables from polar teeth, including first molars, third premolars, canines, first maxillary incisors, and second mandibular incisors, were included. These teeth are the most developmentally stable, showing greater resistance to environmental influence on phenotypic expression (Butler 1939; Dahlberg 1945; Stojanowski et al. 2017). Traits that were missing values for five or more individuals were removed from the analysis. One individual (Burial 10) of the eleven was also removed because they were missing a significant number of the variables. Measurements were then evaluated for normality using qqplots (car R package; Fox and Weisberg 2019), and three variables were removed due to plots with irregular shapes.

At this point, ten odontometric variables remained in the dataset. These included the mesiodistal CEJ diameters of the first maxillary molar, third maxillary premolar, maxillary canine, and mandibular lateral incisor; the buccolingual CEJ measurements for the first maxillary molar, maxillary canine, maxillary central incisor, mandibular third premolar, and lateral mandibular incisor; and the maximum buccolingual crown diameter of the mandibular incisor. Measurements were tested for associations with age-at-death of the individuals in the sample using Spearman's statistic (stats R package; R Core Team 2021) to ensure they reflected underlying genetic patterns rather than factors such as dental wear (Pilloud and Kenyhercz 2016). No variables needed to be removed based on age associations because correlation coefficients all had strengths below 0.55, suggesting age was not a significant contributor to variation. All ten individuals had observations recorded for at least five of the ten traits.

Many biodistance statistics require traits to vary independently of one another, an assumption odontometric datasets often do not meet due to genetic integration of many dental phenotypes (Stojanowski et al. 2017). To ensure trait independence, Principal Components Analysis (PCA) was used to reduce the dataset to a small number of uncorrelated variables (stats R package; R Core Team 2021). Since PCA only works with complete data, missing values (26 percent of the dataset) were estimated first using k-Nearest Neighbor imputation (k=4, VIM R package; Kowarik and Templ 2016), which has been successful in osteological samples (Kenyhercz and Passalacqua 2016). Then, the data were transformed using the geometric mean (compositions R package; van den Boogaart et al. 2021) to reduce the potential influence of sex on tooth size. Like age, sex is a demographic variable that can obscure patterns of relatedness because metrics of the permanent teeth frequently exhibit sexual dimorphism (Pilloud and Kenyhercz 2016).

PCA of these data resulted in four dimensions with eigenvalues above one that accounted for 87.7 percent of the original variance. An inter-individual distance matrix was produced using Euclidean distance of these four principal components (cluster R package; Maechler et al. 2021), and distance relationships were visualized with a dendrogram (stats R package; R Core Team 2021).

Results and Discussion

Figure 10.1 shows the dendrogram produced from cluster analysis of the odontometric data. Individuals 6, 11, 14, and 15 form a cluster within the dendrogram differentiated from the rest of the burials. Another cluster is formed with Individuals 2, 8, and 12. These patterns provide support for the idea that individuals in multiple burials may have been more closely related to each other than to other individuals at the site. Burials 8 and 12 were one of the proposed related pairs and they share terminal branches on the tree, showing greater phenotypic similarity, and by extension genetic closeness, between them. Burials 6 and 11, and Burials 14 and 15, were the other individuals with suggested relationships due to shared archaeological context. Although Burials 11 and 14 share terminal branches in the dendrogram of biological distances, suggesting greater biological affinity to each other than the hypothesized relations to Burials 6 and 15, respectively, the figure still supports a closer relationship between the individuals who share a grave than to most other individuals in the analysis.

Several possibilities could account for the imperfect clustering of Burials 6/11 and 14/15 even in the case they represent close kin. One consideration is that biodistance analyses are most useful for identifying overall patterns of relatedness, rather than specific relationships. Thus, family members will not necessarily show the smallest distances. For example, dental nonmetric biodistance studies of known relatives have shown that while genetic kin show smaller distances than nonrelatives on average, unrelated pairs can also show small distances since phenotypic data are not as precise as genetic data

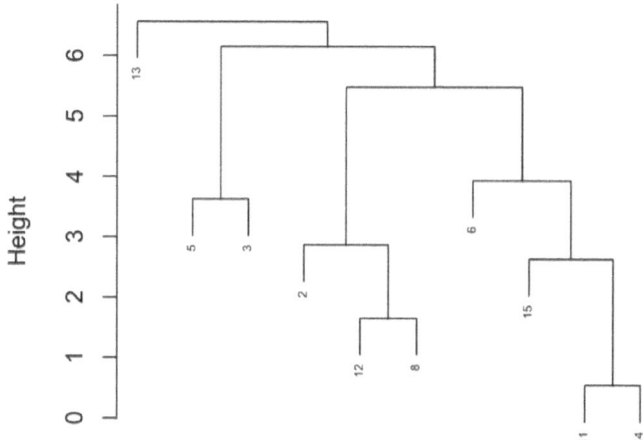

Figure 10.1. Dendrogram showing biological affinity between individuals at Asistencia San Pedro y San Pablo based on odontometric data.

(Paul and Stojanowski 2017). It is also notable that the four individuals who form the biological cluster in the dendrogram (6/11/14/15) are from the more southern of the two spatial clusters at the site, while all the other individuals in the sample are from the northern cluster. This could indicate the burial clusters more broadly represent closely related individuals rather than just the burial pits. In either case, the biological data do appear to show a relationship with archaeological context where spatial clusters (at either the burial pit or broader plot/row level) include more phenotypically similar individuals.

Analysis of historical records in chapter 11 from the asistencia in comparison to the archaeological and osteological data supports some of the results here. In particular, there is evidence that Individuals 6 and 11 are brothers who died and were buried months apart, thereby lending credence to the idea that family members were intentionally interred together. On the other hand, tentative identifications for Individuals 8, 12, 14, and 15 based on the records analysis do not include known biological kin. Still, relationships between them could not be ruled out due to the incomplete and sometimes inaccurate nature of the mission records. There may be familial relationships that are not visible in the historical documentation, or the biodistance results could represent more distant rather than close genetic kinship. The identifications also have some degree of uncertainty, so future research could examine these potential matches and their relationships further. Ancient DNA research would be particularly useful for this purpose, such as comparing mitochondrial and/or Y-chromosome data for evidence of genetic relatedness.

Overall, results of the current study support the hypothesis that multiple burials represent more closely related individuals, with the caveat that the small sample size and missing data could have a significant randomizing effect on the results. If the asistencia population was intentionally burying family close together, which is also supported by the historic research in at least one instance, this would suggest that biological kinship represents an important facet of mortuary identity. People may have used mortuary associations to signal and commemorate kinship connections that were considered significant among the living.

Whether this represents a continuation of traditional Ohlone burial practices, was a new mortuary custom introduced by the Spanish, or is the by-product of other factors (such as comorbidity within families due to sharing infectious disease and burial within the cemetery according to the timing of death), is unclear and must await future research. Currently, there are few studies in the region that explore intra-site patterns of biological kinship available for comparison. One study at a Middle Period shell mound (CA-ALA-11) did not find evidence for a relationship between spatial proximity and dentoskeletal phenotypic similarity (Broehl 2023). Similarly, an analysis of mitochondrial DNA diversity at the Late Period Yukisma site (CA-SCL-38) found the distribution of maternal lineages lacked spatial patterning (Monroe 2014). However, the study at the Yukisma site identified a few multiple burials with a shared haplotype, suggesting biological kin were interred together at least occasionally and it was not an entirely new custom at the asistencia. Due to the paucity of such research, the frequency and circumstances for kin co-burial is unknown. Application of biodistance methods to other precolonial and colonial-period cemeteries would help show whether such mortuary structuring was more widely distributed during the Mission Period and whether such practices changed over time. The hope is that this study will encourage other similar analyses in the future to further our understanding of kinship among Ohlone populations and of cemetery layout and structure.

Acknowledgments

I would like to express my thanks to the Amah Mutsun Tribal Band of Mission San Juan Bautista for supporting this research and hope it has provided useful insight. Thanks also to the editors and Marin Pilloud for helpful comments and encouragement that improved this chapter.

References

Blom, Deborah E., Benedikt Hallgrímsson, Linda Keng, María C. Lozada C., and Jane E. Buikstra
1998   Tiwanaku 'Colonization': Bioarchaeological Implications for Migration in the Moquegua Valley, Peru. *World Archaeology* 30: 238–261.

Broehl, Kristen A.
2023   Biological Distance Analysis of Identity, Postmarital Residence, and Population Structure at the CA-ALA-11 Shellmound. PhD dissertation, Department of Anthropology, University of Nevada, Reno.

Butler, Percy M.
1939   Studies of the Mammalian Dentition—Differentiation of the Post-canine Dentition. *Proceedings of the Zoological Society of London B* 109:1–36.

Dahlberg, Albert A.
1945   The Changing Dentition of Man. *Journal of the American Dental Association* 32: 676–690.

Dempsey, Paula J., and Grant C. Townsend
2001   Genetic and Environmental Contributions to Variation in Human Tooth Size. *Heredity* 86(6): 685–693.

Fox, John, and Sanford Weisberg
2019   *An R Companion to Applied Regression.* 3rd ed. Sage, Thousand Oaks, CA.

Gomes, Cláudia, Gerard Remolins, Ana María López-Parra, Juan F. Gibaja, Maria Fondevila, Flavio De Angelis, Virginia Veltre, M. Eulàlia Subirà, Carlos Baeza-Richer, Diana Guerrero, Sara Palomo-Díez, Cristina Martínez-Labarga, Elena Labajo-González, Maria Victoria Lareu, Bernardo Perea-Pérez, and Eduardo Arroyo-Pardo
2020   Paleogenetic Evidence of a Pyrenean Neolithic Family: Kinship, Physical Appearance and Biogeography Multidisciplinary Analysis. *Journal of Archaeological Science* 123:105226.

Hanihara, Tsunehiko, and Hajime Ishida
2005   Metric Dental Variation of Major Human Populations. *American Journal of Physical Anthropology* 128:287–298.

Hill, Kim R., Robert S. Walker, Miran Božičević, James Eder, Thomas Headland, Barry Hewlett, A. Magdalena Hurtado, Frank Marlowe, Polly Wiessner, and Brian Wood
2011   Co-residence Patterns in Hunter-Gatherer Societies Show Unique Human Social Structure. *Science* 331(6022): 1286–1289.

Hillson, Simon, Charles FitzGerald, and Helen Flinn
2005   Alternative Dental Measurements: Proposals and Relationships with Other Measurements. *American Journal of Physical Anthropology* 126:413–426.

Howell, Todd L., and Keith W. Kintigh
1996   Archaeological Identification of Kin Groups Using Mortuary and Biological Data: An Example from the American Southwest. *American Antiquity* 61:537–554.

Hubbard, Amelia R., Debbie Guatelli-Steinberg, and Joel D. Irish
2015   Do Nuclear DNA and Dental Nonmetric Data Produce Similar Reconstruc-

tions of Regional Population History? An Example from Modern Coastal Kenya. *American Journal of Physical Anthropology* 157(2): 295–304.

Irish, Joel D., Adeline Morez, Linus Girdland Flink, Emma L.W. Phillips, and G. Richard Scott

2020   Do Dental Nonmetric Traits Actually Work as Proxies for Neutral Genomic Data? Some Answers from Continental- and Global-level Analyses. *American Journal of Physical Anthropology* 172:347–375.

Jacobi, Keith P.

2000   *Last Rites for the Tipu Maya: Genetic Structuring in a Colonial Cemetery.* University of Alabama Press, Tuscaloosa.

Johnson, Kent M., and Kathleen S. Paul

2016   Bioarchaeology and Kinship: Integrating Theory, Social Relatedness, and Biology in Ancient Family Research. *Journal of Archaeological Research* 24:75–123.

Kenyhercz, Michael W., and Nicholas V. Passalacqua

2016   Missing Data Imputation Methods and Their Performance with Biodistance Analyses. In *Biological Distance Analysis: Forensic and Bioarchaeological Perspectives*, edited by Marin A. Pilloud and Joseph T. Hefner, 181–194. Academic Press, San Diego.

Kowarik, Alexander, and Matthias Templ

2016   Imputation with the R Package VIM. *Journal of Statistical Software* 74(7): 1–16.

Maechler, Martin, Peter Rousseeuw, Anja Struyf, Mia Hubert, and Kurt Hornik

2021   *cluster: Cluster Analysis Basics and Extensions.* R package version 2.1.2. https://CRAN.R-project.org/package=cluster.

McIlvaine, Britney Kyle, Lynne A. Schepartz, Clark Spencer Larsen, and Paul W. Sciulli

2014   Evidence for Long-term Migration on the Balkan Peninsula Using Dental and Cranial Nonmetric Data: Early Interaction between Corinth (Greece) and Its Colony at Apollonia (Albania). *American Journal of Physical Anthropology* 153:236–248.

Meyer, Christian, Robert Ganslmeier, Veit Dresely, and Kurt W. Alt

2012   New Approaches to the Reconstruction of Kinship and Social Structure Based on Bioarchaeological Analysis of Neolithic Multiple and Collective Graves. In *Theoretical and Methodological Considerations in Central European Neolithic Archaeology*, edited by Jan Kolár and František Trampota. BAR International Series 2325. British Archaeological Reports, Oxford.

Monroe, Cara

2014   Correlating Biological Relationships, Social Inequality, and Population Movement among Prehistoric California Foragers: Ancient Human DNA Analysis from CA-SCL-38 (Yukisma Site). PhD dissertation, Department of Anthropology, University of California, Santa Barbara.

Moorrees, Coenraad FA, and Robert B. Reed

1964   Correlations among Crown Diameters of Human Teeth. *Archives of Oral Biology* 9:685–697.

O'Donnell, Lexi, and Michael A. Schillaci

2021   Inferring the Relationships of the Gallina and Pottery Mound Pueblo Populations Using Craniometric and Dental Morphological Biodistance. *KIVA* 87:97–128.

Paul, Kathleen S., and Christopher M. Stojanowski
2017   Comparative Performance of Deciduous and Permanent Dental Morphology in Detecting Biological Relatives. *American Journal of Physical Anthropology* 164:97–116.

Paul, Kathleen S., Christopher M. Stojanowski, and Michelle M. Butler
2013   Biological and Spatial Structure of an Early Classic Period Cemetery at Charco Redondo, Oaxaca. *American Journal of Physical Anthropology* 152:217–229.

Paul, Kathleen S., Christopher M. Stojanowski, Toby E. Hughes, Alan H. Brook, and Grant C. Townsend
2020   Patterns of Heritability across the Human Diphyodont Dental Complex: Crown Morphology of Australian Twins and Families. *American Journal of Physical Anthropology* 172:447–461.

Pilloud, Marin A., and Michael W. Kenyhercz
2016   Dental Metrics in Biodistance Analysis. In *Biological Distance Analysis: Forensic and Bioarchaeological Perspectives*, edited by Marin A. Pilloud and Joseph T. Hefner, 135–155. Academic Press, San Diego.

Pilloud, Marin A., and Clark Spencer Larsen
2011   "Official" and "Practical" Kin: Inferring Social and Community Structure from Dental Phenotype at Neolithic Çatalhöyük, Turkey. *American Journal of Physical Anthropology* 145:519–530.

Posit Team
2022   *RStudio: Integrated Development Environment for R.* Posit Software, PBC, Boston. http://www.posit.co/.

R Core Team
2021   *R: A Language and Environment for Statistical Computing.* R Foundation for Statistical Computing, Vienna, Austria. https://www.R-project.org/.

Rathmann, Hannes, Hugo Reyes-Centeno, Silvia Ghirotto, Nicole Creanza, Tsunehiko Hanihara, and Katerina Harvati
2017   Reconstructing Human Population History from Dental Phenotypes. *Scientific Reports* 7:1–9.

Stojanowski, Christopher M., Kathleen S. Paul, Andrew C. Seidel, William N. Duncan, and Debbie Guatelli-Steinberg
2017   Heritability and Genetic Integration of Tooth Size in the South Carolina Gullah. *American Journal of Physical Anthropology* 164:505–521.

Stojanowski, Christopher M., and Michael A. Schillaci
2006   Phenotypic Approaches for Understanding Patterns of Intracemetery Biological Variation. *Yearbook of Physical Anthropology* 49:49–88.

Stojanowski, Christopher M.
2005   Biological Structure of the San Pedro y San Pablo De Patale Mission Cemetery. *Southeastern Archaeology* 24:165–179.

Suchey, Judy Myers
1975   Biological Distance of Prehistoric Central California Populations Derived

from Non-Metric Traits of the Cranium. PhD dissertation, Department of Anthropology, University of California, Riverside.

Townsend, Grant C., and Tasman Brown
1978   Heritability of Permanent Tooth Size. *American Journal of Physical Anthropology* 49:497–504.

van den Boogaart, K. Gerald, Raimon Tolosana-Delgado, and Matevz Bren
2021   *compositions: Compositional Data Analysis.* R package version 2.0–2. https://CRAN.R-project.org/package=compositions.

11

Peopling the Past

Life Histories of Native Residents of the Asistencia de San Pedro y San Pablo

Lee M. Panich, Beth Armstrong,
and Christopher Canzonieri

The chapters in this volume illustrate how bioarchaeological and mortuary studies can provide detailed information about the challenges and opportunities faced by Ohlone people in the early colonial period. Drawing on the findings regarding the fifteen Ohlone ancestors whose remains were encountered at the former site of the Asistencia de San Pedro y San Pablo, this chapter combines the rich archaeological and historical records to offer life histories for certain individuals buried in the outstation's cemetery. We believe over half the burials (n=8) can be linked to individuals whose lives were recorded in the baptismal and death records for Mission San Francisco de Asís, allowing us the unique opportunity to give names to particular burials. In this way, we hope to further honor the lives of Native Californians who were directly impacted by the Franciscan mission system.

Previous research has suggested that Native people may have been drawn to San Pedro y San Pablo due to its coastal location and the relative freedom it afforded compared to the main missions at San Francisco, Santa Clara, and in the later years of the outstation's existence, Santa Cruz (Milliken et al. 2009; Newell 2009). Yet, life at the Asistencia de San Pedro y San Pablo posed very real challenges to Native people's health, as discussed in the preceding chapters. Mission records suggest that a total of 152 Native people were buried there, most between 1787 and 1792, though the cemetery seems to have been in use as late as 1800 (Early California Population Project 2022). The fifteen individuals described in this volume therefore represent nearly 10 percent of the total population present in the asistencia's cemetery. Given these factors, we turned to the death records from Mission San Francisco to see if we could identify specific individuals.

Methods and Results

To evaluate possible matches, we drew on skeletal age-at-death estimations as well as bioarchaeological and proteomic sex estimations (chapters 3 and 4), to develop demographic profiles for the individuals under consideration. We also considered archaeological context to further refine the parameters of our search—for example, double burials that might match individuals of corresponding age and sex who were recorded in the death register as being buried simultaneously or in rapid succession. Last, the cemetery appears to have grown in a patterned fashion, with individuals added on the margins of the existing cemetery, creating a link between time and location within the cemetery (i.e., graves near one another likely date close in time). This pattern, which is generally consistent with the presumed filling of nearby Mission Santa Clara (Hylkema 1995), may also help narrow possible identifications.

To assess mission sacramental records, we used a combination of the two extant mission record databases for Alta California: the Early California Population Project, which is freely accessible online, and the Microsoft Access database compiled by the late Randall Milliken (see discussion in Peelo et al. 2018). We also checked key details against the original physical records held in San Francisco. Similar methodologies for reconstructing life histories and familial relationships were previously published for Mission San Francisco (e.g., Cordero 2015; Milliken 1995; Newell 2009). For ease of citation, we use the Early California Population Project (2022) abbreviation and numbering system throughout this chapter. Taken together, the historical and bioarchaeological records offer a rich context for those Ohlone ancestors who lived, worked, and died at the site. Results are presented in table 11.1. We give the rationale for the identifications as follows:

- Among the possible double interments were Burials 8 and 12. Burial 8 was a mature adult male who died above the age of forty-five, whereas Burial 12 was an adult female who died between the ages of twenty and twenty-five. Given that they were buried next to each other, we examined the death records for individuals matching those profiles who were buried within a short time of each other. Although the biodistance study (chapter 10) suggests a close relationship between these two individuals, we could not identify any corresponding pairs in the mission records. The best match involves the case of Olcóx (Spanish name

Table 11.1. Potential matches between archaeological data and historical data for individuals buried at San Pedro y San Pablo

	Archaeological Data			Historical Data					
Burial Number	Prot. Sex Estimation	Osteo. Age Estimation	Native Name	Spanish Name	Origin	Baptism #	Death #	Death Date	Age at Death
2	Male	13–17	Unknown	Jose Manuel	Yelamu/Pruristac	42	298	11/4/1789	~12
6	Male	18–25	Yunnénis	Rosendo	Chiguan	544	254	8/30/1788	~17
8	Male	>45	Olcóx	Cirino	Punta de Almejas	464	214	8/13/1787	~56
9	Male	2–2.5	Unknown	Mauricio	San Pedro y San Pablo	556	282	4/21/1789	2.5
11	Male	4–8	Julirbe	Primo	Chiguan	639	283	4/22/1789	7–8
12	Female	20–25	Jagessém	Margaritta de Escocia	Chiguan	546	212	8/14/1787	~27
14	Female	5–7	Unknown	Maria Athanasia	San Mateo / Pruristac	420	399a	1/5/1792	~6.5
15	Male	13–17	Tarsi	Aparicio	Unknown	963	398a	1/4/1792	12–13

Note: Prot. = Proteomic; Osteo. = Osteological.

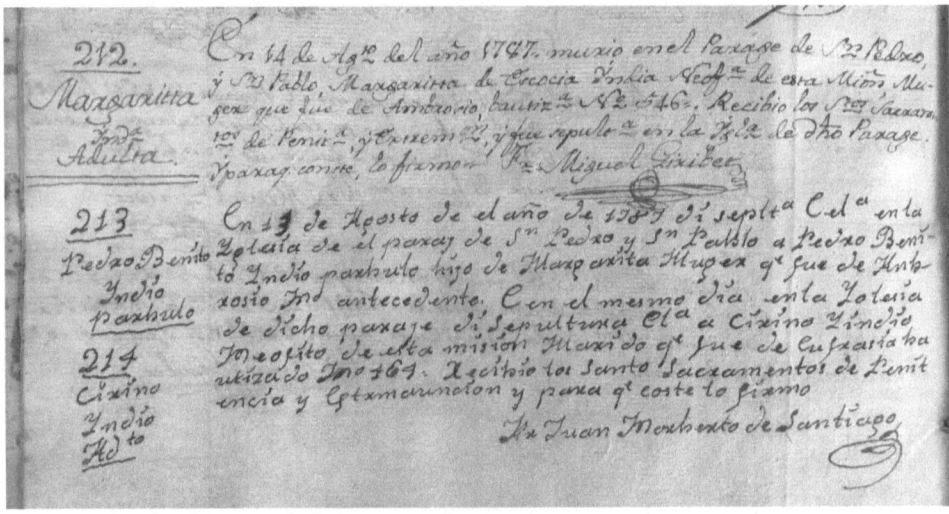

Figure 11.1. Entries in the Mission San Francisco death records for Olcóx (Spanish name Cirino, SFD Death 214) and Jagessém (Spanish name Margaritta, SFD Death 212). Courtesy of the Office of the Curator, Old Mission Dolores, the Archdiocese of San Francisco.

Cirino, SFD Death 214) and Jagessém (Spanish name Margaritta, SFD Death 212) who largely conform to the bioarchaeologial information for Burials 8 and 12, respectively. They died only one day apart in August 1787 (figure 11.1). Based on her baptismal information, Jagessém is estimated to have been twenty-seven years old when she died. This is generally within the possible age range of Burial 12, and the missionaries, moreover, were wildly inconsistent with the ages they assigned to Native individuals in the sacramental registers.

- A potential triple burial includes Burials 9 and 11, two boys aged two to two and a half years and four to eight years respectively. These burials are particularly interesting in that they both were interred with jet beads and crosses, among other funerary offerings. Here again, we looked for age and gender matches from a short period of time. The details correspond well to Mauricio (SFD Death 282) and Julírbe (Spanish name Primo, SFD Death 283). These two boys—a nephew and uncle—of matching ages died on successive days in April 1789 (figure 11.2). The two, moreover, were part of an elite family, a detail that may account for the similarities in funerary offerings. The third associated interment, a young adult male aged eighteen to twenty-five (Burial 6), generally matches the details for Mauricio's father Yunnénis, who died

Figure 11.2. Entries in the Mission San Francisco death records for Mauricio (SFD Death 282) and Julírbe (Spanish name Primo, SFD Death 283). Courtesy of the Office of the Curator, Old Mission Dolores, the Archdiocese of San Francisco.

at approximately seventeen years old, a few months prior to his son and brother, Julírbe.

- Another double burial noted archaeologically seems to be present in the mission death records. Burial 14 was a young girl, aged five to seven, and was associated with Burial 15, an adolescent male, aged thirteen to seventeen. Death records 398a and 399a seem to represent this pattern. Those individuals, María Athanasia and Tarsi, died just one day apart at San Pedro y San Pablo in January 1792, perhaps as some of the first to perish during the wave of deaths that swept the asistencia in the first half of 1792. Here, we note that the biodistance study posits that Burial 14 could have been in the lineage that included Burials 6 and 11 described above. Yunnénis and Julírbe did have a third sibling, Tursucsé, who died at San Pedro y San Pablo as a six-year-old—the same general age as Burial 14. However, Tursucsé is listed in the mission records as a boy (Segundo, SFD Baptism 640, Death 249) and there is no ambiguity in the proteomic sex estimation as female for Burial 14. Thus, while it is possible that the missionaries misgendered Tursucsé, we feel that María Athanasia is a stronger match for Burial 14.

- The final potential match was for Burial 2, an adolescent male who died between the ages of thirteen and seventeen. This individual had a pathology consistent with vertebral tuberculosis. The only individual buried at San Pedro y San Pablo whose death record describes a similar ailment is José Manuel, who died at age twelve after suffering from a palsy.

Other individuals could not be identified because their demographic profiles resulted in multiple possible matches.

- Burial 7 was a newborn, between forty weeks gestational age and two months postpartum. Based on information in the mission death records, nearly two dozen children younger than one year of age were buried at the asistencia. Of those cases, four fit the estimated ages of Burial 7 (table 11.2). One clue to the infants' relative status is that Burial 7 was buried with a sizable quantity of glass beads. Of the possible matches, only one could be linked to known high-status individuals or lineages in the mission records. Santiago, who died at roughly one month of age, was the grandson of Gimás, captain of the Lamchin community from the eastern portion of the San Francisco Peninsula (see SFD Baptism 883). Though other similarly situated individuals in this study were buried with large numbers of beads, we have no additional contextual evidence to confirm this possible match.

- Burials 4 and 16 appear to have been buried together. Burial 4 is thought to have been between fifty and sixty years old at the time of her death, whereas Burial 16 was a second infant between forty weeks gestational age and two months postpartum. Despite Burial 4's relatively advanced age—which may be due to the use of aging standards developed for Western populations—it is worth noting that Burial 16 was located in the thoracic area of Burial 4, potentially indicating a mother and infant who both died in childbirth. Further, these two burials were found stratigraphically superior to Burials 14 and 15. If our identifications are correct, then Burials 4 and 16 would date to after January 2, 1792. Unfortunately, we could not identify any contemporaneous mother and infant deaths in the records for that time period. Pedro Nolasco and Santiago from table 11.2 are both possible matches for Burial 16, but they were clearly not newborns given the evidence from the baptismal and death records. As noted below, there were many adult women buried at the asistencia, complicating the identification of Burial 4. Burial 4, moreover, was buried in a prone position and was aligned differently than other adult burials. Given these details, we leave open the possibility that these two individuals are simply not in the mission death records for San Pedro y San Pablo—either because they were not baptized or possibly because their interments post-date the use of the site as an asistencia.

Table 11.2. Potential matches for Burial 7 and Burial 16

Possible Match	Spanish Name	Parents' Origin	Baptism #	Death #	Death Date	Age at Death
Burial 7	Pacifica	Pruristac	889	350	12/25/1790	~2 weeks
Burial 7	Petronilla	Cotegen	932a	357	2/26/1791	~1 month
Burial 7 or 16	Pedro Nolasco	Yelamu	1072	434	6/7/1792	~2.5 months
Burial 7 or 16	Santiago	Lamchin	2081	1365	10/25/1800	~1 month

Note: Missionaries did not record Native names for these children.

- Burial 13 was an adult woman, estimated to have died between the ages of twenty and twenty-four. Five women in the death records fall with that range, and allowing for a three-year range of variation outside of that window (ages seventeen to twenty-seven) expands the total to twelve possible matches. The burials of these women date to 1789–93, and therefore do not neatly map on to the chronological arrangement seen in the other burials.
- The remaining burials (Burials 3, 5, and 10) are all adult women. Burial 10 died between the ages of approximately forty and forty-four years; Burials 3 and 5 are estimated to have died between the ages of forty-five and fifty years. Allowing for some variation in skeletal aging, there are roughly a dozen women whose ages in the baptismal records could potentially match these burials. Here again, the apparent spatial layout of the cemetery does not provide enough information to make positive identifications in the absence of more specific clues such as pathologies, funerary offerings, or stratigraphic associations that could inform links between the archaeological and historical individuals.

Ohlone Life Histories from the Asistencia de San Pedro y San Pablo

While we could not identify all the individuals whose burials were disturbed, we found matches for more than half. Several of the individuals who appear to be matches between the historical and bioarchaeological records have life histories that intersect—their stories will be presented as a single narrative, followed by those for single individuals. Note that where the Franciscans recorded individuals' Native names, we prioritize those over the Spanish names applied at baptism.

An Elite Ohlone Family: Jagessém, Yunnénis, Julírbe, and Mauricio (Burials 12, 6, 11, and 9)

On June 11, 1786, a twenty-six-year old woman named Jagessém (matching the information for Burial 12) and her brother-in-law Yunnénis (matching the information for Burial 6) were baptized at Mission San Francisco (SFD Baptisms 544 and 546). Both were from the Chiguan village of the broader Ssatumnumo community, whose homelands were along the Pacific coast just north of present-day Half Moon Bay. Their baptism marked an important development in the relationship between their people and the Franciscans. Jagessém's father, Cancégmne, was the leader of the Ssatumnumo community. Jagessém's paternal uncle, Cancégmne's brother, was likewise from the Ssatumnumo community but eventually became the captain of Pruristac, the closest village to the future Asistencia de San Pedro y San Pablo. He was known as Yaguéche and sometimes went by the alias Mossués. Figure 11.3 provides a simplified kinship diagram for this elite family.

Perhaps in an attempt to form an alliance with the Spanish, Yaguéche received baptism at Mission San Francisco in the summer of 1783. Less than a year later, in January 1784, two of his brother Cancégmne's young children—Turumúcssé and Jamlité—were baptized (SFD Baptisms 319, 337, and 338). These were Jagessém's half siblings, though it is unclear if her mother, who was never baptized, had already died or if her father had multiple wives—a distinct possibility given his elite status. A little over a month later, Cancégmne himself and his wife Ssumsin (the mother of Turumúcssé and Jamlité) traveled from the coast to San Francisco to receive baptism (SFD Baptisms 345 and 351).

These decisions came at a great cost. Young Jamlité died at the age of seven in January 1785, just a little over a year after she was baptized. Her mother, Ssumsin, died shortly thereafter. By the end of the summer of 1785, Cancégmne too was dead (SFD Deaths 122, 132, and 142). Though tragic, their deaths reveal something of the porous nature of the colonial frontier in the early years of the Mission Period. Cancégmne and Jamlité were buried at Mission San Francisco, but the death records indicate that Ssumsin became ill while outside of the mission and was likely buried in her home village. This community was said to be some distance beyond Punta de Almejas ("*rancheria mas allá de la Punta de Almejas*"), a description that matches her Ssatumnumo origin. Though the Pruristac captain Yaguéche and his nephew Turumúcssé were still alive, the elite coastal families had already suffered tremendous losses before the founding of the San Pedro y San Pablo outstation.

Simplified Kinship Relationships for Identified Individuals at San Pedro y San Pablo

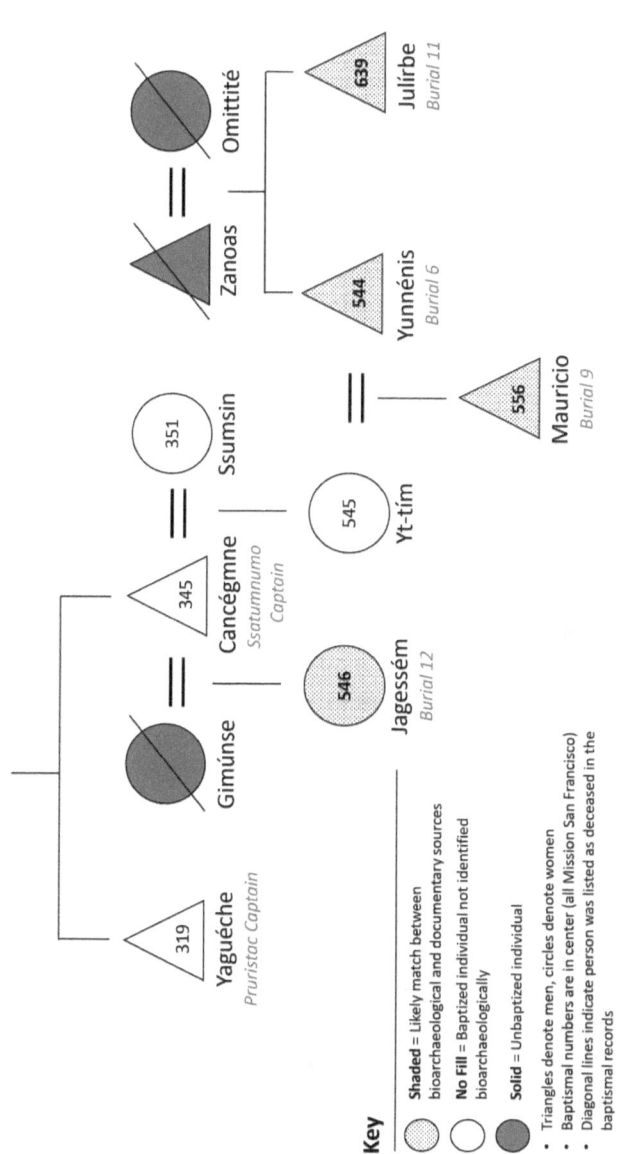

Figure 11.3. Simplified kinship diagram showing the relationships between Jagessém, Yunnénis, Julírbe, and Mauricio—members of an elite lineage who match the details for Burials 12, 6, 11, and 9, respectively.

These events suggest that there was a strong precedent for the survivors of Cancégmne's lineage to become associated with the Franciscan missions, but more than a year passed before they took that step. In June 1786, Cancégmne's daughter Jagessém (Burial 12) was baptized along with her three-year-old son Ulchigt; her half sister, Yt-tím, who was the daughter of Cancégmne and Ssumsin; and her brother-in-law Yunnénis (Burial 6) (SFD Baptisms 543, 544, 545, and 546). These baptisms are the only entries recorded at Mission San Francisco for June of that year and may be related to the onset of construction at the Asistencia de San Pedro y San Pablo, where it appears that all four individuals lived and worked. This supposition is supported by the records related to Mauricio, the newborn son of Jagessém's half sister Yt-tím and her brother-in-law Yunnénis, who was baptized at the asistencia in November 1786 (SFD Baptism 556). A few months later, the younger brother of Yunnénis, a boy named Julírbe, was also baptized. Mauricio and Julírbe match Burials 9 and 11, respectively.

All six of these family members died before the decade was over. Jagessém died on August 14, 1787, one day after her young son Ulchigt (SFD Deaths 212 and 213). Both were buried at the Asistencia de San Pedro y San Pablo. Jagessém's status as the daughter and niece of two important captains—one of whom, her uncle Yaguéche, was still living—is reflected in the belongings laid to rest with her. As detailed in chapter 5, she was buried with nearly three thousand shell and glass beads as well as a groundstone pestle. As shown in studies of her dental calculus, she was also a regular consumer of tobacco, again potentially signaling membership in a high-status lineage (chapter 8). Judging by proteins preserved in her calculus (chapter 7), she was not, however, prone to experimenting with new Spanish-introduced foods. Only proteins consistent with otter and beaver were identified. On the other hand, stress-related immunoglobulins in enamel of her first molar (chapter 4), which would have been deposited over a decade prior to her baptism, were among the highest within the asistencia population. This finding is consistent with several linear enamel hypoplasias that formed on her teeth between the ages of two and four years, suggesting she suffered from one or more severe periods of stress and/or disease as a child.

Yunnénis died a little over a year later, at the age of seventeen or eighteen. His profile matches that of Burial 6. Because his parents were never baptized and were deceased by the time of his baptism, we know little about his traditional background. Still, his status is affirmed by his marriage to Yt-tím, who was the daughter of the Ssatumnumo captain, Cancégmne. That the Franciscans recorded their marriage on the same day that he and Yt-tím were baptized indicates that they were already in a relationship outside of the mission system (SFD Marriage 132). At the Asistencia de San Pedro y San Pablo, his status may have enabled Yunnénis to experiment with new foods and substances brought by the Spanish—metabolomic studies reveal the presence of caffeine in his dental calculus (chapter 8). Likewise, proteomic analyses show the presence of cow's milk and pomegranate (chapter 7). The former may have exposed him to new zoonotic diseases, as proteins consistent with liver fluke were also found in his dental calculus, possibly contributing to his early passing. At the time of his death, he was buried with ninety-three shell and glass beads, as well as a groundstone pestle. He preceded Yt-tím and his son Mauricio in death, as both lived until the Spring of 1789 (SFD Deaths 282 and 284).

Mauricio and Julírbe—nephew and young uncle—died one day apart in April 1789. Mauricio was two and a half while Julírbe was probably just short of eight years old (SFD Deaths 282 and 283). Both were buried at the Asistencia de San Pedro y San Pablo, and match the profiles for Burials 9 and 11, respectively. Mauricio, in particular, shows high levels of proteins expressed during periods of stress, suggesting he was suffering from chronic disease or psychological sources of trauma in the months before his untimely death (chapter 4). Archaeologically, it appears that these two individuals were laid to rest together and had very similar belongings buried with them, confirming the familial connection seen in the documentary record. Of note, the two boys were buried with jet ornaments: each had a carved jet cross and a strand of faceted jet beads. As discussed in chapter 5, these are the only documented jet artifacts recorded to date from a Native Californian context dating to the Mission Period. Isotopic data (chapter 6) indicate that these two boys had unique diets relative to others studied at the site, with a more terrestrial rather than marine focus.

Despite these similarities, the two young boys came from different backgrounds. As the son of Yt-tím, Mauricio was the grandson of Cancégmne, the Ssatumnumo captain—not to mention a relative of Yagueche, the Pruristac captain. In addition to the jet cross and beads, he was buried with nearly a thousand shell and glass beads, which may speak directly to his prominent lineage. Julírbe, for his part, was the brother of Yt-tím's husband Yunnénis. Both Julírbe and Yunnénis were listed as orphans in the mission baptismal records. Therefore, no firm information exists regarding their familial connections, though they were also likely from the Chiguan community. Interestingly, Julírbe tested positive for nicotine but not caffeine in the metabolomic studies, while his brother Yunnénis exhibited the opposite pattern (chapter 8). At the time of his death, Julírbe was buried with a more modest bead assemblage than Mauricio, totaling some 114 shell, glass, and jet beads. Still, both boys were buried with a broad array of beads, each including most of the major typological categories present in the overall mortuary assemblage (see chapter 5, table 5.5). Clearly, they were cherished members of the Ohlone community at San Pedro y San Pablo.

Taken together, these matches add detail to the tragically short lives of members of an elite Native family at the San Pedro outstation. Assuming the matches for Burials 6, 9, and 11 are correct, the difference in time between the burial of Yunnénis and that of his brother and son (who died on consecutive days over seven months later) point toward the importance of social memory when choosing certain burial locations at this Mission Period cemetery.

Clues to Mobility: Olcóx (Burial 8)

Olcóx (a match for Burial 8) was born sometime around 1730, long before the Spanish colonization of Alta California. Though he was later associated with the Ohlone community living in the Cañada de la Punta de Almejas, he likely spent his childhood further inland. As detailed by isotopic studies (chapter 6), Olcóx moved in his adolescence from a slightly more interior area to a more coastal one. This timing could correspond to performing bride service and/or living at his spouse's village for some time after marriage, perhaps until the first child was born. At some point in his early twenties, Olcóx appears to have moved back to a more inland area. He would have been in the prime of his life in 1769 when the first colonial parties passed through the San Francisco Peninsula, and he likely kept a wary eye on the expanding Spanish presence over the next decade and a half.

His children, in contrast, seem to have been more susceptible to the Franciscans' recruitment techniques, which often targeted teenagers and young adults. In 1779, for example, Olcóx watched as his fourteen-year-old son Utála left home to receive baptism at the fledgling mission of San Francisco de Asís. Shortly thereafter, Utála's younger brother—known only as Lucas in the mission records—followed in his footsteps (SFD Baptisms 115 and 125). Perhaps at the urging of her sons, Olcóx's wife Chilssan, who was dreadfully sick, traveled to Mission San Francisco to receive baptism just before her death in the first week of 1781 (SFD Baptism 204, Death 33). Undeterred by that tragedy, Olcóx's teenage daughter Turute took baptism at Mission San Francisco later that year (SFD Baptism 217). Tragically, Utála died at Mission San Francisco in 1784 (SFD Death 94).

Without Chilssan or his children, Olcóx formed a new relationship with a woman named Turjám. Little is known about her background, but both made the journey to Mission San Francisco in the winter of 1786. They were among a group of twenty-five Ohlone individuals baptized on February 5 of that year (SFD Baptism 464 and 475). Most of their party hailed from the western shores of San Francisco Bay, ranging from modern-day San Francisco south to San Mateo; a few were even from the East Bay. Combined with the isotopic data for Burial 8, this may indicate that Olcóx had been living away from the Pacific coast but still retained some affiliation with the community at Punta de Almejas. The marriage of Olcóx and Turjám was recorded the same day as their baptism, suggesting that they were already in a relationship prior to their baptism (SFD Marriage 106).

Given Olcóx's connection to the Punta de Almejas region, it is not surprising that he eventually became associated with the Asistencia de San Pedro y San Pablo, which was founded the same year as his baptism. There, he likely blended old traditions and new, as revealed by the presence of both nicotine and caffeine in his dental calculus (chapter 8). Despite moving throughout the region over the course of his life, Olcóx may have wished to avoid living at Mission San Francisco where his son and first wife had perished. Sadly, his return to the coast was short-lived. Olcóx died in the summer of 1787, just a year and a half after his baptism, and was buried at the asistencia (*"yglesia de el paraj[e] de San Pedro y San Pablo"*) (SFD Death 214).

A Young Orphan: María Athanasia (Burial 14)

On January 5, 1792, the Native residents of San Pedro y San Pablo buried María Athanasia, a young girl aged six or seven (SFD Death 399a). This profile matches the information for Burial 14, which was one of the only burials in this study not to have any funerary offerings. Given the seeming association between grave goods and high-status individuals noted above, this pattern may suggest something about the status of María Athanasia or her lineage.

Unlike many individuals in the early mission records, María Athanasia had parents from two different tribal communities. She was baptized at Mission San Francisco in the spring of 1785, more than a year before the beginning of construction on the San Pedro y San Pablo outstation (SFD Baptism 420). Her parents, Guascám and Camgís, were baptized on February 5, 1786 (SFD Baptisms 465 and 476; and see SFD Marriage 107). They were part of the same mass baptism that included Olcóx (match for Burial 8), and like many from that group, María Athanasia's mother Guascám was from San Mateo, on the western shore of San Francisco Bay. Guascám's twelve-year-old son Chalixsé accompanied her to San Francisco to receive baptism on that same day in February 1786. He too is listed in various records as being from San Mateo. Guascám had another son named Geronimo Emiliano, who had been baptized in 1783 (SFD Baptisms 328 and 473). These boys were María Athanasia's half brothers, and their father likely died before her birth. Her father, Camgís, in contrast to Guascám and her sons, was from the San Pedro Valley, near the site of the future asistencia.

It is also worth noting that María Athanasia lost her mother when she was only three years old. Guascám died in late autumn of 1788 at the Asistencia de San Pedro y San Pablo. María Athanasia's father, Camgís, died in January 1791 (SFD Deaths 260 and 252). This means that for the last year of her life, María Athanasia was effectively an orphan. She did not have any uncles or aunts listed in the records, and her half brother Geronimo Emiliano had died shortly after Guascám and Camgís were baptized in early 1786 (SFD Death 180). It appears that her only living relative at the time of her death would have been her older half brother Chalixsé. By that time, however, Chalixsé was already married to a woman named Queyem and the two were likely living at Mission San Francisco (SFD Marriage 204, Baptism 786). Chalixsé himself died in 1801, apparently as a prisoner at the Santa Barbara Presidio (SFD Death 1385).

An Enigmatic Young Man: Tarsi (Burial 15)

In late August 1791, a young man by the name of Tarsi was baptized at the Asistencia de San Pedro y San Pablo. The Franciscan padre who performed the ceremony noted little about Tarsi's life, save that neither of his parents had been baptized. No other relatives were mentioned, nor was any hint given as to his status or even tribal background. The next time Tarsi appeared in the mission registers—under his Spanish name Aparicio—it was to record his untimely death (SFD Baptism 963, Death 398a). He was buried at the asistencia on January 4, 1792, and the details match the information for Burial 15 in this study. Alongside his body was placed a bundle containing a remarkable array of belongings, including fourteen bird bone whistles, nine obsidian tools (bifaces and projectile points), one chert projectile point, two quartz crystals, two bat ray barbs, and a single Olivella shell bead (see chapter 5). Proteomic analysis shows he experimented with new foods at the asistencia, including cow's milk. Likewise, metabolomic analysis reveals that he was a consumer of nicotine and caffeine (possibly in the form of chocolate). These studies, moreover, point toward a unique—though frustratingly unknown—compound within Tarsi's dental calculus, further setting him apart from others buried at the asistencia (see chapter 8). Clearly, Tarsi was an important young man.

Another mystery about Tarsi is why the records are so silent about his relations. At the time of his baptism, the missionary recorded his unbaptized father's name as Ujul. The only Ujul to appear in any Alta California mission record was baptized at the age of about fifty at the Asistencia de San Pedro y San Pablo on January 10, 1792—less than a week after Tarsi's death. His assigned Spanish name, moreover, was the same one given to Tarsi: Aparicio (SFD Baptism 1031). Though not explicitly stated in the records, there is little doubt that the two men were father and son. Ujul's wife, Jaysutí, was also baptized on January 10, 1792, and their marriage was immediately reconfirmed in the Catholic faith (SFD Marriage 254, and see SFD Baptism 1031). Ujul and Jaysutí were said to be the parents of an eighteen-year-old woman named Eycote, who herself was baptized at the asistencia on the same day as Tarsi in the previous autumn (SFD Baptism 964). She was undoubtedly Tarsi's sister—she was baptized immediately after he was—but strangely, the two are not directly linked in the records, except through their father's Native name.

Tarsi's parents lived only a few years after being baptized. Ujul died in April 1795, while Jaysutí passed away in January 1797. Both were buried at Mission San Francisco (SFD Deaths 821 and 1037). Of the immediate family, Tarsi's sister Eycote lived the longest after baptism, surviving into her early thirties. During the time that she and Tarsi both lived at the asistencia, she married a man named Lámpes from the Oljon community whose homelands were south of San Pedro y San Pablo (SFD Marriage 250, and see SFD Baptism 596). Given that no information exists on the origins of any of Tarsi's blood relatives, this is the only clue as to his tribal origin (early marriages at the Bay Area missions were often endogamous—see Peelo et al. 2018). Eycote was among more than two hundred Native people associated with Mission San Francisco who died in the measles epidemic of 1806 (SFD Death 2148). A possible survivor is José Saturnino, the son of Lámpes and Eycote. He was born at the end of 1797 and does not have a death record linked in either of the two mission record databases, suggesting that he—Tarsi's nephew—may have outlived the mission system (SFD Baptism 1922).

A Case of Tuberculosis? José Manuel (Burial 2)

In January 1778, an Ohlone woman named Cápete brought her infant son to be baptized at Mission San Francisco, where he was given the name José Manuel (SFD Baptism 42). Despite not being baptized herself, this was a familiar practice for Cápete. In the preceding year, her three older children—ages five, nine, and twelve—had already been baptized, soon after the founding of the mission near her homeland along the shores of San Francisco Bay (SFD Baptisms 9, 23, and 28). By the beginning of 1778, the father of those children was deceased, and Cápete was no longer in a relationship with José Manuel's father, Hetecsé, an Ohlone man from the community of Pruristac.

As a single mother, Cápete seems to have been balancing her independence with the welfare of her children. She herself resisted baptism until the summer of 1779 (SFD Baptism 107).

No information exists about José Manuel's life as a boy growing up in the Franciscan mission system. He was undoubtedly affected by the untimely deaths of two of his three half siblings, in 1779 and 1786 (SFD Deaths 20 and 193). His maternal grandmother, Ruxníc, eventually accepted baptism only to perish after a year and a half living at the mission (SFD Baptism 314, Death 160). All three were buried at the main mission. At some point, however, José Manuel, left San Francisco for the newly established outstation of San Pedro y San Pablo. It is unknown whether his father, Hetecsé, was still alive, but it seems likely that José Manuel moved to be closer to his paternal relatives living near the coast. He died at the asistencia in November 1789, just a few days shy of his twelfth birthday. The details of his life match Burial 2 from this study.

The notion that José Manuel retained family—and possibly even his father—at or near San Pedro y San Pablo is born out by the fact that he was buried with over two hundred shell beads (chapter 5). Adding to the overall picture, José Manuel's death record indicates that he suffered from an "ayre perlatico" (SFD Death 298). While not a medical diagnosis that would be used today, this phrase corresponds to contemporary anatomical and folk medicine and likely indicates that José Manuel was suffering from some sort of paralysis that would have been accompanied by tremors or even seizures. The death record, moreover, suggests that this condition may have affected his ability to speak. Bioarchaeologists investigating Burial 2—the apparent match for José Manuel—noted a pathology consistent with vertebral tuberculosis. By the time of the individual's death, the disease had progressed to the point where several vertebral bodies had collapsed. In combination with pelvic and femoral pathologies (discussed in chapter 3), the bioarchaeological record corresponds well to the historical suggestion that José Manuel was paralyzed. High levels of immunoglobulins recorded in his enamel also indicate high stress over an extended period of time, and that his body was working hard to combat this chronic infection (chapter 4).

Cemetery Layout and Growth

Estimating dates of death for individuals provides insight into how the cemetery at the Asistencia de San Pedro y San Pablo evolved over time. Figure 11.4 shows the plan map of the utility trench, populated now with our identi-

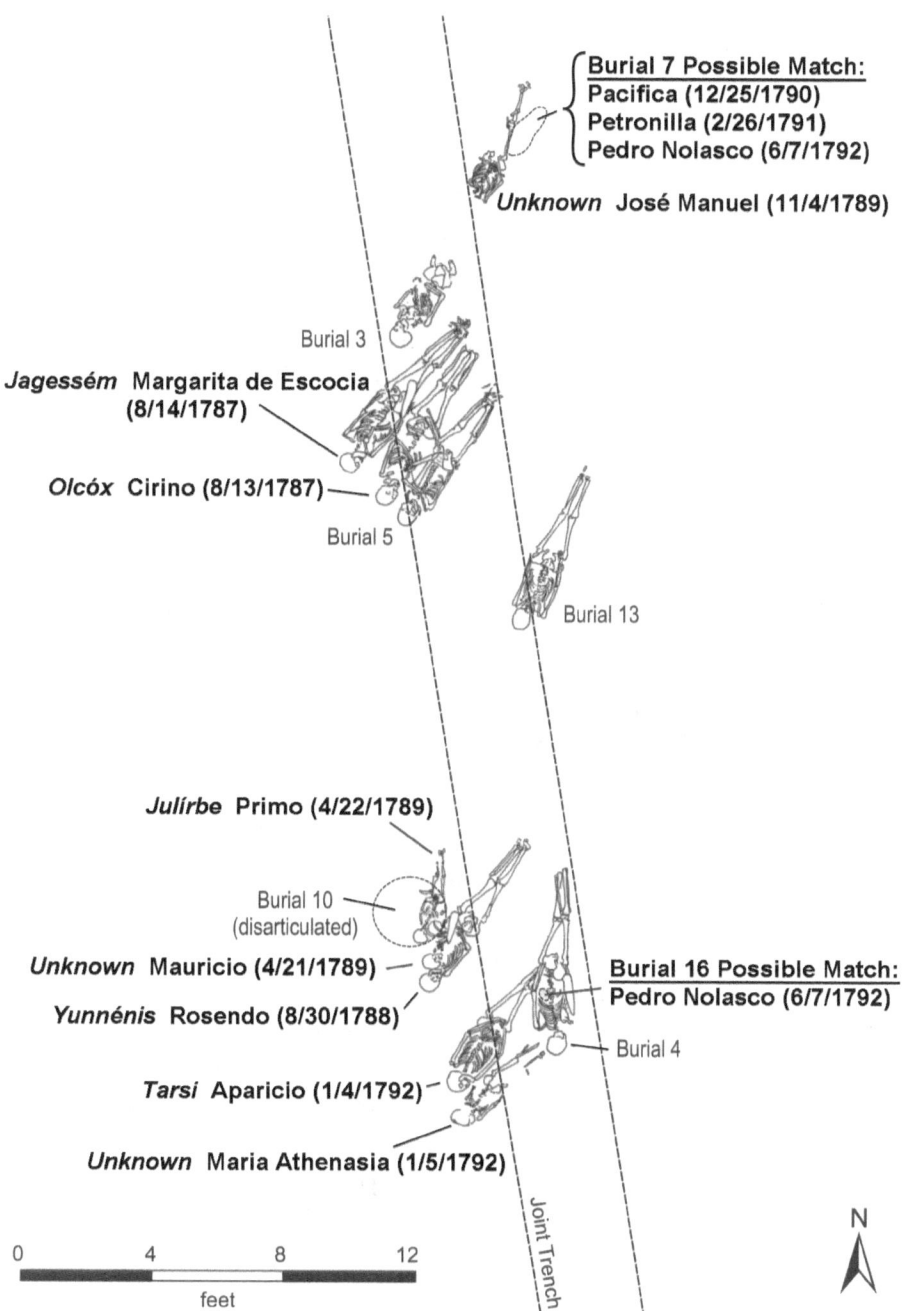

Figure 11.4. Plan map of burials with traditional Ohlone names in italics (when known), Spanish baptismal name, and date of death. Possible matches also given for Burials 7 and 16.

fications of eight individuals, and possible matches for two additional people (Burials 7 and 16). Included in the map are both the Ohlone names of individuals, when given in baptismal or death records, as well as the Spanish baptismal name, and date of death.

As shown, there is a general increase in the date of death from the center of the trench, near Jagessém and Olcóx (buried in the summer of 1787), to both the north and south. This suggests that the cemetery grew in size by adding recently deceased individuals along the outside edges of the existing set of graves. This pattern implies a cemetery that did not have a preplanned and linear layout, for example, where individuals were added accretionally based on a grid system. Instead, individuals seem to have been added based on available above-ground space, avoiding existing marked graves, and/or kin relations with people who were previously buried in the cemetery. As mentioned earlier, a similar system seems to have been in place at Mission Santa Clara (Hylkema 1995).

Conclusions

The use of the historical and archaeological record together offers a unique insight into the lives of the Native Californians who lived, worked, and died at the Asistencia de San Pedro y San Pablo. Despite some lingering ambiguities, we are confident that we have identified several of the Ohlone ancestors who were disturbed by the construction activities at the site. Their life histories offer an important perspective on the challenges faced by Ohlones and other Native Californians during the early years of the Franciscan mission system. All died prematurely, several as young children, a tragic testimony to the realities of colonialism in Alta California. Yet, this research shows how families remained together despite this hardship, and in many cases laid their loved ones to rest with markers of their status and identity. These continuing bonds are perhaps best represented by the example of José Manuel, who must have required near constant care due to his condition. These stories also reveal how individuals, couples, and whole lineages adapted aspects of their precontact community structure and residential mobility to remain connected to one another despite the far-reaching social changes wrought by the missions. By building these interpretive bridges across diverse lines of evidence, we hope to honor the individuals we identified, and by extension all the Native Californians who were buried at the Asistencia de San Pedro y San Pablo.

Acknowledgments

We thank Andrew Galvan for facilitating access to the Mission San Francisco sacramental records and Isa Cruz for her suggestions about interpreting seventeenth-century medical conditions. We appreciate the insights of the other authors in this volume whose studies helped refine the identifications presented here.

References

Cordero, Jonathan F.
2015 Native Persistence: Marriage, Social Structure, Political Leadership, and Intertribal Relations at Mission Dolores, 1777–1800. *Journal of California and Great Basin Anthropology* 35:133–149.
Early California Population Project
2022 Edition 1.1. General Editor, Steven W. Hackel. University of California, Riverside and The Huntington Library, Art Museum, and Botanical Gardens, San Marino, California.
Hylkema, Mark G.
1995 *Archaeological Investigations at the Third Location of Mission Santa Clara de Asís: The Murguía Mission, 1781–1818 (CA-SCL-30/H)*. Oakland: California Department of Transportation, District 4, Environmental Planning.
Milliken, Randall
1995 *A Time of Little Choice: The Disintegration of Tribal Culture in the San Francisco Bay Area, 1769–1810*. Ballena Press, Menlo Park, CA.
Milliken, Randall, Laurence H. Shoup, and Beverly R. Ortiz
2009 Ohlone/Costanoan Indians of the San Francisco Peninsula and Their Neighbors, Yesterday and Today. Report to the National Park Service, Golden Gate National Recreation Area, San Francisco.
Newell, Quincy D.
2009 *Constructing Lives at Mission San Francisco: Native Californians and Hispanic Colonists, 1776–1821*. University of New Mexico Press, Albuquerque.
Peelo, Sarah, Lee M. Panich, Christina Spellman, John Ellison, and Stella D'Oro
2018 Marriage and Death in the Neophyte Village at Mission Santa Clara: Preservation of Ancestral and Elite Communities. In *Forging Communities in Colonial Alta California*, edited by Kathleen L. Hull and John G. Douglass, 162–188. University of Arizona Press, Tucson.

12

Persistence of Traditional Lifeways, and Change, during the California Mission Period at Asistencia de San Pedro y San Pablo

Jelmer W. Eerkens, Lee M. Panich,
Christopher Canzonieri, and Christopher Zimmer

Collaboration between the Most Likely Descendants, San Mateo County Parks, CRM professionals, and university researchers provided an unprecedented opportunity to apply cutting-edge archaeometric and bioarchaeological, as well as more traditional osteological, historical, and contextual studies, to the human remains unearthed during construction at the site of the former Asistencia de San Pedro y San Pablo. While one of the goals of the volume was to identify individuals and reconstruct certain aspects of their life histories, as described in chapter 11, another was to examine the degree to which a range of traditional practices and behaviors either persisted, or changed, for Ohlone within the missions. Each author was asked to explore this topic within the purview of their respective analysis.

All human societies segregate and organize themselves around particular traits of individuals, often seen as inherent to the person at a moment in time and space. Age, gender, race, social class, religion, and language are common traits used to accomplish this in cultures around the world. These traits affect all manner experiences an individual will have in life. For example, in the United States today, age dictates whether one is legally allowed to vote, drive a car, or drink alcohol. Details in how traits are categorized differ from culture to culture (i.e., some cultures may recognize two and others three or more genders). Regardless of how a culture decides which traits are important, such categorization often enhances or restricts access to particular resources or rituals for individuals. Such essentializing traits certainly existed in Ohlone societies, as well as among Spanish colonizers. The intersection of these contrasting Ohlone and Spanish methods of social identity construction is a particularly interesting line of inquiry, as it would have greatly affected the experiences of baptized Ohlone individuals within the mission system.

In bioarchaeological studies, we are often unable to know which traits an ancient society used in social identity construction. Cross-culturally, we know that age, gender, and social status are among the most common. Fortunately, aspects of these three traits are often measurable through archaeometric, skeletal and/or mortuary analyses.

One advantage of the bioarchaeological approach followed here is that we are able to examine persistence and change at the scale of the individual, rather than the population at large, as would be the case for materials discovered in general midden contexts or communal features like those that have been examined at nearby mission sites (e.g., Panich et al. 2014, 2018; Peelo et al. 2018). Aggregating individuals by age, sex, and social status, we are able to contextualize how particular segments of the population, females vs. males, young vs. old, and elite vs. non-elite, engaged in new behaviors or had access to new types of resources brought by the Spanish, or not. Together, we believe this approach sheds light on how Ohlone society within the mission system was structured, and how this may have contrasted with precontact social organization, and our understandings of Spanish ideas about social organization.

The sample of fifteen individuals in this analysis is certainly small for partitioning the burial population into these different categories, particularly intersections of them (i.e., young female elite vs. old female non-elite). Nevertheless, we attempt to summarize the findings along these lines. We hope that future research on other Mission Period populations, if such opportunities arise, might follow up on these issues and test our hypotheses using novel data sets.

Persistence vs. Change by Sex

A combination of osteological and proteomic analyses allowed us to estimate sex for nearly every individual in the population (chapters 3 and 4). Only two infants who lacked teeth could not be assigned to a sex category. The ability to include children in these analyses allowed for the investigation of how sex intersected with age and status, to affect the lived experiences of individuals, especially access to novel Spanish-introduced products. As a result, we were able to examine the degree to which males and females persisted, or not, in certain traditional practices.

Proteomic analyses of dental calculus (chapter 7) identified a range of food items preserved in dental calculus. The majority of these items would have been available to people in precontact times, including deer, otter, and beaver. Every individual included in the study contained proteins associated with at least one of these three foods. Assuming the majority of these proteins became embedded in the calculus following baptism, this indicates a strong degree of persistence of precontact Ohlone dietary practices within the mission.

However, proteomic analyses also identified two classes of food that were clearly imported by the Spanish, cow's milk and pomegranate. Proteins associated with these foods embedded in dental calculus thus represent access to and/or experimentation with new sources of food. Here, there are slight differences in how males and females accessed these foods. Of the three males included in the calculus proteomic study, two tested positive for cow's milk, while only one of the six females did. This result is consistent with the findings by stable isotopes (see below), which suggested baptized males ate greater quantities of terrestrial foods. In addition, calculus from two of the three males tested positive for pomegranate, while only three of the six females did. Overall, all three males have evidence for one of these two novel products, while only three of six females do.

The sample sizes are too small for rigorous statistical analysis (i.e., Chi-square tests would not reveal "significant" p-values). However, the results do point to possible sex-linked differences in access to novel foods. Overall, it appears that males had greater access to new foods than females. We speculate that within the patriarchal Spanish worldview, friars may have differentially encouraged men to try, or supplied them with, mission-produced foods. Perhaps they thought that by getting men to accept these products, that other Ohlone would follow suit. This pattern may also relate to the gendered nature of life in the missions. Only Native men were able to serve in important roles such as interpreters, pages, sacristans, or even cowboys (Lightfoot 2005: 70–71). It is possible that access to new foods was simply part and parcel of Native men's differential engagement with the colonial system.

There also appear to be slight differences in how these sex-linked biases apply to animal versus plant products. The data suggest that males were more likely to experiment with, or had access to, introduced animal products, while females were more likely to incorporate novel plant foods. These slight differences could represent a "mapping on" of traditional tasks, which are known from ethnographic sources to be sex-linked (i.e., hunting vs. gathering), onto subsistence-related tasks within the mission system. Historically, only certain Native men served as vaqueros, or cowboys, in the California mission system—a role that was both gender-based and likely conferred certain social status when combined with horseback riding (Panich 2017). At San Pedro y San Pablo, it seems that baptized Ohlone males were tasked more often with caring for animals, including milking cows, while females were more frequently tasked with attending to gardens and orchards. These activities may have afforded males opportunities to drink extra milk, and females opportunities to consume extra fruit and vegetable products while working in those locations (e.g., directly eating fruits that had fallen off trees).

These trends were repeated in the metabolemic studies of dental calculus (chapter 8). Caffeine was a common biomolecule recovered in the study, with four of ten individuals testing positive. As caffeine is not present in native Central Californian plants, this indicates a willingness to experiment with novel food items, likely in the form of processed cacao (e.g., mole, chocolate). Three of the five males included in the study tested positive for caffeine, while only one of five females did. Again, this implies that males had greater access to the novel products that contained caffeine. By contrast, access to the more traditional product of tobacco is more evenly split, as indicated by the presence of nicotine, with three of five males and two of five females testing positive.

The metabolemic study also pointed to broader differences in the suite of biomolecules present in male vs. female dental calculus. Although the majority of those compounds were not specifically identified (as opposed to caffeine and nicotine), and we cannot ascribe particular behavioral differences to this pattern, most males and females were separated in a PCA analysis of metabolemic compounds. This implies that males and females within the mission system, and perhaps prior to their being baptized as well, were engaging in activities that introduced different compounds into the mouth. This could represent ingestion of different kinds of foods, but could also be related to consumption of medicines or performing tasks that involved use of the teeth (e.g., basketweaving, textile production). This latter possibility is consistent with ethnographically documented gender roles in Native California and in the Franciscan mission system (Lightfoot 2005: 67), again, a mapping on and continuance of traditional practices within the mission system.

Likewise, stable isotope analyses of collagen from tooth sections that formed before an individual entered the mission system, versus collagen that formed after an individual was within the mission, also reveal patterning in diet by sex. Results suggest that male diets were more dynamic across the pre– to post–Mission Period, while female diets were more stable. In particular, while precontact male diets were generally heavy in high trophic-level marine foods, their diets within the mission seem to have transitioned to greater incorporation of terrestrial foods. As shown above, 67 percent of males included in the proteomic studies tested positive for cow's milk, while only 20 percent of the females did. By contrast, precontact females seem to have accessed less marine food than males. But within the mission system, females continued to eat similar quantities of these marine-derived foods. These isotopic differences again suggest that males within the mission system had greater access to novel foods and dietary regimes than females, and witnessed a greater degree of dietary change than females. This finding also comports with historical records indicating that tending cattle within the missions was primarily tasked to male individuals (Hackel 2005). Historical records indicate that some males were involved in trapping and hunting of beaver and otter to supply the Spanish with pelts. However, judging by the proteins present in calculus, the meat from these traditionally caught animals was eaten and shared widely among the Native community associated with the asistencia, males and females. These findings point to a continuance of certain aspects of traditional hunting, trapping, and meat consumption.

Element analyses (chapter 9) did not point to any systematic differences by sex in the degree to which baptized individuals were exposed to heavy metals, though the sample size was limited to just five of the individuals. The results did show that both males and females were exposed to higher amounts of copper, zinc, and iron relative to precontact individuals. Such exposure likely came through the use of new introduced metal tools, including cooking, serving, and drinking vessels, and possibly consumption of some of the new foods discussed above, especially beef and dairy.

Overall, the various studies in this volume point to important differences in how males and females persisted in traditional activities within the mission system. Although members of both sexes in this population show some evidence for dietary and behavioral change from precontact lifeways, as well as evidence for persistence (i.e., consumption of otter and beaver), our findings suggest that females were more likely to maintain traditional practices and males were more likely to adopt novel lifeways.

Persistence vs. Change by Age

The burial population from the asistencia naturally segregates into a set of individuals who died under age twenty-five (n=10, including two infants), and a set that died after age thirty-five (n=5). We use that natural division here to examine patterning in persistence vs. change by ontogenetic age. We collapsed the sex categories noted above in the summaries below. However, we note that there is a slight overrepresentation of males within the younger cohort within the dental calculus studies, and that the two infants were not included in any of the information below.

The calculus proteomic data indicate that both young and old were consuming traditional foods, including deer, otter, and beaver. On the other hand, there was a slight tendency for younger individuals to test positive for cow's milk, where two of four younger people (both males), but only one of five older people did (a female). Pomegranate seems to have been more evenly distributed by age, where two of four younger and three of five older people tested positive for these fruit proteins.

Data from metabolemics suggest a different pattern for access to novel caffeine-containing foods. Only one of six younger people tested positive for caffeine, while two of four older people did. Yet, access to the more traditional tobacco, as evidenced by nicotine, is more evenly distributed, with three of six younger people and two of four older people testing positive.

Stable isotope data suggested that all individuals within the population continued to eat significant quantities of marine foods, but that there is a shift toward a greater terrestrial component within the asistencia. Further, within the population, it appears that younger individuals, particularly those under age twelve, had the most divergent diets relative to precontact dietary practices. There, a terrestrial dietary focus seems to have characterized the youngest children, while collagen that we estimate to have formed after entering the mission from younger adults points to continued consumption of at least some marine foods.

Finally, the heavy metal analyses do suggest some differences by age in exposure to copper, zinc, and iron. Here, the youngest individuals, teenaged Tarsi and child María Athanasia, show generally lower levels of copper and zinc compared to the adults, including Burial 3, Yunnénis, and Olcóx. This suggests that older individuals had greater access to foods prepared or stored in metal containers.

Overall, then, there seems to be only a slight distinction for persistence vs. change by age. The data suggest that both young and old had access to novel dietary items, with a slight bias toward younger individuals being more dynamic in their incorporation of novel food items relative to older adults. The main exception here is in the form of access to caffeine-containing products, presumably cacao, which seem to have been reserved more for older individuals within the mission. It is possible that either friars or Ohlone elders may have restricted access to cacao by age. Chocolate—taken as a beverage—was a standard part of the colonial diet in Alta California, and there is some evidence that missionaries and soldiers may have restricted its usage among Native people to those who were most inclined toward Euro-American lifeways (Graham and Skowronek 2016). At the remote outpost of San Pedro y San Pablo, that practice may have simply meant that adults, especially adult men (per discussion above), rather than children, were able to indulge in the consumption of chocolate. Assuming these cacao-based products were prepared or stored in iron, copper, or brass vessels, such as the chocolateras found in some California mission contexts (Graham and Skowronek 2016; Simmons and Turley 1980), this line of reasoning also explains the higher levels of these metals in the enamel of older individuals within the population.

Persistence vs. Change by Social Class

Social class and/or status is often marked in death by investment in the funerary context (Bartel 1982; Binford and Brown 1971; O'Shea 1984). In many societies such status is materialized by placing goods within the grave, especially items that reflect the social connections the person had in life. The latter often include exotic goods that reflect links or ties to distant but important individuals, cultures, rituals, or landscapes. Research in precontact California has a long history of investigating beads, especially Olivella and clam disk beads, in mortuary contexts (Brown et al. 2023; Groza et al. 2011; Milliken and Bennyhoff 1993), and the quantity of these items are often regarded as marking social status.

Within the San Pedro y San Pablo population, there are nine individuals who were buried with high numbers of beads (greater than ninety beads) and/or other unusual items (in the case of Tarsi; see chapter 5). These include José Manuel (Burial 2), Burial 5, Yunnénis (Burial 6), Burial 7, Mauricio (Burial 9), Julírbe (Burial 11), Jagessém (Burial 12), Burial 13, and Tarsi (Burial 15). On the other hand, five individuals have very few grave goods: Burial 3, Burial 4, Olcóx (Burial 8), Burial 10, and María Athanasia (Burial 14). We use these distinctions to examine "higher status" and connected individuals, from those who were apparently of "lower status" and relatively unconnected.

Proteomic analyses of calculus show that both high- and low-status individuals accessed traditional foods, including otter, deer, and beaver. However, three of five high-status individuals tested positive for cow's milk, while none of the four lower-status individuals did. This may indicate that higher-status individuals, including both males and females, may have had differential access to novel mission animal products. On the other hand, access to pomegranates seems to have been more equal between higher-status (three of five tested positive) and lower-status (two of four) individuals.

Metabolemic studies show that access to caffeine-producing products was more equal between higher-status (two of six tested positive) and lower-status (two of four) individuals. As well, assuming exposure to heavy metals was primarily through metal chocolateras, we did not see differences in the density of heavy metals across the social status categories. Access to traditional tobacco was also equal across higher-status (three of six tested positive) and lower-status (two of four) individuals. Likewise, stable isotope analyses do not indicate significant differences in diets within the mission between higher- and lower-status individuals. Higher-status individuals do not show systematically greater access to marine (or terrestrial) food products. This finding tracks well with complementary archaeological data from mission sites where Native residents prepared communal meals, such as stews (Noe 2022). Together, the information on status indicates that, outside of access to cow's milk, which as noted above may have been linked to sex-biased tasks within the asistencia, there are no clear differences in access to novel foods and resources associated with the quantity of beads or exotic items placed in the grave. This finding suggests that many of the status differences Ohlone recognized within their community, and marked by including grave goods at death (the continuation of a traditional practice), were either not recognized by friars within the mission, or at least did not result in differential treatment. While historical records show that the eighteenth-century Spanish worldview certainly recognized status disparities among individuals, they likely did not extend such social identities to baptized Ohlone within the mission. It is possible that friars considered all Ohlone to be equally inferior. Alternatively, perhaps friars did not wish to promote jealousy or other internal divisions within the baptized community by providing access to certain resources to particular individuals based on a status system they did not understand or recognize (as opposed to age and sex, which they did understand).

In terms of funerary offerings, we note two patterns that may relate to status. One has to do with beads. Of particular interest is that some but not all of the children were buried with sizable quantities of beads, which were a marker of wealth in local Native Californian societies during precontact times and into the colonial period (Milliken et al. 2007; Panich 2014). This pattern is especially evident for Mauricio and Julírbe (Burials 9 and 11), young boys with largely matching burial assemblages of shell, glass, and jet beads, and who can be linked to a known lineage headed by two community captains. Burial 7, an infant, also had a large number of glass beads though their identity remains unknown. The other children, María Athanasia (Burial 14) and Burial 16, were completely lacking in beads or other funerary offerings.

This uneven distribution suggests that status was inherited within the Ohlone community rather than ascribed.

Of the adults with large bead assemblages, the association between beads and status is reinforced. This is particularly true for Yunnénis and Jagessém (Burials 6 and 12), who were part of the same elite extended family as Mauricio and Julírbe. Here, moreover, bead wealth decreased with distance from the lineage captain. Jagessém, daughter of a captain, had the most beads of any individual in this study, whereas Yunnénis, whose brother had married into the lineage, had a relatively modest funerary assemblage. Last, the kinds of beads buried with particular individuals may also be meaningful. Aside from Burial 7, whose historical identity could not be discerned, all the individuals with notable quantities of glass beads were from the high-status lineage. Mauricio and Julírbe had the only jet beads yet recorded from a contemporary mortuary context in the entire region, perhaps also pointing toward the association between introduced beads and status (and see Panich 2014).

Age at weaning may also relate to status. The weaning data from the Asistencia de San Pedro y San Pablo generally conform to the patterns seen in the funerary offerings. Olcóx (Burial 8) was weaned relatively early and did not have any appreciable grave goods deposited with him at the time of his death many decades later. This latter finding may underscore the durability of inherited social position among Ohlone people. A slightly different pattern is present for José Manuel (Burial 2). He also seems to have been weaned relatively early, and he was buried with a modest bead assemblage. These beads, however, were nearly all shell beads (as opposed to glass or jet), perhaps reinforcing the correlation between novel bead types and status. Mauricio (Burial 9), in contrast, was the grandson of a captain and was still breastfeeding at the time of his death at age two and a half when he was buried with an elaborate assemblage of shell, glass, and jet beads. While we know little about the ancestry of Mauricio's father (Burial 6), Yunnénis was weaned late compared to others in this study, suggesting that he may have been destined at birth to assume a leadership position. This may account for his marriage to Yt-tím, the daughter of a captain.

The adolescent Tarsi (Burial 15) suggests that funerary offerings may relate to other vectors of social identity. Tarsi has no known ties to local Native leadership. He was weaned relatively late in his childhood, like other high-status individuals in this study. Where his story diverges is in his burial assemblage. It included only one shell bead, but nonetheless had an array of objects—bird bone whistles, projectile points, quartz crystals, and bat ray barbs—that were absent from any of the other burials at the asistencia. Given that these belongings appear to have been kept in a pouch placed on Tarsi's abdomen, it is possible that his status derived not from political power—as in the case of the lineages of village captains—but rather from proximity to religious or spiritual power.

These inferences about status may also intersect questions about how gender operated among Ohlone communities in late precontact and early colonial times. Whereas the distribution of beads suggests that political status was heritable, information on weaning ages points toward gendered investments in young people, even among important lineages. Jagessém (Burial 12), for example, seems to have been weaned early, at only a year and a half of age. If captainship was passed down patrilineally, she may not have received as much maternal investment in the form of breastfeeding, and was therefore weaned earlier. Her elaborate funerary offerings speak to her status relative to Ohlone individuals outside of her lineage, but the weaning data may suggest that within her own family she was subordinate to her brothers and other male family members.

Conclusions

The recovery of fifteen burials from the Asistencia de San Pedro y San Pablo offered a novel opportunity to learn more about the lives of Ohlone ancestors who were thrust into the Spanish mission system during its early years of operation. There is no doubt that these individuals and families suffered greatly from the impacts of the mission system, as evidenced by skeletal pathologies, other health indicators, and the disproportionate number of children buried in the asistencia's cemetery. This finding is not surprising, as previous bioarchaeological and demographic studies in Alta California have amply demonstrated the negative effects of missionization for Native Californians (Jackson 1994; Jones et al. 2021). Though regional and site-specific differences exist, bioarchaeological analyses from the Spanish colony of La Florida similarly demonstrate that Native health declined in step with their participation in the mission system (Stojanowski 2013). Indeed, such patterns are present throughout the Spanish Borderlands of North America (Baker and Kealhofer 1996).

Despite the hardships they faced, Ohlone ancestors at San Pedro y San Pablo seem to have deliberately chosen to live there rather than at the main mission sites of San Francisco, Santa Clara, and eventually Santa Cruz. The reasons behind this choice are complex, but likely involved the ability to remain close to family and friends, proximity to ancestral homelands along the coast, and perhaps a greater degree of freedom in everyday life. This latter possibility is suggested by the prevalence of tobacco use and the persistent consumption of traditional foods by many of the individuals in this study. Similarly, Native people at San Pedro y San Pablo laid their loved ones to rest with a wide array of belongings, including beads, groundstone pestles, and other items. The use of funerary offerings was in keeping with widespread mortuary traditions among Ohlone communities but would have been expressly prohibited by Catholic doctrine of the time. Interestingly, there is good evidence for all of these same practices—tobacco use, consumption of traditional foods, and the persistence of grave goods—at nearby missions such as Santa Clara (Cuthrell et al. 2016; Hylkema 1995; Panich 2015; Potter et al. 2021). However, the short duration of occupation at San Pedro y San Pablo combined with the ability to identify specific historical individuals offered the unprecedented opportunity to refine the temporal and cultural understanding of how Ohlone people, like other Native Californians, resisted the imposition of the mission system.

Findings in this volume suggest that Ohlone engaged with Spanish culture and worldviews in a mixed fashion. In other words, there is evidence for both persistence and change. Given the nature of archaeological inquiry, our results are necessarily focused on the more material and durable aspects of people's lives. Thus, behaviors surrounding diet, health, and medicinal plant usage figure prominently in our research, while language and clothing are missing. Nevertheless, based on evidence collected, it is clear that a number of traditional dietary, behavioral, and mortuary practices continued among the individuals included in the research. For example, outside of the two infants who were likely still breastfeeding, consumption of native animals and plants was evident in every individual studied.

Results from the studies in this volume suggest that social status does not seem to have had much influence in the degree to which people adopted, or not, novel Spanish practices. On the other hand, women, and to some degree older men, were more likely to persist in these traditional practices, while males, especially boys and younger adult men, seem to have either more readily adopted, or at least had greater access to, the many novel foods Spanish colonizers brought with them. At the asistencia, our evidence shows these products included cow, pomegranate, and cacao. Judging from Yunnénis, who seems to have contracted liver fluke from his interactions with cows, such behaviors also carried health risks to individuals.

In sum, the positive and collaborative interaction between the people who participated in the Asistencia de San Pedro y San Pablo project, provided a wealth of new information about the process of missionization in California, at least for people buried at the site. We were privileged to work with so many professionals, each with amazing sets of knowledge and expertise.

In conducting the studies, we hope to have honored the ancestors by giving names to some of the skeletal remains and reconstructing parts of their life histories during what was a tumultuous and difficult time for Native people. We hope the results of these studies are of value to other Ohlone and Native communities, and to those with interests in California's human history. Finally, we note that archaeological science is an iterative process that builds upon previous findings and continually refines our knowledge and understanding about the past. New analytical methods open up new windows onto the experiences of our ancestors. Should future construction or other activity result in the unanticipated exposure of Mission Period individuals at other locations, we hope that the studies set forth in this volume can provide a framework for new studies, to honor and help remember other individuals, to test some of the ideas proposed in this volume, and to deepen our connection to the past.

References

Baker, Brenda J., and Lisa Kealhofer
1996   *Bioarchaeology of Native American Adaptation in the Spanish Borderlands.* University Press of Florida, Gainesville.
Bartel, Brad
1982   A Historical Review of Ethnological and Archaeological Analyses of Mortuary Practice. *Journal of Anthropological Archaeology* 1: 32–58.
Binford, Lewis R., and James A. Brown
1971   Approaches to the Social Dimensions of Mortuary Practices. *Memoirs of the Society for American Archaeology* 25: 6–29.
Brown, Kaitlin M., Marirose Meyer, Elena Hancock, Nicolasa I. Sandoval, and Glenn J. Farris
2023   Status and Social Stratification at Mission La Purísima Concepción: An Intra-Site Investigation of Residential Space within the Chumash Ranchería'Amuwu. *International Journal of Historical Archaeology* 27: 506–542.
Cuthrell, Rob Q., Lee M. Panich, and Oliver R. Hegge
2016   Investigating Native Californian Tobacco Use at Mission Santa Clara, California, through Morphometric Analysis of Tobacco (Nicotiana spp.) Seeds. *Journal of Archaeological Science: Reports* 6: 451–662.
Graham, Margaret A., and Russell K. Skowronek
2016   Chocolate on the Borderlands of New Spain. *International Journal of Historical Archaeology* 20: 645–665.
Groza, Randall G., Jeffrey Rosenthal, John Southon, and Randall Milliken
2011   A Refined Shell Bead Chronology for Late Holocene Central California. *Journal of California and Great Basin Anthropology* 31: 135–154.
Hackel, Steven W.
2005   *Children of Coyote, Missionaries of Saint Francis: Indian–Spanish Relations in*

Colonial California, 1769–1850. University of North Carolina Press, Chapel Hill.

Hylkema, Mark G.
1995   *Archaeological Investigations at the Third Location of Mission Santa Clara de Asís: The Murguía Mission, 1781–1818 (CA-SCL-30/H)*. Oakland: California Department of Transportation, District 4, Environmental Planning.

Jackson, Robert H.
1994   *Indian Population Decline: The Missions of Northwestern New Spain, 1687–1840*. University of New Mexico Press, Albuquerque.

Jones, Terry L., Al W. Schwitalla, Marin A. Pilloud, John R. Johnson, Richard R. Paine, and Brian F. Codding
2021   Historic and Bioarchaeological Evidence Supports Late Onset of Post-Columbian Epidemics in Native California. *Proceedings of the National Academy of Sciences* 118(28): e2024802118.

Lightfoot, Kent G.
2005   *Indians, Missionaries, and Merchants: The Legacy of Colonial Encounters on the California Frontier*. University of California Press, Berkeley.

Milliken, Randall T., and James A. Bennyhoff
1993   Temporal Bead Changes as Prehistoric California Grave Goods. In *There Grows a Green Tree: Papers in Honor of David A Fredrickson*, edited by Greg White, Pat Mikkelsen, William R. Hildebrandt, and Mark E. Basgall, 381–395. Center for Archaeological Research at Davis, Davis, California.

Milliken, Randall T., Richard T. Fitzgerald, Mark G. Hylkema, Randy Groza, Tom Origer, David G. Bieling, Alan Leventhal, Randy S. Wiberg, Andrew Gottsfield, Donna Gillete, Viviana Bellifemine, Eric Strother, Robert Cartier, and David A. Fredrickson
2007   Punctuated Culture Change in the San Francisco Bay Area. In *California Prehistory: Colonization, Culture, and Complexity*, edited by Terry L. Jones and Kathryn A. Klar, 99–124. Altamira Press, Lanham, MD.

Noe, Sarah J.
2022   Zooarchaeology of Mission Santa Clara de Asís: Bone Fragmentation, Stew Production, and Commensality. *International Journal of Historical Archaeology* 26: 908–950.

O'Shea, John M.
1984   *Mortuary Variability: An Archaeological Investigation*. Academic Press, New York.

Panich, Lee M.
2014   Native American Consumption of Shell and Glass Beads at Mission Santa Clara de Asís. *American Antiquity* 79(4): 730–748.
2015   "Sometimes They Bury the Deceased's Clothes and Trinkets": Indigenous Mortuary Practices at Mission Santa Clara de Asís. *Historical Archaeology* 49(4): 110–129.
2017   Indigenous Vaqueros in Colonial California: Labor, Identity and Autonomy. In *Foreign Objects: Rethinking Indigenous Consumption in American Archaeology*, edited by Craig N. Cipolla, 187–203. University of Arizona Press, Tucson.

Panich, Lee M., H. Afaghani, and N. Mathwich
2014   Assessing the Diversity of Mission Populations through the Comparison of Native American Residences at Mission Santa Clara de Asis. *International Journal of Historical Archaeology* 18: 467–488.

Panich, Lee M., Rebecca Allen, and Andrew Galvan
2018   The Archaeology of Native American Persistence at Mission San José. *Journal of California and Great Basin Anthropology* 38(1): 11–29.

Peelo, Sarah, Linda J. Hylkema, John Ellison, Clinton M. Blount, Mark G. Hylkema, Margie Maher, Tom Garlinghouse, Dustin McKenzie, Stella D'Oro, and Melinda Berge
2018   Persistence in the Indian Ranchería at Mission Santa Clara de Asís. *Journal of California and Great Basin Anthropology* 38(2): 207–234.

Potter, James M., Tiffany Clark, and Seetha Reddy
2021   Subsistence and Ritual: Faunal and Plant Exploitation at the Mission Santa Clara de Asís Ranchería (CA-SCL-30H). *California Archaeology* 13(2): 203–225.

Simmons, Marc, and Frank Turley
1980   *Southwestern Colonial Ironwork: The Spanish Blacksmithing Tradition.* Museum of New Mexico Press, Santa Fe.

Stojanowski, Christopher M.
2013   *Mission Cemeteries, Mission Peoples: Historical and Evolutionary Dimensions of Intracemetery Bioarchaeology in Spanish Florida.* University Press of Florida, Gainesville.

APPENDIX

Images of Human Skeletal Remains

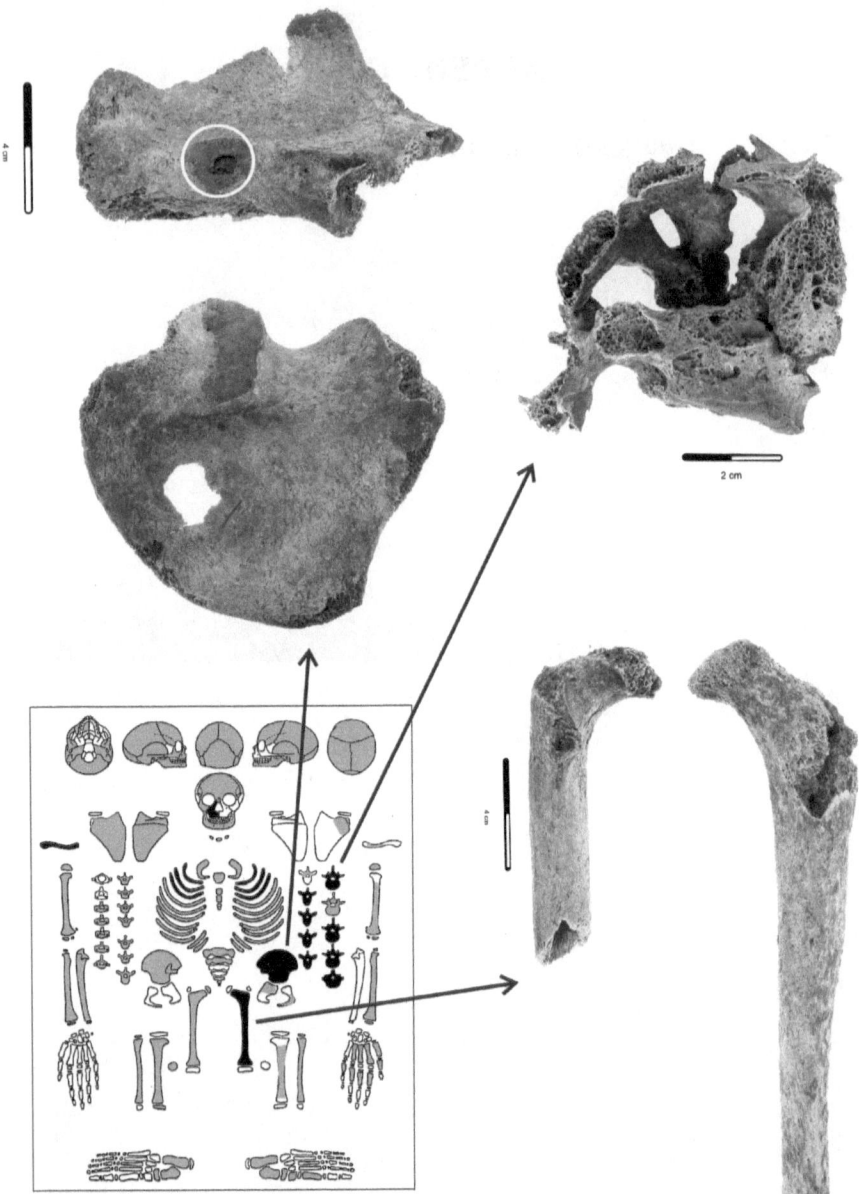

Figure A.1. Preservation of Burial 2 with pathological alterations shaded in black. Pathological alterations at the lower thoracic and lumbar vertebrae, lytic lesion at the right ilium, and morphological changes in femora angle are depicted by arrows.

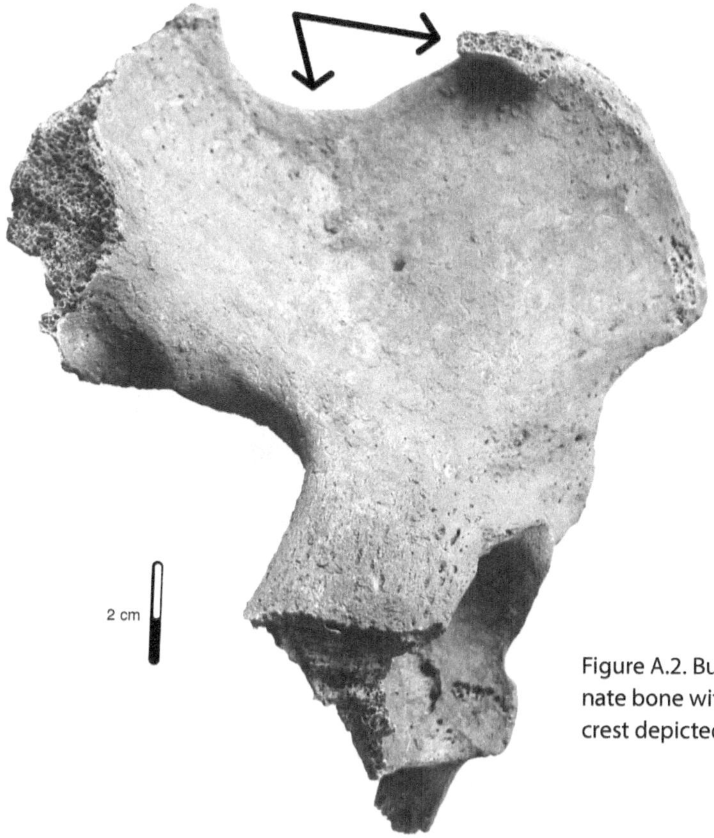

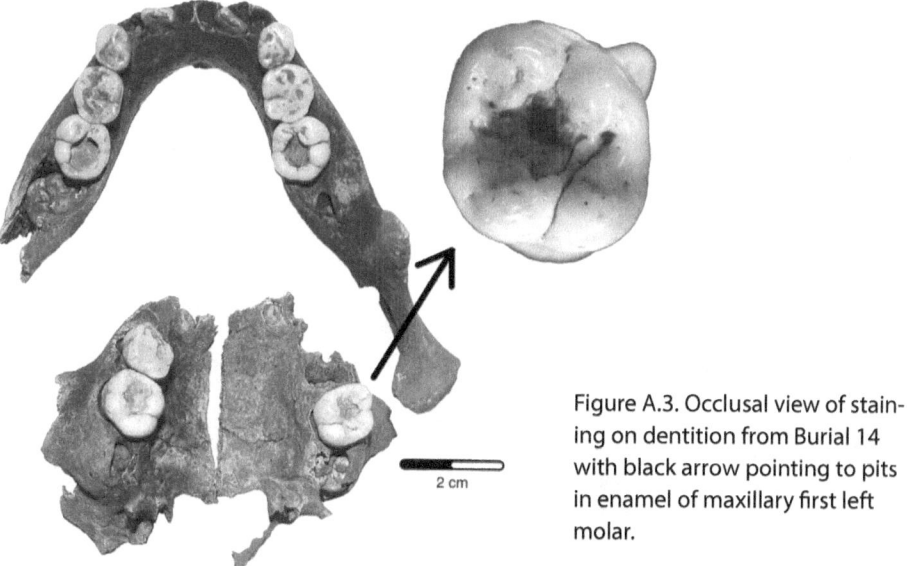

Figure A.2. Burial 3, right innominate bone with alterations at iliac crest depicted by arrows.

Figure A.3. Occlusal view of staining on dentition from Burial 14 with black arrow pointing to pits in enamel of maxillary first left molar.

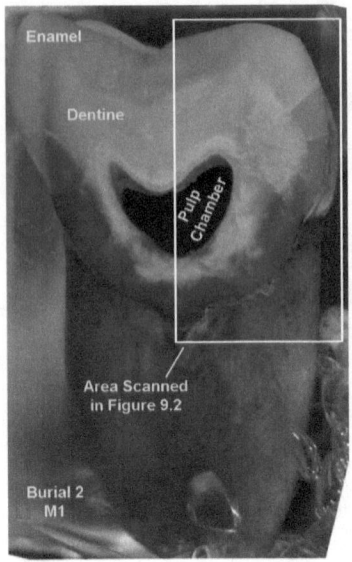

Figure A.4. Cross section of first molar of Burial 2, showing area scanned by LA-ICP-MS in Figure 9.2.

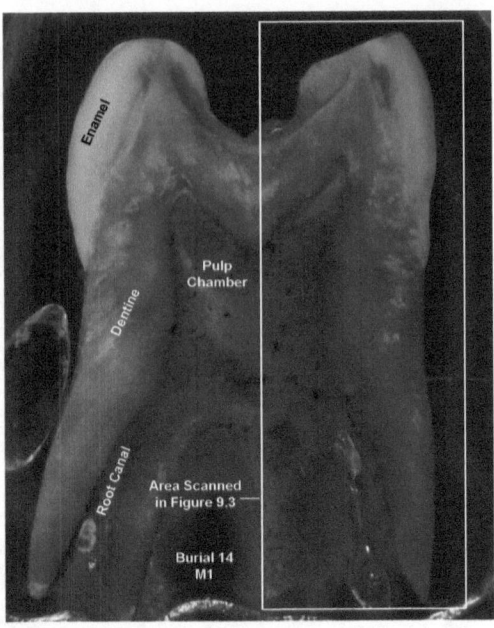

Figure A.5. Cross section of first molar of Burial 14, showing area scanned by LA-ICP-MS in figure 9.3. Note incomplete apical root tip, which was still growing at time of death.

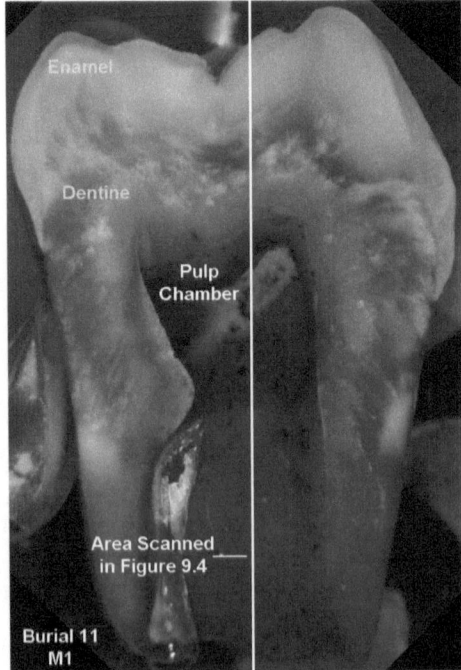

Figure A.6. Cross section of first molar of Burial 11, showing area scanned by LA-ICP-MS in figure 9.4. Note incomplete apical root tip, which was still growing at time of death.

CONTRIBUTORS

Monica V. Arellano represents the Muwekma Ohlone Tribe of the San Francisco Bay Area on the State of California's Native American Heritage Commission's Most Likely Descendant list. She has served as Tribal Vice Chairwoman for the tribe and is also the vice president of Muwekma Ohlone Tribe, Inc., the Tribe's Cultural Resources Management firm.

Beth Armstrong is an independent researcher, archaeologist, and longtime member of the California Archaeological Site Stewardship Program (CASSP).

Christine Austin is assistant professor in the department of environmental medicine and public health at the Icahn School of Medicine at Mount Sinai. Her research projects include developing biomarkers of human exposure to metals, chemicals, diet, and stress, in diverse matrices such as teeth, hair, and placenta.

Anna Berim manages the Tissue Imaging, Metabolomics and Proteomics Laboratory at Washington State University. Her research focuses on flavonoid metabolism, particularly in the mint family, and application of metabolomics and lipidomics in plant biochemistry.

Kristen A. Broehl-Droke is an assistant teaching professor of anthropology at Emory University. Her research focuses are in bioarchaeology and forensic anthropology, especially using biodistance analysis to explore relationships between biological and cultural affinity in past populations.

Tammy Buonasera is an assistant professor of anthropology at the University of Alaska Fairbanks. Her research focuses on biomolecular archaeology (proteomics, lipid analysis, and stable isotopes), to reconstruct past diets and health, and economic and social aspects of food processing.

Kyle Burk is a researcher specializing in proteomics in the department of environmental toxicology at University of California Davis.

Alyson Caine is a visiting assistant professor of anthropology and archaeology at Dickinson College. Her research focuses on social inequality, representation, and social identity as embodied in skeletal remains.

Christopher Canzonieri is a senior project archaeologist and bioarchaeologist at Basin Research Associates with over twenty-five years of experience in California. His research focuses on health and paleopathology in California.

Austin Cole is a spectroscopist and laboratory manager of the UC Davis Interdisciplinary Center for Plasma Mass Spectrometry at the University of California Davis.

Jelmer W. Eerkens is a professor of anthropology at University of California, Davis, where he directs the Archaeometry Lab. His research focuses on human health, diet, and technological innovation especially in small-scale societies.

David R. Gang is a professor in the Institute of Biological Chemistry at Washington State University. His research examines the production, evolution, and function of secondary metabolites in plants and microbes as it pertains to agriculture, human health, and bioenergy.

Alan Leventhal is an emeritus lecturer of anthropology at San Jose State University. His research interests center around the San Francisco Bay, evolution of complex nonagricultural hunting-gathering societies, social stratification, stone tool technologies, skeletal biology, ancient DNA and stable isotope studies, contemporary Native American issues, and federal recognition for California Indian tribes.

Diana Malarchik is a PhD student in anthropology at UC Davis. Her research focuses on health and diet in historic populations, especially nineteenth-century immigrants in San Francisco, using osteological, stable isotope, and proteomic methods.

Christine Marshall is a staff archaeologist at Basin Research Associates. She specializes in bioarchaeology and paleopathology and has experience in North America, Europe, and Africa, focusing especially on post–New Kingdom periods in Egypt.

Jason Miszaniec is a postdoctoral research associate and museum scientist at the University of Wisconsin–Madison. His research focuses on zooarchaeology, especially the study of fish and ancient fisheries in the Arctic.

Lee M. Panich is a professor of anthropology at Santa Clara University. He employs a combination of archaeological, ethnographic, and archival data to examine the long-term entanglements between California's Indigenous societies and colonial institutions, particularly the Spanish mission system.

Glendon Parker is an adjunct associate professor of environmental toxicology at UC Davis. His research focuses on the development of techniques that obtain useful genetic data from forensically informative proteomic datasets.

Tanya M. Smith is a professor in the Australian Research Centre for Human Evolution and the Griffith Centre for Social and Cultural Research at Griffith University. Her research focuses on the growth and structure of teeth.

Melody Tannam is a biological anthropologist and GIS specialist at Basin Research Associates. She has over thirty years of bioarchaeological experience working in North America and Europe.

Shannon Tushingham is an associate curator and Irvine Chair of Anthropology at the California Academy of Sciences. She is an anthropological archaeologist with research broadly centered on human-environmental relationships and the evolutionary archaeology of hunter-gatherer-fishers in western North America.

Christopher Zimmer represents the Amah Mutsun Tribal Band of Mission San Juan Bautista on the State of California's Native American Heritage Commission's Most Likely Descendant list. He represented the interests of the tribe and worked with archaeologists at the Asistencia San Pedro y San Pablo (CA-SMA-71/H).

Mario Zimmermann is an assistant clinical professor in anthropology at Boise State University. His research focuses on paleoethnobotany and chemical residues studies as these inform on ancient foodways and ethnopharmacology.

INDEX

Page numbers in *italics* refer to illustrations (*i*) and tables (*t*)

Abalone: red (*Haliotis rufescens*), 25, 42, 43, 84, 85, 90
Abella, Ramón, 102
Abscesses: dental, 39
Acorns, 24, 120, 144
Adolescents, 198. *See also* Nonadults
Adults, 35, 38, 39, 41, 43–44, 46, 76, 198, 234; caffeine and nicotine markers, 165, 231–32
Africa: anti-parasitic treatment in, 168
Age-at-death estimates, 34, 46, 208; average, 53–54; of adults, 38, 39, 41, 42, 43, 44; of nonadults, 37, 40, 42, 43
Agriculture, 11, 13, 45
Alkaloids, metabolites of, 161
Alta California: bioarchaeology, 235; tobacco in, 23–24
Amah Mutsun Tribal Band of Mission San Juan Bautista, 1, 19, 21
Amazon: tobacco use in, 168
Amelogenesis imperfecta, 49
Amelogenin peptides, 76, 79
Amino acids: in proteomic contexts, 140–41
Ancestors: remembrance and celebration, 4–5
Ancient DNA (aDNA) analysis, 34, 59
Animals: isotopic signatures of, 116–17, 121–22. *See also various types*
Annadel quarry: obsidian from, 25
Anti-parasitic treatments, 168
Aparicio (Tarsi): funerary assemblage with, 99–100; identifying, 211; life history, 220–21. *See also* Burial 15
Apple, 24
Aramai, 12
Archaeology: at Sánchez Adobe (CA-SMA-- 71/H), 16–21
Asistencia de San Pedro y San Pablo, 1, 13, 14, 83; archaeology of, 16–21; baptisms at, 221; cemetery at, 207–8, 222–24; establishment of, 7, 9–10; structure of, 11–12
Assimilation, 62
Asteraceae, 25
Atole, 190
Atropine, 162

Bacterial species: in dental calculus, 142–43; identification of, 143–44
Baptisms, 4, 10–11, 12, 214, 218–19, 221, 222
Barley, 11, 24, 115, 19
Basketry: biochemical markers for, 170
Bat rays: barbs, 40, 100, 105
Bead money, 84
Beads, 3, *91i*, 101, 216, 218; glass, 17, 37, 39, 42, 43, 44, 84, 90–94, 101, 104, 105; jet, 42, 43, *91f*, 94–95, 100–101, 105, 217; shell, 17, 25, 37, 38, 39, 41, 42, 43, 44, 84, 85–90, 92, 100, 104, 105, 222; social status and, 232, 233, 234
Beans, 11, 24, 115
Bears, 121
Beaver (*Castor canadensis*), 144, 146, 148, 151, 152, 153, 216, 232
Beef: zinc in, 191, 192
Belize: Tipu Mayan cemetery in, 197
Benedict XIII: on tobacco use, 160
Berries, 24
Bifaces, 95, *100i*
Biochemical analysis: of dental calculus, 157–58
Biodistance analysis: dental traits, 3, 196–198; methods, 198–200; results, 200–201
Biomarkers, 3, 170; in dental calculus, 161–63, 164–69
Biomolecular signatures: in dental calculus, 138–39, 140
Birds, 24, 120, 150
Black Drink, 169
Blacksmithing, 190

Bodie Hills: obsidian from, 95, 96
Bone, *124t*, 126, 130; proteomic studies, 148–49; stable isotope studies, 114, 115, 229–30
Bone tools, 84
Bone tubes, 105
Boscana, Gerónimo, 84
Bos taurus, 14, 24, 119; diet, 122, 131, 144; Mission Period use of, 151, 152, 153, 230, 236; and *Mycobacterium bovis*, 51–52; proteomic identification, 146, 149
Botanical remains, 24–25. *See also various species*
Brass, 191, 192
Brown, Alan K., 16
Burials, 60; at Asistencia de San Pedro y San Pablo, 11, 12, 13, *20i*, 35; demographics of, 14, *36t*, 45–47; reburial of, 21. *See individual burials by number*
Burial 2 (José Manuel), 198, 212, 234; dental enamel analysis, 182, *244i*; description of, 35, 37; enamel studies, 78, 80; heavy metal accumulation, 183, 186–87, 188; isotopic life history, 126, *127i*; LEH, 56, 61; life history, 221–22; pathologies, 47, *242i*; shell beads, 89, 232; tuberculosis, 51, 52, 59, 60–61, 78
Burial 3, 38, 49, 164, 165, 198, 213, 232; heavy metal accumulation, 183–84; trauma, 58, *243i*
Burial 4, 39, 50, 153, 165, 212, 232; childbirth death of, 47, 101
Burial 5, 41, 49, 52, 198, 213
Burial 6 (Yunnénis), 42, 52, 152, 165; biodistance analysis, 200, 211; and Burial 11, 198, 201; dental enamel study, 182–83; funerary goods, 101, 232, 234; isotopic life history, 126, *127i*, 128
Burial 7, 94, 128, 212; beads in, 101, 232, 233; description of, 37–38
Burial 8 (Olcóx), 41, 49, 153, 164, 165, 198, 232, 234; biodistance analysis, 200, 201; heavy metal accumulation, 183–84; identity of, 208, 210; isotopic life history, 126, *127i*; life history, 218–19
Burial 9 (Mauricio), 42, 128, 217, 234; enamel studies, 78–79, 80; identity of, 210–11; funerary offerings with, 62, 89, 94, 101, 217–18, 232
Burial 10, 43, 213, 232
Burial 11 (Julírbe), 43, 79, 128, 164, 182; biodistance analysis, 200, 211; and Burial 6, 198, 201; heavy metal accumulations, 184–85, 186, 187, 188, 189; identity of, 210–11; jet beads and cross, 94, 101, 217–18, 232, 233
Burial 12 (Jagessém), 164, 198, 210, 235; biodistance analysis, 200, 201; and Burial 8, 198, 208; description of, 43–44; dental disease, 49, 61, 62, *244i*; enamel studies, 78, 80; funerary goods with, 101, 232, 234; life history, 214, 216
Burial 13, 44, 198, 213, 232; isotopic life history, 126, *127i*, 128
Burial 14 (María Athanasia), 198, 211, 212, 232, 233; biodistance analysis, 200, 201; dental enamel analysis, 182, *244i*; description of, 40, 62; dental disease, 49, *243i*; heavy metal accumulations, 183, 184–85, 187, 189; life histories, 219–20
Burial 15 (Tarsi; Aparicio), 40, 52, 152, 164, 165, 198, 211; biodistance analysis, 200, 201; funerary assemblage with, 99–100, 232; life history, 220–21; social identity, 234–35
Burial 16, 101, 128, 233; childbirth death, 47, 101, 212; description of, 39–40

CA-ALA-11: dental disease, 55
CA-ALA-329: dental calculus analysis, 141
CA-ALA-483: dental disease, 55
CA-ALA-613/H: dental disease, 55
Cabbage: wild (*Brassica oleracea*), 144
Cacao (*Theobroma cacao*): biomarker, 162, 229; caffeine biomarker for, 169–70; use of, 171, 231–32, 236
CA-CCO-548: dental disease, 55
Caffeine, 162; biochemical evidence of, 165, 169–70, 217, 220, 229, 231, 233
Callianax biplicata, 25, 88. *See also* Olivella beads
Camgís, 219, 220
Cancégmne, 101, 214, 216
Canids, 122
Cápete, 221–22
Capra hircus, 153; in diet, 122, 144; proteomic identification, 146, 148, 149
Carbon isotopes, 115–16, *118i*, *123i*; and dietary signatures, 128, 129; weaning estimates, *125t*, 126
C_3 plants, 115, 116; in diets, 119, 121–22
C_4 plants, 115–16; in diets, 119, 122
Carious lesions, 34, 44, 49–50, 55–56

Index · 253

CA-SCL-128, 130
CA-SCL-287, 130
CA-SCL-674: carious lesions, 55
CA-SFR-191, 130, 141; heavy metal analysis, 180, 182, 184
CA-SRI-2: carious lesions, 55–56
CA-SRI-41: carious lesions, 55
Cast iron pans, 191
Cattle (*Bos taurus*), 14, 24, 119; diet, 122, 131, 144; Mission Period use of, 151, 152, 153, 230, 236; and *Mycobacterium bovis*, 51–52; proteomic identification, 146, 149
Cemeteries: mission-era, 16, 17, 207; structure of, 208, 222–24
Ceramics, 189–90; tin- or lead-glazed, 23, 192
Ceremony: tobacco used in, 168
Cervus canadensis, 24, 120, 144, 146, 148
Chalixsé, 219–20
Charquin: resistance by, 12–13
Chenopodium spp., 25; *quinoa*, 143
Chert, 96, 100; projectile points, 40, 95
Chicken (*Gallus gallus*), 24, 119; diet, 122, 131; proteomic studies, 144, 150
Chiguan, 12, 13, 214, 217
Childbirth: deaths in, 101, 212; dangers of, 47, 54; tobacco taboos, 160
Children: burials, 40, 43, 169, 198, 212; diet, 131, 231, 232; funerary offerings, 233–34; morbidity and mortality, 3, 13–14, 61; nicotine signatures, 167–68; tuberculosis, 51, 80
Chilssan, 218
Chocolate. *See* Cacao
Chocolate pots (*chocolateras*), 23, 169, 190, 233
Chromatography, 3, 21; UPLC-MS, 158, 161–67
Chronic ailments, 22, 49
Chumash: Olivella beads, 25
Clamshell disk beads (CSDB), 84, 85, 151; in burials, 37, 41, 42, 43, 44, 101; at Mission Santa Clara, 86–87; production and distribution of, 87–88
Cirino (Olcóx), 208, 210, 232, 234. *See also* Burial 8
Coastal Contracting Stem Cluster, 95
Coast Ranges: obsidian from, 25
Coffee (*Coffea arabica*), 162, 169
Colonialism, 2, 236
Comales de fierro, 190–91
Cooking: metal tools in, 176–77, 190–91
Copper (Cu), 23; as essential metal, 177, 178–79; exposure to, 182, 183, 184, 192, 231; in food preparation, 176, 190, 191; levels of, 185–86, 188–89
Corporal punishment, 58
Cotegen, 12, 13
C-reactive protein (CRP), 76, *77t*, 78, 80; psychosocial stress, 72–73, 79
Cremations, 102, 104
Cribra orbitalia (CO), 61
Crops, 11, 113; C_3 and C_4, 115–16; fertilized, 122
Crosses, 85, *91i*, 94, 100–101; in burials, 11, 42, 217
CRP. *See* C-reactive protein

Dairy products: proteomic identification of, 148, 150, 151; zinc in, 191, 192
Datura: biomarkers, 162
Death records, 3–4, 208, 210; demographics of, 13–14
Deaths, death rates, 11, 12, 22, 84
Deer (*Odocoileus virginianus*), 24, 120, 144, 146, 148, 149; Mission period use, 151, 153, 232
Demographics: average age-at-death, 53–54; burial, *36t*, 45–47; of death records, 13–14
Dental attrition, 49
Dental calculus, 3, 21, 49, 159, 179, 229; biochemical analyses, 157–58; biomarker data, 161–70; cow's milk proteins in, 52, 217, 231; diet, 114, 228; peptides in, 138–39; proteomic analysis, 141–43; species identified in, 143–44, 145–50
Dental disease(s), 34, 47, *48t*, 49–50; in burials, 37, 39, 40, 41, 43, 44, *243i*; in Precontact and Mission Period, 55–57
Dental enamel, 3, 40, 61, *244i*; diet and, 114–15; essential metals in, 177–78; heavy metal analysis of, 180–89; metals in, 176–77; proteomic analyses, 71–72, 75–80
Dental hypoplasia, 78, 80
Dental microwear, 114
Dentin: heavy metal accumulations in, 186, 187–89
Depopulation: Mission Period, 45, 53
Diagenesis, 187
Diet(s), 3, 21, 24–25, 50, 56, 113, 119, 138, 144, 217, 236; age and, 230–32; deficiencies in, 61, 62; dental calculus indicators, 148–51; faunal, 120–22, *123i*; gender differences in,

228–30; human, 124–29, 130–31; precontact, 117, 143; and tooth growth, 114–15
Disease(s), 12, 21, 22, 48t, 54, 78; dental, 47, 49–50, 55–57; infectious, 51–52, 53, 69; joint and trauma, 50–51, 57–58; osteological analyses, 34–35, 45
DNA analysis, 34
Domestic work, 45
Dung: nitrogen in, 116

Early California Population Project, 208
Earthenwares: lead-glazed, 17, 23
Elites: Ohlone, 214–18
Elk (*Cervus canadensis*), 24, 120, 144, 146, 148
Enamel. *See* Dental enamel
Enamel hypoplasia, 34, 49
Enculturation, 83
Epidemics, 22, 54, 221
Ethnobotanical practices, 157
Euro-Americans: heavy metals analysis, 181; stable isotope analysis, 119, 131
Europeans: tobacco use, 159–61
Evangelization, 157
Excelsior point, 95
Exchange networks, 96, 103, 104–5
Eycote, 221

Families, 4, 21, 60
Faunal assemblages, 24; diet, 120–22, *123i*, 131; stable isotope data, 119–22
Fasciola: gigantica, 144; *hepatica*, 144, 148, 150, 152, 168, 217, 236
Females, 13, 35, 38, 39, 47, 198; adults, 41, 43–44, 79; biomarker data, 166, 170; diet, 129, 131, 228, 229–30; nonadults, 40, 46; proteomic studies, 74–76; stable isotope data, 122, 124
Femurs: stature estimation, 34
Fertilizer: nitrogen, 116–17
Fish, 24, 120, 153
Flaked stone, 84, 95–97, 105. *See also* Projectile points and preforms
Fluke: giant liver (*Fasciola gigantica*), 144; liver (*F. hepatica*), 144, 150, 152, 168, 217, 236
Foods, foodways: age changes in, 230–32; heavy metal exposure, 176, 189–90, 191–92; macrobotanical evidence, 113–14; Mission-era, 11, 24–25, 236; nitrogen in, 116; sex-linked differences in, 228–29; social status and, 232–33

Fowl: peptide signals of, 150, 153
Fractures: avulsion, 38, 50; compression, 39, 50; healed, 38, 58
Frailty, 60–61
Franciscans, 7, 160; Mission system, 2, 11, 84; on mortuary practices, 102–3
Fruits, 24, 115, 150, 162
Funerary offerings/objects, 21, 35, 83, 103–4, 216, 217, 220, 222, 236; assemblages, 98–101; in burials, 40, 43, 44; flaked stone, 95–97; glass beads, 90–94; ground stone, 97–98; jet beads and crosses, 94–95; persistent practices, 60, 84, 102; shell beads, 85–90; social status and, 232, 233–35

Gallus gallus, 24, 119; diet, 122, 131; proteomic studies, 144, 150
Galvan, Andrew, 19
Gardens, 229
Gas chromatography-mass spectrometry (GC-MS), 161
Gastrointestinal infections: *Mycobacterium bovis* and, 52
GC-MS. *See* Gas chromatography-mass spectrometry
Gender roles: and foodways, 228–29
Geronimo Emiliano, 219–20
Gimás, 212
Glass beads, 17, 37, 39, 42, 43, 44, 84, 93t, 104, 105; types of, 90, *91i*, 92, 94, 101
Goat (*Capra hircus*), 153; in diet, 122, 144; proteomic identification, 144, 146, 148, 149
Goosefoot (*Chenopodium californicum*), 143, 144
Grains, 24
Grapes (*Vitus*): domesticated (*vinifiera*), 143, 144, 146, 148, 162; native (*californica*), 143, 144, 146, 150
Grasses, 24, 120
Grave goods. *See* Funerary offerings
Ground stone, 17, 84, 97–98, 105
Guascám, 219, 220

Half Moon Bay, 12
Haliotis rufescens, 25, 42, 43, 84, 85, 90
Hares, 120
Haro, Francisco de, 15
Hawikku, 197
Health, 3, 21, 45, 47, 216; average age-at-death,

Index · 255

53–54; Precontact–Mission Period comparisons, 55–57
Heavy metals, 3, 21; in dental enamel studies, 180–89; exposure to, 23, 178, 231, 232, 233; food preparation and, 176, 189–90
Heirlooming: of obsidian artifacts, 96
Hernández de Toledo, 160
Hetecsé, 221, 222
Him'Ren Ohlone (Ramona Garibay), 141
Historical records, 113, 208
Historic Period, 59; heavy metal exposure, 181, 184
Honed stone, 40
Honeybee (*Apis cerana*), 144
Horse: diet, 122
Huchen/salmon (*Salmo/Huchen/Oncorhynchus*), 146
Hunter-gatherers: dental diseases, 55
Hunting, 24; Mission period, 151, 152, 153
Hypomaturation amelogenesis imperfecta, 40
Hypoplasia: dental, 78

Immunoglobulin gamma (IgG), 76, 77(table), 78, 80; and psychosocial stress, 72–73, 79
Immune systems, 72
Individuals, 35; identifying, 3–4, 208–13, 237; life histories of, 214–22; resilience, 60–61; social identity, 226–27
Indoctrination, 45
Infants: Burial 7, 37–38, 212; Burial 9, 42; Burial 16, 39–40; mortality rates, 46–47
Infectious disease, 34, 59
Interment: extended, 35
Iron (Fe): in enamel, 177–78; levels of, 182, 183, 190–91, 192, 231; toxicity, 179–80
Iron grills: in food preparation, 176

Jagessém (Margaritta), 101, 232; identification of, 210, 224; life history of, 214, 216, 235. *See also* Burial 12
Jamlité, 214
Jaysutí, 221
Jet: beads and crosses, 42, 43, *91f*, 94–95, 100–101, 105
Joint changes, 38
Joint disease, 34, 50, 57–58

José Manuel, 22, 212; life history, 221–22; social status, 232, 234. *See also* Burial 2
José Saturnino, 221
Julírbe (Primo), 210, 216, 217, 232, 233, 234. *See also* Burial 11

Kelp, 120
Kinship, 101, *215i*; biodistance analysis, 196–98, 201–2
Kyphosis: tuberculosis and, 51, 52

Labor, 11, 22, 45; and trauma, 50–51
Laboratories for Molecular Anthropology and Microbiome Research, 34–35
La Florida, 235, 95
Lámpes, 221
Land: San Pedro y San Pablo, 14
Land grants: petitions for, 14, *15*
Laser Ablation-Inductively Coupled Plasma-Mass Spectrometry Imaging (LA-ICP-MS): dental enamel study, 181–82, 184–89
Laudanum: biomarkers, 162
Lead (Pb): accumulation of, 185–86; exposure to, 178, 182, 183, 184, 192
LEH. *See* linear enamel hypoplasia
Leporids: stable isotope analysis, 121–22
Lesions, 49; lytic, 37, 52; periapical, 34, 41, 55; periodontal, 34
Life expectancy, 14, 45
Life histories: individuals, 3, 207, 214–22, 224, 237
Linear enamel hypoplasia (LEH), 37, 44, 49, 55, 56, 61, 62
Livestock, 113, 119, 128, 149, 229
Living conditions: and death rates, 22
Lucas, 218
Lupin: white (*Lupinus albus*), 144
Lytic lesions, 37, 52

Macrobotanical remains, 113–14
Maize (*Zea mays*), 11, 24, 116, 119, 130; in animal diets, 122, 131; proteomic identification of, 144, 150
Majolica, 17, 189
Males, 47, 79, 198; adult, 35, 41, 42, 46; biomarker data, 166–67; diet, 129, 131, 229–30; gendered roles, 228–29; nonadult, 37, 40, 42, 43, 46; proteomic studies, 74–76; stable isotope data, 122, 124

Mammals, 24; marine, 120, 121
Manzanita, 120
Margarita (Jagessém), 101, 210, 232. *See also* Burial 12
María Athanasia, 211, 231, 232, 233; life histories, 219–20. *See also* Burial 14
Marine foods, 24, 116, 117, 120, 191; in human diet, 122, 124, 126, 128, 130–31, 229, 230, 231
Marriage(s), 12, 126, 219
Mauricio, 210, 216, 217, 232, 233, 234. *See also* Burial 9
Measles epidemic, 221
Medicinal practices, 3; tobacco in, 158–59, 160, 168
Medieval Climatic Anomaly, 55
Mercury (Hg): exposure to, 178, 182, 183, 184, 192
Metabolemic indicators, 158, 166–67, 233; sexual differences in, 170, 229
Metals, 22–23; essential, 177–78; food preparation, 176–77; heavy, 178–79; toxicity, 179–80
Metates: basalt tripod, 97–98i, 169
Milk: cow's, 52, 152, 217, 228, 229, 230, 232, 236; proteins, 148, 151
Millet, 116
Milliken, Randall: database, 208
Mink (*Neovison vison*), 146, 148, 151
Mission Carmel, 160
Mission Diet, 128
Mission Dolores. *See* Mission San Francisco de Asís
Mission La Purísima, 104
Mission Period, 17, 45, 59, 62; average age-at-death, 53–54; dental disease, 55–57; diet, 128, 130–31, 143–44, 150–51; food preparation, 176, 189–91; heavy metal analysis, 180, 182–83; joint disease and trauma, 57–58; Olivella bead chronology, 88–89; proteomic studies, 141–42, 146–48; tobacco use, 159, 160
Mission San Diego, 104
Mission San Francisco de Asís, 10, 13, 23, 54, 101, 102, 103 104, 108, 189; and Asistencia San Pedro y San Pablo, 56–57; baptisms at, 214, 218–19; Cápete's family at, 221–22; establishment, 7–8
Mission San Francisco Solano, 104
Mission San Gabriel, 104
Mission San José, 21, 23, 104, 105; obsidian from, 26, 96, 97; bird bone tubes from, 168–69
Mission San Juan Bautista, 1, 19
Mission Santa Catalina de Guale (Georgia), 95
Mission Santa Clara, 12, 23, 24, 26, 90, 85, 92, 96, 98, 104, 105, 119, 169, 189, 236; archaeology at, 21, 22; burial practices, 35, 102, 224; clamshell disk beads, 86–87, 88; stable isotope analysis, *118i*, 130
Mission Santa Cruz, 12, 21, 23, 85, 92, 96, 190
Mission Soledad, 104
Mission system, 2, 15, 24, 45, 62; autonomy in, 160, 235–36; gender roles, 228–29; historical records, 3–4; native responses to, 83–84
Mitenne: resistance to, 12–13
Miwok, 14
MLD. *See* Most Likely Descendants
Monitoring: archaeological, 19
Mono Glass Mountain: obsidian from, 95
Monterey Chert, 95, 96
Morbidity: children, 13–14
Morphine, 162
Mortality, mortality rates: children, 13–14, 61; infant, 46–47; Mission Period, 45, 83
Mortuary practices, 35, 105; artifact assemblages, 98–101; Ohlone, 102–3, 236; persistent traditional, 103–4, 236
Mossués (Yaguéche), 10, 214, 217
Most Likely Descendants (MLD), 1, 19
Mourning: Native vs. Spanish views, 84, 102–3
Mussel (*Mytilus californianus*), 144
Muwekma Ohlone, 141
Mycobacterium spp., 59; evidence of, 37, 60–61, 78, 80, 222; transmission of, 51–52

Napa Valley: obsidian from, 19, 25, 95, 96
Native American Heritage Commission, 1, 19
Neonates: Burial 7, 37–38; Burial 16, 39–40
Neovison vison, 146, 148, 151
Newborns: death rates, 13–14
New Spain: cacao in, 169; tobacco in, 160–61
Nicotiana, 23; biochemical evidence of, 162, 216, 229, 231 233; *glauca*, 24, 168, 169; *rustica*, 168; *tabacum*, 24, 168, 169; use of, 158–61, 167, 235
Nicotine, 162; biochemical evidence of, 164–65, 167–69, 217, 220, 231
Nitrogen: in fertilizers, 116–17

Nitrogen isotopes, 116, *118i, 123i;* and dietary signatures, 128–29; weaning estimates, *125t,* 126
Nolasco, Pedro, 212
Nonadults, 35, 37–38, 39–40, 43, 45, 198, 231; nicotine signatures, 167–68; proteomic analyses, 34, 42, 76; sex distribution, 46–47
Northern California: Olivella beads from, 89

Oak, 25; valley (*Quercus lobata*), 144, 150
Obsidian, 3, 19; in Burial 15, 40, *100i;* dating, 95–96, 97; sources, 25–26
Odocoileus virginianus, 24, 120, 144, 146, 148, 149; Mission period use, 151, 153, 232
Odontometric variables, 198; cluster analyses, 199–200
Ohlone communities, 1, 9, 13, 182; chronic psychosocial stress, 72–73; diet, 24–25; elites, 214–18; Mission Period foodways, 189–91; mortuary practices, 102–3, 236; Pruristac, 10–11; territory, 101—2; tobacco use, 23, 158–59
Ohlone Indian Tribe: monitors, 19
Olcóx (Cirino), 208, 210, 224, 232, 234; life history of, 218–19. *See also* Burial 8
Olivella (*Callianax biplicata*) beads, 17, 25, 85, 151; in burials, 37, 38, 39, 40, 41, 42, 43, 44, 84, 100; chronology, 88–89; sources of, 89–90
Oljon, 12, 13, 221
Orchards, 11, 24
Osteoarthritis (OA), 34, 50
Osteological studies, 3, 45; methods, 33–35
Osteomyelitis, 59
Osteophytic formation, 39, 41
Otters: sea (*Enhyrda lutris kenyoni*), 24, 120, 144, 146, 148, 151, 152, 153, 216, 232
Oysters, 191

Paleopathological studies, 3, 21
Palóu, Francisco, 10
Parasites, 168; in dental calculus, 148, 150, 152
Partial Least Square-Discriminant Analyses (PLSDA), 162; results, 164–67
Paseo, 103
Pathologies: dental disease, 47, 49; Mission Period, 54–59; skeletal, 33, 37, 38, *48t, 242i, 243i*
Peaches, 24
Pear, 24

Peptides, peptide sequences, 145–46; bacterial species identification, 143–44; in dental calculus, 138–39
Periapical lesions, 34, 41, 49, 55, 184
Periodontal disease, 34, 49, 55; in burials, 39, 41, 42, 43, 184
Periosteal reactions, 59, 61
Peru: medicinal tobacco use, 168
Pestles, 39, 42, 44, *97i,* 101, 216, 217
Phenotypes: dental, 196–98
Pigs (*Sus scrofa*), 119; proteomic identification, 144, 146
Pipes, 23, 158, 159, 169
Plants, 119, 130, 159, 170. *See also by type*
Plaque, 49; calcified, 139–40
PLSDA. *See* Partial Least Square-Discriminant Analyses
Point Año Nuevo, 23
Pomegranate (*Punica granatum*), 24, 144, 146, 148, 150, 153, 217, 228, 231, 236
Pomponio, 14
Population dynamics, 11–12
Porotic hyperostosis (PH), 61
Posole, 190
Postmortem damage: to burials, 37, 38, 44
Pott's disease, 51, 59
Precontact period: dental disease, 55–57; diet, 130, 149–50; heavy metal analysis, 180, 182, 184; obsidian artifacts, 95, 96; proteomic analysis, 141–42, 144, 148; yaupon holly use, 169
Pregnancy, 47
Primo, 22
Primo (Julírbe), 210, 216, 232. *See also* Burial 11
Projectile points and preforms, 40, 95–96, *100i*
Pronghorn, 144, 146
Proteomic analyses, 34, 77–80, 231, 232; amino acids, 140–41; dental calculus, 141–43, 228; methods, 73–74; Mission Period samples, 146–48; sex estimations, 21, 37, 38, 39, 40, 41, 42, 43, 44, 71–72, 74–76; species identification, 143–46
Pruristac, 9; and Asistencia de San Pedro y San Pablo, 157–58; baptisms, 10–11; people from, 12, 13, 214
Pseudoarthrosis, 38, 50
Psychosocial stress: immune system responses to, 72–73

Punica granatum, 24, 144, 146, 148, 150, 153, 217, 228, 231, 236
Punta de Almejas, 10; people from, 12, 218, 219

Quadrangle, 17
Quartz crystals, 40, *100i*
Quercus, 25; *lobata*, 144, 150
Queyem, 220
Quince, 24
Quinoa (*Chenopodium quinoa*), 143
Quiroste, 12–13

Rabbits, 24, 120
Ramona Garibay (Him'Ren Ohlone), 141
Rancheria (Mission Santa Clara): clamshell disk beads, 86–87; *Haliotis rufescens* beads, 90
Rancho Petaluma: obsidian from, 97
Recycling: obsidian artifacts, 96
Regional interaction spheres, 25
Resilience, 56, 60
Resistance, 2; by Charquin, 12–13
Ritual power, 235
Rosaries, 42, 43, 94–95
Royal New Hispanic Tobacconist, 160
Ruxníc, 222

Sainz de Lucio, Juan, 102
Salmon: pink (*Oncorhyncus gorbuscha*), 144
Sánchez, Francisco, 10, 15
Sánchez Adobe, 10, 15–16
Sánchez Adobe Park Historic District (CA-SMA-71/H), 1, 10, 21; dental disease, 55–57
San Francisco: City Cemetery individuals, 181, 184; Euro-Americans, 119, 131
San Francisco Bay Area, 2, 7, 10, 104
San Francisco State University, 16
San Gregorio, 12
San Joaquin Valley: Native cemeteries, 104
San Mateo, 13, 219
San Mateo County Historical Association, 1
San Mateo County Department of Parks, 1
San Mateo County Park, 10
San Mateo Junior College, 16
San Pedro Valley, 220
San Pedro y San Pablo de Patale mission (Florida), 197
San Sabá (Texas): *comales* at, 191
Santa Barbara Channel, shell from, 25, 90
Santa Barbara Presidio, 169, 220

Santa Rosa Island: *Haliotis* bead production, 90
Santiago, 212
Saxidomus sp., 84. *See also* Clamshell disk beads
Scopolamine, 162
Sea lions, 120
Seaweed, 120
Serra, Junípero, 160
Serum albumin, 76, 77, 80
Sex estimations, 3, 34, 36, 38, 46–47, 227–28; proteomic studies, 71–72, 74–76, 79
Sheep (*Ovis*), 148; domestic (*aries*), 144, 153; bighorn (*canadensis*), 146, 149–50
Sheep/goat, 24, 122
Shellfish, 24, 120
Shell middens, 16, 19
Shells, 190; beads, 17, 25, 84, 101, 105. *See also* Clamshell disk beads; *Haliotis rufescens*; Olivella beads
Sierra Nevada: obsidian from, 96
Síi Túupentak (CA-ALA-565/H): infant weaning rates at, 47
Skeletal remains: study methods, 33–35
Social identity: constructing, 226–27; Tarsi, 234–35
Social memory, 218
Social status, 3; and foodways, 232–33; funerary goods and, 233–35; of individuals, 212, 214, 216
Southern California: Olivella beads in, 89, 90
Spain: jet from, 94; tobacco use, 160–61
Spiritual power, 235
Ssatumnumo community, 214
Ssumsin, 214, 216
Stable isotope analyses, 21, 114, 129–31, 218; analyses, 119–20; and diet, 228, 229–30, 231, 233; faunal assemblages, 120–22, *123i*; human remains, 122, 124–29; model, 115–19
Stature estimations, 34, 41, 42, 44
Stone: polished, *100i*
Stressors, stress, 4; childhood, 61, 80, 216; health indicators, 56, 78; psychosocial, 72–73
Sugar cane, 116
Sulfur, 117
Sus scrofa, 119; proteomic identification, 144, 146
Syphilis, 59

Taboos: tobacco-related, 160
Tarsi (Aparicio), 211, 231; funerary assemblage

with, 99–100, 232; life history, 220–21; social identity, 234–35. *See also* Burial 15
Tartaric acid, 162
Tea (*Camellia sinensis*), 169
Teeth, 117; biodistance analysis, 196–200; growth layers, 114–15, *244i*; stable isotope data, 119, 120, 124–26; traits, 3, *244i*; wear, 56
Terrestrial foods, 120; in human diet, 122, 124, 229, 231
Theobroma cacao: biomarker, 162, 229; caffeine biomarker for, 169–70; use of, 171, 231–32, 236
Tipu Maya: dental phenotype study, 197
Tivela sp., 84. *See also* Clamshell disk beads
Tobacco (*Nicotiana*), 23; Aztec (*rustica*), 168; biochemical evidence of, 158, 162, 216, 229, 231, 233; domesticated (*tabacum*), 24, 168, 169; Native American use of, 158–59; in New Spain, 160–61; tree (*glauca*), 24, 169; use of, 167–69, 235
Trade, trade networks, 25–26; cacao and yaupon holly, 169; Mission Period, 151–52; obsidian, 96; shell beads, 90
Trauma, 34, 58; and labor practices, 50–51
Triticum aestivum, 11, 24, 115, 119, 150
Tuberculosis (*Mycobacterium* sp.), 59; evidence of, 37, 60–61, 78, 80, 222; transmission of, 51–52
Turjám, 218–19
Tursucsé, 211
Turumúcssé, 214
Turute, 218

Ujul, 220–21
Ulchigt, 216
Ultra Performance Liquid Chromatography-Mass Spectrometry (UPLC-MS), 158; analysis using, 161–67

Urban VII: anti-smoking edict, 159–60
Utála, 218

Vigil, Desiree, 19
Vineyard, 11
Violence: and blunt force trauma, 58
Vitus: californica, 143, 144, 146, 150; *vinifiera*, 143, 144, 146, 148, 162

Weaning practices, 47, 56; and social status, 234, 235; stable isotope values, *125t*, 126
Weathering: of skeletal remains, 34, 38, 39, 40, 41, 42, 43, 44
Wheat (*Triticum aestivum*), 11, 24, 115, 119, 150
Whistles: bird bone, 40, *100i*, 122
Windover Pond site (Florida): phenotype analysis, 197
Women. *See* females

XRF studies, 96

Yaguéche (Mossués), 10, 214, 216, 217
Yaupon holly (*Ilex vomitoria*), 169
Yerba Buena Cemetery: dental enamel studies, 181
Yt-tím, 216–17, 234
Yunnénis, 210–11, 214, 232, 234; life history of, 214, 216–17. *See also* Burial 6

Zea mays, 11, 24, 116, 119, 130; in animal diets, 122, 131; proteomic identification of, 144, 150
Zimmer, Christopher, 19
Zinc (Zn): as essential metal, 177, 178, 179; in foods, 191, 192; levels of, 176, 182, 183, 184, 185–88, 231

www.ingramcontent.com/pod-product-compliance
Lightning Source LLC
Chambersburg PA
CBHW030822230426
43667CB00008B/1339